The

WESTMINSTER
CONFESSION
of FAITH

Other works by Dr. Surrendra Gangadean & The Logos Foundation:

Philosophical Foundation: A Critical Analysis of Basic Beliefs

History of Philosophy: A Critical Analysis of Unresolved Disputes

Theological Foundation: A Critical Analysis of Christian Belief

Philosophical Foundation: Trivium Study Guide

The Logos Papers: To Make the Logos Known

The Westminster Shorter and Larger Catechisms:
A Doxological Understanding

On Natural and Revealed Theology:
Collected Essays of Surrendra Gangadean

The Logos Curriculum:
Grammar Catechisms: Philosophical, Theological, and
Historical Foundations

Fundación Filosofica: Un Análisis Crítico de Creencias Básicas

DOXOLOGICAL REFORMED SERMON SERIES:

The Book of Revelation: What Must Soon Take Place
Doxological Postmillennialism

The Biblical Worldview: Creation, Fall, Redemption
Genesis 1–3: Scripture in Organic Seed Form

The Unity of the Church: That They May Be One That the
World May Believe

PHILOSOPHICAL FOUNDATION DIALOGUE SERIES:

Introduction to Philosophy: The Basic Things Are Clear to Reason

The

WESTMINSTER
CONFESSION
of FAITH

A Doxological Understanding

SURRENDRA GANGADEAN

A DIVISION OF THE LOGOS FOUNDATION
Phoenix, Arizona

The Westminster Confession of Faith: A Doxological Understanding

Copyright © 2004, 2024 Surrendra Gangadean

Logos Papers Press 2024
Phoenix, Arizona
logospaperspress.com

Printed in the United States of America

Scriptures quotes are taken from the KING JAMES VERSION (KJV): KING JAMES VERSION, public domain, except where cited.

Cover Design: Beth Ellen Nagle
Typesetting: Matthew P. Hicks & Brian J. Phelps
Front Cover Image: Jovannig/stock.adobe.com
Back Cover Image: Jankost/stock.adobe.com

Library of Congress Cataloging-in-Publication Data pending

Gangadean, Surrendra, 1943–2022.
    The Westminster confession of faith: a doxological understanding
    Includes bibliographical references, footnotes, index,
    and glossary.
    ISBN: 979-8-9867472-6-2 (hbk.)
    ISBN: 979-8-9867472-5-5 (pbk.)
    ISBN: 979-8-9867472-7-9 (e-book)

1. Westminster Standards 2. Theology—Westminster Confession of Faith 3. Theology—Reformed 4. Historic Christianity 5. Theology—Doxological I. Title

Ad Majorem Dei Gloriam!

For the Greater Glory of God

CONTENTS

THE CONFESSION OF FAITH

APPENDICES

EDITOR'S PREFACE

D R. SURRENDRA GANGADEAN (1943–2022) taught a course on the Westminster Confession of Faith with study questions in 2004-2005 for adherents and members of Westminster Fellowship Church, of which he was Pastor. This class provided the occasion for developing a commentary on the Westminster Confession of Faith, published posthumously. The study questions and audio recordings from that class serve as the primary content for this book, while The Logos Foundation Editorial Board incorporated portions of some of his other writings to provide a more comprehensive exposition of the subject. The use of additional sources centered upon those doctrines that Dr. Gangadean focused on in his life's work in natural, revealed, and philosophical theology. Doctrines contained within the Westminster Confession of Faith (the Confession) that have undergone extensive discussion during and after the Reformation received less elaboration in this work. The latter topics of the Confession surrounding soteriology, religious worship, ecclesiology, the sacraments, and eschatology, among others, will be addressed extensively in subsequent books. This commentary is intended to bring into focus the foundational doctrines needing the greatest attention in our time and address those challenges through Rational Presuppositionalism[1] and the doxological focus of the Confession.[2]

The Westminster Confession of Faith: A Doxological Understanding is an example of Dr. Gangadean's incisive analysis, which, through clarity of focus and economy of words, provides the necessary insight to understand, defend, and advance the Christian faith against the mounting challenges of Modernity and Postmodernity. These challenges can be identified as follows: (1) the relation between faith and reason, (2) the knowability of God and the proofs for God's existence, (3) the goodness of God in the face of evil, (4) the doctrine of original sin, (5) the justice of God, and (6) the justification for the exclusivist claims of

---

1. Appendix 5.
2. Appendix 2.

Christianity. Each one of these challenges and their corollaries must be taken captive so as to overcome unbelief in the Church and in the world.

The Logos Foundation Editorial Board believes that a doxological understanding of the Westminster Confession is needed to prepare God's people for works of service. Faithful work in the kingdom requires *maturity* in the faith, *fruitfulness* in our lives, *unity* in the Church, and the *fullness* of Christ to be attained by filling the earth with the knowledge of God. This can only be accomplished by building on the foundational truths of the faith. Foundation comes from three sources: *philosophical*—from the clarity of general revelation; *theological*—from the biblical worldview of creation–fall–redemption; and *historical*—from the cumulative insight of the Church's creeds and confessions.

After his conversion to Christianity, Dr. Gangadean labored to lay the foundations in these three areas, with each having complementary texts: The philosophical includes *Philosophical Foundation: A Critical Analysis of Basic Beliefs* and *History of Philosophy: A Critical Analysis of Unresolved Disputes*. The theological includes *Theological Foundation: A Critical Analysis of Christian Belief*. The historical is represented in *The Westminster Confession of Faith: A Doxological Understanding* and *The Westminster Shorter and Larger Catechisms: A Doxological Understanding*. Additionally, *The Logos Papers: To Make the Logos Known* is a collection of 150 of Dr. Gangadean's occasional papers articulating these foundations and addressing both internal and external challenges to the faith from all three. These six books are complementary in their content, in that they share methodology (Rational Presuppositionalism), focus (Doxological Reformed), and aim (Doxological Postmillennialism).

The Logos Foundation Editorial Board deliberated extensively on how to make the 2004–2005 study of the Confession available to the larger body of Christ. A balanced format was aimed at through several stages of preparation: transcription of the audio recording, teaching in the classroom setting (at Logos Preparatory Academy), church instruction (during Sabbath School), and discussions at Logos Theological Seminary. *The Westminster Confession of Faith: A Doxological Understanding* retained much of Dr. Gangadean's spoken format with minor editorial changes to allow for readability. Additional resources were added to prepare the way for the reader to engage with the material more fully. This includes an introductory exposition of the Historic Christian Faith, summary answers at the end of each question, footnote references to Dr. Gangadean's other works, several appendices of core doctrines presupposed in the work, a glossary of terms, and an index. In this work, the reader is given a window into the greatest insights of the Westminster Confession and access to a well-laid foundation with sufficient strength to withstand and overcome the challenges to the faith, by taking thoughts captive and making them subject to Christ.[3]

Other study guides on the Westminster Confession of Faith by A. A. Hodge, G. I. Williamson, and R. C. Sproul are valuable works worthy of consultation. Yet, they have not identified the doxological focus of the Westminster Standards so as to provide a conclusive response to the challenges of our age. Understanding the Reformed Faith is four-fold: traditional, soteriological, worldview, and doxological. Only the doxological understanding incorporates the assumptions and doctrines required to formulate answers that take into account the persistent and cumulative effect of challenges to the coherence of the faith since the rise of the Modern world. The doxological understanding affirms the doctrine of the clarity of general revelation and the inexcusability of unbelief (1.1), the use of reason (the light of nature and good and necessary consequence) to understand general and special revelation (1.1, 1.6), the doxological focus on the knowledge of the glory of God (SCQ. 1, 101; the Confession 4.1, 5.1), divine sovereignty in creation–fall–redemption, and the law of God for all of life. Readers who engage diligently with this work can trace the way these assumptions and doctrines are woven systematically into every response. The concern for consistency in thought and analysis permeates Dr. Gangadean's work; this commentary is no exception.

The Logos Foundation Editorial Board is dedicated to making available Dr. Gangadean's extensive body of work, projected to be at least 100 books, over the next decade. We also intend to identify his unique contributions to philosophy, theology, religious studies, and the humanities. In God's providence, most of Dr. Gangadean's work was preserved in various formats, and we hope to bring the totality of his work to the awareness of the larger body of Christ and those seeking answers to basic questions. While Dr. Gangadean developed all that is being published under his name, he was not able to bring all the material to its final printed form during his lifetime. Resting upon God's

---

3. *2 Corinthians 10:4-5.*

upholding, The Logos Foundation Editorial Board desires to publish all of his work. Yet, we are mindful that our formulation falls short of the clarity, sharpness, and poetic quality of Dr. Gangadean's writing. We claim no originality; we seek to give honor to whom honor is due, and we take full responsibility for any errors.

—THE LOGOS FOUNDATION
EDITORIAL BOARD
Phoenix, Arizona
November 2023

THE WESTMINSTER ASSEMBLY
The Doxological Focus on the Glory of God

THE REFORMATION (1517–1648) ATTEMPTED to restore the Church to the Historic Christian Faith based upon the historically cumulative insight of earlier Church councils. It specifically responded to the challenges of sacramentalism and synergism addressed in the Councils of Jerusalem and Orange.

The Westminster Confession of Faith (the Confession) built upon earlier creeds of the Reformation: Augsburg (Lutheran), Thirty-Nine Articles (Anglican), Belgic (French), Helvetic (Swiss), Heidelberg (German), and Dort (Dutch). It is the last and most conscious and consistent creed of the Reformation and of Church history thus far.

The Westminster Standards (the Confession and its Catechisms) affirm the clarity of general revelation and the inexcusability of unbelief,[1] the use of reason (the light of nature and good and necessary consequence) to understand general and special revelation,[2] the doxological focus on the knowledge of the glory of God,[3] divine sovereignty in creation–fall–redemption, and the law of God for all of life.

Reformation soteriology has been summed up in the *ordo salutis*—the order of the application of redemption: effectual calling (regeneration), conversion (repentance and faith), justification (based on Christ's righteousness received by faith alone), adoption (having all the privileges of the children of God), sanctification (being made holy through knowing the truth), and glorification (the removal of all sin at death and the removal of death by the resurrection of the body).

In response to the challenge of Arminian semi-Pelagianism at Dort, the Confession affirmed (from Dort) the doctrines of Total Depravity, Unconditional Election, Limited Atonement, Irresistible Grace, and Perseverance of the Saints.

---

1. *The Westminster Confession of Faith (WCF.) 1.1.*

2. *WCF. 1.1, 1.6.*

3. *The Westminster Shorter Catechism Questions (SCQ.) 1, 101; WCF. 4.1, 5.1.*

The spirit of the theology of the Reformation has been summed up in the affirmation of the Five Solas: *Sola Scriptura* (by Scripture alone), *Sola Fide* (by faith alone), *Sola Gratia* (by grace alone), *Solus Christus* (by Christ alone), and *Soli Deo Gloria* (for the glory of God alone).

Uncritically held assumptions remain in the Church and have been the source of divisions in the Church which have scandalized the world. The Church must acknowledge the nature of the spiritual warfare between belief and unbelief present at every level, enter into the process of much discussion by which the Holy Spirit leads the Church into all truth, and take every thought captive raised up against the knowledge of God from unbelief, both in the Church and in the world.

INTRODUCTION

The Westminster Confession of Faith,
Its Relation to Other Creeds,
and Levels of Understanding

QUESTION 1

What is a confession of faith?
How is it an ordinary means of salvation?

A *confession of faith* is a summary of what the pastor-teachers[1] have achieved in understanding the Scriptures in light of the challenges raised to the Church in history. The first of these challenges occurred in Acts 15, when Jewish believers raised questions about how we are to be saved in light of the transition from the Old to the New Testament. In response to this challenge, the pastor-teachers, along with the apostles, gathered together, and after much discussion, came to an agreement which was sent out to the Churches.[2] The process of much discussion by pastor-teachers is the ordinary way the Church grows in its understanding of doctrine and achieves the unity of the faith.

---

1. By pastor-teachers is meant the leaders of the Christian Faith who have engaged with the most pressing theological issues in the history of the Church. They have served as the instrument of the Holy Spirit to respond to challenges of the Faith. "So Christ himself gave the apostles, the prophets, the evangelists, the pastors and teachers, to equip his people for works of service, so that the body of Christ may be built up until we all reach unity in the faith and in the knowledge of the Son of God and become mature, attaining to the whole measure of the fullness of Christ" (Ephesians 4:11-13 NIV). The progress of the Faith in Church history is not merely the contributions of great men, but the work of the Holy Spirit working through men through the process of much discussion. All those involved are counted among the pastor-teachers.

2. *Acts 15:23-31.*

Today the Church is badly divided, indicating that it has not built on the work of the pastor-teachers in the past. In studying the work of the Westminster Divines, we can grow in our understanding of challenges that have been answered and of those that remain. Within Christendom, the three major denominational differences are Roman Catholicism, Eastern Orthodoxy, and Protestantism. Within each of these, there are many variations. The extent and depth of the divisions within the body should call us to engage more thoughtfully with the content of the Westminster Standards. We must keep as a constant in our minds that in its statements, the Westminster Confession of Faith is either speaking positively in favor of a view or responding to a challenge. The Confession, along with the accompanying Shorter and Larger Catechisms (together, The Westminster Standards), is the high-water mark of the Historic Christian Faith because it responded to all the relevant challenges up to the time of its writing (1648). A thoughtful study of the Standards requires that we penetrate the material at the level of challenges and responses to the Faith.

It is the Lord's intention that the Church respond to challenges, through the process of much discussion by the pastor-teachers, as the ordinary means by which it grows in its understanding of the Faith and that by which fullness of the truth is to be attained. Our Lord said that He would "send the Holy Spirit to lead the Church into all truth."[3] Acts 15 affirms, "it seemed good to the Holy Spirit and to us."[4] The process in Acts 15 is a paradigm example of how the Holy Spirit leads the Church into all truth.

Ordinary means are the God-ordained means to exercise dominion over an area of life or discipline. Ordinary means entail making use of the means provided by God to grow in wisdom. Building on the historically cumulative insight achieved in Church history, through the work of the pastor-teachers, in response to challenges, is the God-ordained way to attain maturity, fruitfulness, unity, and fullness in Christ.[5] If our goal in understanding the Faith is doxological, to give all glory to God, as opposed to merely soteriological (centered on salvation—in

---

3. *John 16:13.*

4. *Acts 15:28.*

5. *Ephesians 4:11-13*; Surrendra Gangadean, "Paper No. 54: From Foundation to Fullness: A Biblical Worldview for Maturity, Fruitfulness, Unity, and Fullness," in *The Logos Papers: To Make the Logos Known* (Phoenix: Logos Papers Press, 2022), 287-292.

the minimal sense of justification, so that we may go to heaven), then we will see the need to become established in the Faith in its full sense of the term,[6] to attain to the full measure of the stature of Christ.[7] The councils and creeds of the Church, which are consistent with the truth of God are the work of the Holy Spirit leading the Church into all truth—apart from this, we cannot expect to attain maturity in the Historic Christian Faith. In light of this context, it is fitting and proper that it is asked: What is our understanding of the Westminster Confession of Faith and Catechisms? And what is our understanding of the work of the Holy Spirit leading the Church into all truth up to the development of the Westminster Standards (1648)? The Standards is a comprehensive work that has built on what came before and summarizes all that is true in previous councils and creeds. It is an enduring work that prepares us to address subsequent challenges in the modern world.[8]

QUESTION 2

What is the relation of the Westminster Confession to preceding creeds?

A *creed* is a statement of belief, from the Latin word *credo*, which means, "I believe." The word *confession* is used synonymously with *creed*. The Westminster Confession of Faith and the Shorter and Larger Catechisms were written at the end of the Reformation period (1643–1648), which also coincided with the beginning of the Modern period (1648–1950). In summing up the most prominent challenges that came into the Church up to that time, they particularly addressed the challenge of the sacramental system of the Roman Catholic Church of Medieval Europe. Although the Westminster Assembly faithfully answered the

---

6. Gangadean, "Paper No. 98: Faith and the Word of God," in *The Logos Papers*, 511-514.

7. *Ephesians 4:13*.

8. Gangadean, "Paper No. 58: The Spiritual War (Church and World)," in *The Logos Papers*, 317-322.

challenges of its time, many more significant challenges have developed since (in 370+ years), from both Modernity (1648–1950) and Post-modernity (1950–present),[9] which the Church (in council or creed) has yet to meaningfully answer (systematically and comprehensively). Accordingly, the Confession is the last of the creeds and there is no other since that time that has attained the lofty heights, in its degree of excellence, precision, and depth of thought, reached by the Confession.[10] Subsequent creeds, such as The London Baptist Confession of 1689, used the majority of the content of the Confession but set aside important components instead of building on it. The exclusion of these elements from the Confession has served as a source of division in the Reformed Faith ever since.[11]

---

9. Gangadean, "Paper No. 16: The Historic Christian Faith," in *The Logos Papers*, 103-114.

10. Since the Westminster Confession of Faith is the highest expression of Historic Christianity, the founding pastor of Westminster Fellowship (WF), Surrendra Gangadean, adopted the WCF as the doctrinal basis for WF. See Appendices 1–3 for a fuller explanation of the distinctives of Westminster Fellowship.

11. The London Baptist Confession of 1689 retained much of the WCF, yet proceeded to replace two significant epistemic statements. One deals with the relationship between general revelation (GR) and special revelation (SR), and the other speaks about the use of reason in interpreting the Scriptures. WCF 1.1 begins by affirming the clarity of general revelation and proceeds to explain the need for Scriptures to provide knowledge of God's will for redemption. The WCF moves from GR to SR, thus setting the context for the need for redemption from the failure to know God in the created order. The Baptist Confession reverses the order and gives an implied primacy to SR over GR. The changed statement reads as follows: "The Holy Scripture is the only sufficient, certain, and infallible rule of all saving knowledge, faith, and obedience, although the light of nature, and the works of creation and providence do so far manifest the goodness, wisdom, and power of God, as to leave men inexcusable" (BC 1.1). This change reverses the logical and historical order acknowledged in the WCF. This move marks the tendency in theology, since the Baptist Confession, to appeal to SR as the more reliable source of knowledge, which by implication is seen as more clear and more certain than GR. As the challenges of the modern world mount, the Church has increasingly appealed to SR for its answers, yet that comes at the cost of neglecting GR and the clarity of God's existence contained therein.

The second statement is in regards to the use of reason to interpret SR. The original statement in the WCF reads as follows: "The whole counsel of God concerning all things necessary for His own glory, man's salvation, faith, and life, is either expressly set down in Scripture, or by good and necessary consequence may be deduced from Scripture" (WCF 1.6). It was changed to the following: "The whole counsel of God concerning everything essential for His own glory and man's salvation, faith, and life is either explicitly stated or by necessary inference contained in the Holy Scriptures." (BC 1.6). The change from "good and necessary consequence" to "necessary inference" restrains interpretation to a more literal and textual basis. The larger and broader context of the clarity of general revelation in which Scripture is given is set aside for an exclusively SR context. "Good and necessary consequence" is an application of presuppositional thinking. In it, the less basic

The content of the confessions and creeds provides a cumulative development of the Historic Christian Faith. Each one responded to the most pressing challenges that divided the Faith in their time. As the gospel spread worldwide, believers had to contend with competing worldviews and faulty assumptions used to dilute, distort, and undermine the truth of the gospel. Contending with unbelief gave rise to the creeds and councils that constitute the Holy Catholic and Apostolic Faith. It is important that before addressing the content of the Confession, we gain an understanding of the main doctrines formulated in the creeds and councils that preceded the Westminster Standards. The creeds and confessions/councils explained below have positively strengthened the formulation of the Faith; together, they constitute the Holy Catholic and Apostolic Faith.[12]

Historic Christianity makes explicit the teaching of Scripture and its practice in liturgy; it cannot be used to set aside the truth from either general revelation or from Scripture, which are more basic. Among the several councils in the history of the Church, not all the content in the confessions and creeds has undergone the same degree of discussion. Some theological topics were central, such as the Trinity in Nicea or the Incarnation in Chalcedon. Some related topics were not yet challenged at that time in history; hence, less attention was given to them. And therefore, their formulation does not carry the same weight as the most debated parts do. In other words, not everything contained in every creed or council underwent the process of much discussion. Some assumptions were not subject to intellectual scrutiny at that time in history. As such, those parts of a confession do not have the same degree of authority as compared to those portions that did undergo the process of much discussion. Theological topics that have not undergone much discussion allow for uncritically held assumptions to persist. Those assumptions are later, in the course of history, brought under scrutiny and give rise to the need to formulate a response that takes into account the intellectual challenges that have arisen in God's providence. Historic Christianity continues to respond to challenges

---

ideas are interpreted in light of the more basic ones. In the context of hermeneutics, the context of the clarity of general revelation is logically and historically prior to SR and, therefore, it is presupposed in the content transmitted in SR. As such, it must not be excluded.

12. Gangadean, "Paper No. 16: The Historic Christian Faith," in *The Logos Papers*, 103-114.

as God makes them increasingly relevant in history. This is part of the process of the Holy Spirit leading the Church into all truth; the Church is to take every thought captive that raises itself up against the knowledge of God and make them subject unto Christ.[13]

The progress attained through creeds and councils remains. The fundamental truths reached and settled after much discussion are foundational to the Faith. Later confessions cannot set aside what has been agreed upon in Historic Christianity without addressing prior deliberation.[14] We are morally responsible to not lightly and thoughtlessly disregard the work of God accomplished in history through the pastor-teachers. We should think long and hard (critically) before calling into question what has been agreed upon through the process of much discussion. Historic Christianity includes more than the early councils and creeds discussed below, but they contain the fundamental teachings, so they constitute building blocks of momentous importance.

The First Council at Jerusalem: Sacrament and Salvation

The first Church Council at Jerusalem (A.D. 51) dealt with the question of sacrament and salvation: Is circumcision necessary for salvation? Against the teaching that one must be circumcised and obey the law to be saved, the Council answered: "We gave no such command."[15] Underlying this conflict was the error of literalism. Hebraic literalism, not distinguishing sign and reality, led to ceremonial legalism and has been a major stumbling block to faith past and present.[16] This council rejected the insistence that sacraments are necessary for salvation, and the Historic Christian Faith affirms this teaching.

The Apostles' Creed: Gnosticism and Dualism

The Apostles' Creed (A.D. 180) summarizes the Church's response to the challenge to the truth from the Greek worldview of epistemological

---

13. *2 Corinthians 10:4-5.*

14. Gangadean, "Paper No. 113: Historic Christianity," in *The Logos Papers*, 587-589.

15. *Acts 15:24.*

16. Gangadean, "Paper No. 60: The Spiritual War (Part II)," in *The Logos Papers*, 329-330.

gnosticism[17] (vs. the clarity of general revelation), metaphysical dualism (both matter and spirit are eternal), and ethical dualism (separating the soul from the hindrances of the body). Against metaphysical dualism, the Church affirms God as Creator of heaven and earth. God in the flesh (the Incarnation) is real, not apparent, and bodily existence continues forever (in the resurrection).

The Nicene Creed: The Trinity

At Nicea (A.D. 325), the Church summarized its understanding that God is one over and against misunderstanding, which has survived in several forms throughout history (Arianism, Socinianism, Deism, Unitarianism, Judaism, and Islam). What is one is a unity, and unity is a unity of diversity. God the Most High is a unity of the highest reality, that of Persons. "In the unity of the Godhead there be three persons, of one substance, power, and eternity: God the Father, God the Son, and God the Holy Ghost: the Father is of none, neither begotten, nor proceeding; the Son is eternally begotten of the Father; the Holy Ghost eternally proceeding from the Father and the Son."[18]

The Council of Carthage: The Canon of the New Testament Scripture

At the Council of Carthage (A.D. 397), the Church identified all the books and only the books that constitute the Scripture of the New Testament, the Word of God written, the rule of faith and life for all Christians. Scripture in every age must be spoken in the name of God (consistent with clear general revelation and with any prior special revelation). Scripture, as redemptive revelation, is given only by God, and being given by God, is kept pure and entire by God in every age so that nothing is to be added to it or taken away from it, contrary to all other claims. Both the Old and New Testaments were received by the testimony of the Church.

---

17. Epistemological gnosticism is the belief that knowledge is only for some, not all human beings. The nature of this knowledge is esoteric rather than knowledge about the basic things regarding God and man, and good and evil.

18. *WCF* 2.3.

The Council of Chalcedon: Christ Is God and Man

At the Council of Chalcedon (A.D. 451), the Church affirmed the doctrine of Christ as fully God and fully man. In the Incarnation, "two whole, perfect, and distinct natures, the Godhead and the manhood, were inseparably joined together in one person, without conversion, composition, or confusion."[19] The doctrine of Christ as God and man affects every aspect of understanding the person and work of Christ as Creator of all things, upholder of all things, redeemer of all things, and heir of all things.[20]

The Council of Orange: Sin and Salvation

At the Council of Orange (A.D. 529), the Church affirmed the doctrine of sin (man is fallen in Adam) and salvation (man is saved by grace) in response to Pelagian and semi-Pelagian error. The Church affirmed the distinction of liberty and ability in the four-fold state of man: (1) before the Fall, it was possible to sin; (2) after the Fall, it is not possible not to sin; (3) after regeneration, it is possible not to sin; (4) in man's glorified state, it is not possible to sin. While ability changes, liberty (doing what I want) does not change. Grace is given by God, sovereignly, as He wills. Grace is not dependent on man's willing, but by grace man is made willing. All acts by which we are saved—whether we "believe, will, desire, strive, labor, pray, watch, study, seek, ask, or knock"[21]—are by grace, the gift of God, not of ourselves, so that no man can boast.

---

19. *WCF 8.2.*

20. *Hebrews 1:1-3.*

21. *Council of Orange, Canon 6.*

THE FIVE SOLAS: Summary of the Reformation Principles

The Five Solas were derived from the creeds of the Reformation: The Westminster Confession built upon Augsburg (Lutheran), Thirty-Nine Articles (Anglican), Belgic (French), Helvetic (Swiss), Heidelberg (German), and Dort (Dutch).

Sola Scriptura: The Authority for Faith Is Scripture Alone

The authority of Scripture as special revelation is opposed to the authority of all other forms of special revelation (including the opinions of men or of private spirits). *Sola Scriptura* is not opposed to the use of reason in making good and necessary consequence, but assumes it. *Sola Scriptura* is not opposed to the clarity of general revelation, but assumes it. *Sola Scriptura* is not opposed to historically cumulative insight, the work of the Holy Spirit leading the Church into all truth, summed up in its creeds and confessions/councils, but anticipates it. *Sola Scriptura* requires all of the Scriptures and only the Scriptures, understood with good and necessary consequence, to be used in interpreting the Scriptures. Interpretation, therefore, is contextual, not literal or allegorical (in light of foreign assumptions).[22]

Sola Fide: Justification Is by Faith Alone

Justification is based on a person having righteousness. This righteousness is from Christ, whose righteousness is perfect and complete, and not from oneself. Christ's righteousness is imputed to the believer. This act of imputation assumes that Adam's sin is imputed to all men and that man's sin is imputed to Christ. The righteousness of Christ is received by faith alone. Justification is not sanctification; imputation of righteousness is not infusion of righteousness; forgiveness of sin is not cleansing from sin, but cleansing flows from forgiveness.

---

22. By foreign assumptions is meant the use of assumptions that are inconsistent with the biblical worldview of creation-fall-redemption, along with related and presupposed doctrines and beliefs.

Sola Gratia: Salvation Is by Grace Alone

Salvation is by grace alone, from beginning to end, without any admixture of human works. Both faith and works that glorify God are by grace. The grace of salvation is sovereignly bestowed, by God's predestination, apart from any condition in the person. The context of the bestowal of grace is summed up in the acronym TULIP.[23] In the order of application of redemption (*ordo salutis*), God's act of effectual calling (regeneration) precedes man's conversion (repentance and faith). Predestination is not opposed to but upholds freedom—properly understood as liberty to do what one desires, rather than ability to do otherwise.

Solus Christus: Salvation Is by Christ Alone

Salvation is through Christ alone, and not through Christ and the Church as mediator of grace. Salvation is through Christ alone and not through Christ and the merits or intercession or mediation of any other. Salvation is through Christ alone and not through Christ and any practice of penance in this life or in the next or through any supposed good deeds. Salvation is through Christ alone and not apart from Christ; there is no salvation without atonement, or without the vicarious atonement of Christ. Salvation is through Christ alone and in this life alone, after which is the final judgment, which vindicates the divine justice in judging man in unbelief.

Soli Deo Gloria: All of Life Is for the Glory of God Alone

God's glory, which is intrinsic in His being, cannot be added to but is only manifest in, by, unto, and upon all His creatures.[24] God manifests His glory in all His works of creation and providence, which purpose is extended to the fall of man.[25] Man's chief end is to glorify and enjoy God in all that by which He makes Himself known, in all His works of creation and providence.[26] The purpose of the work of dominion in the creation mandate and of the work of Christ in making disciples of all

---

23. Gangadean, "Paper No. 18: Salvation by Grace," in *The Logos Papers*, 119-122.

24. *WCF. 2.2.*

25. *WCF. 4.1, 5.1, 6.1.*

26. *SCQ. 1, 101; WCF. 4.1, 5.1.*

nations is the knowledge of God, which is eternal life.[27] The outcome of Christ's work through the Church is that the earth will be filled with the knowledge of the Lord as the waters cover the sea.[28]

THE SYNOD OF DORT: The Sovereignty of God in the Salvation of Man

TULIP is an acronym for the five points addressed in the Canons of Dort.

Total Depravity

Sin affects the whole (total) heart of man so that no one seeks God, no one understands, and no one is righteous.[29] Sin (moral evil) has become rooted in self-deception and self-justification so that the curse of toil and strife, and old age, sickness, and death was imposed by God to restrain, recall from, and remove moral evil in man.[30] While sin is total in extent, sin varies in degrees (men are more or less conscious and consistent in their unbelief), and it may increase to ever-deeper depravity. The sin of not seeking results in culpable ignorance of what is clear about God and the moral law. Inconsistencies within one's understanding result in inconsistencies within one's feelings and within one's actions. The understanding of fallen man (learned or unlearned) is deficient so that it is knowing the truth that makes one holy and sets one free.[31]

Unconditional Election

Election unto salvation is not based on any condition (past, present, or future) in man, but wholly on God's purpose, which is, in wisdom, to make His glory known. Election unto salvation is not apart from or against secondary causes such as seeking and understanding or repentance and faith; predestination is not of ends without means, but of both ends and means. Election of men presupposes the Fall

---

27. *Genesis 1:28; Matthew 28:20; John 17:3.*
28. *Isaiah 11:9.*
29. *Romans 3:10-11.*
30. *Genesis 3.*
31. *John 17:17; 8:32.*

(infralapsarianism) either to leave one in sin and death or to restore one to life and righteousness. Unconditional election is not arbitrary regarding justice; spiritual death is always due to sin, and mercy never sets aside justice, but satisfies justice through vicarious atonement by Jesus Christ. God has mercy on whom He chooses. Showing mercy to some is not unfair to others; what is unfair is to deny justice to any.

Limited Atonement

The intent and effect of Christ's atonement makes salvation actual for the elect, not merely possible for all, but actual for none. It is the revealed will of God that no one *should* sin and that all who sin *should* repent of sin and come to salvation. It is the decreed will of God to *permit* sin and the persistence of some in sin against calls to repentance. It is the decreed will of God (by promise) that good *will* overcome evil, that all nations *will* be blessed, that all nations *will* be discipled, and that the earth *will* be filled with the knowledge of the Lord as the waters cover the sea.[32] It is by the decree of God that the limit of atonement *does* include the salvation of the whole world as the kingdom of God grows to its fullness. The decree of God to save the world reveals the length, breadth, depth, and height of the love of God for mankind."[33]

Irresistible Grace

The grace of salvation is prevenient to the time of one's salvation; it operates to preserve and prepare a person for salvation. Salvation begins with effectual calling in which a person is raised from spiritual death to life, which is to be regenerated by spiritual rebirth or to be recreated as a new creature in Christ. Regeneration is wholly of God and not from man, either positively (by man's will cooperating with God's will) or negatively (by man's will not resisting God's will). By regeneration, a person is made both willing and able to seek and to understand and to do the will of God so that regeneration precedes and *naturally* results in repentance and faith. The grace of salvation continues after regeneration throughout one's life to make a person willing and able to know and do the will of God.

---

32. *Isaiah 11:9.*

33. *John 3:16; Ephesians 2:14-21.*

Perseverance of the Saints

Those who are effectually called (regenerated) are kept by the power of God unto salvation. A person who is outwardly called (but not effectually called) may fall away from their profession of faith. A person who is effectually called may fall away for a time or be left to walk in darkness, but is never utterly destitute of the seed of God.[34] Assurance of salvation is not of the essence of faith; a true believer may lack assurance but may through the right use of ordinary means attain assurance.[35] Assurance based on false teaching or practice is presumptuous. Perseverance of believers is not *regardless* of sin, but a *perseverance* and growth in faith and righteousness.

QUESTION 3

Identify levels of understanding the Reformed Faith. Explain the most basic level.

Four distinct levels of commitment to the Reformed Faith, from less to more deeply founded, are identified below in order that believers might become more conscious and consistent in understanding and see the need for a deeper foundation for the Historic Christian Faith.

1. *Traditional Reformed:* This level includes those brought up in Reformed churches as covenant children, having had exposure to the Reformed teaching, and who absorbed it by an acquaintance, not by explicitly examining the Reformed Faith. In other words, *Traditional Reformed* is a minimal level attained by upbringing, not thorough reflection. Many hold to the Confession by traditional exposure to the content, and remain there. Although this is how some come to the Reformed Faith, one should go beyond this level of understanding.

---

34. *WCF 18.4.*
35. *WCF 18.3.*

2. *Soteriological Reformed:* This level emphasizes salvation and includes those who call themselves five-point Calvinists (TULIP). They hold to the *ordo salutis* (the order of application of salvation) and the Five Solas of the Reformation (*Sola Scriptura, Sola Fide, Sola Gratia, Solus Christus, Soli Deo Gloria*). This is a common way many become involved with the Reformed Faith as it centers primarily on the doctrine of salvation. While this understanding is necessary for our faith, its scope does not extend to the biblical worldview and the moral law as applied to culture.

3. *Worldview Reformed:* This level is more invested in the cultural implications of Reformed theology and is connected with the work of Abraham Kuyper's *Lectures on Calvinism*. It is a distinct level from *Soteriological Reformed* as it seeks to implement the ethical implications of the biblical worldview (creation–fall–redemption) to culture and its institutions and focuses on kingdom living. In the words of Abraham Kuyper, "There is not a square inch in the whole domain of our human existence over which Christ, who is Sovereign over all, does not cry: Mine!"[36] *Worldview Reformed* seeks the Lordship of Christ in all areas of life. However, it falls short of the *Doxological Reformed* level as it does not affirm the clarity of God's existence and the goal of filling the earth with the knowledge of God.

4. *Doxological Reformed:* This level is the deepest (most basic) and most comprehensive level of understanding the Reformed Faith. Doxology is giving glory to God. The doxological understanding of Reformed theology focuses on and magnifies the fullness of the knowledge of the glory of God as stated in Isaiah 11:9(b): "For the earth shall be full of the knowledge of the Lord, as the waters cover the sea." The Westminster Standards emphasize the glory of God and the doxological focus of the Standards draws out the implications of this emphasis for all of life. Several statements from the Standards, taken together, are the basis for a doxological understanding of theology:

Westminster Confession of Faith (the Confession) 1.1 emphasizes the clarity of general revelation and the inexcusability of man's unbelief: "Although the light of nature, and the works of creation and providence

---

36. James D. Bratt, *Abraham Kuyper: A Centennial Reader* (Grand Rapids: William B. Eerdmans Publishing Company, 1998), 461.

do so far *manifest the goodness, wisdom, and power of God*, as to leave men inexcusable . . ."[37]

The Confession 2.2 emphasizes the manifestation of God's glory in, by, unto, and upon the created order: "God has all life, *glory*, goodness, blessedness, in and of Himself; and is alone in and unto Himself all-sufficient, not standing in need of any creatures which He has made, nor deriving any glory from them, but only *manifesting His own glory* in, by, unto, and upon them."

The Confession 3.3 emphasizes that God decrees all things for the praise of His glory: "By the decree of God, for the manifestation of *His glory*, some men and angels are predestinated unto everlasting life [to the praise of His *glorious* mercy]; and others foreordained to everlasting death [to the praise of His *glorious* justice]."

The Confession 4.1 emphasizes that God created to make His glory known: "It pleased God the Father, Son, and Holy Ghost, for the *manifestation of the glory* of His eternal power, wisdom, and goodness, in the beginning, to create, or make of nothing, the world, and all things therein whether visible or invisible, in the space of six days; and all very good."

The Confession 5.1 emphasizes that God rules to make His glory known: "God the great Creator of all things doth uphold, direct, dispose, and govern all creatures, actions, and things, from the greatest even to the least, by His most wise and holy providence, according to His infallible foreknowledge, and the free and immutable counsel of His own will, to the *praise of the glory* of His wisdom, power, justice, goodness, and mercy."

The Confession 6.1 emphasizes that God permitted the Fall and sin for His own glory: "Our first parents, being seduced by the subtlety and temptation of Satan, sinned, in eating the forbidden fruit. This their sin, God was pleased, according to His wise and holy counsel, to permit, having purposed to order it to *His own glory.*"

---

37. Emphasis added here and on the following points.

The doxological focus is further expressed in the Shorter Catechism. The answer to Shorter Catechism Question (SCQ.) 1, regarding the chief end of man, is a summary statement of the doxological focus: "Man's chief end is to *glorify God*, and to enjoy Him forever."[38]

The answer to SCQ. 46, regarding the First Commandment, emphasizes that we are to worship and glorify God accordingly: "The first commandment requires us to know and acknowledge God to be the only true God, and our God; and to *worship and glorify* Him accordingly."

Finally, the answer to SCQ. 101, regarding the First Petition of the Lord's Prayer, emphasizes that we are to glorify God in all that by which He makes Himself known: "In the first petition, which is, *Hallowed be thy name*, we pray that God would enable us, and others, to *glorify* Him in all that whereby He makes Himself known; and that He would dispose all things to His own *glory*."

The preceding selections from the Confession and the three Shorter Catechism questions unfold the meaning of *Doxological Reformed*. The doxological focus is the most basic and, therefore, fundamental understanding of the Westminster Standards despite not being commonly identified or taught in many Reformed circles. The doctrine of the clarity of God's existence (clearly revealed in and understood from the creation) and the earth being filled with the knowledge of God is distinctive of the doxological level of Reformed theology. The focus/goal of all of human life is to know God and make him known.

---

38. Benjamin B. Warfield in his essay "The First Question of the Westminster Shorter Catechism" draws attention to the doxological aim of this question. He states: "No Catechism begins on a higher plane than the Westminster 'Shorter Catechism.' Its opening question . . . sets the learner at once in his right relation to God. Withdrawing his eyes from himself, even from his own salvation, as the chief object of concern, it fixes them on God and His glory, and bids him seek the highest blessedness in Him." He continues: "The Westminster Catechism cuts itself free at once from this entanglement with lower things and begins, as it centers and ends, under the illumination of the vision of God in His glory, to subserve which it finds to be the proper end of human as of all other existence, of salvation as of all other achievements. To it all things exist for God, unto whom as well as from whom all things are; and the great question for each of us accordingly is, How can I glorify God and enjoy Him forever?" Warfield further explains that "The peculiarity of this first question and answer of the Westminster Catechisms, it will be seen, is the felicity with which it brings to concise expression the whole Reformed conception of the significance of human life." Benjamin Warfield. *The Westminster Assembly and its Work* (Michigan: Baker Books, 2003), p 380.

OUTLINE OF QUESTIONS

Introduction: The Confession, Its Relation to Other Creeds, and Levels of Understanding

1. What is a confession of faith? How is it an ordinary means of salvation?

2. What is the relation of the Westminster Confession to preceding creeds?

3. Identify levels of understanding the Reformed Faith. Explain the most basic level.

Chapter 1: Of the Holy Scripture

4. Explain the opening words of the Confession (assumptions and implications).

5. Explain the necessity of special revelation and Scripture. 1.1

6. Identify the content of Scripture positively and negatively. 1.2, 3

7. Explain the objective and subjective aspects of the authority of Scripture. 1.4, 5

8. Explain the assumptions and implications of the sufficiency of Scripture. 1.6

9. What is meant by the perspicuity of Scripture? 1.7

10. Explain the inspiration, transmission, and translation of Scripture. 1.8

11. How is Scripture to be interpreted? What is required, and what is forbidden? 1.9

12. What is the final authority in religious controversies? What is opposed by this? 1.10

Chapter 2: Of God, and of the Holy Trinity

13. What is God? What are the incommunicable, natural, and moral attributes? 2.1

14. Explain the aseity and sovereignty of God. 2.2

15. What are the ontological and economic aspects of the Trinity? 2.3

Chapter 3: Of God's Eternal Decree

16. What is decreed by God? How are second causes decreed? On what basis? 3.1, 2

17. How is God's decree applied to men and angels for life and death? 3.3, 4

18. How is God's decree applied to mankind for life? What is God's purpose? 3.5

19. What is the order of God's decree for the elect? 3.6

20. How is God's decree applied to mankind for death? What is God's purpose? 3.7

21. How is the mystery of predestination to be handled with special care? 3.8

Chapter 4: Of Creation

22. Explain the nature and purpose of creation. 4.1

23. Describe the nature of man in original creation. 4.2

Chapter 5: Of Providence

24. What is the extent, basis, and purpose of God's providence? 5.1

25. Explain first and second causes in ordinary and extraordinary providence. 5.2, 3

26. What is the providence of God with respect to sin in general? 5.4

27. What is the providence of God with respect to sin in believers? 5.5

Chapter 17: Of the Perseverance of the Saints

76. What is the perseverance of the saints? 17.1

77. On what does perseverance depend? 17.2

78. How does perseverance appear to be qualified? 17.3

Chapter 18: Of the Assurance of Grace and Salvation

79. Is the assurance of being in a state of grace presumptuous? 18.1

80. On what factors is the infallibility of assurance based? 18.2

81. Explain the necessity, means, obligation, and effects of assurance. 18.3

82. How and to what extent may assurance be shaken? 18.4

Chapter 19: Of the Law of God

83. What is the original character, content, and consequence of God's law? 19.1

84. What is the relation of this law to the law given at Sinai? 19.2

85. What is the purpose and permanence of the ceremonial and the civil law? 19.3, 4

86. What obligation is there to the moral law under the gospel? 19.5

87. Of what use is the moral law to the true believer? 19.6

88. What is the relation between law and grace? 19.7

Chapter 20: Of Christian Liberty, and the Liberty of Conscience

89. In what does Christian liberty consist? 20.1

90. What is the basis of true liberty of conscience? 20.2

91. How is Christian liberty abused? 20.3

92. How is Christian liberty related to civil and ecclesiastical authority? 20.4

Chapter 21: Of Religious Worship, and the Sabbath Day

93. How is worship regulated by general and special revelation? 21.1

94. To whom is religious worship to be given? 21.2

95. What are the requirements in worship for prayer? 21.3, 4

96. What are the ordinary and special forms and content of worship? 21.5

97. How is God to be worshiped in spirit and truth under the gospel? 21.6

98. What is the requirement of time and day for worship under the gospel? 21.7

99. How is the Sabbath day kept holy unto the Lord? 21.8

Chapter 22: Of Lawful Oaths and Vows

100. What is an oath and when is it warranted? 22.1, 2

101. What is the attitude toward and content of an oath? 22.3, 4, 5

102. What is acceptable and forbidden in an oath? 22.6, 7

Chapter 23: Of the Civil Magistrate

103. What is the origin and function of the civil magistrate? 23.1

104. What is the relation of the believer to the State and to war? 23.2

105. What is the relation of the Church and the State? 23.3

106. What honor is due to the magistrate? 23.4

Chapter 24: Of Marriage and Divorce

107. What is marriage and why was it ordained? 24.1, 2

108. Who can marry and what is it to be married in the Lord? 24.3, 4

109. What are the grounds for divorce and remarriage? 24.5

110. What due process is to be observed in divorce? 24.6

—

THE
CONFESSION
OF FAITH

—

Chapter 1

OF THE HOLY SCRIPTURE

QUESTION 4

**Explain the opening words of the Confession
(assumptions and implications).**

*I. Although the light of nature, and the works of creation and
providence do so far manifest the goodness, wisdom, and power of
God, as to leave men unexcusable . . .*

The opening words of the Westminster Confession of Faith assume
the clarity of general revelation[1] and the inexcusability of unbelief. The
clarity of general revelation affirms that the basic things about God and
man and good and evil are clear to reason. General revelation is what
can be known about God by all men, everywhere, and at all times. It
manifests the wisdom, power, and goodness of God in its fullness. The
clarity of general revelation is maximally clear.[2] It is known by reason
inferentially, being deduced (understood) from the things that are made.
The existence and nature of God is objectively clear and accessible to
any that care to know by seeking diligently,[3] and is so clearly revealed
as to leave men without excuse. We are inexcusable (*anapologia*) for

---

1. Gangadean, "Paper No. 35: The Clarity of General Revelation (Applied to GR-SR-HC)," 195-200; "Paper No. 41: What is Clear About God," 225-229; "Paper No. 112: Why General Revelation Is Basic in the Christian Worldview," in *The Logos Papers*, 583-585; Surrendra Gangadean, *The Westminster Shorter and Larger Catechisms: A Doxological Understanding* (Phoenix: Logos Papers Press, 2023), 111-112; Appendix 4.

2. *Romans 1:20.*

3. *Hebrews 11:6.*

our unbelief. We are guilty before God for failing to know and acknowledge Him as the only true God.[4] Our failure to know the clarity of general revelation is without excuse (culpable ignorance), which is morally blameworthy and, therefore, sin. Sin is a denial of the clarity of general revelation by failing to seek, understand, and do what is right.[5] Sin is shutting one's eyes, closing one's ears, and hardening one's heart in the face of God's clear objective revelation. The inexcusability of unbelief assumes that the acts of God reveal the nature of God and that, therefore, creation is revelation.[6] Every being acts according to its nature and reveals its nature by its acts. Therefore, all things that exist and are ruled by God reveal the divine nature. There is no revelation of God apart from His **works of creation and providence.** There is no direct seeing of God.[7]

While some believers occasionally acknowledge the clarity of general revelation, the classical proofs for God offered historically have been less than adequate. To show that there is something higher than the mind (Augustine), or that there is a first cause of motion (Aquinas), is not to show God the Creator. The teleological argument by itself shows only a designer, not the Creator. The ontological argument (Anselm) by itself shows, at best, that there must be something eternal, not that *only* some (God) is eternal. A recent form of the transcendental argument for God argues from the Triune God of the Scriptures rather than from general revelation. This way of argument fails to see that reason is both transcendental (self-attesting—as the laws of thought) and ontological (applies to *being* as well as to thought). Reason applies to God's being in that He is not both eternal and non-eternal, at the same time and in the same respect.

The inexcusability of unbelief entails that we can show—give proof of—what is clear from general revelation. To know that God exists, in the strong sense of "know," which is necessary for inexcusability, requires

---

4. *The Shorter Catechism Question (SCQ.) 46.*

5. *Psalms 14:1-3, 53:1-3; Romans 3:10-12.*

6. Surrendra Gangadean, *Philosophical Foundation: A Critical Analysis of Basic Beliefs,* Second Edition (Phoenix: Public Philosophy Press, 2022), 3-5, 287-292.

7. Gangadean, "Paper No. 106: The Good and Heaven," in *The Logos Papers,* 547-556; Surrendra Gangadean, *On Natural and Revealed Theology: Collected Essays of Surrendra Gangadean* (Phoenix: Logos Paper Press, 2023), 9-22.

having rational justification for one's belief, which constitutes proof.[8] The classical arguments for the existence of God have come short of proof. Objections have been raised against them, which call for a comprehensive response in a logically cumulative sequence. *Philosophical Foundation: A Critical Analysis of Basic Beliefs* provides proof by the epistemological method of Rational Presuppositionalism.[9] A sequence of arguments are given to show that only some is eternal: Matter exists, and matter is not eternal; The soul exists, and the soul is not eternal. *Philosophical Foundation* also addresses the principal counterarguments to belief in God as Creator in the problem of origin and the problem of evil. By combining revised forms of the ontological, cosmological, and teleological arguments, the eternal power and divine nature of God are clearly seen (further outlined below).

Prior to addressing arguments for the clarity of general revelation, it is important to note that some have sought to bypass the need for proof by appealing to direct knowledge of God. This view claims that all men have an immediate knowledge of God, which is other than an acquired or an inferred knowledge. This position is sometimes referred to as the *sensus divinitatis* (the Sensus Divinitatis view) and has been appealed to by several in the Reformed community (Calvin, Hodge, Van Til, Plantinga, Sproul, and Oliphint.) There are differences among those holding the Sensus Divinitatis view regarding the content of this knowledge, how it arises, and whether it is present as a propensity or an actuality.

The Sensus Divinitatis view assumes common sense realism, which assumes that appearance is reality, and that there is an external physical world. When objections arise against an immediately held, non-inferred (intuitive) belief in God or the external world, it is not evident to the Sensus Divinitatis position that in order to maintain belief in the face of objections, intuition must override reason. Rather, reason demands evidence, and intuitive belief is not a sufficient basis for the knowledge of God. Furthermore, an immediately held belief in God, in the face of what seems to be rational *prima facie* objections to that belief, is not warranted. Some, though not all, holding to the Sensus Divinitatis

---

8. Gangadean, "Paper No. 3: The Principle of Clarity," 15-20; Gangadean, "Paper No. 72: What is Knowledge? (Concise Version)," in *The Logos Papers*, 381-383; also see Appendix 5.

9. Appendix 5.

view attempt to establish moral accountability based upon immediate knowledge by claiming that knowledge of God gets through, and is suppressed, leaving men without excuse. This view assumes that if one does not have knowledge, one cannot be held responsible or that one is not culpable for the failure to acquire knowledge. But failure to seek and to understand describes a universal, basic, moral failure. Christ's prayer, "Father, forgive them, for they know not what they do,"[10] assumes ignorance is culpable.

The Sensus Divinitatis view assumes that knowledge of the truth does not set a person free and that moral bondage is not due to a lack of knowledge. To avoid denying that freedom comes through knowledge, a distinction has to be made in differing kinds of knowledge. But if knowledge is based on understanding the truth that sets one free, can there be any knowledge based on misunderstanding or lack of understanding?

The idea of inexcusability and suppression of the truth has been variously understood. To give an account of how a belief originates is not the same as an account of suppression of truth and inexcusability. A belief is suppressed by (or rejected for) an alternative belief for which one presumably has reasons. If it is clear that there are no reasons in support of one's unbelief, then unbelief is inexcusable. To merely reaffirm that "everyone deep down knows God" does not show clarity by showing the inexcusability of unbelief.

As mentioned above, the clarity of general revelation can be shown through Rational Presuppositionalism. The major steps in showing the clarity of general revelation proceed from the more basic to the less basic. Each subsequent argument presupposes and builds upon the previous arguments in a logically cumulative sequence. The following is a summary of the approach developed in *Philosophical Foundation* and *Theological Foundation*[11]:

1. Show the necessity for clarity in general against skepticism, and the necessity for clarity in particular for Christian theism against fideism.

---

10. *Luke 23:34.*

11. Surrendra Gangadean, *Theological Foundation: A Critical Analysis of Christian Belief* (Phoenix: Logos Papers Press, 2024).

2. Show, by ontological argument, that there must be something eternal. This is a paradigm of what is clear to reason. Rational Presuppositionalism requires agreement here before going any further in metaphysics. If this cannot be known, nothing can be known, and dialogue is not possible.

3. Show, by cosmological arguments, that only some (God) is eternal; that is, show theism vs. all forms of non-theism. This requires showing that matter exists and that matter is not eternal, that the soul/spirit exists and the soul is not eternal.

   To show that the material world is not eternal, it must be shown that the material world is not self-maintaining (vs. material monism—all forms of scientific materialism and cosmological naturalism).

   To show that the soul exists, it must be shown that the mind is not the brain. To show that the individual soul exists, it must be shown that there is not one mind only and its ideas (vs. spiritual monism—absolute or Vedantic idealism).

   To show that the material world exists (vs. ordinary idealism), it must be shown that the cause of what is seen is not my mind or another mind, but outside all minds.

   To show that the soul is not eternal (vs. all forms of dualism—Greek, Indian, Persian, Mormon, and reincarnation), it must be shown that the soul experiences unique events such as learning and growth.

4. Show, by teleological argument, that the natural order is by design (that is, show special creation) vs. all forms of evolution—natural and theistic.

5. Show, by teleological argument, that, in divine providence, moral and natural evil serve the divine purpose (that is, show the Ironic Solution to the problem of evil) vs. naturalistic and free will solutions.

6. Show that the moral law, structured into human nature by creation, is clear, comprehensive, and critical, the same in content as the law given by special revelation.

7. Show the necessity, content, origin, and existence of special revelation (vs. deism). Further, show the transmission, completion, translation, clarity, sufficiency, and interpretation of special revelation.

8. Show Christian theism (vs. all forms of non-Christian theism—that is, Judaic and Islamic theism), based on general and on special revelation.

9. Show the response to past challenges to Christian theism, based on general and on special revelation, and summed up in the ecumenical and historical creeds (Gnosticism, Trinity, Incarnation, predestination).

10. Show the response to continuing external and internal challenges to Christian theism (faith vs. reason, otherworldliness and secularism vs. knowledge of God, continuing divisions within theism vs. unity of the faith).

Proof by reason and argument, as listed above, raises immediate questions regarding skepticism about reason. In the history of philosophy and theology, many claims have been made in the name of reason that, upon analysis, have fallen short of proof. Since reason is **the light of nature** in man, a brief apology correcting failures in the use of reason in the history of ideas is needed.

Reason itself becomes a source of skepticism when it is misused or not fully used. It is misused when used as a source of truth rather than as a test for meaning. It is not fully used when it is used to construct a worldview and not first used critically as a test for the meaning of one's own basic belief. The antinomy of trusting in reason to know the truth and not trusting in reason to know the truth is grounded in the failure to use reason critically. There are several uses of reason which are to be distinguished and used in order, proceeding from the more basic to the less basic use.

Reason has been misused as a source of truth. Certain convictions are treated as self-evident to reason, and foundational, requiring no further need for defense. Descartes' *cogito ergo sum* is said to be self-evident every time it is thought. Thomas Jefferson took it as self-evident that all men are created equal. These views may be true, but the question is, are they self-evident? Are alternative views immediately self-contradictory? Are Hindu, Buddhist, or Naturalist views of the self immediately self-contradictory? Or do they require at least a few steps in reasoning to show they are contradictory? If so, how would Descartes show the steps in reasoning leading to self-contradiction in alternative views? In showing one's view of the self, must the existence of God first be addressed, and does this require attention, in proper order, to the ontological, cosmological, and teleological arguments? Clarity is not incompatible with a step-by-step approach in argument and seems to require it if thinking is presuppositional—proceeding from what is more basic to what is less basic.

Reason has not been fully used if it is not first used critically at the basic level. Reason is said to have reached its limits when more basic issues of permanence and change, unity and diversity, substance, and causality, are not first settled. Yet, these are the transcendentals that make thought possible.[12] Reason is used to form concepts that grasp the essence of things, the set of qualities that all members have, which they always have, and which distinguish them, by the law of identity, from non-members. Essences can be questioned where permanence (i.e., there must be something eternal) has not been settled. To question the ontological possibility of the relationship between *a* and *non-a* is to question the possibility of unity of diversity and whether anything can exist at all, a point not disputed by many. It is not to be assumed that the relationship between *a* and *non-a* is necessarily exclusionary (as being and non-being), but it may be complimentary (as wise and happy), or inclusive (as infinite and finite). Without permanence, essence, unity, and identity, concepts are empty, and words become meaningless. To deny the precondition for being and thought, to deny the ontological status of reason, to deny the Logos in the world, is to leap into the abyss of personal and cultural nihilism.

Many have said reason cannot grasp reality for any number of reasons. Aquinas, going back to Aristotle's Unmoved Mover, and later, Kant encountered an antinomy regarding time and creation: the world had a beginning (in time), and, there never was a time when the world did not exist. The antinomy assumes that time itself did not begin with creation, an assumption arising from a failure to understand the nature of time as relative to change. Kant assumed reason cannot grasp the world (*a priori* categories are mind-imposed on the world as we know it). Yet to distinguish first among things-in-themselves (a chair-in-itself is not a table-in-itself) and then to make the chair-in-itself

---

12. Surrendra Gangadean, *History of Philosophy: A Critical Analysis of Unresolved Disputes* (Phoenix: Public Philosophy Press, 2022), 25-44.

the cause of what appears, however much the mind shapes its input, is to know much about the *noumenal* world, making it not totally unknown. Mahayana sutras decry the intellect as getting stuck in antinomies: "Everything has a cause" and "nothing has a cause"; "Everything is eternal" and "nothing is eternal." But this is merely to assume that all is one and that contraries are indeed contradictories. Again, it is thought that reason cannot grasp reality. For example, categorical reason cannot grasp the being of Christ as both infinite and finite. One must transcend categorical reason for a transcategorical reason, or for meditative reason, or for a higher "double-bracketed" [[reason]]. But this is to assume a rational opposition between the infinite and the finite, rather than saying the infinite does and must include the finite. The same is to be said of reason in relation to the *Tao* (Lao Tzu), or Anaximander's *apeiron*, or Shankara's Nirguna Brahman—convictions arrived at by not critically examining assumptions.

Reason has also been the subject of debate regarding its role in religious beliefs, particularly in Christian theism. The contention has been between the magisterial and the ministerial uses of reason. It is acknowledged by those who uphold the ministerial use of reason that reason is necessary to receive revelation (the formative use of reason). It is also acknowledged that reason is useful in giving reasons for the truth of revelation. But it must never be the magistrate over or judge of the truth of revelation. It is a maidservant, not a mistress, and the strongest condemnation is reserved for the arrogation of the role of magistrate by reason. It is of use in systematizing truth (the constructive use of reason). And it is used to interpret Scripture and to support one interpretation over and against another interpretation (the interpretive use of reason). It may even be used to critically test alternative beliefs for coherence of meaning. But here, the line is drawn by those regarding reason as servant, not judge. They claim it cannot—it shall not—be used to judge the truth of revelation. Is this line being arbitrarily drawn?

It should be granted here, over and against deists (Herbert) and dogmatic rationalists (Wolff), that special revelation is necessary and does not and cannot *originate* from reason. But since reason is necessary to receive *and to understand revelation*, revelation must necessarily pass the minimal test of intelligibility. What is contradictory and is seen as contradictory is unintelligible and cannot be thought and, therefore, cannot be believed. What is an actual and what is an apparent contradiction must be discerned, often with much effort, to uncover hidden assumptions. To separate the formative and interpretive uses of reason is artificial, and to apply the critical use of reason to other Scriptures and not to one's own Scripture is arbitrary in the extreme. As an alternative to several forms of Sensus Divinitatis—whether a vague higher being (Calvin), or basic theism (Hodge), or full theism (Oliphint), or the Triune God (Van Til)—one can posit innate (non-empirical) concepts that are applied either to God or to the creation (e.g., finite or infinite, temporal or eternal, changing or unchanging). All men have these concepts. How they should be applied (whether only to God or to the creation) is clear to reason.

The Confession is arranged presuppositionally by addressing what is more basic first. Before addressing the content of Scripture, the Westminster Divines addressed the light of nature, and the works of creation and providence—which are within the domain of general revelation, and general revelation is within the domain of natural theology. Natural theology precedes revealed theology, and it provides the basis for its necessity.[13] In other words, general revelation is prior to and necessary for the existence of special revelation (Scripture).

The second assumption of the opening words of the Westminster Confession is that special revelation assumes the clarity of general revelation.[14] Special revelation,[15] given by God and committed to writing, *is* Scripture and is set over and against all other claims of special revelation (including the opinions of men or of private spirits). This is how the doctrine of *Sola Scriptura* should be understood. Scripture is not set in opposition to reason (the light of nature) in making good and necessary consequence, but assumes it. Scripture is not opposed to clear general revelation because Scripture presupposes the existence of reason and general revelation; therefore, Scripture must be consistent with both. Special revelation is redemptive revelation; it assumes the reality of sin in the failure to see what is clear from general revelation.[16]

---

13. Gangadean, *On Natural and Revealed Theology*, 149-165.

14. Gangadean, "Paper No. 112: Why General Revelation Is Basic in the Christian Worldview," in *The Logos Papers*, 583-585.

15. Gangadean, "Paper No. 87: Scripture," in *The Logos Papers*, 455-458.

16. Gangadean, "Paper No. 146: The Biblical Worldview (Part VI)," in *The Logos Papers*, 741-745; Gangadean, *The Westminster Confession*, Question 24; Appendix 7.

Therefore, *Sola Scriptura* is not set against reason and the clarity of general revelation, but presupposes both as its most basic context.[17]

The third assumption of the opening words of the Confession is about the content of general revelation. It encompasses the **works of creation and providence**—more specifically, how these reveal God's **goodness, wisdom, and power.** These specific attributes can and should be derived from general revelation, which shows not merely a bare existence of a divinity, but the existence and nature of God.[18] We should show the eternal power of God, and by implication, that human beings are inexcusable for not seeing the eternal power of God. In thinking, we begin with basic questions regarding the nature of being: What has the power of self-existence, and what does not? What is real? What is eternal? The pastor-teachers are calling us to engage with these fundamental questions. In our study of the Confession, we will build on the clarity of God's existence and understand our inexcusability in our failure to know what is clear. We will see the implications of clarity and inexcusability regarding providence as it relates to the problem of evil (the curse) in the world. From providence, we will point out how original creation was very good, and how the goodness of original creation is also affirmed in Scripture. The same truth is affirmed in both general and special revelation, but it can be known from providence first. We should know the goodness of God from creation and how that affects providence, how it relates to natural evil, what natural evil is, and what natural evil implies about the covenant by which we are represented. We should be able to show from providence that, because of the act of another, we are affected (covenant representation). These are some of the things that we should be able to show from general revelation.[19]

---

17. The opening words of *Genesis* "In the beginning God created . . ." presupposes the existence of God, a belief in the existence of God and divine revelation, including the context and purpose of revelation, and an understanding of what "God" means. This, in turn, presupposes an understanding of Spirit, infinite, eternal, and unchangeable. These presuppose an understanding of being, qualities, essence, etc. Later statements in the earliest chapters presuppose an understanding of good and evil and of life and death. Understanding *Genesis 1–3* in this way, then, becomes the basis of understanding all that comes later in *Genesis* and throughout the Scriptures to the last book.

18. *Romans 1:18-20.*

19. Gangadean, "Paper No. 3: The Principle of Clarity," in *The Logos Papers*, 15-20; Gangadean, *History of Philosophy*, 48-69; Gangadean, *On Natural and Revealed Theology*, 149-165; Appendix 6.

The fourth assumption of the opening words of the Confession concerns the relationship between reason and general revelation. The concept of **the light of nature** is distinguished from **the works of creation and providence**. They are not to be equated. The light of nature is to be understood as reason, and the works of creation and providence is to be understood as general revelation. Understanding the light of nature as *reason* is another distinct contribution of the Confession. It is an assumption incorporated within the rest of the work. The Confession affirms our nature as fundamentally rational, made in the image of God, and endowed with the ability to use reason to understand the nature of the things created. Reason is the Word of God in man.[20] The Word of God comes *to* man and *into* man in several ways (explained throughout the Gospel of John). The life of the logos is in all men as light.[21] The light of nature is the light of reason, by which we see/understand the invisible things about God. Reason in man is ineradicable and irresistible. Man is created by God, in His own image, to know God. By reason, all other forms of revelation are understood: in creation (general revelation); in history (special revelation in Scripture); in person (incarnate in Jesus Christ); in the Church (in its councils and creeds—the work of the Holy Spirit through the pastor-teachers); and in believers (through regeneration and sanctification). Reason is the most basic form of the Word of God for human knowledge; it is the self-attesting form of the Word of God present in all men.

There are common Christian misconceptions about reason that ought to be addressed at this point, as they are widespread. First, it is said that reason is fallen, that the effects of the Fall (or noetic effect) of sin blinds man and distorts his reason. In response, it can be said that reason is not affected by the Fall any more than our sight is affected by the Fall. The Fall affected our willingness to use reason, not reason itself. Second, it is said that reason is autonomous, that it is used to support vain philosophy, and that in the name of reason, men have turned away from God. In response, it can be said that since reason is the Word of God in men, it cannot be opposed to Scripture, and that one has to deny reason to avoid seeing God. Those who deny God in the name of

---

20. Gangadean, "Paper No. 45: The Logos Theses," 257-259; Gangadean, "Paper No. 48: Reason and the Word of God," 267-269; Gangadean, "Paper No. 92: The Relevance of Reason," in *The Logos Papers*, 485-491.

21. *John 1:4.*

reason have failed to use reason fully and are morally culpable for that failure. Third, it is also said that Scripture is the authority, not reason. Since Scripture is sufficient, reason is not necessary. In response, it can be said that reason is the laws of thought. It is necessary to understand God's self-revelation in nature/creation and in Scripture. Reason is necessary to expose inconsistencies both in false prophets and in false interpretations of Scripture.[22]

Instead of rejecting reason as the light of nature based on historical misconceptions, the role of reason in man should be further understood—whether in the Fall, in conversion, or in apologetics. Man, in himself, is now fallen; he fails to use reason self-critically or fully. This failure is in man, not in reason. Reason in itself (as the laws of thought) is not and cannot be fallen. In salvation, man is restored to the life of reason by regeneration, and sanctified through trials of faith leading to deeper understanding. In apologetics, by reason, man is to demolish arguments and every pretension that exalts itself against the knowledge of God, take every thought captive to the obedience of Christ, and silence what opposes the Word of God.[23]

The Confession is the work of the Holy Spirit through the pastor-teachers in Church history, given to us to become established. How well established would we be if we understood these ideas and implications? *Individually*, we would not be tossed to and fro by every wind of doctrine,[24] nor would we waver in our resolve to seek God diligently. Instead, we would be established in personal maturity. *Collectively*, the Church would not be badly divided, disregarded, and scorned by others. It would assume its proper role as the pillar and ground of the truth, as the redemptive institution that preserves what is best (salt) and exposes unbelief by knowledge of the truth (light).[25] We cannot get to the position of being salt and light in the culture without the work of

---

22. These are some of the common objections against reason. For a fuller exposition, see: Gangadean, "Paper No. 111: Common Christian Misconceptions About Reason," in *The Logos Papers*, 579-582.

23. *2 Corinthians 10:4-5.*

24. *Ephesians 4:14.*

25. Gangadean, "Paper No. 33: The Church (Concise)," 189-190; Gangadean, "Paper No. 36: The Pillar and Ground of the Truth," 201-206; Gangadean, "Paper No. 44: Reason in Itself," 255-256; Gangadean, "Paper No. 58: The Spiritual War (Part I)," 317-322; Gangadean, "Paper No. 60: The Spiritual War (Part II)," 329-330; Gangadean, "Paper No. 61: The Present and Future State of the Church," in *The Logos Papers*, 331-333.

the pastor-teachers. This is the ordinary way provided by God for the Church to attain the unity of the faith. Consequently, knowledge of the Confession is essential in preparing us for the work of the kingdom.

SUMMARY ANSWER

The first assumption of the opening words of the Confession is the relation between the clarity of general revelation and the inexcusability of unbelief. The second assumption is that special revelation assumes the clarity of general revelation. The third assumption is the content of general revelation, including both creation and providence, and all that can be known in each. The fourth assumption is that the light of nature is the logos in man as reason and that there is a relation between reason and general revelation. Implications of the opening words include: God's nature is knowable from general revelation; original creation was very good; covenant representation—natural evil was imposed because of the act of another; natural evil is imposed as a merciful call back from moral evil; and evil is permitted to serve the good.

QUESTION 5

Explain the necessity of special revelation and Scripture.

I. Although the light of nature, and the works of creation and providence do so far manifest the goodness, wisdom, and power of God, as to leave men unexcusable; yet are they not sufficient to give that knowledge of God, and of His will, which is necessary unto salvation. Therefore it pleased the Lord, at sundry times, and in divers manners, to reveal Himself, and to declare that His will unto His Church; and afterwards, for the better preserving and propagating of the truth, and for the more sure establishment and comfort of the Church against the corruption of the flesh, and the malice of Satan and of the world, to commit the same wholly unto writing: which makes the Holy Scripture to be most necessary; those former ways of God's revealing His will unto His people being now ceased.

Special revelation **is necessary unto salvation.** The word **necessary** is essential to understanding the purpose of special revelation. Special revelation is the only way to know how we can be saved. Special revelation assumes that we need redemption, that we have sinned, and that we have come short of the glory of God by failing to see what is clear from general revelation.[26] It is in this context that we are to speak of the need for special revelation. God gave special revelation at different times and in different ways (**at sundry times, and in divers manners**), and God had it preserved in writing, which is the transition from the necessity for special revelation to the existence of Scripture.[27] Scripture is special revelation in written form. Why was it written down? God committed it unto writing **for the better preserving and propagating of the truth,** and for the **establishment and comfort of the Church.**

---

26. *Romans 1:18-20, 2:12-14, 3:10-12*; Gangadean, "Paper No. 56: The Gospel (Summary)," in *The Logos Papers*, 303-313.
27. Gangadean, "Paper No. 12: The Necessity for Scripture," in *The Logos Papers*, 75-77.

Given the reality of sin, it is necessary to commit Scripture unto writing in order to protect and preserve it. And Scripture is complete—**those former ways of God's revealing His will unto His people being now ceased.** With redemption accomplished—the promise being fulfilled in the person and work of Christ—there is no need for any further revelation. Being complete, special revelation is now ceased.[28]

The questions that naturally occur in relation to Scripture are: (1) Since I believe in God (e.g., deists), why do I need Scripture? (2) How do we know that we have the Word of God? (3) How do we know that it has not been corrupted? Or that a gospel or book has not been excluded? Or that a non-inspired book has been added? In other words, how do you know that Scripture has been preserved pure and entire?

The Confession was written at the beginning of Modernity (1648). These questions have been raised most pointedly by deists, naturalists, anti-theists, and postmodernists, after the writing of the Confession, and thus require our attention. Becoming more conscious and consistent in the faith requires answering challenges as they manifest themselves prominently in history. The necessity for special revelation has been the subject of much contention, but no step-by-step proof has been provided. Therefore, the necessity for special revelation, along with related questions, will be briefly addressed.

Understanding the necessity for Scripture is the first step in the process of rationally going from general revelation to special revelation. It is a ten-fold step-by-step process from the more basic to the less basic. After *Necessity,* there is understanding the *Content, Origin, Existence, Transmission, Completion, Translation, Clarity, Sufficiency,* and *Interpretation* of Scripture.[29]

General revelation requires special revelation. Original creation was very good. It was absent of any moral or natural evil. That God created the world without evil can be shown from the nature of God. We could and should have known the doctrine of the goodness of creation from clear general revelation by analyzing the very terms involved in the problem of evil: If God is all good and all powerful, why is there evil? This is called the *could–would–must–did* argument. By understanding

---

28. Gangadean, "Paper No. 122: Contra Charismatic Distinctive," in *The Logos Papers*, 651-653.

29. Gangadean, "Paper No. 11: From General Revelation to Special Revelation," in *The Logos Papers*, 69-73; Gangadean, *Theological Foundation.*

the implications that follow from God's infinite power and infinite goodness, we can prove that original creation was very good:

> Since God is infinite in power, He *could* create a world without evil.
>
> Since God is infinite in goodness, He *would* create a world without evil.
>
> Since God *could* and *would* create a world without evil, He *must* have.
>
> Therefore, God *did* create a world without evil. Hence, original creation was very good.

The existence of moral evil, its inherent consequence of spiritual death in man (justice), and the existence of natural evil as a merciful call back from moral evil (mercy), require special revelation/Scripture to show how God can be both just and merciful to man in sin.

Moral evil is an act contrary to human nature as a rational being. It is the failure to use reason to see what is clear. It is to not seek, not understand, and not do what is right.[30] It is to neglect, avoid, resist, and deny reason (NARD) in the face of what is clear about God. If there is no clear general revelation, there is no inexcusability (sin).[31] The inherent consequence of moral evil (NARD) is meaninglessness, boredom, and guilt. This is spiritual death ("the wages of sin is death"; "in the day that you eat you shall surely die"; "you that were dead in your trespasses and sins"[32]). The just punishment for sin is inherent in sin and therefore present, now and always, not merely future and imposed (the popular view of hell).[33]

Natural evil is suffering from circumstances—toil and strife, and old age, sickness, and (physical) death. It can be intensified corporately to war, famine, and plague. Natural evil is not original in creation (*could–would–must–did* argument). Natural evil is not inherent in moral evil; spiritual death is inherent in moral evil, not physical death. Natural evil is therefore imposed by an act of God. Natural evil as imposed is not inherent and, therefore, is not punishment. Natural evil is not imposed

---

30. *Romans 3:10; Psalm 14:1-3, 53:1-3.*

31. *Romans 1:20.*

32. *Romans 6:23; Genesis 2:17; Ephesians 2:1.*

33. Gangadean, "Paper No. 4: The Cornerstone," in *The Logos Papers*, 21-25. Provides an explanation of good and evil understood from general revelation, special revelation, and Historic Christianity.

arbitrarily; it is imposed because of the moral evil of one person.[34] Natural evil is not imposed unnecessarily, but because of the depth of moral evil (failure to know what is clear coupled with self-deception and self-justification concerning this failure). Natural evil is imposed as a call back from moral evil; suffering is a call to stop and think; it serves to restrain, recall from, and remove moral evil. Physical death is a call back from sin and its inherent consequence (spiritual death). Natural evil imposed as a call back is, therefore, mercy, not justice (punishment). Natural evil as mercy requires special revelation (Scripture) to show how God can be both just and merciful at the same time: Mercy cannot set aside God's justice; mercy must satisfy justice since God is infinite, eternal, and unchangeable in His justice. Scripture is necessary to show how God is both just and merciful to man in sin.

SUMMARY ANSWER

Special revelation is necessary to know how we can be saved from root sin (the failure to see what is clear from general revelation). Special revelation is given as redemptive revelation. The need for redemptive revelation can be known from the existence of natural evil. Physical death is not natural/original (if God is all good and all powerful, then He could, would, must, and therefore did create the world without evil). Natural evil is due to moral evil: Natural evil assumes moral evil; natural evil is imposed as a merciful call back from moral evil; physical death calls us back from spiritual death (the inherent consequence of moral evil). If natural evil and moral evil exist, then justice and mercy exist. Mercy must satisfy justice (versus mercy setting aside justice). Special revelation must show how God is both just and merciful to man. If natural evil is by one representing all, then special revelation is necessary to show righteousness by one representing all. Redemptive revelation in the Old Testament describes the person and work of the Messiah to come, while the New Testament shows how Jesus fulfilled and is fulfilling what was written of the Messiah. God committed special revelation unto

---

34. Gangadean, "Paper No. 147: The Biblical Worldview (Part VII)," in *The Logos Papers*, 747-757.

writing for the preservation and propagation of the truth and the establishment and comfort of the Church.

QUESTION 6

Identify the content of Scripture positively and negatively.

II. Under the name of Holy Scripture, or the Word of God written, are now contained all the books of the Old and New Testaments, which are these: Of the Old Testament: Genesis, Exodus, Leviticus, Numbers, Deuteronomy, Joshua, Judges, Ruth, I Samuel, II Samuel, I Kings, II Kings, I Chronicles, II Chronicles, Ezra, Nehemiah, Esther, Job, Psalms, Proverbs, Ecclesiastes, The Song of Songs, Isaiah, Jeremiah, Lamentations, Ezekiel, Daniel, Hosea, Joel, Amos, Obadiah, Jonah, Micah, Nahum, Habakkuk, Zephaniah, Haggai, Zechariah, and Malachi. Of the New Testament: The Gospels according to Matthew, Mark, Luke, and John, The Acts of the Apostles, Paul's Epistles to the Romans, Corinthians I, Corinthians II, Galatians, Ephesians, Philippians, Colossians, Thessalonians I, Thessalonians II, Timothy I, Timothy II, Titus, Philemon, The Epistle to the Hebrews, The Epistle of James, The first and second Epistles of Peter, The first, second, and third Epistles of John, The Epistle of Jude, The Revelation of John. All which are given by inspiration of God to be the rule of faith and life.

III. The books commonly called Apocrypha, not being of divine inspiration, are no part of the canon of the Scripture, and therefore are of no authority in the Church of God, nor to be any otherwise approved, or made use of, than other human writings.

Positively, the content of Scripture includes **all the books of the Old and New Testaments.** The canon of the Old Testament was received by the testimony of the Church under the Old Testament. The canon of the New Testament was received by the testimony of the Church under the New Testament. At the Council of Carthage (A.D. 397), the

Church identified all the books and only the books that constitute the Scripture of the New Testament, the Word of God written, **the rule of faith and life** for all Christians. Scripture in every age must be spoken in the name of God (consistent with God's nature, His revelation in the creation, and any prior special revelation).[35] Scripture, as redemptive revelation, is given only by God, and being given by God is kept pure and entire by God in every age, so that nothing is to be added to it or taken away. Scripture includes all of the 66 books of the Bible, only these books, and nothing more. This means that nothing has been left out, and nothing has been added.

How can we know we have all and only the true Scripture? Could some books have been left out? This question can be answered by understanding the content and relation between general and special revelation. A prerequisite in discerning the content of special revelation is that it must be consistent with what is clear from general revelation. From general revelation, it is clear that only some is eternal, that God the Creator exists.[36] It is also clear that original creation was very good, devoid of any natural evil (*could–would–must–did* argument[37]). By one man (Adam), as representative head, physical death entered the world and passed to all. By one man (Christ), as representative head, physical death will be removed (by the resurrection).

One could never know, apart from special revelation, how another man would be found who will take away the sin of the world. Only special revelation makes known the mystery of the Incarnation of the one who comes to take away the sin of the world. Only the Scriptures affirm what is true about God from the creation. Only Genesis 1–3 affirms God the Creator, man's purpose (the knowledge of God through the work of dominion), man's destiny (the earth being filled with the knowledge of God), and the original goodness of creation.[38] Only Genesis 1–3 affirms that all are affected by one (covenant representation and the fall of man). Only Genesis 1–3 affirms man's redemption through the curse and promise (mercy satisfies justice through vicarious

---

35. *Deuteronomy 18:22.*

36. For a complete proof for the existence of God, see: Surrendra Gangadean, *Philosophical Foundation: A Critical Analysis of Basic Beliefs.*

37. pp. 15-16

38. *Genesis 1:4, 10, 12, 18, 21, 25, 31.*

atonement vs. setting aside divine justice). Therefore, only in Genesis 1–3 is given as the foundation of Scripture in organic seed form. Scripture builds on, is to be understood by, and is the development of what is revealed in Genesis 1–3.

How can we know that the Scripture is complete? Scripture is redemptive revelation—it is based on promise and fulfillment. The promise is for another to come in the place of Adam to *undo* what Adam did and to *do* what Adam failed to do. Scripture in the Old Testament tells of the person and work of the Messiah to come. The New Testament shows how Jesus of Nazareth fulfilled, and is fulfilling, what was written of the Messiah. When the promise is fulfilled, then special revelation (Scripture) is complete. If Christ has come, then the promise is fulfilled. Christ has come if the Spirit has been sent. It is the work of the Messiah (anointed by the Spirit) to send the Spirit after His death and resurrection. The Spirit has come if the kingdom of God is expanding to all nations. Since the kingdom is expanding into all nations, the promise is fulfilled. Stated syllogistically: If the promise is fulfilled, then special revelation is completed. The promise is fulfilled. Therefore, special revelation is completed.

Negatively, the books of the *Apocrypha* are not included in the Bible. The Roman Catholic Church has included the *Apocrypha* as Scripture, but the Protestant Church has not. The people of God, the Jewish people (the Hebrews) under the Old Testament, were entrusted with identifying the Scriptures prior to the coming of Christ. They did not include the *Apocrypha*. The Roman Catholic Church does not have the authority to identify anything as Scripture outside of what has been previously canonized. The word *Apocrypha* has come to mean non-scriptural or non-canonical; it ought not to be accepted as Scripture. The books of the *Apocrypha* were written pre-Christ—between the Book of Malachi and the coming of Christ. Additionally, no post-Christ books are identified as *Apocryphal*. The Jews identify the Old Testament canon as it exists today and only those books. If anyone had the authority to add to the Scripture, it would have been the Jewish people, and they never did. They developed the *Talmud* (the *Mishna*, and the *Gemara*), but it was never included in the *Torah*, and they never adopted it as part of Scripture. The Jewish religious teachers may give tradition greater authority than Scripture,[39] but tradition is not considered to be Scripture. The Jews make a distinction between the inspiration of Scripture and the works of tradition. Finally, the *Apocryphal* writings were not quoted by Christ or any of the New Testament writers, and they are not consistent with prior revelation.

SUMMARY ANSWER

Positively, special revelation is the Bible. It consists of 66 books and only the books of the Old Testament (39) and New Testament (27). Special revelation is complete because the promise is fulfilled.

Negatively, the books of the Apocrypha are excluded. They do not claim inspiration, were excluded from the canon by the people of God in the Old Testament, were not quoted by Christ or the New Testament writers, and are not consistent with prior revelation.

QUESTION 7

Explain the objective and subjective aspects of the authority of Scripture.

IV. The authority of the Holy Scripture, for which it ought to be believed, and obeyed, depends not upon the testimony of any man, or Church; but wholly upon God (who is truth itself) the author thereof: and therefore it is to be received, because it is the Word of God.

---

39. *Mark 7:6-8.*

V. We may be moved and induced by the testimony of the Church to an high and reverent esteem of the Holy Scripture. And the heavenliness of the matter, the efficacy of the doctrine, the majesty of the style, the consent of all the parts, the scope of the whole (which is, to give all glory to God), the full discovery it makes of the only way of man's salvation, the many other incomparable excellencies, and the entire perfection thereof, are arguments whereby it does abundantly evidence itself to be the Word of God: yet notwithstanding, our full persuasion and assurance of the infallible truth and divine authority thereof, is from the inward work of the Holy Spirit bearing witness by and with the Word in our hearts.

We may know both objectively and subjectively that the Old and New Testaments are Scripture. Objectively, the Holy Scripture is, in fact, the Word of God; it does not depend on **the testimony of any man, or Church, but wholly upon God Himself. It is to be received because it is the Word of God,** which is the objective, external source of the authority of Scripture. Since God is the author of Scripture, God endows the Scripture with objective authority. This authority exists irrespective of whether anyone sees it or not. Yet, how do we know that we have the Word of God? The Confession speaks of the objective authority of the Scripture as self-attesting. It is not immediately, directly self-attesting as is reason (as the laws of thought),[40] but is self-attesting through arguments. Arguments are the objective ground for determining the authority of Scripture.

The objective authority of the Word is self-attesting through the following arguments: (1) **The testimony of the Church** (the work of the Holy Spirit leading the Church into all truth), (2) **the heavenliness of the matter** (as redemptive revelation), (3) **the efficacy of the doctrine** (the rule of faith and life), (4) **the majesty of the style** (the sublime expression of truth), (5) **the consent of all the parts** (the internal consistency of redemptive content and void of contradictions), (6) **the scope of the whole (which is, to give all glory to God),** and (7) **the full discovery it makes as the only way of man's salvation** (vicarious atonement by a covenant representative). The effect of the authority of the Word is its power to change human lives. The Word has the power to change

---

40. Gangadean, *Philosophical Foundation*, 298-299.

lives in a particular way that other Scriptures do not. For example, the Hindu Scriptures may bring about a change in a person's life by their considering the self as one with the being of God. Instead, the Holy Scripture brings change through the conviction of humility rooted in our dependent creatureliness before God the Creator.

Furthermore, Scripture must have objective content that is consistent with what can be known of God from the creation (general revelation). The Confession says that we are to be moved by the evidence of **the scope of the whole (which is, to give all glory to God).** This passage calls attention to the necessity for Scripture to be spoken in the name of God—that is, it must be consistent with the glory of God and affirming of God's attributes—His wisdom, power, holiness, justice, goodness, and truth, in an infinite, eternal, and unchangeable way.[41] If a purported Scripture does not affirm these attributes of God, it is lacking. It cannot be Scripture and, therefore, should not be considered Scripture. The Confession refers to the redemptive content of Scripture in **the full discovery it makes of the only way of man's salvation.** The purpose of Scripture is to show how God can be both just and merciful to man in sin. The Scripture and *only* the Scripture reveal His plan of salvation.

There is objective content to Scripture that can be brought under intellectual scrutiny and withstand challenges against it. Furthermore, we can provide responses that overcome objections to Scripture. We know the Bible is Scripture—the Word of God—by a threefold criterion:

(1) The Bible is spoken in the name of God, consistent with God's essence, nature, and attributes.

(2) The Bible is consistent with what can be known from clear general revelation—that only God the Creator is eternal, that original creation was without natural evil, and that all humans have been affected by the act of one person.[42]

---

41. Gangadean, *The Westminster Catechisms*, 119-122.
42. Gangadean, "Paper No. 35: The Clarity of General Revelation (Applied to GR-SR-HC)," 195-200; Gangadean, "Paper No. 41: What is Clear About God," 225-229; Gangadean, "Paper No. 112: Why General Revelation Is Basic in the Christian Worldview," in *The Logos Papers*, 583-585; Gangadean, *The Westminster Catechisms*, 111-112; Appendix 4.

(3) The Bible shows (in light of what is clear about God) the only way of salvation—how God is both just and merciful to man in sin.[43] It shows how mercy satisfies, versus sets aside, divine justice.

Other Scriptures do not show the need for vicarious atonement to satisfy divine justice. Vicarious atonement is a basic doctrine by which we can distinguish between Christianity and Islam.[44] Both worldviews claim that God is both just and merciful. In Christianity, the mercy of God satisfies the divine justice through the atoning sacrifice of Christ. In other words, mercy perfectly satisfies the demands of justice. In Islam, although claiming to affirm both, the mercy of God cancels the requirement of justice, overrides it, and sets it aside. In Islam, mercy does not satisfy the demands of justice, which is contrary to the central teaching of Biblical Judaism and Christianity. Islam professes to build on the Old Testament and the New Testament, yet denies what is central to both: In the Old Testament, it denies vicarious atonement on *Yom Kippur* (the Day of Atonement) and in the New Testament, which fulfills the Old Testament, it denies the death of Christ on the cross to atone for the sin of the world. If there is no redemption in Islam, then God is not great in justice and mercy, and *"Allahu Akbar!"* is empty of meaning. In Islam, justice is not satisfied, but is disregarded by mercy. This leads to a fundamental problem in Islam—God cannot be infinite in justice if the requirements of justice are not satisfied. This is the most basic disagreement between Christianity and Islam. In Christianity, atonement is the heart of the doctrine of redemptive revelation. The centrality of atonement is what the Confession means by **the full discovery it makes of the only way of man's salvation.**

The Confession goes on to say, **the many other incomparable excellencies, and the entire perfection thereof, are arguments** (note the word "arguments") **whereby it doth abundantly evidence itself to be the Word of God.** Again, "evidence itself" means Scripture is self-attesting through arguments. Thus, the Scripture is not immediately self-attesting. Only reason, as the laws of thought, is immediately self-attesting—it cannot be questioned because, as the laws of thought, it makes questioning possible. But, as is noted above, the Confession

---

43. Gangadean, "Paper No. 114: The Gospel: For Everyone," in *The Logos Papers*, 591-594.

44. Gangadean, "Paper No. 91: Christianity and Islam," in *The Logos Papers*, 479-484.

specifies seven arguments for Scripture by which it evidences itself to be the Word of God.

The Bible does not appeal to experience as in the case of Mormonism, which claims the evidence for the truth of their Scriptures is a "burning in the bosom." The Mormon appeal to special experience is an appeal to experience apart from the Word, rather than understanding what is contained within the Word. In Evangelical circles, the claim that we are to believe the Bible fideistically (without proof or understanding), apart from arguments, is likewise a mistake. Over and against appeals to experience or to faith in a fideistic sense, the Confession brings into focus the need for arguments to prove the self-attesting nature of the Word of God. The lack of awareness among believers of the objective content of Scripture is widespread and is notably why the Church at large has been unable to answer the challenges of Modernity. The Church's inability to respond to challenges regarding the necessity and existence of Scripture has weakened its witness. If we are to go on to maturity, we need to answer these basic questions faithfully, by the cumulative insight provided to us by the work of the Spirit in Church history.

A further argument for Scripture is **the consent of all the parts.** We can search the Scripture and find no contradictions within. There may be alleged contradictions, but upon analysis, these are only apparent and not actual contradictions. For example, some claim that Genesis chapter 2 is a second creation account when, in fact, it is a further development of Genesis 1. If we understand Genesis 1–3, we can easily understand what comes after in Scripture, because Genesis 1–3 contains the biblical worldview in an organic seed form.[45] The biblical worldview of creation–fall–redemption is tightly put together and includes all the basic components of redemptive revelation.[46] Through the enabling of the Holy Spirit, we come to see the redemptive content of Scripture.

When we see what is objectively clear, we will see that Scripture gives all glory to God. Nowhere does Scripture give glory to man or to other creatures. Nor does Scripture compromise God's glory by saying He is less than wise, or less than fully just. Only the Scripture discloses the way of salvation, which involves the Incarnation of the Son of God

---

45. Surrendra Gangadean, *The Biblical Worldview: Creation, Fall, Redemption: Genesis 1–3: Scripture in Organic Seed Form* (Phoenix: Logos Papers Press, 2024).

46. Gangadean, "Paper No. 13: The Biblical Worldview (Concise)," 79-80; Gangadean, "Paper No. 14: The Biblical Worldview (Expanded)," in *The Logos Papers*, 81-89.

in human nature. The Incarnation had to be communicated through special revelation; we could not have figured it out on our own. It had to be revealed by special revelation along with other revealed truths such as the Trinity and specific aspects of eschatology.[47]

From general revelation alone, we can go as far as to say that we need someone to represent us. We can see that help is needed and that God sends help by imposing natural evil as a call back from moral evil. If natural evil is a call back (mercy), the question arises: How is God going to be just and merciful to man in sin? We need another human representative, but all human beings born of man are born in trespasses and sin. Where will we get this human representative? No human being could figure this out. No one can draw the inference that the Lord will provide a savior through the Incarnation, nor can we know that there is a Trinity apart from God revealing it. The Incarnation and the Trinity are revealed only through special revelation.

The Scripture reveals the only way for man's salvation, which includes the idea of a covenant, that Christ comes to *undo* what Adam did (according to the first covenant) and to *do* what Adam failed to do. The first covenant is not set aside, which is attested to by the fact that all are born into a world with physical death.[48] Natural evil is imposed on the world because of the moral evil of another. However, even when this reality is explicitly stated in Scripture, we tend not to pay attention to it.

The subjective conviction of the authority of Scripture is through the work of the Holy Spirit. God is the author of Scripture,[49] there is objective content in the Word, and God, the Spirit who inspired it, subjectively works in our hearts so that we might understand the content. The Confession says, the **full persuasion and assurance of the infallible truth and divine authority thereof, is from the inward work of the Holy Spirit bearing witness by and with the Word in our hearts.** Persuasion is not apart from the Word; it is **by and with the Word**, enabling us to see what is objectively revealed.

---

47. Surrendra Gangadean, *The Book of Revelation: What Must Soon Take Place: Doxological Postmillennialism* (Phoenix: Logos Papers Press, 2024).

48. pp. 15-16

49. Gangadean, "Paper No. 12: The Necessity for Scripture," in *The Logos Papers*, 75-77.

SUMMARY ANSWER

The objective authority of Scripture consists of it being authored by God, given by God, and it is to be received because it is the Word of God. Scripture is self-evidently the Word of God through arguments. The arguments from the Confession are sevenfold:

1. The testimony of the Church (the work of the Holy Spirit leading the Church into all truth).

2. The heavenliness of the matter (as redemptive revelation).

3. The efficacy of the doctrine (the rule of faith and life).

4. The majesty of the style (the sublime expression of truth).

5. The consent of all the parts (the internal consistency of redemptive content and void of contradictions).

6. The scope of the whole (the doxological focus—to give all glory to God).

7. The full discovery it makes of the only way of man's salvation (vicarious atonement by a covenant representative).

There is a threefold criterion from general revelation in answering the question: How do we know the Bible is the Word of God (special/redemptive revelation)?

1. It is spoken in the name of God.

2. It is consistent with what can be known from clear general revelation.

3. It shows (in light of what is clear about God) the only way of salvation—how God is both just and merciful to man in sin.

The subjective authority of Scripture consists of our coming to know the objective truth of Scripture through the inward work of the Holy Spirit, bearing witness by and with the Word in our hearts.

QUESTION 8

Explain the assumptions and implications of the sufficiency of Scripture.

VI. The whole counsel of God concerning all things necessary for His own glory, man's salvation, faith and life, is either expressly set down in Scripture, or by good and necessary consequence may be deduced from Scripture: unto which nothing at any time is to be added, whether by new revelations of the Spirit, or traditions of men. Nevertheless, we acknowledge the inward illumination of the Spirit of God to be necessary for the saving understanding of such things as are revealed in the Word: and that there are some circumstances concerning the worship of God, and government of the Church, common to human actions and societies, which are to be ordered by the light of nature, and Christian prudence, according to the general rules of the Word, which are always to be observed.

Section 1.6 uses the phrases: **expressly set down** and **by good and necessary consequence**. "Expressly set down" refers to the explicitly stated words in the Scripture. For example, the New Testament does not explicitly give a command to baptize infants; it is not *expressly* set down. Some have used this fact to justify rejecting paedobaptism (infant baptism).[50] Literalism is a misapplication of the sufficiency of Scripture. In holding to the sufficiency of Scripture, we should be mindful that we can have a very limited, somewhat mechanical, view of interpretation. Those who adhere to literalism in their hermeneutics err by affirming only what has been expressly set down. The Confession does not limit the sufficiency of Scripture to what is expressly set down. It says it is *either* **expressly set down** *or* **by good and necessary consequence may be deduced from Scripture**. To deduce by good and necessary consequence means that we are to use reason to understand the implications of Scripture. The Confession refers to using good and

---

50. Gangadean, "Paper No. 140: Argument for Paedobaptism," in *The Logos Papers*, 703-704.

necessary consequence as deductions or inferences of reason to be made from what is stated in the Scriptures. When the Confession speaks of the sufficiency of Scripture, it is not setting Scripture over and against reason, because the interpretation of Scripture involves making good and necessary consequence that presuppose the use of reason.[51]

The doctrine of clarity and inexcusability is deduced from Romans 1:18-20. Other doctrines, such as the Trinity, are not expressly set down in Scripture, but by good and necessary consequence can be deduced from Scripture. Some details about Christ's incarnation, His dual nature—being both God and man—are expressly set down in Scripture, but *how* that is so (the Incarnation) is not expressly set down, and that is what was worked out in the Council of Chalcedon and affirmed in the Confession. The Incarnation needed to be addressed because non-believers challenged the rationality of the Incarnation. Some may ask: "Would not God have saved us much trouble if He just explained the Trinity? Moreover, would not God have saved us much trouble if He had just explained what atomic energy is, and how DNA works? Why did God not do that? That would have saved us a lot of pain and heartache. Why did God not just whisper it into the ear of a scientist?" The answer is that God wants us to exercise dominion—to exercise our understanding. Some things are clear. For example, the existence of God is clear, yet many dispute that God exists. "Why did God not give us the proof in the Bible?" Moreover, when we affirm the clarity of God's existence and provide proof, it causes difficulty in the hearer—not because it is objectively difficult to know that God exists—but because it is subjectively difficult since fallen human beings are resistant to the truth. It is objectively clear, and God wants us to use our reason to see what is clear, just as He wants us to use our reason to see how He and only He is eternal. Through inferential knowledge from the things that are made (creation), we come to know Him, which is part of diligently seeking and knowing Him.

The difficulty in understanding inferred doctrines comes at the subjective level, not at the objective level of doctrinal truth. This is to speak of the *perspicuity* of Scripture or *clarity* of Scripture. Not only is general revelation clear, but Scripture is also clear—objectively clear—in itself. But Scripture becomes unclear as it is resisted in light of our sin

---

51. Gangadean, "Paper No. 15: Hermeneutics," in *The Logos Papers*, 91-101.

of not seeking and not understanding, which is compounded by our self-deception and self-justification concerning this failure.

Scripture, as special revelation, is set over and against other claims of special revelation (e.g., the Book of Mormon, the Quran, the Vedas, etc.), which is how the sufficiency of Scripture should be understood. The sufficiency of Scripture is not set over and against reason or general revelation, but over and against any other forms of special revelation. The Confession affirms this when it states: **unto which nothing at any time is to be added, whether by new revelations of the Spirit, or traditions of men.** All other claims of special revelation are excluded. There have been teachings and traditions brought into the Church that are not taught in Scripture, such as the immaculate conception and assumption of Mary, purgatory, supererogation, and papal infallibility. These doctrines have divided the Church and should not have been accepted. Where did these doctrines come from? They constitute a new special revelation. Scripture is sufficient; nothing is to be added. What if someone comes up with a new charismatic revelation, and says that God showed them that we are to go to Africa as missionaries next year? Some things are known by good and necessary consequence, but particular things about the future are not known.[52]

The sufficiency of Scripture is set over and against new revelations of the Spirit, which is not to be confused with the illuminating work of the Holy Spirit, bringing us to a saving understanding of what is revealed in the Word. The knowledge necessary for our salvation is in the Scriptures, but we often fail to see it, and rather than repenting and seeking diligently, many opt for seeking extra-biblical revelation. To go outside of the revealed will of God in Scripture is to bypass what God has revealed of Himself in the Scriptures. Instead, we should pray, seek the Lord, and ask Him for illumination, not in something extraordinary, but in what is contained in the Scriptures themselves—for the answer lies therein. The sufficiency of Scripture and the perspicuity of Scripture go hand in hand. What is necessary for us to know regarding salvation is contained in the Scriptures and is accessible to all who seek it through the illuminating work of the Spirit.

---

52. Gangadean, "Paper No. 122: Contra Charismatic Distinctive," in *The Logos Papers*, 651-653.

The Confession proceeds to draw out implications regarding the use of good and necessary consequence by stating **there are some circumstances concerning the worship of God, and government of the Church, common to human actions and societies** (referring to general revelation) in which wisdom is to be applied. Some aspects of worship are left to the exercise of practical wisdom, including things such as the time to meet for worship, the furniture to be used, the arrangement of the chairs, whether to increase the sanctuary size, etc. We do not go to the Urim and Thummim with a special request to answer such questions. Practical matters are **to be ordered by the light of nature, and Christian prudence, according to the general rules of the Word, which are always to be observed.** Again, the sufficiency of Scripture denies the need for any additional revelation.

The sufficiency of Scripture presupposes the use of reason to understand the meaning of revelation and the prior context of general revelation. In addition, the general principles contained in Scripture should be used as general rules for practical matters regarding the worship of God. Understanding the sufficiency of Scripture in light of reason, general revelation, and Christian prudence is set over and against those holding to literalism, who operate only by what is explicitly set down in Scripture.[53] Not all things are expressly set down in Scripture. For example, how should we worship God? Does it expressly say that we should sing in worship, or is that a general revelation awareness? Scripture gives us the content of what is to be sung in worship—the Book of Psalms—but it does not tell us explicitly to sing because singing praise is derived from general revelation. A further implication is that since we have been given a book of songs in Scripture, then we should sing from that book. That the psalms should be sung in worship is an implication derived by good and necessary consequence. The psalms provide the *content* of worship, not the *circumstance* of worship. This is an example of how we deduce implications from the content of Scripture through the use of good and necessary consequence.

---

53. Literalism is the belief that understanding a text is free of interpretive assumptions; that preceding layers of context are not necessarily relevant; that meaning is explicit only and not also by inference; that understanding language figuratively is to be avoided whenever possible. For further understanding of literalism as applied to Church history, see: Gangadean, "Paper No. 60: The Spiritual War (Part II)," in *The Logos Papers*, 329-330.

SUMMARY ANSWER

Scripture presupposes the use of reason to understand the meaning and implications of its statements. Some things are expressly stated in Scripture, and others are deduced by good and necessary consequence—they are inferred. Assumption: The revelation is complete (no additional revelation is needed) and sufficient to provide knowledge regarding faith (doctrine) and life (application).

Implications: There is no need for other special revelations or traditions of men. Some Christian doctrines (e.g., the Trinity, Incarnation, and infant baptism) are inferred through the use of good and necessary consequence—the use of reason to understand the implications of Scripture. Some alleged Christian doctrines not found in Scripture expressly or inferred are not to be believed (e.g., the immaculate conception and assumption of Mary, purgatory, supererogation, and papal infallibility). Some aspects of the worship of God, the government of the Church, and ethics are to be ordered by the light of nature (reason) and Christian prudence, consistent with general and special revelation.

QUESTION 9

What is meant by the perspicuity of Scripture?

VII. All things in Scripture are not alike plain in themselves, nor alike clear unto all: yet those things which are necessary to be known, believed, and observed for salvation, are so clearly propounded, and opened in some place of Scripture or other, that not only the learned, but the unlearned, in a due use of the ordinary means, may attain unto a sufficient understanding of them.

The *perspicuity* of Scripture is clearly stated in the Confession. Not all things are **alike plain in themselves, nor alike clear unto all**. For example, the references regarding the man of sin or antichrist—are those clear? How about the doctrine of predestination—is that clear?

In saying that **all things in Scripture are not alike plain in themselves, nor alike clear unto all,** does not mean that things are not plain, but when contextualized, they may be seen as plain. Moreover, what is not clear at one time to a person may become clear later as more basic pieces of interpretation fall into place. At some point, one may not understand the doctrine of predestination, but once assumptions and objections concerning the nature of God and man, freedom, and the use of reason to see what is clear are responded to, it can become quite clear. We may reflect and be surprised that we did not understand what is now very clear to us. When certain truths and assumptions fall into place, then it is clear. It continues by saying, **those things which are necessary to be known, believed, and observed for salvation, are so clearly propounded, and opened in some place of Scripture or other, that not only the learned, but the unlearned, in a due use of the ordinary means, may attain unto a sufficient understanding of them.** The Scriptures can be known and understood by all.[54] We do not need a special guide to the Scriptures. Having the Confession does not negate searching the Scriptures to see "if these things are so."[55] In other words, there is clarity to the Scriptures, and we need to learn to make use of the ordinary means that the Lord has established to come to a deeper understanding of its objective content.

Again, not all things are **alike clear**—less basic beliefs depend on more basic beliefs. For example, we could not get to the belief that "God exists" without prior arguments. But once the arguments are understood, it is a simple step to see how it is clear that God exists.[56] If we can know that only some is eternal, then it is a simple step to say that God the Creator exists. The Confession states that all can know the redemptive content of Scripture—both the learned and unlearned. The ordinary means can allow all to understand, if those means are used faithfully. This truth has not been upheld in the history of the Church. What has happened in the history of the Church is that some have said, "You cannot understand this; we will tell you what it means." The Medieval Catholic Church did not allow the Scriptures to be in

---

54. Gangadean, "Paper No. 15: Hermeneutics," in *The Logos Papers*, 91-101.

55. *Acts 17:11.*

56. Gangadean, *Philosophical Foundation*, 71-161; Gangadean, *History of Philosophy*, 47-58; Gangadean, *The Westminster Catechisms*, 111-112; Gangadean, "Paper No. 3: The Principle of Clarity," 15-20; Gangadean, "Paper No. 102: The Clarity of General Revelation," in *The Logos Papers*, 527-529.

the hands of the people, to be searched by all. In Gnosticism in the early Church, there was an appeal to secret knowledge which was only attainable by a few. The Confession affirms the basic things are clear, and everyone can and should read the Scriptures.[57]

The encouragement to read the Scriptures is not to be taken for granted. Some have objected by saying, "Look at what has happened to the Protestants, they allowed access to the Scriptures, and they have gone every which way with it—we really need to get back to the Roman Catholic Church and the *magisterium*." In response, it must be noted that the Confession states that **the unlearned, in a due use of the ordinary means**, are to read the Scriptures. And for that matter the *learned*, who often bring foreign assumptions to the interpretation of Scripture (e.g. allegoricalism) not consistent with general revelation or the biblical worldview of creation–fall–redemption, are to make due use of the ordinary means as well. For example, liberal theology has strayed and departed from the basic things about God (the Trinity), Christ (the Incarnation), and the inerrancy of Scripture. So, the problem is not with the degree of learning that a person has, but whether that person has made use of the ordinary means to see what is clear. The ordinary means consist of prayer, personal devotions (Scripture is to be read by all and searched by all), family devotions (reading of Scripture, singing, and praying), regularly attending worship, observing the sacraments, tithing, fellowshipping, church membership, submitting to godly oversight, meditating on the Law day and night, and building upon the Historic Christian Faith.

The Scripture is to be read by all and searched by all. This is why believers in Protestant churches are encouraged to read the Scriptures. And we should further point out that the Protestant Church has become badly divided not because believers read the Scripture, but because we do not read the Scripture with the due use of ordinary means. Due use of ordinary means includes understanding the way to interpret Scripture (hermeneutics and epistemology)—by contextual interpretation—understanding the less basic in light of the more basic.[58]

---

57. Gangadean, *Philosophical Foundation*, 3-5, 287-292.

58. For further elaboration on contextual interpretation, see: Gangadean, "Paper No. 15: Hermeneutics," in *The Logos Papers*, 91-101. For further understanding of epistemology, see: Gangadean, *Philosophical Foundation*, 3-68.

The elementary teachings are easily knowable by good and necessary consequence. Yet those basic truths have been obscured by the antinomy of literalism and allegoricalism in hermeneutics. Literalism, based on non-rational empiricism, fails to distinguish interpretation based on the biblical worldview of creation–fall–redemption (Rational Presuppositionalism applied in contextualism) from interpretation based on non-biblical or foreign/unwarranted (gnostic) assumptions used by allegoricalism. Literalism neglects, avoids, resists, and denies the logical distinction of less and more basic. It cannot understand the distinction because it undermines it. It renders the distinction meaningless by making all things equally basic. In seeking to preserve literal meaning, without contextual interpretation, literalism loses all meaning. Allegoricalism uses a foreign interpretative framework to provide a deeper meaning as a response to the arbitrary constraints of literalism. Literalism and allegoricalism are antinomies that derive their strength from their mutual failure.[59] The excesses of each compel the other to double down in their views. In order to overcome the uncritically held assumptions of both, contextualism applies Rational Presuppositionalism to hermeneutics.

Contextual interpretation is opposed to both literalism (which treats context as non-existent or irrelevant) and to allegoricalism (which rejects that interpretation is bound by the clarity of general revelation, or maintains that there is no clear general revelation, or that we cannot know what is clear from general revelation). Contextualism uses good and necessary consequence derived from several ordered layers of context: first, clear general revelation; second, the biblical worldview of creation–fall–redemption in Genesis 1–3; third, the historical context of redemptive revelation; fourth, the book in historical context; then chapter; then verse; then word. We understand Scripture, not by any church's teaching, but by interpreting what is less basic in light of what is more basic—what logically comes after by what is logically prior. We understand Scripture (the Word of God written) in light of reason (the Word of God in all men)[60] and the clarity of general revelation (the

---

59. Gangadean, *The Book of Revelation*. The Book of Revelation serves as the most illustrative work to explain and expose the limitations and difficulties brought about by either literalism or allegoricallism in interpreting Scripture. Dr. Gangadean's Doxological Reformed Sermon Series provides a stark contrast to the failed antinomy (literalism and allegoricalism) in favor of contextualism.

60. *John 1:4.*

Word of God in creation), through good and necessary consequence. We understand redemption in light of the Fall, and the Fall in light of creation. We understand man's purpose as a rational creature in light of God's purpose: that creation is revelation, necessarily, intentionally, and exclusively, and that all things are directed to the good—the knowledge of the glory of God. Contextual interpretation applied to the philosophical, theological, and historical foundations enables us to see how the basic truths of Scripture are elementary and easily knowable.

The revelation in Scripture is cumulative—it builds on prior revelation and understanding. Contextual interpretation, when applied to what comes before, enables the anticipation of subsequent revelation. The content of latter revelation (e.g., the Book of Revelation) is anticipated by prior revelation and confirms what was to be expected.[61] What began in the Garden of Eden is brought to full expression in the City of God—from creation to the kingdom's consummation, the truth of God is clear, and we are morally accountable to know and build upon it.[62]

SUMMARY ANSWER

The basic things about God and man and good and evil are clear to all who seek to know. Some things are clear to all in Scripture. The basic things are clear to all. Some things are not clear in themselves nor alike clear unto all. When the basic truths of Scripture are understood (the biblical worldview,[63] the Seven Pillars,[64] and the Principle of Clarity[65]), the less basic truths become clear in context through the use of good and necessary consequence (e.g., covenant representation, predestination, and eschatology). The illumination of the Spirit through the use of ordinary means leads to knowledge of the truth of God contained in Scripture. The

61. Gangadean, *The Biblical Worldview*.

62. Gangadean, *The Book of Revelation*.

63. Gangadean, "Paper No. 13: The Biblical Worldview (Concise)," 79-80; Gangadean, "Paper No. 14: The Biblical Worldview (Expanded)," in *The Logos Papers*, 81-89.

64. Gangadean, "Paper No. 37: The Seven Pillars," 207-210; Gangadean, "Paper No. 36: The Pillar and Ground of the Truth," in *The Logos Papers*, 201-206.

65. Gangadean, "Paper No. 3: The Principle of Clarity," 15-20; Gangadean, "Paper No. 35: The Clarity of General Revelation (Applied to GR-SR-HC)," 195-200; Gangadean, "Paper No. 53: Common Ground (Part IV)," in *The Logos Papers*, 283-286.

ordinary means consist of prayer, personal devotions (Scripture is to be read by all and searched by all), family devotions (reading of Scripture, singing, and praying), regularly attending worship, sacraments, tithing, fellowshipping, church membership, submitting to godly oversight, meditating on the Law day and night, and building upon the Historic Christian Faith.

Historic denials of the perspicuity of Scripture were notable in Gnosticism in the early Church, where appeal to secret knowledge was only attainable by few; and in the magisterium of the Medieval Catholic Church, where the teaching authority resided in the Church and the laity was discouraged from searching the Scriptures.

QUESTION 10

Explain the inspiration, transmission, and translation of Scripture.

VIII. The Old Testament in Hebrew (which was the native language of the people of God of old), and the New Testament in Greek (which, at the time of the writing of it, was most generally known to the nations), being immediately inspired by God, and, by His singular care and providence, kept pure in all ages, are therefore authentical; so as, in all controversies of religion, the Church is finally to appeal unto them. But, because these original tongues are not known to all the people of God, who have right unto, and interest in the Scriptures, and are commanded, in the fear of God, to read and search them, therefore they are to be translated into the vulgar language of every nation unto which they come, that, the Word of God dwelling plentifully in all, they may worship Him in an acceptable manner; and, through patience and comfort of the Scriptures, may have hope.

Scripture is inspired by God in the original languages of Hebrew and Greek. Translations of Scripture are not inspired, only the original languages are. What is meant by inspiration? Inspiration is not a mechanical operation apart from the mindset and time of the person writing the Scriptures. However, inspiration is not limited only to the writer's historical context and understanding. For example, the prophet Amos, writing in 8th century B.C., was not limited to his particular historical context and understanding. Inspiration means that God works to clearly reveal the truth, and nothing but the truth, in and through human vessels, even when the water (the Word) takes the shape of the vessel (the writer). This means that the writing style of Isaiah is different from that of Amos, but it is 100% water, not in the least bit changed because of the person through whom it comes. Jonah's form of writing is different from Jeremiah's in terms of the experiences, thoughts, and feelings of each. Ezekiel speaks using imagery in a way that Isaiah does not. This allows for variations of many kinds. Biblical inspiration is not a mechanical theory of inspiration as in the Islamic sense of dictation by God. Biblical inspiration is much richer and fuller. God prepared the vessel of revelation, and God ordained all the various ways in which revelation may be communicated. Although there are many ways in which the Word may be communicated, the form does not change the content; the revelation is what God intended. Whether it is done through symbol, prose, or poetry, it is the same inspiration. That every word of Scripture is inspired by God is spoken of as the plenary or full inspiration of Scripture. Every word is God-breathed, down to the last colon and semi-colon, "Not one jot or one tittle shall in any way pass from the law until everything is fulfilled."[66] We should affirm the full inspiration and inerrancy of Scripture, not just that the words, in general, are true, but that Scripture is inerrant in the original.

Secondly, Scripture is fully inspired (plenary). Many in the history of the Church have tried to find errors and contradictions in the Bible. The supposed contradictions and errors cannot withstand critical scrutiny—when the claims are examined, the apparent error or contradiction can be answered. This includes asking questions about how something is stated, or its placement in one gospel as compared to other gospels. Apparent anomalies can be addressed through contextual interpretation by understanding the point that is being made in the gospel. Furthermore, we should understand that the gospels are not written in chronological sequence, unless it explicitly makes a

---

66. *Matthew 5:18.*

point of chronology. For example, what happened when Jesus cursed the fig tree,[67] and what was said when? Sometimes we have to put the chronology back together by taking two or three gospels and analyzing their content to understand their complementarity. Apparent errors are alluded to—claims are made by people who easily and quickly question the Scriptures, yet upon analysis, these *prima facie* arguments do not withstand contextual scrutiny. As another example, some have asked, "How long did it take for the Israelites to cross the Red Sea, and how many people crossed that distance?" The claim is made that it is not physically and mathematically possible for them to have crossed the Red Sea. Statements and inquiries of this kind are often made because the basic things are not kept in mind.

Before addressing the translation of Scripture, the question of inspiration and original copies should be understood further. We do not have any of the original copies of Scripture. Yet, copies of the original manuscripts have been preserved, though there are variations among these copies of the original. As an illustration, let us say that ten people are taking notes from what is being taught, and some differ on the punctuation or have misspellings—we can do redactions and put the various notes together and clearly see the content. Similarly, we have copies of the original manuscripts with minor variations, yet when we compare them, we have no problem understanding the meaning and original statements of the Scripture. The Confession says that these were **immediately inspired by God, and, by His singular care and providence, kept pure in all ages.** With respect to the transmission of Scripture, we assert that God gives Scripture, and because God gives it, we should infer that God preserves it.[68] From the inspiration of Scripture, we should infer—by good and necessary consequence—the preservation of it. This is how we proceed from the more basic (Scripture is given by God) to the less basic (if God gave Scripture, then He would preserve it). Since Scripture (as redemptive revelation) is given in light of moral evil in man, and it is given to restore man from evil, it is therefore preserved from man's neglect, avoidance, resistance, and

---

67. *Mark 11:12-25; Matthew 21:18-22.*

68. Gangadean, "Paper No. 11: From General Revelation to Special Revelation," in *The Logos Papers*, 69-73.

denial of the truth of God. The Scriptures have been preserved by God pure and entire—all of the Scriptures and only the Scriptures.

Can Scripture be translated? is like asking: Are concepts universal? Words express concepts and judgments which are cognitive, meaning they are true or false. Concepts are universal, they apply to all members of a class of beings, and they are the same in all thinkers.[69] Words are conventional, in that they differ from language to language. The universality of concepts makes translation from one language to another possible. Concepts or ideas remain the same, but in translating, the word may change from one language to another. Furthermore, since all persons are to read Scripture, it must be translated. Since the Scriptures are inspired (God-breathed), are preserved by God, and their content is for all, then translations are necessary and desirable.

Some people claim that the Scriptures should only be read in the original language—anything less will not convey its true meaning. Furthermore, they say if we do not know the original Greek and Hebrew, we are unqualified to interpret the Scriptures. Others say that Scriptures are not to be translated. For example, in Islam, since the Quran was originally given in Arabic, Allah intended it to be read only in Arabic. On the contrary, we should argue that since Scripture uses human language, and is given for human redemption, then it can and should be translated into the common languages of the people. Furthermore, translations are opposed to the use of paraphrases in the place of translations.

As mentioned before, the original Scriptures are inspired and inerrant, and since redacted copies were preserved, we can consult those redacted manuscripts to discern the original content. In light of the ancient manuscripts, differing approaches to translation can be used. The two most common approaches are formal equivalence (literal word-for-word) and dynamic equivalence (thought-for-thought). For example, the King James Version is a literal word-for-word translation, where if a word is not in the original, the word is placed in italics. The New International Version is dynamic, where the idea or conceptual understanding is given priority. Consulting different translations may help to understand the meaning intended to be conveyed.

---

69. Gangadean, *Philosophical Foundation*, 51-54; Gangadean, *History of Philosophy*, 28-29.

SUMMARY ANSWER

Inspiration: Scripture in the original languages is fully inspired (God-breathed) and inerrant (void of contradictions). The revelation came through human vessels, and while expressing the uniqueness of each vessel, it remained fully inspired. God prepared the vessel and ordained providentially all the ways in which the revelation was communicated. It resulted in a richer and fuller revelation (vs. dictation).

Transmission: Although none of the original manuscripts are available, we possess many copies of the originals to verify the accuracy of their content. The argument for transmission is: If Scripture is given by God, then it is preserved by God. Scripture is given by God. Therefore, Scripture is preserved (pure and entire) by God.

Translation: Since concepts are universal, we can translate from one language to another. And since all are commanded to read the Scripture, it must be translated.

QUESTION 11

How is Scripture to be interpreted?
What is required and what is forbidden?

IX. The infallible rule of interpretation of Scripture is the Scripture itself: and therefore, when there is a question about the true and full sense of any Scripture (which is not manifold, but one), it must be searched and known by other places that speak more clearly.

In approaching Scripture, questions arise regarding its content. For example, how do we know that Adam and Eve were historical persons? Or how do we prove that Genesis was not written poetically or mytho-poetically? The context must be used to discern how we are to interpret the passage. For instance, in the Book of Genesis, we have a clear genealogy provided for Adam's descendants, which we can trace back step-by-step to the beginning of mankind. There are no jumps in the genealogy. The genealogical context makes clear, by good and necessary consequence, that the creation of man and the account in the Garden of Eden is intended as literal and biological. When we read that Adam begat so and so, and people multiplied on the earth, the context of the passage helps to bring out the intended sense and meaning.

If necessary, in interpreting Scripture, we should look at **other places that speak more clearly.** A commonly controverted topic is the doctrine of predestination. We encounter verses that might seem to go in two possible directions. When this occurs, we should search out other verses that speak more clearly to overcome any ambiguity. **The infallible rule of interpretation of Scripture is the Scripture itself.** The less clear is interpreted in light of what is more clear (presuppositionally).[70] How do we interpret the Book of Revelation? We should go back to the biblical worldview given in Genesis 1–3, understand the curse and the promise, and how that is being worked out in history.[71] The biblical worldview is clear by good and necessary consequence. The Scriptures are given in an organic seed form—it is a unity that grows. The basic framework for understanding the Scriptures is stated in Genesis 1–3 and increasingly expressed throughout the Scriptures.[72] The curse and the promise are given in Genesis 3, yet without a proper understanding of them (which requires a proper understanding of the creation of man and the Fall), we will have difficulty interpreting the later books, such as the content of the Book of Revelation. If we understand the curse and the promise when we come to the Book of Revelation, we can see the continuity and unity of content and understand its meaning more clearly.

The general rule of interpretation is that we are to interpret the less basic in light of more basic by using presuppositional thinking.[73] We should understand the meaning of Scripture in context. There are several levels of context to consider: We should look at a *word* in the context of a *sentence*, a sentence in the context of a *paragraph*, and a paragraph in the context of the *book* as a whole, which includes an introduction,

---

70. Gangadean, "Paper No. 15: Hermeneutics," in *The Logos Papers*, 91-101.

71. Gangadean, *The Book of Revelation.*

72. Gangadean, *The Biblical Worldview.*

73. Appendix 6.

conclusion, and the type of revelation. Furthermore, we examine each book in light of larger sections of Scripture. We should understand later portions of Scripture in light of earlier portions, always keeping in mind the purpose of Scripture as redemptive revelation, and what it reveals about the nature of God. Moreover, we interpret the Scripture in light of what is clear from *general revelation*.

How do we interpret the passage: "In the beginning, God created the heavens and the earth"? Some things from general revelation should be in place before reading the Scriptures. In keeping with the contextual interpretation of Scripture, we should not take things literally out of their context, nor should we put them into our own context. We should not bring in a foreign context when reading the Bible. We should likewise not bring in a scientific context to interpret the Scriptures. But, conversely, we may read science in light of what is clear from general revelation. We interpret empirical claims in light of what is philosophically established through the use of reason.[74]

What is forbidden in the interpretation of Scripture? What is forbidden is using assumptions foreign to Scripture, apart from Scripture, or using what is outside of clear general revelation in an attempt to interpret the Scriptures. Some may emphasize only Scripture (scripturalism), forgetting the context of the clarity of general revelation. To avoid this, it is important to keep in mind the use of good and necessary consequence. Scripture speaks of the clarity of general revelation, and because it speaks of it, we must use it. Scripture assumes the knowledge of God as the good when we begin reading that "In the beginning, God created the heavens and the earth." Genesis 1:1 does not provide a definition of God as infinite. It does not define what spirit is. It expects the reader to have this knowledge before reading the Scriptures. In other words, Scripture assumes the clarity of general revelation so that men are inexcusable.[75]

---

74. For a further exposition and critical analysis of assumptions in science, see: Gangadean, *Philosophical Foundation*, 86-100.

75. Gangadean, "Paper No. 35: The Clarity of General Revelation (Applied to GR-SR-HC)," in *The Logos Papers*, 195-200; Appendix 6.

SUMMARY ANSWER

The infallible rule of the interpretation of Scripture is the Scripture itself. The general rule of interpretation is contextual/presuppositional interpretation: the less basic in light of the more basic (or what is less clear in light of what is more clear). Applied thus: a word in the context of a sentence; a sentence in the context of a paragraph; a paragraph in the context of the book—in terms of introduction and conclusion; a book in the context of all that came before—later portions of Scripture in the context of earlier portions; and Scripture itself in the context of clear general revelation.

There are seven layers of context for interpretation:

1. Clear general revelation (what can be known of God by all from the creation).

2. Biblical Worldview (Genesis 1–3). '

3. Historic Christianity (historically cumulative insight—creeds and councils).

4. Book (introduction, conclusion, and type of revelation).

5. Paragraph (place in the book).

6. Sentence (place in the paragraph).

7. Word (place in a sentence).

Excluded in the interpretation of Scripture is the use of all assumptions inconsistent with clear general revelation and special revelation. This includes literalism and allegoricalism.[76]

---

76. See Glossary.

QUESTION 12

What is the final authority in religious controversies?
What is opposed by this?

X. The supreme judge by which all controversies of religion are to be determined, and all decrees of councils, opinions of ancient writers, doctrines of men, and private spirits, are to be examined, and in whose sentence we are to rest, can be no other but the Holy Spirit speaking in the Scripture.

The Scripture is the final authority in religious controversies. The Scripture is the final judge, not the decrees of councils nor the opinions of ancient writers. The decrees of councils are to be examined in light of Scripture. The opinions of ancient writers, such as Augustine, Tertullian, or Jerome, or great theologians such as Calvin or Luther are not ultimate authorities. Nor should we claim as authoritative a new revelation of the Spirit. Theologians are claimed as representatives by the Roman Catholic Church (Tertullian, Jerome, Augustine of Hippo, Gregory the Great, Thomas Aquinas, and Albertus Magnus), Eastern Orthodoxy (John Chrysostom, Basil the Great, Gregory of Nazianzus, Origen of Alexandria, and Athanasius of Alexandria), and by Protestantism (John Wycliffe, John Huss, Martin Luther, John Calvin, John Knox, Thomas Cranmer, Menno Simmons, Charles Hodge, Karl Barth, and Cornelius Van Til). Yet, no councils, creeds, or great theologians are to be taken as ultimate authorities to settle disputes. Nor are we to appeal to the doctrines of men as authoritative, such as celibacy, which has historically been adopted by the Roman Catholic Church while lacking scriptural justification.

How should we proceed in settling controversies of faith that cause division? We should go to the Scriptures to settle doctrinal disputes, understood as the Confession says, "either expressly set down in Scripture, or by good and necessary consequence may be deduced from Scripture," and "some circumstances . . . which are to be ordered by the light of nature."[77] Scripture does not exclude reason; it assumes it. Scripture does not exclude general revelation; it assumes it.

SUMMARY ANSWER

Scripture is the final authority in religious controversies (vs. councils, creeds, opinions of great theologians, doctrines of men, private spirits, or any assumption inconsistent with clear general revelation or Scripture).

---

77. *WCF. 1.6.*

Chapter 2

OF GOD, AND OF THE HOLY TRINITY

QUESTION 13

What is God?
What are the incommunicable, natural, and
moral attributes?

I. There is but one only, living, and true God, who is infinite in being and perfection, a most pure spirit, invisible, without body, parts, or passions; immutable, immense, eternal, incomprehensible, almighty, most wise, most holy, most free, most absolute; working all things according to the counsel of His own immutable and most righteous will, for His own glory; most loving, gracious, merciful, long-suffering, abundant in goodness and truth, forgiving iniquity, transgression, and sin; the rewarder of them that diligently seek Him; and withal, most just, and terrible in His judgments, hating all sin, and who will by no means clear the guilty.

The Westminster Shorter Catechism asks: What is God? And then summarizes what is stated in the Confession, "God is a Spirit, infinite, eternal, and unchangeable in His being, wisdom, power, holiness, justice, goodness, and truth."[1] This is the divine nature that is clearly revealed in the creation (through the things that are made) and known

---

1. *SCQ. 4.*

from general revelation.[2] Important distinctions in the attributes of God are made here. The Confession says: **There is but one only, living, and true God.** There is one God, which is referred to as the unity of the Godhead or the unity of God. Then the Confession says He is **infinite in being and perfection, a most pure spirit.** From these attributes, a summary description is given: **invisible** is a property of spirit, **without body, parts, or passions,** are properties of an infinite spirit. The Confession goes on to say He is unchangeable—**immutable,** and He is **immense,** or omnipresent because He is infinite in spirit. And then He is **eternal**—without beginning and without end. God is a Spirit, infinite, eternal, and unchanging. These three attributes are the incommunicable attributes.

The Confession goes on to say that God is **incomprehensible,** which does not mean that He cannot be known, but that He cannot be known exhaustively or fully by finite beings. We do know in part now and will continue to grow in knowledge given our finite, temporal, and changeable nature. Yet, we do not, and will not have exhaustive knowledge of anything, including the finite, much less God Himself. In understanding this, we begin to understand the infinite depth of His being. God is infinite in power and wisdom: He is **almighty, most wise, most holy, most free, most absolute.** The Shorter Catechism sums this up well: "being, wisdom, power." These are the natural attributes of God. He has being because He exists. He has wisdom because He chooses means for the end of bringing glory to Himself. He has power to create and rule according to His purposes.

Having named the attributes of God, the Confession speaks about God working His purposes and plan. It says, **working all things according to the counsel of His own immutable and most righteous will, for His own glory.** God is sovereign and, by implication, rules in everything that comes to pass. In answering the question "What is God?", the content of the beginning of Chapter 2 of the Confession and Shorter Catechism Question 4 correlate with and reinforce one another.

How do we distinguish between the incommunicable, natural, and moral attributes of God? The incommunicable attributes are attributes that God and only God has. These attributes are His infinitude,

---

2. For an exposition of the attributes of God from clear general revelation, see: Gangadean, *The Westminster Catechisms,* 119-122.

eternality, and unchangeability. These attributes go together, and while they are distinguishable, they are inseparable. What is meant by in-communicable is that God has these attributes, and God does not communicate them; in fact, He *cannot* communicate them to another being. God cannot bring a being into existence that is eternal (without beginning),[3] because if something is brought into being, by nature it is temporal. The eternality of God is incommunicable, which heightens the otherness of God, the holiness of God (in one sense). God is wholly different from all other beings. God is eternal, and only God is eternal. And we should add that it is clear that God is eternal and that nothing else is eternal.[4] If there must be something eternal, and matter exists and matter is not eternal, and the soul exists and the soul is not eternal, it becomes clear that God and only God is eternal. Materialists grant the attribute of eternality to the physical universe by claiming that the physical universe is self-existing and self-maintaining. Upon reflection we should see that the universe does not keep itself going and, there-fore, it is not eternal.[5] The attribute of eternality is incommunicable.

God is not simply infinite. To assume such is a mistake, and a very serious mistake that has been made in the history of thought. God is infinite, which means encompassing all that exists. However, if misap-plied, infinitude without qualification ends in pantheism, as in the case of Lao Tzu's *Tao*. If we conceive of God as simply infinite and beyond all names (*nirguna brahman*), then we fall into all kinds of strange doc-trines.[6] Rather, we should understand infinitude as an attribute of an attribute—infinitude is applied to other attributes of God. For example, God is not merely wise, He is infinitely wise. Nor is He merely just, but infinitely just. Nor is He merely powerful, but infinitely powerful. Infinite, eternal, and unchangeable are incommunicable attributes, and they are attributes of attributes, as they qualify other attributes. These attributes provide the basis for distinguishing God from all that is not

---

3. For a systematic explanation of eternal, see: Gangadean, *Philosophical Foundation*, 56-59; Gangadean, *History of Philosophy*, 35-40.

4. For a complete proof and response to objections regarding the existence and nature of God, see: Gangadean, *Philosophical Foundation*, 71-161; Gangadean, *History of Philosophy*, 47-58.

5. For the full presentation of the arguments against material monism, see: Gangadean, *Philosophical Foundation*, 71-100.

6. Gangadean, *History of Philosophy*, 39.

God—only God is infinite, eternal, and unchangeable. All else is finite, temporal, and changeable.

By way of contrast, let us examine the nature of man. Man has wisdom—this is part of being made in the image of God—but man does not have it in an infinite, eternal, and unchangeable way. Rather, He has it in a finite, temporal, and changeable way. Man is finite, temporal, and changeable in being, wisdom, power, holiness, justice, goodness, and truth. Together, these constitute the larger aspect of human nature. The attributes that follow after "temporal" are considered natural and moral attributes. The communicable attributes (finitude, temporality, and changeability) qualify man's natural (being, wisdom, power) and moral attributes (holiness, justice, goodness, and truth). Man is always and will always remain finite, temporal, and changeable, as man was created (had a beginning).

In understanding the nature of God and His incommunicable attributes, questions may be raised regarding God's freedom. Since He is infinite, then can He do all things? Since God is infinitely, eternally, and unchangeably wise, can He make a mistake? Can He lie? Does freedom mean the ability to do otherwise, or does it mean doing what we want or please?[7] In response, God does whatsoever He pleases. His freedom has no reference to the ability to do otherwise. God's actions are only bound by His nature, and He only acts as He pleases. God is infinite, eternal, and unchangeable in truth; therefore, He cannot lie. Scripture says explicitly that He cannot lie.[8] This does not mean that He is not free (regarding ability); instead, God is free in the sense that He does what He wants in speaking Truth (doing what He pleases).

Misunderstanding the attributes of God leads to various misconceptions of God's divine nature, resulting in distortion and division throughout the centuries.[9] For example, in pantheism, all is God, thus all is eternal. In deism, God creates but does not rule, thus God is amoral. In Islam, the mercy of God sets aside the need for vicarious atonement. And in the popular view of God in Roman Catholicism,

---

7. Gangadean, *Philosophical Foundation*, 66; Gangadean, *History of Philosophy*, 153-154, 113-114; Gangadean, "Paper No. 97: Freedom and Predestination," in *The Logos Papers*, 509-510.

8. *Numbers 23:19; Titus 1:2; Hebrews 6:18.*

9. For a fuller explanation of the misconceptions of the divine nature, see: Gangadean, *Philosophical Foundation*, 185-198.

Mary is more approachable than God as "mediatrix." If she is more approachable, what becomes of the infinite compassion of God? These are just a few of the many implications that follow from misconceiving God's divine nature.

The moral attributes of God are to be understood in light of the incommunicable attributes of God. The goodness of God is noted near the end of this section in the Confession: **most loving, gracious, merciful, long-suffering, abundant in goodness and truth, forgiving iniquity, transgression, and sin; the rewarder of them that diligently seek Him.** All of these attributes are connected by the root idea that God is good. There are many dimensions of the goodness of God, starting with His being the rewarder of those that diligently seek Him.[10] Goodness also implies He is forgiving, long-suffering, gracious, and merciful.[11] The goodness of God is expressed in Scripture in the direst of ways: "While we were still sinners, Christ died for us."[12] It is one thing if someone does a wrong in general, but when that person wrongs us, and we not only forgive, but do good to them, we see the grace of God present in us. God forgives us through the atoning sacrifice of His Son, which is a special dimension of the mercy of God.

On the other side of goodness is the justice of God. The Shorter Catechism states that God is infinite, eternal, and unchangeable in His being, wisdom, power, holiness, and then the *justice* and *goodness* of God. These two attributes are particularly highlighted in the Confession Section 2.2, and again in the next chapter, "Of God's Eternal Decree."[13] When God decrees, He does so for the display of His grace, which is one dimension of His goodness, or for the display of His justice.

The Confession continues, **and withal, most just, and terrible in His judgments, hating all sin, and who will by no means clear the guilty.** These reflections on the nature of God should bring sobriety to our minds. We should allow these ideas to penetrate our minds. The way that we conceive of God will have implications for how we understand who God is and how we should approach Him. Knowing God's attributes will also help us understand the radical difference between the

---

10. *Hebrews 11:6.*

11. *Exodus 34:6-8.*

12. *Romans 5:8.*

13. *WCF. 3.*

god of Islam and the God of Christianity. When the question is asked: "Who is God?", we should respond—God is a Spirit, infinite, eternal, and unchangeable in His attributes, underscoring the goodness of God as well as the justice of God. All believers, as children of God, must reckon with God's nature, specifically His goodness, justice, and mercy.

SUMMARY ANSWER

God is a Spirit, infinite, eternal, and unchangeable in His being, wisdom, power, holiness, justice, goodness, and truth. The incommunicable attributes are attributes that God and only God has. These include His being infinite, eternal, and unchangeable. Although they are distinguishable, they are inseparable. Infinitude and unchangeability spring from eternality. Incommunicable implies the logical impossibility of communicating or giving them to another being—God cannot create (bring into being) an eternal being (uncreated being). Eternality, infinitude, and unchangeability belong only to God. The natural attributes are being, wisdom, and power. And the moral attributes are holiness, justice, goodness, and truth. The natural and moral attributes are shared with human beings as made in the image of God.

QUESTION 14

Explain the aseity and sovereignty of God.

II. God has all life, glory, goodness, blessedness, in and of Himself; and is alone in and unto Himself all-sufficient, not standing in need of any creatures which He has made, nor deriving any glory from them, but only manifesting His own glory in, by, unto, and upon them. He is the alone fountain of all being, of whom, through whom, and to whom are all things; and has most sovereign dominion over them, to do by them, for them, or upon them whatsoever Himself pleases. In His sight all things are open and manifest; His knowledge is infinite, infallible, and independent upon the creature, so as nothing is to Him contingent, or uncertain. He is most holy in all His counsels, in all His works, and in all His commands. To Him is due from angels and men, and every other creature, whatsoever worship, service, or obedience He is pleased to require of them.

The aseity of God is His self-sufficiency and completeness. God as self-sufficient means that all of God's actions proceed from within Himself and not from any outside cause. The aseity of God enables us to understand how and why God acts. He acts for the manifestation of His own glory. The Confession explains this doctrine in the following way: **God has all life, glory, goodness, blessedness, in and of Himself; and is alone in and unto Himself all-sufficient, not standing in need of any creatures which He has made, nor deriving any glory from them, but only manifesting His own glory in, by, unto, and upon them.** This section is important for understanding the doxological focus of the Confession.[14] God does not derive glory from His creatures but manifests His glory in them, by them, unto them, and upon them. This is a total and complete description of the glory of God in relation to the creature. Humans, as created beings, cannot add to the glory

---

14. Levels of Understanding The Reformed Faith (pp. xxix-xxxii); Appendices 1-2; Gangadean, "Paper No. 115: Doxological Christianity," in *The Logos Papers*, 595-596.

of God. God does not derive any glory from the creation, so there is nothing that the creation and human beings can give to God. He has everything to give, and the creation and humanity have everything to receive. We say that we should give praise to God, but giving praise is not to be understood in any sense that God is lacking or in need of something. God is complete in Himself. **He is the alone fountain of all being, of whom, through whom, and to whom are all things; and has most sovereign dominion over them, to do by them, for them, or upon them whatsoever Himself pleases.** The aseity of God—the self-sufficiency and completeness of God—is naturally connected with the sovereignty of God over all His creatures.

What is emphasized in the latter part of the Confession 2.1 is the goodness and justice of God. These two attributes are not often affirmed together. Imagine if we started ordinary discussions with the common understanding that God is both good and just. How much more would there be upon which we could agree? If we contrast the view that God is infinitely good and infinitely just with other views, such as the popular view of God, we see that many deny the sovereignty of God. In our fallen state, we like to think that a loving God provides opportunities to all, and that God would not be good if He did not provide opportunities for everyone. Someone might say, "It is not nice for God to choose one person and leave another." Doctrinal implications follow very quickly from such statements. Others may question: "Why would God want the death of Christ? That is not nice." But if God is most just and will not by any means clear the guilty,[15] then someone must stand in the place of the guilty. If we understand that God is infinitely just, then the doctrine of vicarious atonement follows without difficulty. God is infinitely just and makes man in His own image. Justice is a moral attribute given to man. If we properly understand the justice of God, we would see that vicarious atonement—payment is through the death of another—is required. Furthermore, we would see that justice requires payment in kind. We see the highest expression of God's goodness and mercy in and through His justice on the cross.

God rules over His creatures according to His own will. **In His sight all things are open and manifest, His knowledge is infinite, infallible, and independent upon the creature, so as nothing is to Him contingent,**

---

15. *Exodus 34:7.*

or uncertain. He is most holy in all His counsels, in all His works, and in all His commands. To Him is due from angels and men, and every other creature, whatsoever worship, service, or obedience He is pleased to require of them. On the face of it, God requiring worship may seem arbitrary. Yet, it is not so. God made mankind and accordingly He requires worship and service. God made human beings utterly dependent upon Him for all that is good. Thus, He can ask Abraham to offer up his only son whom he loves, in the context of saying, "it is through Isaac your seed will be called."[16] If God is pleased, He may require of Abraham the sacrifice of Isaac. The command to Abraham was not arbitrarily given, but was given in the context of redemption and disclosing the content of redemptive revelation. Through the act of Abraham, God reveals that He will offer up His own son. Abraham, as a prophet, enacts the fulfillment of the atoning sacrifice of Christ. Thus, Abraham offering up his son is pointing to the reality to be fulfilled.[17]

God's counsel is holy and wise; it is not arbitrary. Whatever pleases God is subject to His counsel according to His most holy and wise nature. We should affirm that God does whatever He pleases, but we must also understand what pleases Him. If God says, "I want you to endure this trial and to learn and be cleansed from sin," then we should submit. If God calls believers to do what is required according to His Word, then believers should submit to God and do it because He is infinitely wise, holy, good, and just. Because of who God is, we ought to place full trust in Him. At times, believers are double-minded and feel very differently, but we should know that what comes to pass is the will of God, and since obedience is required according to the Word of God, we must submit to the will of God.

SUMMARY ANSWER

Aseity means the completeness of God. God is not lacking anything, nor can anything be added unto God: praise, honor, or glory. God is complete in and of Himself. All God does is caused

---

16. *Genesis 21:12;* For a fuller account on how to understand Abraham's sacrifice of Isaac, see: Gangadean, *Philosophical Foundation*, 121-127; Gangadean, *History of Philosophy*, 163-166; Gangadean, "Paper No. 128: Abraham's Faith," 665-666; Gangadean, "Paper No. 129: Faith and Reason in the Life of Abraham," in *The Logos Papers*, 667-669.

17. *John 8:56.*

from within Himself, not by external factors. All that God demands is what pleases Him, and what pleases God is in accord with His infinite nature. Therefore, we should submit to whatever He requires, for it is intended for our good and His glory.

QUESTION 15

What are the ontological and economic aspects of the Trinity?

III. In the unity of the Godhead there be three Persons, of one substance, power, and eternity: God the Father, God the Son, and God the Holy Ghost: the Father is of none, neither begotten, nor proceeding; the Son is eternally begotten of the Father; the Holy Ghost eternally proceeding from the Father and the Son.

The formulation of the Trinity was concluded in the Council of Nicea in A.D. 325. The Trinity was affirmed by the work of the pastor-teachers after much discussion. It was rechallenged but reaffirmed in the Council of Constantinople in A.D. 381. God is one in unity, and there is but one living and true God. The Confession says, **In the unity of the Godhead there be three Persons, of one substance, power, and eternity.** Following the explanations provided in the previous sections, we can begin to understand more fully Section 2.2, which says God is complete in Himself. There is an eternal fellowship in God: The Father glorifies the Son, the Son glorifies the Father, what results is a relationship between the Father, Son, and Holy Spirit. They are three distinct persons, yet one God. Some may ask: "How can God be one and three?" The response is, **in the unity of the Godhead there are three Persons.** There is one God, three persons, not three gods. If we understand what is meant by "God is one,"[18] our understanding is not strained. The Trinity is very much what we should expect—without saying that we can predict or deduce the Trinity from general revelation. The mystery of the Trinity

---

18. Gangadean, *History of Philosophy*, 40.

revealed in special revelation is most consistent with reason. The Trinity is not deduced by reason, but it is most consistent with reason *after* it has been revealed in special revelation. The highest reality (what is eternal) is personal, not just a principle, and since God is the highest reality, God is a unity of diversity, not just within the differences between wisdom, power, justice, and goodness. There is diversity in the attributes of God, but the Trinity is a diversity of persons.[19]

The Trinity, being a mystery, is impossible to know apart from Scripture. Once revealed, we can and should understand it in part (like other Biblical mysteries). The Trinity is what we should have expected for the following reasons:

1. Being is a unity of diversity.

2. The highest being is a unity of the highest diversity.

3. The highest diversity is between persons.

4. Therefore, the highest unity would be the unity of persons.

5. Therefore, God as the highest being is a unity of persons.

There is one God, three persons, **in the unity of the Godhead there are three Persons, of one substance, power, and eternity** and these are identical. This is called the ontological Trinity. The Father, Son, and Holy Spirit coexist eternally. However, there is a relationship and an order within the Trinity; this is the economic aspect of the Trinity. The Confession names each person, **God the Father, God the Son, and God the Holy Ghost.** The Confession then speaks about the relationship between the three persons: **The Father is of none, neither begotten, nor proceeding; the Son is eternally begotten of the Father**—sonship is eternal sonship, an eternal relationship—with **the Holy Ghost eternally proceeding from the Father and the Son.** There is an order within the Trinity without subordinating one person to another. They are equal in power and glory.

The Confession 2.3 corresponds with the answer to Question 6 of the Shorter Catechism, which states: **There are three persons in the Godhead; the Father, the Son, and the Holy Spirit; and these three are one God, the same in substance, equal in power and glory.** Notice that the economic relationship within the Godhead is addressed in the

---

19. Gangadean, *The Westminster Catechisms*, 122-125.

Confession but it is not addressed in the Shorter Catechism. The economic relationship is significant because man is made in the image of God, and the tri-unity of God is reflected in human beings. Humans are one person with a triune personality. Human beings have the three principles of knowledge, holiness, and righteousness—intellect, emotion, and will—and there is an order between them without subordinating one to another. If the order in personality were understood, it would lead to great unity in the Church. If the relationship between prophet, priest, and king was properly understood, the Church could attain a very high degree of unity. Remember, these personality differences are what was troubling the church in Corinth in the claims, "I am of Paul, I am of Apollos, I am of Cephas."[20] Each of these people reflect either the prophetic, priestly, or kingly orientation. Each human personality is either predominantly prophetic, priestly, or kingly—as each is gifted differently—but God intends the diversity in the three personalities to be complementary and used for the unity of the Church.

God is Triune, and prior to further discussion of the Trinity, we must agree on the attributes of God because all three persons have all of these attributes—each of the attributes belong to God *per se*. The nature of God, His being, and attributes (incommunicable and communicable attributes) are presupposed in our discussion of the Trinity. The attributes of God are more basic than the discussion of the Trinity. People tend to proceed to the question of the Trinity without first understanding the meaning of "one"—of the unity of diversity.[21] Because the meaning of "one" goes unaddressed, many difficulties in understanding the Trinity arise. The failure to address what is more basic translates into overlooking the nature of God prior to engaging in discussion of the Trinity. The question of God's attributes, such as "is God infinitely merciful and infinitely just?", is a prior question. That is why God's attributes are discussed in the first section "On God" (2.1).

Understanding the nature of God as infinitely just and merciful would settle the most significant dispute between Christianity and Islam. This division would be resolved by simply affirming that God

---

20. *1 Corinthian 1:12.*

21. Gangadean, *History of Philosophy*, 39–40.

is infinite, eternal, and unchanging in justice and goodness.[22] The divisions with Judaism can likewise be resolved by affirming that God's justice requires payment in kind.[23] Furthermore, when we understand sin and death, we will understand what God requires as the penalty for our sin. By implication, if we affirm that these attributes are clear from general revelation, then agreement would be secured. If we proceed presuppositionally, step-by-step from the more basic to the less basic, it follows that we can do the work God calls us to do in discipling the nations[24] and in taking thoughts captive.[25]

The Confession continues, **the Son is eternally begotten of the Father.** This relationship is like a parent bringing forth a child. Jacob begat Joseph—begotten—he is brought forth as a son. Yet the Son of God is **eternally begotten.** The Son is of the Father, but the Father is not of the Son. They are equally co-eternal and equal in power. **Begotten** is an eternal relationship. It is a timeless relationship; it is not a relationship in time, for one cannot be a father without there being a son. One is not a father before there is a son. It is a relational term and, for God the Father, it is a timeless term. This is contrary to the misuse of the term by Arians in the early church who openly proclaimed: "If the Father begat the Son, then He who was begotten had a beginning in existence, and from this, it follows there was a time when the Son was not." They misunderstood the relationship of father-son by attaching a chronological understanding rather than a timeless relational understanding to the Father and Son. Misconceptions of concepts lead to further misunderstandings in doctrine. In saying that they are **of one substance,** God is one individual being that is a unity of diversity. The Father, Son, and Holy Spirit are equally spirit and have no parts. The word *substance*, in the Greek use of the term, is substance of a single being.

---

22. Gangadean, *Philosophical Foundation*, 191-192; Gangadean, "Paper No.91: Christianity and Islam," in *The Logos Papers*, 479-484.

23. Gangadean, *Philosophical Foundation*, 193-194.

24. *Matthew 28:20.*

25. *2 Corinthians 10:4-5.*

SUMMARY ANSWER

Ontologically, the three persons of the Trinity are equal in substance and attributes. They are one being—The Godhead. They share the same spiritual substance and each has the same incommunicable and moral attributes. This is set in contrast to various forms of subordination: Monarchianism (modalism or adoption of Christ), Arianism (only the Father is eternal), Unitarianism (no Trinity), deism (God does not act in creation), and Islam (God's will is absolute).

Economically, each person of the Trinity has a different function. There is a distinct order within the Trinity (vs. modalism). The three persons of the Trinity relate in two ways:

(1) In relation to themselves: God the Father eternally begets the Son; the Son is eternally begotten of the Father; and the Holy Spirit eternally proceeds from the Father and the Son.

(2) In relation to creation and providence: God the Father decrees in creation and elects in redemption. God the Son is the eternal Word of God that makes God known in creation and became incarnate to satisfy the requirements of divine justice to accomplish the salvation of the elect. God the Holy Spirit applies redemption to the elect in justification and sanctification.

Chapter 3

OF GOD'S ETERNAL DECREE

QUESTION 16

What is decreed by God?
How are second causes decreed?
On what basis?

I. God, from all eternity, did, by the most wise and holy counsel of His own will, freely, and unchangeably ordain whatsoever comes to pass: yet so, as thereby neither is God the author of sin, nor is violence offered to the will of the creatures; nor is the liberty or contingency of second causes taken away, but rather established.

II. Although God knows whatsoever may or can come to pass upon all supposed conditions, yet has He not decreed anything because He foresaw it as future, or as that which would come to pass upon such conditions.

The Confession says God decreed **whatsoever comes to pass.** Everything in the universe that comes about is decreed/ordained by God. It is not that it merely comes to pass, but God decrees it—He ordains it. That God decrees all of what comes to pass immediately raises the question, "Does He decree evil?" The Westminster Divines address the question directly by saying, **yet so, as thereby neither is God the author of sin . . .** "Since sin exists, did God ordain it?" Yes, God ordained it. "Is He the author of sin?" The answer is no. An explanation as to why God is not the author of sin is needed. The following statements help to make the answer clearer. The Confession says, **nor is violence offered to the will of the creatures**—God does not override the will of the creature—**nor is the liberty or contingency of second causes taken away, but rather established.** This passage requires that we understand the distinction between primary and secondary causes, and how secondary causes are decreed.

God as Creator is the first cause. It is He who brought all else into being. All beings have existence, a nature, and each acts according to its nature. The nature of beings are second causes. For example, God created humans with a rational nature, and He sustains us so that our nature remains intact—inviolable—for human nature is finite, temporal, and changeable. When humans act out of their nature, they are a cause. When the Confession says, **God... ordain whatsoever comes to pass** so that **the liberty or contingency of second causes** are not **taken away, but rather established,** it is precisely because God decrees whatsoever comes to pass that nothing can interfere with the nature of another thing. God so sustains the world that the nature of each thing remains fixed. All created natures are finite, temporal, and changeable; human nature is changeable, yet fixed because God upholds it along with all other second causes.

Some may ask: "How is it that second causes are decreed?" Second causes are decreed precisely because God creates and upholds the world, and there are real beings in the world, and beings act consistently with and out of their nature—contingently or freely. The liberty or contingency of second causes are not taken away. When stones fall, they fall according to the laws of gravity. And, God sustains the world so that all things act according to their natures, i.e., stones operate like stones, rabbits operate like rabbits, etc. God creates the nature of things, and each being acts out of its nature as sustained by God; beings acting according to their natures are second causes. They are not taken away but established by God's decree.

The question remains, on what basis does God decree? God does not decree on the basis of foreseeing what would happen in the future, so that God foresaw it and then ordained it. **God knows whatsoever may or can come to pass upon all supposed conditions, yet has He not decreed anything because He foresaw it as future, or as that which would come to pass upon such conditions.** The basis of God's decree is not in foreseeing. God's decree is His purpose and plan. Having created things with certain natures, He rules them in such a way that His plan is fulfilled. His plan is not made by foreseeing the future, but rather what comes about in the future is according to His plan. Many Christians have questions about God's sovereignty, generally because it is misunderstood. Let us first try to understand God's sovereignty, then after we understand it, we can see if questions remain about the truthfulness of the doctrine of sovereignty.

We have established that God decrees everything and He does not violate but establishes second causes, not based on foreseeing, but by foreordaining. He has a plan, and things will come to pass according to His plan. Who will you marry? What is your future job? How many children will you have?—all of this is foreordained. What God has joined together, let not man put asunder. While **God ordains whatsoever comes to pass**, we are to operate by the revealed will of God and not seek to peer into His hidden will. The revealed will of God is His will and purpose revealed in the content of general and special revelation; it encompasses the dominion mandate,[1] the great commission,[2] and the law of God that is written in our hearts which is summarized in the Ten Commandments.[3]

SUMMARY ANSWER

God decrees whatsoever comes to pass for the praise of His own glory—including evil. However, God is not the author of sin. God as the primary cause does not override the nature of secondary causes (nature of things created) but rather establishes them. God sustains the world enabling second causes to act according to their nature—without interference.

God decreed upon the basis of His own will and purpose—no external factors determine God's decrees. He did not decree because He foresaw. He decreed because He was pleased to decree.

---

1. *Genesis 1:26-28.*

2. *Matthew 28:18-20.*

3. *Deuteronomy 30:11-14; Romans 2:14-15; Exodus 20.*

QUESTION 17

How is God's decree applied to men and angels for life and death?

III. By the decree of God, for the manifestation of His glory, some men and angels are predestinated unto everlasting life; and others foreordained to everlasting death.

IV. These angels and men, thus predestinated, and foreordained, are particularly and unchangeably designed, and their number so certain and definite, that it cannot be either increased or diminished.

The doxological theme of the Confession is developed and elaborated from 1.1 to 2.2, and now we see it enlarged in 3.3. **By the decree of God, for the manifestation of His glory, some men and angels are predestinated unto everlasting life; and others foreordained to everlasting death.** The implications of God's sovereign rule are becoming more explicit as we go through the Confession. It is one thing for God to ordain whom we will marry; it is another to ordain who will have life and who will remain dead in sin. The Confession, following Scripture, affirms that God ordains life and death. To underscore this fact the Confession goes on: **These angels and men, thus predestinated, and foreordained, are particularly and unchangeably designed. . . .** This is not a general predestination, like "10 will be elected out of 100." Rather, God's predestination is particular, such as, "Jacob I have loved and Esau I have hated."[4] There is no switching places. That is what is meant by **particularly and unchangeably designed, and their number is so certain and definite, that it cannot be either increased or diminished.** The Confession is saying that not one will be lost,[5] not one added.

Much care and effort must be employed in understanding what is being said about predestination in these passages of the Confession.

---

4. *Romans 9:13*
5. *John 10:27-28.*

Those who reject predestination generally misunderstand it, so we must handle this matter carefully. Predestination is applied to life and death; to some, not all, it is particular and unchangeable and cannot be increased or decreased. Some might ask, What if there are 56 persons who are elected and another person says, "Can I please be included?" Examples like this are counterfactual conditions. Election does not happen this way, though some people think of it like this. It is also inappropriate to think, "I know this person is elect, but I am not sure about this other person." These are inappropriate ways of thinking about predestination and the decrees of God.

SUMMARY ANSWER

Predestination is not general but specific to the individual. God, according to His mercy, chose some to everlasting life, and left others, according to His justice, in their state of death. Justice is getting what we deserve. Justice treats equals equally. Justice requires punishment for all who sinned. Since all have sinned, all deserve to be forsaken by God—let go in their sin. Mercy is freely given. Mercy is getting what we do not deserve. In election, God forgives some out of His mercy. Election rests entirely in God and not in anything foreseen in or done by the creature. It is solely an act of sovereign choice—out of free grace and love.

QUESTION 18

How is God's decree applied to mankind for life? What is God's purpose?

V. Those of mankind that are predestinated unto life, God, before the foundation of the world was laid, according to His eternal and immutable purpose, and the secret counsel and good pleasure of His will, has chosen, in Christ, unto everlasting glory, out of His mere free grace and love, without any foresight of faith, or good works, or perseverance in either of them, or any other thing in the creature, as conditions, or causes moving Him thereunto; and all to the praise of His glorious grace.

Predestination unto life is according to God's free grace and love. It is not due to anything in the creature whatsoever.[6] If we ask, "Why is it that one person comes to believe instead of another?" the answer is that it is because of God's free grace and love. What is God's purpose in predestinating some unto life? Please note, predestination unto life is **all to the praise of His glorious grace.** Grace is the deepest, richest level of mercy. And God's grace is glorified, revealed, and magnified in His greatness, in the predestination unto life.

---

6. Election unto salvation is not based on any condition (past, present, or future) in man, but wholly on God's purpose, which is, in wisdom, to make His glory known. Election unto salvation is not apart from or against secondary causes such as seeking and understanding or repentance and faith; predestination is not of ends without means, but of both ends and means. Election of men presupposes the Fall (infralapsarianism) either to leave one in sin and death or to restore one to life and righteousness. Unconditional election is not arbitrary regarding justice; spiritual death is always due to sin, and mercy never sets aside justice, but satisfies justice through vicarious atonement by Jesus Christ. God has mercy on whom He chooses. Showing mercy to some is not unfair to others; what is unfair is to deny justice to any.

SUMMARY ANSWER

God's purpose in predestination unto life is to magnify His glorious grace. Grace is the richest, deepest, and fullest expression of mercy. Predestination unto life is out of God's free grace and love, without any foresight of faith or good works, or perseverance in either of them, or any other thing in the creature, as conditions or causes moving Him thereunto.

QUESTION 19

What is the order of God's decree for the elect?

VI. As God has appointed the elect unto glory, so has He, by the eternal and most free purpose of His will, foreordained all the means thereunto. Wherefore, they who are elected, being fallen in Adam, are redeemed by Christ, are effectually called unto faith in Christ by His Spirit working in due season, are justified, adopted, sanctified, and kept by His power, through faith, unto salvation. Neither are any other redeemed by Christ, effectually called, justified, adopted, sanctified, and saved, but the elect only.

Section 3.6 of the Confession is very explicit about the order of the decree for the elect. Care must be taken to avoid related issues regarding God's decree where mistakes may arise. God has a purpose and uses means in election: **As God has appointed the elect unto glory, so has He, by the eternal and most free purpose of His will, foreordained all the means thereunto.** God does not foreordain an end apart from the means. Partial predestination is held in Islam[7] and in some popular Christian thinking. This is the view that God foreordains ends apart from means. In contrast, the Confession affirms that God's

---

7. In Islam, the end is decreed apart from the means (second causes *in* the nature of things). The Islamic view of ends without means is *partial* predestination and results in paradoxes of freedom and responsibility. Rather than question uncritically held assumptions about freedom and divine omnipotence, Islam moves to give up reason.

predestination is full. He foreordains not just the end, but how that end will be accomplished.

What is the order of God's decree? The Confession states: **Wherefore, they who are elected**, notice very carefully, are those who are *fallen in Adam.* Does God decree the election of those who are not fallen (is election prior to the Fall?), or does He decree election out of those who are fallen? The Confession affirms the latter—in the order of His plan—election is out of those who are fallen. Election of men, either to leave one in sin and death or to restore one to life and righteousness, presupposes the Fall. This position is known as infralapsarianism. If we reverse the order, and view election as prior to the Fall, we get a very different position that introduces distortions and is problematic. The view that claims election is prior to the Fall is known as supralapsarianism. The Confession affirms election is unto life out of a condition of sin and death. Once the Fall occurs, in the plan of God, out of fallen mankind God chooses to bring some to life purely out of His free grace. This is the order of God's decree.

Notice, the second sentence in this section says, **Wherefore, they who are elected, being fallen in Adam, are redeemed by Christ**, which is redemption accomplished. Redemption is then applied when they **are effectually called unto faith in Christ by His Spirit.** Christ on the cross accomplished redemption and the Spirit applies it to individuals by **working in due season,** such that they are **justified, adopted, sanctified, and kept by His power, through faith, unto salvation.** God chooses out of those who are fallen, accomplishes redemption in Christ, and applies redemption to the believer's heart by His Spirit, so that one is granted repentance and faith, and then justification, adoption, and sanctification. All of these are the means by which God brings the elect to grace. Moreover, God does not ordain the end apart from the means. We should not say that "It doesn't matter whether I believe or not because I am one of the elect." Redemption does not work that way. This view is called partial predestination and it is a distortion of the truth.

For those able to be outwardly called by the gospel (not someone who is mentally impaired or an infant), God does not call the elect to Himself apart from regeneration, repentance, and faith. God never works in such a way that some person calls upon Christ to be saved, and God says, "You are not one of the elect." It never works that way. It is never the case in Christianity, holding to biblical predestination, that someone wants to be saved and cannot be saved. In Islamic partial predestination, it may actually be the case that one wants to be saved and cannot be. In the *Rubaiyat,* Omar Khayyam has a stanza that says: "Ah Love! Could you and I with Fate conspire to grasp this sorry Scheme of Things entire, Would not we shatter it to bits and then remould it nearer to the Heart's Desire!"[8] Khayyam says that he desires a different outcome, but fate prevents it, so there is a disconnect between what we want and what we get. That never happens in divine predestination. We always get what we want. The non-believer left to himself wants to go his own way, and he gets it. In contrast, the believer, because God has regenerated him/her, desires to know God, and he/she gets to know God. The predestination of ends is never apart from means, which includes desire at some point. This is what is meant by the order of decree for the elect (ends and means—*ordo salutis*[9]). This section of the Confession concludes with: **Neither are any other redeemed by Christ, effectually called, justified, adopted, sanctified, and saved, but the elect only.**

SUMMARY ANSWER

God's predestination is full—it includes means and ends. God does not predestine ends apart from means; it is never the case that someone wants to be saved and cannot be saved. Infralapsarianism: Election unto life comes after the Fall in Adam. God, purely out of grace, redeems some out of the condition of sin and death. Imputation: The sin of Adam in the Fall is imputed to all, redemption is accomplished in Christ, and Christ's righteousness is imputed (applied) to the elect by the Holy Spirit. The Order of Salvation (*Ordo Salutis*): regeneration, repentance and faith, justification, adoption, sanctification, and glorification.

---

8. Omar Khayyám, *The Rubáiyát of Omar Khayyám* (Boston: Little Brown and Company, 1900).

9. Gangadean, *The Westminster Catechisms*, 41-49.

QUESTION 20

How is God's decree applied to mankind for death? What is God's purpose?

VII. The rest of mankind God was pleased, according to the unsearchable counsel of His own will, whereby He extends or withholds mercy, as He pleases, for the glory of His sovereign power over His creatures, to pass by; and to ordain them to dishonor and wrath for their sin, to the praise of His glorious justice.

Question 20 parallels questions 17 & 18 regarding the application of God's decree. The decree is first applied to men and angels in general, then to the elect, and then to those left in their sin, which is addressed in section 3.7 of the Confession: **The rest of mankind God was pleased, according to the unsearchable counsel of His own will, whereby He extends or withholds mercy, as He pleases.** God does not extend or withhold justice; He extends or withholds mercy as He pleases, . . . **for the glory of His sovereign power over His creatures, to pass by.** . . . He passes by the rest of mankind, those who are not elect, **to ordain them to dishonor and wrath.** . . . Notice the next three words, . . . **for their sin.** . . . God's wrath is never apart from man's sin, fallen in Adam, not only for imputed sin/guilt but his actual sin. Those God passes by are ordained to dishonor and wrath for their sin, and all of this is **to the praise of His glorious justice.**

Recalling the aseity of God, God manifests His own glory in, by, unto, and upon His creatures; He manifests His justice through some, and His mercy through others. Those through whom justice is manifested can neither demand mercy nor do they desire it. It is never the case that someone desires mercy, and they do not receive mercy. Free will is such that we always get what we want. God leaves human beings to themselves; they turn to their own way; they do not want God. Mankind in unbelief wants to go their own way, and God leaves them to go their own way. God has mercy on some to the praise of the glory of His grace, and God leaves some in sin and death to the praise of the glory of His justice.

SUMMARY ANSWER

God extends justice to all—for our sin—as required by His nature for the praise of His glorious justice. God withholds mercy from some for the revelation of His glorious justice. He may manifest His justice through some, and He may manifest His mercy through others. Those left in sin get the sin they desire, and those desiring mercy get the mercy they desire. We always get what we want. The responsibility for our desires rests in ourselves.

QUESTION 21

How is the mystery of predestination to be handled with special care?

VIII. The doctrine of this high mystery of predestination is to be handled with special prudence and care, that men, attending the will of God revealed in His Word, and yielding obedience thereunto, may, from the certainty of their effectual vocation, be assured of their eternal election. So shall this doctrine afford matter of praise, reverence, and admiration of God; and of humility, diligence, and abundant consolation to all that sincerely obey the Gospel.

The last section of the Confession chapter 3 draws our attention to the reality that, **The doctrine of this high mystery of predestination is to be handled with special prudence and care.** Predestination is a high mystery, yet people often veer in this or that direction with the doctrine without keeping clearly in mind the need to handle predestination with prudence and care. People may draw unnecessary implications and end up in a terrible state of confusion. When in this state, they may throw up their hands and reject the doctrine saying "I cannot believe in a God like that." Moreover, some people presume upon God in ways they should not as if they had the power to dictate how God is to dispense His mercy.

The special prudence and care is **that men, [attend] the will of God revealed in His Word, and [yield] obedience** to His Word. Notice and underscore the words: **the will of God revealed.** The will of God revealed is not the same as the secret or decreed will of God. And vice versa, the decreed will of God is not the same as the revealed will of God. God says: "You shall not lie," which is the revealed will of God. In His decree, God leaves some to themselves, they lie, and He permits it, not with bare permission, but He is pleased to permit it. He permits changeable creatures, being left to themselves, to change from seeking good to seeking evil. The revealed will of God is that none should lie, and the decreed will of God is that some will lie—Satan is a liar and the father of lies.[10] God may, by decree, permit lying—He could stop it if He is pleased, and in some cases, He does stop it. In some cases, He intervenes in the hearts of men and turns them away from falsehood and lying. And in some cases, He leaves them in their falsehood and their lies. God intervenes in the hearts of some based on His mercy.

Election unto salvation applies to some human beings, but it does not apply to angels. Elect angels do not need to be saved, and fallen angels are left in their fallen condition. Human beings are elected by being brought out of sin and death. There is a difference, and the focus here is on election regarding human beings.

God shows His justice and mercy by letting some humans go (justice) and bringing some back (mercy). We should attend to the revealed will of God. God says to repent; that is His revealed will, so we should repent. God says to repent and believe the gospel. God says to seek Him earnestly, "And you will seek Me and find Me, when you search for Me with all your heart."[11] We should pay attention to the revealed will of God, not His secret will. Moreover, on the face of it, we cannot know who is and who is not saved. Neither can we say that someone is beyond redemption. What happens between the bridge and the water, only God knows. We do not have to speculate about who is saved. There is no human and no sin so heinous that God cannot forgive. If Christ can say, "Father, forgive them," of those who crucified

---

10. *John 8:44.*

11. *Jeremiah 29:13.*

Him—the Son of God—then anyone and everyone can be forgiven. We are to attend to **the will of God revealed in His Word, and [yield] obedience thereunto,** and some doing so will, **from the certainty of their effectual vocation, be assured of their eternal election.** We have assurance by God's work in our life and by our love of God. Left to ourselves, we do not love God. We know that we love God when we obey His Word. It is possible to presume upon the grace of God and not have a proper basis for assurance. Some presume by thinking, "I asked Jesus into my heart, I prayed the sinner's prayer, He came into my heart, and I am saved." Many people have this kind of assurance. Rather, we are saved by paying attention to and obeying the will of God revealed. Assurance of our salvation is not based on our profession, but it is based on how we live in obedience to the Word of God.

The Confession continues, **so shall this doctrine afford matter of praise, reverence, and admiration of God.** We understand the doctrine of election as follows: God is the one who brought us to Himself. Left to ourselves, we would be as any other person on the road to perdition. Those who believe should say, "there but for the grace of God go I." When we understand God's love, and our utter dependence upon Him for grace and mercy, we are overcome by praise, reverence, and admiration for God, and we respond with humility. The Confession mentions **humility;** it is God who saves. It mentions **diligence,** as we obey the revealed will of God, **and abundant consolation to all that sincerely obey the gospel.**

If we have the assurance that we are a child of God when we are chastened by God, then chastening does not become disheartening. We may affirm we are loved by God, but He brings hardship into our lives because He wants us to learn, and He ordains that we will learn through hardship. When we recognize that we need hardship we can say God loves us: "For whom the Lord loves He chastens, and scourges every son whom He receives."[12] He chastens us because He wants us to be conformed to His revealed will. We have to work through baggage from our past, and that is why chastening is needed. In addition, we like to think we do the will of God, but often we mislead ourselves by not examining the Scriptures.

---

12. *Hebrews 12:6.*

If we properly understand the doctrine of predestination, it will bring **praise, reverence, and admiration of God; and humility, diligence, and abundant consolation to all that sincerely obey the gospel.** When God says "Do this and do it this way," according to His precepts, ordinances, statutes, and Word, and we do it His way in obedience to Him, we have consolation.

SUMMARY ANSWER

The mystery of predestination must be understood in light of God's revealed will—the Word of God revealed in Scripture. The revealed will of God is not the same as the decreed will of God. The revealed will of God states that all humans as sinners must repent and seek Him diligently. We should attend to the revealed will of God, repent, and live accordingly. The decreed or secret will of God is what will come to pass. Its content is not known to us. Assurance of salvation comes by obedience to His Word. Assurance of salvation apart from the use of ordinary means is mere presumption. If we love God, we obey His Commandments. When properly understood, predestination leads to praise, reverence, and adoration of God. It affords man humility, diligence, and consolation as we seek to obey His will.

Chapter 4

_____

OF CREATION

QUESTION 22

Explain the nature and purpose of creation.

I. It pleased God the Father, Son, and Holy Ghost, for the manifestation of the glory of His eternal power, wisdom, and goodness, in the beginning, to create, or make of nothing, the world, and all things therein whether visible or invisible, in the space of six days; and all very good.

The Westminster Confession of Faith contends with both internal and external challenges to the faith. Chapter four addresses several challenges about the creation while continuing the doxological focus. The chapter opens: **It pleased God the Father, Son, and Holy Ghost, for the manifestation of the glory of His eternal power, wisdom, and goodness, in the beginning, to create, or make of nothing, the world, and all things therein whether visible or invisible, in the space of six days; and all very good.** We can identify several applications from this section, and one of these is the purpose of God in creation: **It pleased God . . . for the manifestation of the glory of His eternal power, wisdom, and goodness . . . to create.** The Confession affirms that creation *is* revelation. Why did God create?[1] To reveal His glory. Creation is revelation *necessarily*; the acts of a being reveal the nature of that being. The acts of God in creation reveal the nature of God. The creation is a manifestation of

---

1. For a general revelation response addressing the question of need in God in the act of creation, see: Gangadean, *Philosophical Foundation*, 144.

the glory of God. God's creation reveals His glory, *intentionally.* Seven times in Genesis chapter one the Lord attests to the goodness of original creation by saying, "it was good," and culminating with "it was very good."[2] Creation is revelation necessarily, intentionally, and we should add, *exclusively.* There is no revelation of the glory of God apart from creation and what happens in creation (providence). Those who think that there is direct knowledge of God apart from creation (the beatific vision) are mistaken.[3] There is no direct vision of God in heaven. Those who believe so attempt to know God as He is in Himself apart from His work of creation and history (providence). If we are to know God, we must do so by understanding the revelation that He has made of Himself. This is very basic and therefore requires due attention. We cannot bypass the purpose of God in creation. We should not bypass history either; what happens in history is connected with and serves God's purpose. Evil cannot frustrate the purpose of God's revelation.[4] Instead, God uses evil to further this purpose. Many inferences may be made from the reality that *creation is revelation.*[5]

If we believe eternal life is knowing God, then we are to approach God as He has revealed Himself. Put another way, the popular doctrine of heaven, which says that "when we die we go to be with the Lord, and we receive the fullness of the blessing," is problematic and incoherent upon analysis.[6] If we go to be with the Lord, do we get the knowledge of God apart from creation? Can we bypass the revelation given on earth and say that we will get another revelation in heaven? What might that revelation in heaven be? Is it revelation of His love? Is it revelation of His love apart from the demonstration of His love in Christ dying and the application of that to sinners in the history of the world?

The second application of the doctrine of creation is that creation is *ex nihilo.* The nature of creation is *ex nihilo*—from nothing. The

---

2. *Genesis 1:4, 10, 12, 18, 21, 25, 31.*

3. Gangadean, "Paper No. 106: The Good and Heaven," in *The Logos Papers,* 547-556; Gangadean, *On Natural and Revealed Theology,* 9-32.

4. Gangadean, *Philosophical Foundation,* 145-161.

5. Appendix 6; Gangadean, "Paper No. 12: The Necessity for Scripture," in *The Logos Papers,* 75-77.

6. Gangadean, "Paper No. 106: The Good and Heaven," in *The Logos Papers,* 547-556; Gangadean, *On Natural and Revealed Theology,* 9-32.

doctrine is stated as follows: **to create, or make of nothing**—it is important that He made of nothing—this is not the Greek dualist view of a divine maker. God is not the maker of a world where He fashions pre-existing material. If He merely made the world (vs. create it) He would not be omnipotent over the things created, which is Plato's concept of God (the *Demiurge*).[7] Original creation is *ex nihilo*; subsequent creation is forming and filling what was created.[8] How did we infer that distinction? Scripture says, "and the world was without form and void."[9] After the original creation *ex nihilo*, God formed the world,[10] and He caused it to be filled. When He created man in His own image, He commanded for man to be fruitful and multiply and replenish the earth, to fill it, and subdue it.[11] Part of subduing the world is the continuing formation of it by mankind through developing the powers latent in the creation. This is a basic piece; this is foundation, and it may take some time to get this foundation well laid in the church and in our lives.

A third application of the doctrine of creation is that creation was **very good**—there was no natural evil originally. There was no death; there was no curse, no thorns and thistles; there was no toil—there was work, but not toilsome work. It was all very good.[12] Notice that the world was created in six days. There have been arguments and different theories about what exactly "six days" means.[13] The sense in the Confession is that the six days are connected with the special acts of God. Some try to argue that the sun did not appear until the fourth day. Subsequently, there was no darkness and light, and therefore Genesis chapter 1 is not referring to solar days. Yet, we get the sense that on the fifth and sixth days the description does include solar days.

---

7. Gangadean, *History of Philosophy*, 87-91.

8. Gangadean, *Philosophical Foundation*, 141-143.

9. *Genesis 1:2.*

10. Gangadean, "Paper No. 142: The Biblical Worldview (Part II)," 711-717; Gangadean, "Paper No. 143: The Biblical Worldview (Part III)," in *The Logos Papers*, 719-724.

11. Gangadean, "Paper No. 144: The Biblical Worldview (Part IV)," in *The Logos Papers*, 725-732.

12. *Genesis 1:4, 10, 12, 18, 21, 25, 31.*

13. For an exposition on subsequent creation, see: Gangadean, "Paper No. 143: The Biblical Worldview (Part III)," in *The Logos Papers*, 719-724.

Regardless, the Confession affirms that Scripture teaches special creation within six days.

Original creation affirms the absence of natural evil. The special creation of each after its own kind took place in the space of six days. There was no natural evil (the curse) before moral evil (the Fall). Furthermore, the Scriptures attest that the creation was pleasing to God by stating that it was "very good." Hugh Ross, who holds to an old earth theory of Genesis,[14] or Meredith Kline, who speaks about the framework hypothesis theory,[15] usually grant natural evil as part of the original creation. That natural evil is original is inconsistent with what the Scripture and the Confession say, which is creation is **all very good**.[16] The accommodation of contemporary views of the age of the earth with the Genesis account cannot succeed because they assume the existence of natural evil prior to moral evil. Moral evil came with the act of Adam and Eve. Prior to the Fall, animals did not devour each other, and neither was physical death in the world. Both man and animals were given vegetation to eat. The curse, including toil and strife, and old age, sickness, and death, was specifically imposed by God after the Fall. The Darwinian framework of origins,[17] which accepts natural evil as original, has penetrated the church and Christian institutions. This saturation is institutional and cultural; it also carries faulty views about God, the creation, and the purpose of evil. The Roman Catholic Church has accommodated evolution. Many Protestant churches and Christian colleges have also accommodated evolution. The Confession denies this accommodation.

SUMMARY ANSWER

Nature of creation: Original creation is *ex nihilo* (out of nothing). Subsequent creation is forming and filling. Original creation was very good—neither natural nor moral evil. There was no natural

---

14. Hugh Ross, *Creation and Time: A Biblical and Scientific Perspective on the Creation-Date Controversy* (Colorado Springs: Navpress, 1994).

15. Meredith G. Kline, *Essential Writings of Meredith G. Kline* (Peabody: Hendrickson Publishers, 2022).

16. Gangadean, "Paper No. 7: The Problem of Evil," in *The Logos Papers*, 33-39.

17. For argumentation regarding the biological data and the incompatibility of historic theism with theistic evolution, see: Gangadean, *Philosophical Foundation*, 90-100.

evil before moral evil. God created in six days (evening and morning). Special creation: each after its own kind. The purpose of God in creation is the manifestation of His glory. Creation is revelation: necessarily (the acts of a being reveal the nature of that being), intentionally (God was pleased with what He created—it was very good), and exclusively (there is no revelation of God apart from God's works of creation and providence).

QUESTION 23

Describe the nature of man in original creation.

II. After God had made all other creatures, He created man, male and female, with reasonable and immortal souls, endued with knowledge, righteousness, and true holiness, after His own image; having the law of God written in their hearts, and power to fulfill it: and yet under a possibility of transgressing, being left to the liberty of their own will, which was subject unto change. Besides this law written in their hearts, they received a command, not to eat of the tree of the knowledge of good and evil; which while they kept, they were happy in their communion with God, and had dominion over the creatures.

Chapter four of the Confession only has two sections. We must pay special attention to understanding the inferences and implications derived from analyzing the content of each section. In Section 4.2, the first point is, He **created man, male and female**—this is the male/female distinction. The second point, is they are created **with reasonable and immortal souls.** Man is a body/soul unity. Notice that man was not alive until God breathed into Adam the breath of life, and man *became* a living creature.[18] That the life is bound up with having a soul has implications for understanding when life begins in the ordinary course of procreation. Some say they do not know when the soul begins, as if the

---

18. *Genesis 2:7.*

soul is something separate from the life of man.[19] Adam and Eve were created with reasonable and immortal souls from the moment of life.

The third point is, they are **endued with knowledge, righteousness, and true holiness**, and are created **after His own image**. As explained earlier, God is a Spirit infinite, eternal, and unchangeable in His being, wisdom, power, holiness, justice, goodness, and truth. Man is created finite, temporal, and changeable in being, wisdom, power, holiness, justice, goodness, and truth, which is the larger aspect of human nature.[20] **After His own image** includes the larger aspect of man in the image of God, which all human beings always retain, even while fallen. All humans are always the image of God (*imago dei*).[21]

The fourth point is, the narrower aspect of the image of God is that man is created **in knowledge, righteousness, and true holiness**. The narrower aspect of man's nature is affected by the Fall. The larger aspect of man in the image of God as finite, temporal, and changeable plus the narrower aspect of man as capable of knowledge, holiness, and righteousness are what make the Fall possible. Man can change from the state of knowing to not knowing, from holiness to unholiness, and from righteousness to unrighteousness. There are other aspects about the nature of man not mentioned in this section of the Confession that can be articulated, but for now, this is sufficient.[22] Four aspects of being made **after His own image** have been noted so far: male and female; body and soul; the larger aspect; and the narrower aspect (knowledge, holiness, and righteousness).

The fifth aspect of the image of God is **having the law of God written in their hearts**[23] and they having the **power to fulfill it**. And sixth, they are changeable. They are **under a possibility of transgressing, being left to the liberty of their own will**. Notice, it says **being left**.

---

19. Gangadean, "Paper No. 27: The Limits of the State," in *The Logos Papers*, 165-169; Gangadean, *Philosophical Foundation*, 237-239.

20. Gangadean, "Paper No. 144: The Biblical Worldview (Part IV)," in *The Logos Papers*, 725-732.

21. Gangadean, *The Westminster Catechisms*, 16-18; Gangadean, "Paper No. 144: The Biblical Worldview (Part IV)," in *The Logos Papers*, 725-732.

22. Surrendra Gangadean, *Man, The Image of God: The Seven Aspects of Human Nature* (Phoenix: Logos Papers Press, 2025).

23. *Deuteronomy 30:11-14; Romans 2:12-14.*

They are mutable and the Confession adds that their will **was subject unto change.** Man is finite, temporal, and *changeable.*

The seventh aspect of human nature is that they were created in a covenant relationship. The Confession says, **Beside this law written in their hearts, they received a command, not to eat of the tree of the knowledge of good and evil, which while they kept, they were happy in their communion with God, and had dominion over the creatures.** Connected with obedience, they were in communion with God.

The eighth aspect of human nature is that they **had dominion over the creatures,** which should be underscored. Dominion over the creatures is actually the first thing mentioned about man in Scripture. God says: "Let us make man in our image . . . with dominion . . ."[24] The Confession includes dominion as part of the image of God. There are many implications about man in the image of God that we can derive from the Confession and apply to challenges in our day.

To anticipate possible questions, the following explanations are provided:

Body/soul unity: Having a body is an integral part of being a human being; it is part of the essence of human nature. To be human is to be a body/soul unity. Physical death was not original but imposed because of sin. Physical death is a natural evil imposed until the overcoming of moral evil (sin) by the rule of Christ. The rending of body and soul in death is removed in the resurrection—then humans remain in the body in perpetuity. The visible body reveals the invisible soul and is the basis of anthropomorphic language in speaking about God: "face to face," "walked with God," "I will stretch out my hand," "sitting at the right hand," etc.

Male/female unity: Both maleness and femaleness equally reflect diverse aspects of what is united in God—Creator and sustainer of the universe. Both are in God, and there is an order (creation is prior). Maleness reflects God as Creator and ruler, while femaleness reflects God as upholder and nurturer. Maleness is inferred from God as Creator (origination, initiation, determination, planning, bringing into being) and femaleness from providence (upholding, directing, disposing, governing, and nurturing). Maleness and femaleness are rooted

---

24. *Genesis 1:26-28.*

in the being of God. They are to be understood in that context—from general revelation (bringing into being and sustaining in being), and special revelation.[25] Man was originally one being (Adam), embodying two principles (male and female). Woman was formed from man—a principle became a person. What became two persons is to be united again in one flesh (by marriage in an economic and ethical unity). The context of this unity is the pursuit of the good—the chief end of man—which is the source of all unity.

The larger aspect of the image of God: God is a Spirit, infinite, eternal, and unchangeable in being, wisdom, power, holiness, justice, goodness, and truth. Man, as made in the image of God, shares in the same moral attributes (wisdom, power, holiness, justice, goodness, and truth) but in a finite, temporal, and changeable way. This is equally true of all human beings, always—pre-Fall, post-Fall, regenerated, glorified, and resurrected. These attributes exist as formal capacities only, and structure human consciousness of self and of God. We must recognize our similarities and our differences in thinking about ourselves and God. God's incommunicable attributes (infinitude, eternality, and unchangeability) are different in kind from our temporality, finitude, and changeability. Humans are to think presuppositionally about God. We are to think about the finite (man) in light of the infinite (God), not the infinite (God) in light of the finite (man) or the finite (man) in light of the finite (nature). We are to think of man as the image of God; we are not to think of God as the image of man. The divine nature, which is infinite, eternal, and unchangeable, is not to be likened to human nature, which is finite, temporal, and changeable.

The triune personality of man: Man is created in knowledge, holiness, and righteousness, called the narrower aspect of the image of God. This aspect has specific content; it was lost in the Fall and restored in regeneration. It reflects the structure of the human heart and is the basis of diverse functions as prophet, priest, and king. Man as a prophet is to understand God's revelation in creation, history, and Scripture so as to attain to the fullness of the knowledge of God. Man as priest is to teach God's revelation so as to bring all men to holiness—the sanctification

---

25. *Genesis 1–2.*

that comes through knowing the truth. Man as king is to rule in God's creation so as to bring all men to righteousness through obeying God's law in all things. In Scripture, these offices are manifested in the person and work of Moses as prophet, Aaron as priest, David as king, and those who continued these offices. The three offices are united doxologically in the work of the kingdom. The order in the Trinity (Father, Son, and Holy Ghost) is reflected in the order of these functions within each person (intellect, emotion, and will) or also described as (mind, soul, and strength). The order should be maintained between persons in any group (prophetic, priestly, and kingly).

Man is created with dominion over the creatures: Man's work of dominion reflects God's dominion in creation; man is to name (grasp the essence of things) and rule (develop all the powers latent in himself and the created order). Man is to name the creation so as to know God, who reveals His glory in creation and providence. Man is to fill everything in every way as the rule of God's kingdom over all. The task of dominion is for the entire human race throughout history. The work will be completed when the earth is filled with the knowledge of God as the waters cover the sea.[26] The Sabbath given to man signifies the goal and completion of this work. Just as God completed His work and then rested, so man (as made in the image of God) will complete his work and then rest.

SUMMARY ANSWER

The nature of man in original creation can be understood in the eight components listed as follows: (1) Male/Female, (2) Body/Soul, (3) Larger aspect (after His own image), (4) Narrower aspect (knowledge, holiness, righteousness), (5) Law written on their hearts with power to fulfill it, (6) Changeable, (7) In covenant relationship, and (8) With dominion over the creatures.

---

26. *Isaiah 11:9.*

Chapter 5

OF PROVIDENCE

QUESTION 24

What is the extent, basis, and purpose of God's providence?

I. God the great Creator of all things does uphold, direct, dispose, and govern all creatures, actions, and things, from the greatest even to the least, by His most wise and holy providence, according to His infallible foreknowledge, and the free and immutable counsel of His own will, to the praise of the glory of His wisdom, power, justice, goodness, and mercy.

Chapter five of the Westminster Confession of Faith concerns the providence of God. It addresses the extent, basis, and purpose of His providence. The extent of God's providence is to **govern all creatures, actions, and things, from the greatest even to the least.** His providence is universal and includes every last detail. It is extensive and intensive. It does not merely include the large or small features of the world, but it is all inclusive. The Confession states that God does **uphold, direct, dispose, and govern** each aspect of creation. Upholding is one aspect of providence, directing is another, disposing is the third, and governing. By considering each we begin to understand the completeness and extent of providence. The basis for providence is God's plan, His decree. The Confession states that God does all things **by His most wise and holy providence, according to His infallible foreknowledge, and the**

free and immutable counsel of His own will. All things unfold in time according to the plan of God.

The purpose of providence is **the praise of the glory of His wisdom, power, justice, goodness, and mercy.** The doxological focus of the Confession is the recognition and emphasis upon the reality that all things work for the praise of His glory.[1] As seen in the previous chapter, God creates for His glory, and He rules for that same purpose. Doxology has to do with the praise of God's glory. The Confession affirms that God's attributes are revealed in creation and providence and that He deserves all praise and glory because of the clear revelation of His attributes. We can and should understand how God's goodness, justice, wisdom, and power are manifest in the created order and in His providential rule.

Implicit in this section of the Confession is the doctrine of fullness,[2] which is that the whole earth is *full* of His glory and human beings are to come to know the revelation of God in creation and to make this glory known. From the doctrines of creation and providence, we should understand how the whole earth is full of His glory. Isaiah 6:3 says, "Holy, holy, holy is the Lord of Hosts; the whole earth is full of His glory." The word "is" means present tense. Furthermore, Isaiah 11:9 states, ". . . the earth shall be filled with the knowledge of God . . ." The words "shall be" are future tense. The implication of these two verses is the glory presently revealed in creation and providence will become known as the work of dominion is advanced. That the earth "is" filled with the glory of God, but also that it "will be filled with the knowledge of the glory of God" is the distinction between objective revelation (what God has revealed of Himself in creation and providence) and subjective revelation (humans coming to understand that revelation).

The doctrine of fullness is also expressed in Habakkuk 2:14, "For the earth will be filled with the knowledge of the glory of the LORD . . ." How do we get from the earth *is* full of His glory by creation and providence to the earth *shall be* full of the knowledge of the glory of God? It is by the work of dominion, originally given to Adam in the Garden,[3] that "the earth shall be full" of the knowledge of the glory of God. As

---

1. Appendix 2.

2. Appendix 4, 8.

3. *Genesis 1:26-28*; Appendix 4; Gangadean, "Paper No. 117: Knowing and Making God Known," in *The Logos Papers*, 599-601.

mankind establishes dominion over the things created, we come to understand the revelation of God in the creation. We cannot attain the knowledge of this glory apart from the work of dominion. We can be certain that the work of dominion will be completed by understanding the meaning of the Sabbath.[4] God creates to reveal His glory, and man's work in dominion is to come to the knowledge of that glory.

Shorter Catechism Question 1 says the chief end of man, the end in itself, the good, "is to glorify God, and to enjoy Him forever."[5] Notice that enjoyment comes in glorifying Him. We glorify God when we come to know His glory and to make it known. Our enjoyment cannot be separated from the work of dominion. Furthermore, though human beings may engage in the work of dominion apart from glorifying God, to do so is inconsistent with our nature and with God's purpose. Many people engage in dominion by common grace, but it is not for God's glory; it is for their own personal gain. Scripture underscores the activity of glorifying God by saying, ". . . whatever you do, do it all to the glory of God."[6] As believers, the engagement with the work of dominion should go beyond personal gain to glorifying God.

SUMMARY ANSWER

Extent: universal down to the last detail—upholding, directing, disposing, and governing all creatures, actions, and things, from the greatest even to the least (completeness). Basis: the plan or council of His own will. Purpose: doxological end—for the praise of His glory through the revelation of His attributes. God creates and rules for this purpose. The earth is full of the glory of God[7] by act of creation and providence, and the earth shall be full of the knowledge of the glory of God[8] through the work given to mankind in the Garden. Man's chief end is to glorify God and

---

4. Appendix 8; Gangadean, *The Book of Revelation.*

5. Gangadean, *The Westminster Catechisms,* 109-111.

6. *1 Corinthians 10:31.*

7. *Isaiah 6:3.*

8. *Isaiah 11:9; Habakkuk 2:14.*

enjoy Him forever.[9] Man glorifies God by coming to know Him in all that whereby He makes Himself known.[10]

QUESTION 25

Explain first and second causes in ordinary and extraordinary providence.

II. Although, in relation to the foreknowledge and decree of God, the first Cause, all things come to pass immutably, and infallibly; yet, by the same providence, He orders them to fall out, according to the nature of second causes, either necessarily, freely, or contingently.

III. God, in His ordinary providence, makes use of means, yet is free to work without, above, and against them, at His pleasure.

In understanding the decree of God, a distinction is made between God acting as the first cause, and God causing things to come about by second causes. Second causes occur according to the nature of things created. Some have mistakenly understood the providence of God in governing all things to mean God immediately and directly, apart from second causes, brings things to pass. This is not the case. God upholds the things He has created according to their inviolable natures so that they operate according to second causes. An ant operates according to its nature, a horse according to its nature, and a tree according to its nature.

God orders second causes to operate **either necessarily, freely, or contingently.** A rock by nature will fall *necessarily*. It acts according to the laws of the physical world. A person acts *freely* according to their desire and not against their desire. We always get what we want. Some things occur without human intention and are caused *contingently*. For example, God decreed that Ahab,[11] the king of Israel, would be killed

---

9. *SCQ. 1.*

10. *SCQ. 101.*

11. *1 Kings 22:29-40.*

in battle, and God brought this to pass. Ahab went into battle—not contrary to his desire, will, and purpose, but he went freely. Someone drew a bow and shot the arrow through the air, and the laws of physics necessarily governed the arrow's movement. He did not aim the arrow at Ahab, he shot at random, which is contingent. According to that contingency (in terms of where he directed the arrow), it moved according to the laws of physics and came through an opening in the armor, and struck Ahab. As the arrow reaches Ahab we observe a combination of causes operating. We see *necessity* in the law of physics and biology; *contingency* in terms of lack of intention of it being the instrument of Ahab's demise. God did not redirect the arrow; He used contingency to bring about His purpose. Furthermore, we see the *freedom* of Ahab in going to battle. Even though God told him through the prophet that he would die, he still went of his own accord. The event of Ahab's death is an illustration of how God brings to pass His purpose through second causes, either necessarily, freely, or contingently.

God ordinarily works through second causes, which the Confession 5.3 calls "ordinary providence." Ordinary providence entails extraordinary providence. **God, in His ordinary providence, makes use of means**—but He **is free to work without, above, and against** ordinary means. Some miracles of God work against ordinary means. In 2 Kings 6:1-6, the sons of the prophets come to Elisha with the desire to build a place in which to dwell: "And when they came to the Jordan, they cut down trees. But as one was cutting down a tree, the iron axe head fell into the water; and he cried out and said, "Alas, master! For it was borrowed.'" In this example, the laws of gravity necessarily caused the axe head to sink into the water. The person was freely chopping wood with the axe. Natural wear caused the axe head to fly off the handle landing in the water and sinking so it could not be found (according to the nature of things). Since the axe was borrowed, the man would get into trouble at its loss, so he cried out to his master to do something. Elisha threw a stick into the water, and the axe head floated.[12] In the floating of the axe head, God worked against the laws of physics. God also acted against the laws of physics when He parted the waters of the Red Sea, when Balaam's donkey spoke, and when Christ turned the water into wine at the wedding at Cana in Galilee. Paul the Apostle

12. *2 Kings 6:1-6.*

wanted to go to Bithynia, and God closed the door, preventing him from going. In Paul's case, God worked against or above ordinary means. We can look at these events and see how God works above, apart, and against ordinary means.

In the providence of God, there are ordinary and extraordinary means. We ought to rely on the use of ordinary means. If we desire a job in a certain area, we have to go through years of preparation, according to our abilities. Then we follow the ordinary course of applying for the job we desire. God may open the door, we may be just the right person, and if not, God closes the door. Some people feel as if God has been working in their life only by extraordinary means as if God shuts every door that we ordinarily think would open. And then, they start relying on God to use extraordinary means in their lives rather than ordinary means. Yet, we should not trust in ordinary means, but we should ask God to bless the use of ordinary means, knowing that ordinary means in themselves will not produce what we desire. Unless the Lord builds the house, they labor in vain that build it.[13] We ought to ask God to bless the gifts He has given us, bless the means, and give us the strength to use the means that we may prosper for the purpose of the kingdom.

SUMMARY ANSWER

Ordinary providence: God (the first cause), brings about His will through secondary causes (the nature of things created) either necessarily, freely, or contingently. Necessarily means according to the nature of a being. Freely means according to the desire of the being. Contingently means occurring without the agent willing the outcome brought about—e.g., death of Ahab. We are to use ordinary means, but we should not trust solely in ordinary means. We ought to pray that God will bless the use of ordinary means. Extraordinary providence: God is free to act without, above, and against ordinary means.

---

13. *Psalm 127:1.*

QUESTION 26

What is the providence of God with respect to sin in general?

IV. The almighty power, unsearchable wisdom, and infinite goodness of God so far manifest themselves in His providence, that it extends itself even to the first fall, and all other sins of angels and men; and that not by a bare permission, but such as has joined with it a most wise and powerful bounding, and otherwise ordering, and governing of them, in a manifold dispensation, to His own holy ends; yet so, as the sinfulness thereof proceeds only from the creature, and not from God, who, being most holy and righteous, neither is nor can be the author or approver of sin.

The Fall is not beyond the providence and plan of God. Sin is included in the providence of God. The first point of this section affirms **the almighty power, unsearchable wisdom, and infinite goodness of God so far manifest themselves in His providence, that it extends itself even to the first fall, and all other sins of angels and men.** Those who say the Fall, or sin, happens independent of God's plan, or that some other being, Satan, or ruler over the earth causes sin, misunderstand divine sovereignty and providence. Sin is included in the providence of God and needs to be understood in that context. The Confession affirms God's providence over sin is **not by a bare permission.** God permits sin, but He does not actively cause sin. God does not barely permit the sins of fallen angels and men, **but such as has joined with it a most wise and powerful bounding, and otherwise ordering, and governing of them, in a manifold dispensation, to His own holy ends.** God permits sin, **not by a bare permission,** but for a purpose—for His holy ends—which is to reveal His glory. And, He does it in a way that **the sinfulness thereof proceeds only from the creature, and not from God, who, being most holy and righteous, neither is nor can be the author or approver of sin.** God permits sin for a purpose, but He is not the author or approver of sin.

It pleased God to reveal His glory by permitting sin. We should add, God is pleased to deepen the revelation of His glory by permitting sin. Sin is contrary to, or the denial of, the glory of God. God may permit the denial of His glory (failing to know and understand) for the purpose of deepening the revelation of His glory. In other words, God, in His infinite deliberate wisdom, uses sin (the denial of His glory) to serve the good (the knowledge of God's glory). The point is that God does not actively bring sin about; He permits it, but **not by a bare permission.** God is grieved with sin, and His wrath is upon sinners. God is ruling over sin, and He is not unable to control it as though it is something beyond His control. God could prevent sin; thus, if sin occurs, it does so by God permitting it. God could uphold a person who is tempted to sin. In light of this, we pray, "lead us not into temptation, but deliver us from evil."[14]

Genesis 6:6 says, "It grieved God that He had made man on the earth."[15] Sin always grieves God. God is unchangeably grieved with sin and, at the same time, God's wrath is connected with sin, even when He permits it. He can be filled with both grief and wrath every day, as He is both just and merciful. These passions and attributes are part of the simplicity of God. The act that fully reveals God's justice is the very same act that fully reveals the mercy of God. There is no tension within God's attributes or passions. When the Confession affirms that God is impassable, it does not mean He has no feelings. God has feelings in an infinite, eternal, and unchangeable way. Human beings, made in the image of God, have feelings in a finite, temporal, and changeable way. Whereas our feelings change, God's do not.

SUMMARY ANSWER

The providence of God extends to all things—including sin. God permits sin not with a bare permission, but with the purpose of His most holy end. Although God ordains and permits sin, He is neither the author nor approver of sin. The responsibility for sin rests fully on the creature. Although always displeased and

---

14. *Matthew 6:13.*

15. *Genesis 6:6.*

grieved by sin, God is pleased to allow sin for the purpose of deepening the revelation of His glory.

QUESTION 27

What is the providence of God with respect to sin in believers?

V. The most wise, righteous, and gracious God does oftentimes leave, for a season, His own children to manifold temptations, and the corruption of their own hearts, to chastise them for their former sins, or to discover unto them the hidden strength of corruption and deceitfulness of their hearts, that they may be humbled; and, to raise them to a more close and constant dependence for their support upon Himself, and to make them more watchful against all future occasions of sin, and for sundry other just and holy ends.

God may leave His children for a season for the purpose of chastening. No one knows how long this season may be. It is for a time, not indefinitely. It is to serve His purpose. He leaves them **to manifold temptations, and the corruption of their own hearts**. We are often not aware of the corruption that remains in our heart. This lack of awareness is due to self-deception. God may leave us to chastise us for our former sins, from the things of our past and the way we used to live. Notice that God chastises believers. Chastening is not the same as punishment. God has forgiven the sin of believers, but we still need to be cleansed from sin. Leaving believers to themselves allows sin to come to the surface, exposing what remains, to chastise them for their former sins, **or to discover unto them the hidden strength of corruption and deceitfulness of their hearts, that they may be humbled.** Believers do not realize the strength of corruption and the deceitfulness of the human heart. When we go through a period of testing, the sin that remains in our heart is made manifest, the realization of which humbles us. Furthermore, if we have sinned in the past and have asked

God for forgiveness, but have not dealt with sin to eradicate it, we will have to come to a deeper repentance.

Secondly, God may leave His children for a season **to raise them to a more close and constant dependence for their support upon Himself.** In our trials we learn to look to God. When it comes to our attention that we repeatedly sin in the same way, we are grieved and humbled. Then we learn to look to God and avoid sin by depending upon Him. Additionally, God may leave His children **to make them more watchful against all future occasions of sin.** We may be careless and casual. In this condition, we may expose ourselves to occasions for sin. Where we previously did not pay attention, we must now pay attention and be alert for such occasions. We may be involved with other people in ways that we think we are not liable to temptation, and in the next turn, we fall into sin. We have to guard against occasions for temptation and sin. What we read, the songs we listen to, and what we watch may cause certain feelings to be stirred and kept alive. In addition, we need to be watchful of future occasions of sin. Some songs may get into our minds, with a mood connected to the song, and in that mood, we look at the world differently. Lastly, God may leave His children **for sundry other just and holy ends.** God leaves believers and permits sin in believers for many just and holy purposes.

SUMMARY ANSWER

God uses sin in believers—by leaving them to themselves for a time—to accomplish several purposes: to deepen our understanding of the hidden strength of corruption and the deceitfulness of our heart; to chastise, humble, and make believers more dependent upon Him; to make believers more watchful against sin and all future occasions of sin; and for many other holy ends.

QUESTION 28

What is the providence of God with respect to sin in non-believers?

VI. As for those wicked and ungodly men whom God, as a righteous Judge, for former sins, does blind and harden, from them He not only withholds His grace whereby they might have been enlightened in their understandings, and wrought upon in their hearts; but sometimes also withdraws the gifts which they had, and exposes them to such objects as their corruption makes occasion of sin; and, withal, gives them over to their own lusts, the temptations of the world, and the power of Satan, whereby it comes to pass that they harden themselves, even under those means which God uses for the softening of others.

God, in wisdom, uses the curse to soften some and harden others depending on the condition of their heart. God cleanses believers through suffering by recalling them and removing the sin that remains in them. Unbelievers, when confronted with the curse, left to themselves, will harden in their unbelief. Rather than being recalled to stop and think and understand the need for repentance, unbelievers become more conscious and consistent in their unbelief. The same means that are used to soften and edify believers are used to compel unbelievers to go deeper into their sin. As described by Isaiah, the very Word of God that is intended to bring us to repentance can have different effects depending on the heart condition of the hearer: "So shall my word be that goes forth from my mouth: it shall not return to me void, but it shall accomplish what I please, and it shall prosper in the thing for which I sent it."[16] The Word serves to bring life unto life and death unto death, depending on the heart condition of the person. All of this is in the providence of God.

---

16. *Isaiah 55:11.*

SUMMARY ANSWER

God leaves the wicked to their sin by withholding His grace. Left to themselves, the wicked harden by going deeper into unbelief. The same means God uses to soften the righteous—the curse and His Word—harden/compel the wicked into their wickedness.

QUESTION 29

What is the providence of God with respect to the Church?

VII. As the providence of God does, in general, reach to all creatures; so, after a most special manner, it takes care of His Church, and disposes all things to the good thereof.

The failure of the Church to seek, know, and understand God as it ought is part of His providence. God brings trials and temptations into the Church, and the Church may be taken captive by them for a time, and then it may come to repentance. Even when the Church is made subject to unbelief and outward oppression, God disposes all things for the good of the Church. If the Church needs cleansing, God will do what is necessary to bring cleansing to the Church. An individual believer is not the same as the Church. Individual believers may die, but the Church goes on in history. An individual may come to a certain maturity in their lifetime. However, the Church as a collective body will reach a higher level of maturity in history.[17] The Church may exist throughout thousands of years and go through history, which might be parallel to individual history, but it is different as a body. Believers in the Church now have access to greater understanding than in the third century. This is because the Church has continued and achieved a greater maturity through the cumulative work of the pastor-teachers being led by the Holy Spirit.

---

17. *Ephesians 4:11-13.*

SUMMARY ANSWER

God in providence upholds the Church to lead it into all glory—
understanding the fullness of God's revelation.

Chapter 6

OF THE FALL OF MAN, OF SIN, AND OF THE PUNISHMENT THEREOF

QUESTION 30

Explain what is the original sin. Why is evil permitted?

I. Our first parents, being seduced by the subtlety and temptation of Satan, sinned, in eating the forbidden fruit. This their sin, God was pleased, according to His wise and holy counsel, to permit, having purposed to order it to His own glory.

The doxological element is again highlighted in Chapter six of the Confession, **Our first parents, being seduced by the subtlety and temptation of Satan, sinned, in eating the forbidden fruit. This their sin, God was pleased, according to His wise and holy counsel, to permit, having purposed to order it to His own glory.** We are to understand that God, in His providence, was pleased to permit the first sin. God upholds, directs, disposes, and governs all creatures, actions, and things from the greatest to the least, so that He could have upheld Adam. Nevertheless, God was pleased to permit Adam's sin. He did so **to His own glory.** Creation is revelation, and providence is a further revelation of His glory. God's providence includes permitting sin to deepen the revelation of His glory. The revelation of His glory is the doxological focus of the Confession as seen in sections 1.1, 2.2, 3.3, 4.1, 5.1, 6.1. These passages, along with the Shorter Catechism

Questions 1, 46, and 101, when combined, provide the doxological focus of the Westminster Standards.[1]

Eating the forbidden fruit is the manifestation of the first sin.[2] The forbidden fruit was the fruit of the tree of the knowledge of good and evil. They were **seduced by the subtlety and temptation of Satan**. We should understand "the subtlety of Satan" in light of the clarity of general revelation. What may be known of God and man, and good and evil, is clear so that men are without excuse.

Specifically, in the temptation, Satan said, "You shall be like God knowing good and evil."[3] God does not know good and evil by discovery; but as Creator, He determines the nature of things, and in determining the nature of things, He determines what is good and evil for those things. Adam and Eve should have known that they were creatures, that the Creator exists, and that they are not the Creator, and so they could not determine good and evil as God does. In the first sin, they put themselves in the place of God to determine good and evil, thus the first sin is autonomy.

Analyzing, in retrospect, they put themselves in the place of God to determine good and evil. The sin is not merely the act of the eating of the fruit, but the eating of the fruit is the manifestation of the sin. Sin occurs before the act of eating, in that they believed what Satan said (the lie). They failed to understand because they had not been seeking God. Sin is not only autonomy in putting ourselves in the place of God to determine good and evil, but it is not seeking, not understanding, and not doing what is right.[4] This is the original sin.[5] The outward act is sin, and the inward desire is sin. All sin is rooted in the failure to know God. In identifying the root of original sin, we can understand the real nature of sin and repent of it. If we do not know the real nature of sin, we cannot understand the consequences of sin. If we do not understand the real nature and consequence of sin, we cannot understand the justice and mercy of God. If we do not have an

---

1. pp. xxix-xxxiii.

2. For a fuller explanation of the sin in the Garden, see: Gangadean, *On Natural and Revealed Theology*, 195-212.

3. *Genesis 3:5.*

4. *Romans 3:10-12; Psalm 14:2-3, 53:1-3;* Gangadean, "Paper No. 8: Belief and Unbelief," in *The Logos Papers*, 41-42.

5. Gangadean, *The Westminster Catechisms*, 144-145.

adequate understanding of sin, we will not have an adequate understanding of many other foundational teachings, particularly our need for salvation in Christ.[6] This is why we put much emphasis on root sin. Understanding sin and death is part of the foundation;[7] as such, much else will be affected by our understanding, or lack of understanding, of the foundation.

The Scriptures define sin as not seeking, not understanding, and not doing what is right. We see this definition of sin in Romans 3:10-12, which comes after Romans 1 and 2. The sins of Romans 1 and 2 are not seeing what is clear about God—His eternal power and divine nature, and the transgression of the law of God written on the heart. Therefore, Romans 3 takes that prior context into account. This definition of sin is also provided in Psalm 14:1-3 and Psalm 53:1-3. In addition, Paul's quoting it in his letter to the Romans, in keeping with the pattern of repetition, accentuates what is important in Scripture. This description helps us to understand what sin is. Sin is not seeking, not understanding, and not doing what is right. These three aspects of sin are related. If we seek, we will understand. If we seek and understand, we will do what is right. When we examine the act of eating the forbidden fruit, it outwardly expressed what was transpiring inwardly. Adam and Eve had put themselves in the place of God to determine good and evil, and they had already determined that something other than the knowledge of God was the good. They had not been seeking the knowledge of God, and therefore not growing in understanding while losing the understanding that they did have, and as a result, they did what was not right by the outward act of eating. Paul sums up all of sin in these three aspects of not seeking, not understanding, and not doing what is right. Obedience is not only in terms of the outward act, but also in the inward reality of seeking.[8]

Sin is not only autonomy—determining good and evil for oneself—but goes back to something prior. God created humans with a certain nature, and if humans act according to their nature, they act rightly. Human nature is made in the image of God with the capacity to understand. To sin is to act contrary to our nature as made in the

---

6. Appendix 7.

7. Gangadean, "Paper No. 37: The Seven Pillars," in *The Logos Papers*, 207-210.

8. *Hebrews 11:6.*

image of God. That sin is an act contrary to our nature is an axiomatic truth that should be known from general revelation prior to coming to Scripture: The good for a being is according to the nature of a being.[9] A rabbit has a rabbit's nature created by God. And to act according to his nature is good for the rabbit. Horses should not act like rabbits; they should act like horses, and neither should horses be treated like rabbits. For man as a rational being, we should use reason to understand. Humans need meaning the way horses need hay. Furthermore, if we go without meaning, our life will become distorted, and we will be deeply affected. Human beings need meaning according to their nature as rational. When we act contrary to our nature made in the image of God, we harm ourselves—sin is self-destructive. Meaning is most beneficial to humans. We would rather give up our life at times to preserve meaning. That is how beneficial it is. We can conclude that sin is an act contrary to human nature; it is not seeking, not understanding, and not doing what is right; it is autonomy; it is to neglect, avoid, resist, and deny (NARD) reason in the face of what is clear. Hopefully, we see the importance of getting a clearer idea of sin.[10]

SUMMARY ANSWER

Original sin is the first sin, the same in all, and the paradigm of sin. From general revelation, sin is an act contrary to our nature. It is to neglect, avoid, resist, and deny—NARD—what is clear about God and man, and good and evil. From special revelation, sin is not seeking, not understanding, and not doing what is right. From Historic Christianity, sin is any want of conformity unto, or transgression of, the law of God. Sin is unbelief—believing what is false. Sin is unrighteousness—doing what is forbidden. Sin is autonomy—the denial of our creaturely dependence on God. Theodicy: God was pleased to permit sin having purposed to order it to His own glory—to deepen the revelation of His own glorious justice and mercy (WCF. 1.1, 2.2, 3.3, 4.1, 5.1, 6.1 and SCQ. 1, 46, 101).

---

9. Gangadean, *Philosophical Foundation*, 171-183.

10. Appendix 6.

QUESTION 31

Explain the consequence of sin.

II. By this sin they fell from their original righteousness and communion with God, and so became dead in sin, and wholly defiled in all the parts and faculties of soul and body.

The consequence of sin is spiritual death. Spiritual death applies particularly to the soul, but it also affects the body, since humans are a body/soul unity. It should be noted that Scripture states that the wages of sin is death,[11] and we should make a distinction between physical and spiritual death. There was no physical death before the Fall; physical death was imposed by God. Spiritual death is the consequence of not seeking and not understanding. What we understand is meaning. The consequence of not understanding is meaninglessness. Not understanding is synonymous with not having faith. Having faith is possessing understanding, for it is by faith that we understand.[12]

Adam and Eve fell into spiritual death—death of the soul—as a result of sin. Spiritual death is synonymous with not using our mind to understand, resulting in meaninglessness. Sin and death affects the other parts of the soul, including our feelings and desires. When we are not seeking God, but seeking something else in the place of God, what we seek cannot satisfy the need for meaning, and boredom is the result. The human soul is triune,[13] which includes the mind (understanding), the feelings (desires), and the will (moral sense of ought). Whereas meaninglessness connects with understanding, and boredom with desire, guilt connects with the will. When we suffer from meaninglessness and boredom, it is because we have done something wrong (not sought, not understood, and not acted rightly). In the condition

---

11. *Romans 6:23.*

12. Gangadean, "Paper No. 21: Faith and Reason in Christianity," in *The Logos Papers*, 135-138; Gangadean, *Philosophical Foundation,* 121-127.

13. Gangadean, *Philosophical Foundation,* 43-45.

of boredom, humans often do things contrary to the law of God for the sake of satisfaction. Both boredom and guilt affect us physically. Thus, spiritual death has an effect on our bodies.

SUMMARY ANSWER

The consequence of sin is spiritual death (meaninglessness, boredom, and guilt). Sin breaks our communion with God, and it carries the noetic effect (defilement of body and soul). The noetic effect affects our willingness to use reason. It affects our understanding of sin, spiritual death, the curse, eternal life, and basic beliefs.[14]

QUESTION 32

What are the objective and subjective effects of original sin?

III. They being the root of all mankind, the guilt of this sin was imputed; and the same death in sin, and corrupted nature, conveyed to all their posterity descending from them by ordinary generation.

IV. From this original corruption, whereby we are utterly indisposed, disabled, and made opposite to all good, and wholly inclined to all evil, do proceed all actual transgressions.

The objective effect of original sin is that the guilt of this sin was imputed to all descended from Adam (the doctrine of imputation). With the guilt of Adam imputed, so is **the same death in sin, and corrupted nature, conveyed to all their posterity descending from them by ordinary generation.** Being born of Adam, humanity is united with Adam by ordinary generation. The same pattern of imputation holds true for Christ. As Adam's guilt is imputed to his offspring, so

---

14. Appendix 7.

Christ's righteousness is imputed to believers who are united to Him through faith.

The Confession section 6.4 describes the subjective effects of original sin in that **we are utterly indisposed, disabled, and made opposite to all good, and wholly inclined to all evil.** This does not mean that humans actually do all evil, but that humans are wholly inclined to all evil. It does not mean that humans do no good, but humans are indisposed to do good. Fallen human beings have a fundamental disposition both negatively and positively. Negatively, humans are indisposed to all good, and positively, humans are inclined to all evil. This disposition is in all human beings as a result of the imputed guilt of Adam and corruption of our nature. And, from this disposition proceeds **all actual transgressions.** Note the distinction that is being made between *original* sin and *actual* sin. There is an additional distinction to be made between actual *root sin* and actual *fruit sin.*

The *Objective* effects of original sin means that our fallenness is a reality whether we feel it or not. The *Subjective* effects of original sin are made manifest in our feelings and in our inclinations. Remember the statement regarding man at the time of the Flood, "every inclination of his thought is only evil continually."[15] When human beings are left to themselves over a period of time, our sinful condition becomes more and more manifest, and it was manifested in its maximal degree before the Flood. At that time, all human beings had corrupt desires and did violence against each other as the original sin manifested itself in actual sin. We should pay attention to the distinction between the *objective* and *subjective* effects of original sin and also between *original* and *actual sin.* As fallen humanity, we are dead in trespasses and sin from birth,[16] because original sin is objectively present by imputation. It is also true that the wages of actual sin is spiritual death.[17] So when we see root sin occurring in Romans 1:18-20 through the failure to seek and understand the clear revelation of God in creation, the result is spiritual death (the wages of sin). In Romans 1:21-32 we see the fruit sin that arises from root sin. Spiritual death accepts of degrees because humans are finite, temporal, and changeable; we should speak of death

---

15. *Genesis 6:5.*

16. *Ephesians 2:1.*

17. *Romans 6:23.*

as increasing. Just as life increases by seeking God through His grace, death increases by persisting in the failure to live according to human nature as rational beings.

SUMMARY ANSWER

Objective effect: imputation of original sin (root sin) through Adam—our covenant representative. Union to Adam is by ordinary generation. Subjective effect: negatively, we are utterly indisposed to all good, and positively, we are wholly inclined to all evil. It does not mean we do all evil, but that we are wholly inclined towards all evil. All actual sin proceeds from original sin. Original sin is to be distinguished from actual sin. Original sin is root sin (failure to seek and understand the knowledge of God), and out of it proceeds fruit sin. Actual sin accepts of degrees, and the consequence of sin accepts of degrees as well.

QUESTION 33

What is the effect of original sin in the regenerate?

V. This corruption of nature, during this life, does remain in those that are regenerated; and although it be, through Christ, pardoned, and mortified; yet both itself, and all the motions thereof, are truly and properly sin.

Regeneration does not remove original sin. The Roman Catholic Church teaches that regeneration occurs with baptism; that baptism is not a sign, but is actual regeneration, and baptism removes original sin. The Confession denies this position and affirms **this corruption of nature**—from original sin—**during this life, does remain in those that are regenerated; and although it be, through Christ, pardoned, and mortified; yet both itself, and all the motions thereof, are truly and properly sin.** Believers have the effects of original sin remaining during this life. Original sin as an attitude is indisposed to consider the glory of God in all things and is inclined towards the self-life (i.e., to consider ourselves first). The sin of autonomy (determining good and evil for ourselves), and all that comes from it, also remains in this life.

One might question whether the Confession accurately addresses the subject of sin. Earlier, an account was provided regarding the original sin in the Garden (eating the forbidden fruit). The act of eating was preceded by a lack of understanding the basic things regarding God and man, and good and evil. We can infer this failure by examining the meaning of the words of the temptation and what must have existentially preceded the eating of the fruit. By examining the temptation through the use of good and necessary consequence, a fuller and clearer understanding of sin and death is attained.[18] Thus we can see that the Confession's depiction of sin is fully consistent with an analysis of sin from the Genesis account.

The analysis of the Fall affirms death in sin as spiritual. Sin affects the faculty of the mind, the faculty of the soul as the seat of affection, and sin affects the will, especially in the moral sense of ought, and it involves guilt. Some might say that we can sin without guilt. Yet, insofar as we must provide excuses to justify ourselves in our sin shows, objectively, there is guilt, and we have to justify ourselves to avoid it.

Scripture describes spiritual death as darkness of mind[19] (outer darkness), burning in desire[20] (burning without satisfaction), and the worm that does not die[21] (the gnawing of conscience and the torment of guilt). These figures of speech are used to describe the condition of spiritual death, which culminate in the bottomless pit[22] (it is unending). Physical figures of speech are used to describe a spiritual condition. The wages of sin is death.[23] These figures of speech are popularly thought of as hell, where the "lake of fire" is taken literally. However, Scripture

---

18. For a fuller explanation of the sin in the Garden, see: Gangadean, *On Natural and Revealed Theology*, 195-212; Gangadean, *The Biblical Worldview*.

19. *Matthew 8:12, 22:13, 25:30.*

20. *Mark 9:46.*

21. *Mark 9:48.*

22. *Revelation 9:2.*

23. *Romans 6:23.*

says the lake of fire is the second death. This phrase is repeated twice in the Book of Revelation.[24]

Generally speaking, the figurative language of "hell" represents destruction, not the cessation of being, but destruction in the sense that all of the efforts of our understanding which resist acknowledging God end in futility and darkness. The more we seek to justify our unbelief before God, the deeper into darkness we go and the more fanciful distinctions we make in order to preserve ourselves against God.[25] There are people who are otherwise quite educated who speak folly, and do not see it as folly, which is an indication of how dark their minds are. Having a Ph.D. does not exempt one from folly. Our learning does not protect us as we may misuse our learning to go more fully into folly becoming blinded to reality. Pharaoh was blinded to the obvious. Caiaphas the high priest asked Jesus to tell the Sanhedren if He was the Christ, the Son of God (which implies that He is God and man), and when Jesus said He was, they charged Him with blasphemy.[26] But the very question showed that Christ was the Son of God. This is an example of how the mind is darkened and cannot see the very obvious.

SUMMARY ANSWER

Regeneration does not remove original sin (vs. Catholic baptismal regeneration). Sin remains in all that are regenerated until death (glorification). As believers, we are inclined to be man-centered rather than God-centered. We are inclined towards regarding the self rather than God. The wages of sin is death expressed in a state of outer darkness—darkness of mind; burning in desire—inflamed; the worm that does not die—tormenting of our conscience; and the bottomless pit—without end.

---

24. *Revelation 20:14, 21:8.*

25. Gangadean, *Philosophical Foundation*, 73-80.

26. *Matthew 26:57-67.*

QUESTION 34

What are the effects of original and actual sin?

VI. Every sin, both original and actual, being a transgression of the righteous law of God, and contrary thereunto, does, in its own nature, bring guilt upon the sinner, whereby he is bound over to the wrath of God, and curse of the law, and so made subject to death, with all miseries spiritual, temporal, and eternal.

Original sin in human nature is an indisposition: **Every sin, both original and actual, being a transgression of the righteous law of God, and contrary thereunto, does, in its own nature, bring guilt upon the sinner.** When the Scripture says that no one seeks God, this is the indisposition of sin, which is not to delight in the Creator but to take delight in the creation. This indisposition brings guilt upon ourselves. We are not to take the name of God in vain.[27] Whosoever takes the name of God in vain, God will not hold him guiltless. When we are not disposed to seek God, it is sin, and we are held guilty. There are times when we should read the Scriptures diligently and study, but we do not. We are indisposed to reading the Scripture and inclined toward sloth. This sin is a transgression of the righteous law of God.

The first commandment, according to the Shorter Catechism, requires us "to know and acknowledge God to be the only true God, and our God, and to worship and glorify Him accordingly."[28] Not knowing God is a transgression of the law of God. We cannot know without seeking. God is the rewarder of those who diligently seek Him.[29] Seeking, knowing, and understanding God is part of obedience to the law of God. Actual sin is preceded by our failure to seek God and to understand God, which results in the failure to do what is right. If we

---

27. *Exodus 20:7.*

28. *SCQ. 46.*

29. *Hebrews 11:6.*

have actual sin at its root, we will have actual sin in fruit. All sin (root and fruit) is contrary to the law of God and brings death.

Humans are **bound over to the wrath of God, and curse of the law, and so made subject to death, with all miseries spiritual, temporal, and eternal.** We need to keep in mind the distinction between temporal miseries and spiritual miseries. We should also note the distinction between spiritual death and physical death. We need to recall that physical death is not punishment for sin, but is a call back. Sometimes the Scripture uses terms for punishment synonymously with chastising (chastening for cleansing purposes). Nevertheless, we are to affirm the distinction between spiritual and physical death.

Humans have original sin, spiritual death that comes with sin, and the effects of death. It should not be surprising to us that the Confession addresses this distinction. Moreover, the Confession address the distinction between both original and actual sin and their effects. This understanding is why the Westminster Confession of Faith is the high-water mark of creedal Christianity. It is the most conscious and consistent understanding of sin and death to date.

SUMMARY ANSWER

The effect of original and actual sin is spiritual death. Root sin is indisposition towards knowing and acknowledging God to be the only true God, and our God, and to worship and glorify Him accordingly.

The objective effect is the imputation of original sin (root sin) through Adam—our covenant representative. The subjective effect of original sin is twofold: negatively, we are utterly indisposed to all good, and positively, we are wholly inclined to all evil. It does not mean we do all evil, but that we are wholly inclined towards all evil. All actual sin proceeds from original sin. The effect of both original and actual sin is spiritual death.

—

Chapter 7

OF GOD'S COVENANT WITH MAN

QUESTION 35

What is the purpose and content of the covenant of works?

I. The distance between God and the creature is so great, that although reasonable creatures do owe obedience unto Him as their Creator, yet they could never have any fruition of Him as their blessedness and reward, but by some voluntary condescension on God's part, which He has been pleased to express by way of covenant.

II. The first covenant made with man was a covenant of works, wherein life was promised to Adam; and in him to his posterity, upon condition of perfect and personal obedience.

In ourselves we are changeable. The purpose of the covenant is to establish man from a state of being changeable in himself to a state where he is unchangeable. The Confession explains, **the distance between God and the creature is so great, that although reasonable creatures do owe obedience unto Him as their Creator, yet they could never have any fruition of Him as their blessedness and reward, but by some voluntary condescension on God's part, which He has been pleased to express by way of covenant.** A covenant is an arrangement made by God with man for the purpose of blessing him. Our first parents, being changeable, would have no guarantee of lasting benefit in God apart from God's arrangement. The lasting benefit of the covenant is that man in himself is changeable, and in the covenant relationship, he is unchanging. This is desirable so that we will never fall away. Humans, left to themselves, are changeable and will always be changeable, but in the covenant, God upholds believers so that they will not change. A permanent relationship established by God through His upholding grace is our blessedness and reward.

The covenant is a special arrangement made by God whereby Adam represents mankind. *The covenant is deduced from Scripture by good and necessary consequence.* The covenant has three parts: representation, probation, and manifestation. In *representation*, Adam is the covenant head of mankind—his actions will affect all. In *probation*, Adam is to continue in perfect obedience—seeking the knowledge of God as the good by carrying out the work of dominion. In *manifestation*, it was revealed that Adam did not continue in perfect obedience—Adam failed to know the distinction between God and man, and good and evil. If Adam had obeyed God, righteousness would have been passed down to all his posterity.

Though the concept of covenant may be deduced by good and necessary consequence, literalists often deny its existence because the word "covenant" is not explicitly used in the opening chapters of Genesis.[1] In Genesis 2 there is a special arrangement made by God with Adam to represent man. Additionally, the effect of Adam's sin is passed down to all posterity. Adam represented humanity, and he was tested as our representative head as a matter of probation. God provides the condition for the effects of this test to be made manifest, which is the purpose of the two trees in the Garden of Eden. The two trees, and particularly, the names of the trees, especially the tree of the knowledge of good and evil, were designed to manifest outwardly, what was going on inwardly. The test is for Adam's representation, his probation, and the manifestation of sin, which is the arrangement that God made. The Confession says, **the first covenant made with man was a covenant of works, wherein life was promised to Adam; and in him to his posterity, upon condition of perfect and personal obedience.** If Adam had obeyed God, he and all those he represented would have been established in righteousness. The first covenant is called a covenant of works because it is connected with Adam's obedience. He was to actively obey the Word of God.

---

1. Gangadean, *The Biblical Worldview: Creation, Fall, Redemption*, Sermon 9.

SUMMARY ANSWER

Purpose: In ourselves, we are changeable. In the covenant, we are unchangeable. The covenant moves man from a state of being changeable in himself to a state where man is unchangeable in the covenant.

Content: The covenant is a special arrangement made by God for Adam to represent mankind. The covenant is deduced from Scripture by good and necessary consequence. The covenant has three parts: representation, probation, and manifestation. In representation, Adam is the covenant head of mankind—his actions will affect all. In probation, Adam is to continue in perfect obedience—seeking to know God as the good by carrying out the work of dominion. In manifestation, it became revealed that Adam did not continue in perfect obedience—Adam failed to know the distinction between God and man, and good and evil. If Adam had obeyed God, righteousness would have been passed down to all his posterity.

QUESTION 36

What is the covenant of grace and its relation to the covenant of works?

III. Man, by his fall, having made himself incapable of life by that covenant, the Lord was pleased to make a second, commonly called the covenant of grace; wherein He freely offers unto sinners life and salvation by Jesus Christ; requiring of them faith in him, that they may be saved, and promising to give unto all those that are ordained unto eternal life His Holy Spirit, to make them willing, and able to believe.

The covenant of grace is intimately connected with the covenant of works. The covenant of grace is made with Jesus Christ, who is the new representative head in the place of Adam and who, by His perfect and personal obedience pays the penalty of the first covenant, and establishes man in righteousness. The covenant of grace *must* be understood in relation to the covenant of works. The covenant of grace is the same covenant only made with a new representative who will *undo* what Adam did (by paying the penalty for sin) and *do* what Adam failed to do (perfect and personal obedience). It is called the covenant of grace because God, by His grace, provides redemption—through vicarious atonement—for those who are in sin and death under the first covenant. The covenant of grace is fulfilled not by any demand outside of God, but by God's mercy through Christ. Christ perfectly obeys and fulfills the covenant of works, and the provision of Christ (by God Himself) to fulfill the covenant of works is called the covenant of grace.

Jesus Christ represents all believers that are united to Him by faith. Just as those who are united to Adam are affected by the covenant of works, those who are united to Christ under the covenant of grace come under the terms of that covenant. The covenants of works and grace are where covenant theology begins. The idea of covenant theology is further emphasized in Genesis 2 in the account of the manner of the creation of woman. Woman is taken out of man, of his flesh, and she is brought to man in the covenant relationship of marriage. The human covenant of marriage is a visible display of the covenant relationship man is to have with God. This is in keeping with the pattern of creation that the visible reveals the invisible. The covenant of grace removes the failure under the covenant of works and fulfills the benefits of that covenant. The Confession says, **Man, by his fall, having made himself incapable of life by that covenant, the Lord was pleased to make a second, commonly called the covenant of grace; wherein He freely offers unto sinners life and salvation by Jesus Christ; requiring of them faith in Him, that they may be saved, and promising to give unto all those that are ordained unto eternal life His Holy Spirit, to make them willing, and able to believe.**

The covenant of works and grace continue throughout history. All those who are outside of Christ are under the covenant of works. All those who are in Christ are under the covenant of grace. The covenant of grace fulfills the requirements of the covenant of works, which is why Christ had to fulfill all righteousness, obey the law to its utmost, and then die. Christ had to die to pay the penalty of those condemned under the covenant of works. Moreover, Christ had to fulfill the requirements of the covenant of works, just as it was given to Adam, to bring life to human beings. It is a covenant of grace in that the fulfillment of all righteousness is provided wholly by God. Genesis 3 contains the promise that the seed of the woman shall crush the head of the serpent (the covenant of grace was given and initiated in Genesis 3:15). Adam was saved by the covenant of grace. When Adam obeyed God under the conditions of the curse, calling his wife's name Eve, he put his faith in what God had promised and thereby was saved through Christ. The covenant of works and the covenant of grace have been in effect since Genesis 2–3. Cain did not put his faith in the promise and therefore continued under the covenant of works, perishing under it. Every human being, at this very moment and all through history, is either under the covenant of works or under the covenant of grace.

SUMMARY ANSWER

The covenant of works is stated in Genesis 2, and the covenant of grace in Genesis 3. The covenant of grace must be understood in connection with the covenant of works. The covenant of grace is made with Jesus Christ. Christ is to undo what Adam did (by paying the penalty for sin) and do what Adam failed to do (by perfect and personal obedience until the earth is filled with the knowledge of God). Christ, in faithfulness, fulfilled the covenant of works. It is upon His perfect obedience and payment of divine justice at Calvary—by His death—that His righteousness is imputed to us in the covenant of grace. All humanity is under one of the two covenants. All represented in Adam are united to Adam; likewise, all represented in Christ are united to Christ by faith. The covenant of grace removes the failures under the covenant of works and fulfills the benefits of that covenant. The covenant of works and covenant of grace continue until the end of history. Unbelievers are under the covenant of works while believers are under the covenant of grace. Adam was saved under the covenant of grace, while Cain died under the covenant of works.

QUESTION 37

How is the covenant of grace administered in the Old Testament?

IV. This covenant of grace is frequently set forth in Scripture by the name of a testament, in reference to the death of Jesus Christ the Testator, and to the everlasting inheritance, with all things belonging to it, therein bequeathed.

V. This covenant was differently administered in the time of the law, and in the time of the gospel: under the law, it was administered by promises, prophecies, sacrifices, circumcision, the paschal lamb, and other types and ordinances delivered to the people of the Jews, all foresignifying Christ to come; which were, for that time, sufficient and efficacious, through the operation of the Spirit, to instruct and build up the elect in faith in the promised Messiah, by whom they had full remission of sins, and eternal salvation; and is called the Old Testament.

Section 7.4 of the Confession transitions from the idea of the covenant of grace to the idea of the testament in speaking about the death of Christ, who is the testator, and the inheritance that comes from the death of Christ. **This covenant of grace is frequently set forth in Scripture by the name of a testament, in reference to the death of Jesus Christ the Testator, and to the everlasting inheritance, with all things belonging to it, therein bequeathed.** This one covenant of grace is set forth as a testament in two different forms (Old Testament and New Testament), yet it is the same covenant of grace. We are not to make the mistake many evangelicals have made over the years by identifying the Old Testament with the covenant of works. The Old Testament is under the covenant of grace. The old administration of the covenant of grace started in Genesis 3. The idea of the covenant does not begin with Moses or Abraham; it begins in Genesis. Dispensationalists have tried to argue that there are different covenants and dispensations showing different requirements under different covenants. The promise is one and the same from Adam on. There are not different blessings, such as earthly blessings and spiritual blessings, in different eras. It is not one covenant of grace and then a subsidiary covenant of works after the covenant of grace was made. The covenant of works goes all the way back to Adam. Speaking of the covenant otherwise are confusions in popular Christianity that need to be addressed.

The Confession goes on, **this covenant was differently administered in the time of the law, and in the time of the Gospel: under the law it was administered by promises, prophecies, sacrifices, circumcision, the paschal lamb, and other types and ordinances delivered to the people of the Jews, all foresignifying Christ to come.** The covenant of grace is not just for the Jews, but goes back to Adam when God provided the coats of skin.[2] It goes back to Abel when he offered the sacrifice. The covenant of grace was administered through these types and shadows. They were **all foresignifying Christ to come; which were, for that time, sufficient and efficacious, through the operation of the Spirit, to instruct and build up the elect in faith in the promised Messiah, by whom they had full remission of sins, and eternal salvation; and is called, the Old Testament.** The Holy Spirit worked in Adam's heart, Abel's heart, and in Noah's heart to help them see that these sacrifices were foresignifying Christ, the promised Messiah, the seed of the woman who was to come. The Holy Spirit enabled them to understand the meaning of the sacrifice and to receive full remission of sins and eternal salvation; they did not receive some other blessing.

SUMMARY ANSWER

The covenant of grace begins in Genesis 3 and continues in effect until Christ. Under the law, it was administered by promises, prophesies, sacrifices, circumcision, the paschal lamb, and other types and ordinances—all foresignifying Christ to come. Believers in the Old Testament were enabled by the Holy Spirit to understand the symbolism of the Jewish law as a forerunner of Christ. Believers in faith, under the covenant of grace, receive full remission of sin and salvation. All believers under the Old

---

2. *Genesis 3:21.*

Testament and New Testament are counted righteous by the imputed righteousness of Christ in the covenant of grace. There is no other name under heaven given among men by which we must be saved.

QUESTION 38

How is the covenant of grace administered in the New Testament?

VI. Under the Gospel, when Christ, the substance, was exhibited, the ordinances in which this covenant is dispensed are the preaching of the Word, and the administration of the sacraments of Baptism and the Lord's Supper: which, though fewer in number, and administered with more simplicity, and less outward glory, yet, in them, it is held forth in more fullness, evidence and spiritual efficacy, to all nations, both Jews and Gentiles; and is called the New Testament. There are not therefore two covenants of grace, differing in substance, but one and the same, under various dispensations.

Dispensationalism is a popular view within the Christian community. Dispensations, as taught in the Scripture and the Confession, are different administrations of one and the same covenant of grace. Dispensations should not be understood as if different covenants are administered differently before and after the coming of Christ. Dispensationalists differ from the Confession based on their literalist hermeneutics, especially in not applying good and necessary consequence.[3] Sometimes a literalist interpretation claims that the use of a different word means there is a difference in a concept or in reality. However, different words may often convey the same concept. Dispensationalists make a distinction between the kingdom of heaven and the kingdom of God as if they were different realities. Different words are used, but they refer to the same concept. Different words are used to refer to the

---

3. *WCF. 1.6.*

kingdom because of the Jewish belief that we are not to take the name of God in vain, therefore the word "God" is replaced with "heaven" in the Gospel of Matthew. The literalist's tendency to reduce the content of a text to its explicit form leads them to believe that words and concepts are synonymous, and that unless the word is present, the concept/idea is not. For example, since the word "covenant" is not explicitly/literally used in Genesis 2, the idea of covenant is denied.

Dispensationalists apply a different hermeneutic principle. They say that in addition to salvation, there are temporal blessings given through the Mosaic economy, and if we obey the regulations given by Moses, we would have blessings in the land. According to them, this is different from the covenant of grace, which has spiritual blessings, not temporal earthly blessings. Dispensationalists do not see the connection between earthly blessings and spiritual blessings. If we understand what "the" blessing is—the knowledge of God—we would see the connection between earthly and spiritual blessings, because the blessing was always connected with the earth and having dominion. God did not give the Jews earthly physical blessings apart from spiritual blessing. To fail to affirm so misses the idea of the knowledge of God as the blessing, and to miss the relation between earthly and heavenly blessings. We could overcome this misunderstanding if we have the more basic in place. What needs to be asked of the dispensationalists is what is the blessing of God? What is eternal life? We will need to seek agreement on the blessing before understanding the covenant. Eternal life comes through the work of dominion.[4] The work of dominion cannot be set aside as though there is some other way to know God. There is no knowledge of God directly in heaven nor apart from the work of dominion.[5] The good is not something other than the knowledge of God.[6] This is the prior issue to be addressed. Doctrine is a system that proceeds from the more basic to the less basic; if we understand the more basic, we will understand the less basic. This is part of the process of learning to think presuppositionally. God would have us think about the basic things, understand, and draw implications. There is one covenant of

---

4. Appendix 4.

5. Gangadean, "Paper No. 106: The Good and Heaven," in *The Logos Papers*, 547-556; Gangadean, *On Natural and Revealed Theology*, 9-32.

6. Gangadean, *Philosophical Foundation*, 208-212.

grace with different dispensations or administrations quite naturally before and after Christ came.

SUMMARY ANSWER

The covenant of grace under the New Testament is administered by the preaching of the Word, the sacraments of Baptism and the Lord's Supper: which, though fewer in number, and administered with more simplicity, and less outward glory, yet, in them, it is held forth in more fullness, evidence, and spiritual efficacy, to all nations, both Jews and Gentiles. There are not therefore two covenants of grace, differing in substance, but one and the same, under various dispensations.

Chapter 8

OF CHRIST THE MEDIATOR

QUESTION 39

What is the office of mediator?

I. It pleased God, in His eternal purpose, to choose and ordain the Lord Jesus, His only begotten Son, to be the Mediator between God and man, the Prophet, Priest, and King, the Head and Savior of His Church, the Heir of all things, and Judge of the world: unto whom He did from all eternity give a people, to be His seed, and to be by Him in time redeemed, called, justified, sanctified, and glorified.

It pleased God, in His eternal purpose, to choose and ordain the Lord Jesus, His only begotten Son, to be the Mediator between God and man. The office of the mediator is to stand between God and man. The Confession further explains the office of the mediator by specifying Christ is the Prophet, Priest, and King.[1] As the Prophet, He announces the promise and pronounces the curse. As the Priest, He makes us holy, and as the King, He rules until He subdues all of His enemies. Section 8.3 speaks about the *office* of mediator, **which office He took not unto Himself**, and then in Section 8.4, **this office the Lord Jesus did most willingly undertake.** He did not take up the office of mediator of Himself, but He did willingly undertake the office.

The first point is that the **mediator** is **between God and man.** The second is that He is **Prophet, Priest, and King.** The third is that He is **Head and Savior of His Church;** fourth, He is **Heir of all things;** and

---

1. Gangadean, *The Westminster Catechisms*, 163-168.

fifth, He is **Judge of the world.** Furthermore, unto this mediator God gave **a people, to be His seed, and to be by Him in time redeemed, called, justified, sanctified, and glorified.** We might say that a people is given to Him to be a seed as Adam was given a seed, to be (by Him) in time redeemed—this involves being called, justified, sanctified, and glorified. This is a summary of the office of the mediator.

SUMMARY ANSWER

The office of mediator is the mediation between God and man. He is the Prophet (announcing the promise and pronouncing the curse), Priest (making us holy), and King (ruling until all enemies are subdued to Him), the Head and Savior of His Church, the Heir of all things, and Judge of the world.

QUESTION 40

Who is the person of the mediator?

II. The Son of God, the second person in the Trinity, being very and eternal God, of one substance and equal with the Father, did, when the fullness of time was come, take upon Him man's nature, with all the essential properties, and common infirmities thereof, yet without sin; being conceived by the power of the Holy Ghost, in the womb of the virgin Mary, of her substance. So that two whole, perfect, and distinct natures, the Godhead and the manhood, were inseparably joined together in one person, without conversion, composition, or confusion. Which person is very God, and very man, yet one Christ, the only Mediator between God and man.

In approaching the person of the mediator, we should ask: What is required of the mediator between God and man? And, who is sufficient to undertake the office of mediator? A mediator must represent both God and man. The one to fulfill this office cannot merely be a man, and it cannot merely be God, if He is to represent both. This is a puzzle and struggle to be confronted. The mediator is to redeem man. **The Son of God, the second person in the Trinity, being very and eternal God, of one substance and equal with the Father, did, when the fullness of time was come, take upon Him man's nature, with all the essential properties, and common infirmities thereof, yet without sin.** He is God the Son who takes to Himself human nature. The Son of God can represent both God and man, because it is not man who takes to himself the divine nature, but it is God who must take to Himself human nature.

Man cannot take to himself the divine nature because he is finite, and the finite cannot include the infinite. Hinduism would like to say it goes both ways—if God can take to Himself human nature, then human beings can take to themselves the divine nature. This is not possible because the finite does not and cannot include the infinite.[2] The infinite is so much greater than the finite can ever be. Yet, the infinite can and does take to itself the finite because the infinite already includes the finite. Infinite knowledge includes finite knowledge. The relation between the infinite and the finite is not symmetrical, it is asymmetrical. Some have struggled over this question saying, "How is it possible for someone to be both God and man? It is beyond reason." And some suppose that if we say it is rational for Christ to be both God and man, it must be "rational" in some special sense of the word.[3] Yet, it is not contrary to reason to think that the infinite can take to itself the finite because infinite already includes finite. God knows everything humans know and knows how humans know. If He did not know this, then He would not be infinite in knowledge.

---

2. Gangadean, *History of Philosophy*, 108-110; Gangadean, *Philosophical Foundation*, 27-31.

3. Ashok Gangadean, *Between Worlds—The Emergence of Global Reason* (New York: Peter Lang, 1998), 179-180. "Christ-being is dialectical in the sense that if taken in essential terms as one being which is both finite and infinite at the same time (two natures) it presents itself to understanding as being contradictory . . . Christ-being may be taken of an exemplar of all beings . . . It is transcategorical, like all beings . . . It is only in this way that the Christ can be the real mediator, the savior." Ashok Gangadean, *Meditative Reason—Toward Universal Grammar* (New York: Peter Lang, 1993), 103-118. But if the infinite is not opposed to, but is inclusive of the finite, unlike black and non-black, why should Christ-being be considered contradictory to reason in the ordinary sense of reason? Until it is shown to be contradictory, one is not obligated to consider "global" reason. Meditative or global reason appears to make the move to give up "categorical" reason for the same reason as others in the monist "all is one" tradition.

God's taking to Himself human nature was accomplished by Christ's **being conceived by the power of the Holy Ghost, in the womb of the virgin Mary, of her substance**—her humanity—**So that two whole, perfect, and distinct natures, the Godhead and the manhood**—the divine nature and human nature—**were inseparably joined together in one person.** This formulation of the dual nature of Christ was worked out in the earlier creeds and is reiterated in the Confession. Notice the further explanation—**without conversion**—the infinite did not become finite, and the finite did not become infinite; one was not converted into the other; and these two natures were joined together without **composition, or confusion**—not half God and half man; He is not a human body with a divine soul—that would be a composition. He is a human body and human soul, and divine nature. Specifying, **without conversion, composition, or confusion** means that each nature does what is distinct to that nature. **Which person is very God, and very man, yet one Christ, the only Mediator between God and man.** Again, because He is both God and man He is able to fulfill the office of mediator.

Who could have known this reality prior to it being revealed to us? The dual nature of Christ is what is called a mystery of the faith. A mystery is what was formerly hidden and is now revealed.[4] Who would have known the Trinity or the Incarnation apart from special revelation? Believers in the Old Testament knew of the coming Messiah and of the Holy Spirit. David prayed, "take not your Holy Spirit from me."[5] They knew about the Spirit and knew the Spirit came upon prophets, priests, and kings when they were anointed. Moreover, they knew the Messiah would be anointed with the Spirit. This is what "Messiah" means—anointed. The oil of anointing was symbolic of the Spirit coming upon them. They did not know it as clearly and fully as we do now, but they knew it sufficiently for salvation. The Spirit enabled them to know the things they needed. The mediator is God the Son, who took to Himself human nature. He is two whole, perfect, and distinct natures, the Godhead and the manhood, inseparably joined together in one person—two natures, one person. Having two natures is something that can be understood by analogy in human beings. Human

---

4. *Colossians 1:26.*

5. *Psalm 51:11.*

beings partake of both animal nature in our bodies and in angelic nature in having spirit and rationality. A human being has two natures in one person. The concept of dual natures should not be foreign to us.

SUMMARY ANSWER

The office of the mediator brings reconciliation between God and humanity. It cannot be a man merely, and it cannot be God merely. A mediator is to take upon both divine and human nature. Yet man cannot take upon himself divine nature (the finite cannot include the infinite), but God can take on human nature (the infinite includes the finite). Only God can condescend by taking on human nature. Hence the Son of God took upon Himself man's nature, with all the essential properties, and common infirmities thereof, yet without sin; being conceived by the power of the Holy Ghost, in the womb of the virgin Mary, of her substance. So that two whole, perfect, and distinct natures, the Godhead and the manhood, were inseparably joined together in one person, without conversion (one nature does not change and become another), composition (Christ is not partly God and partly man), or confusion (each nature acts distinctly according to its own essence). Which person is very God, and very man, yet one Christ, the only Mediator between God and man.

The mystery of the Incarnation, although unknowable by reason from general revelation, is in accordance with reason once revealed. We can understand it by analogy to our humanity. We are the composition of two natures: spiritual nature in terms of spirit and rationality and animal nature in terms of the body.

QUESTION 41

Explain the intent of the anointing of the Mediator.

III. The Lord Jesus, in His human nature thus united to the divine, was sanctified, and anointed with the Holy Spirit, above measure, having in Him all the treasures of wisdom and knowledge; in whom it pleased the Father that all fullness should dwell; to the end that, being holy, harmless, undefiled, and full of grace and truth, He might be thoroughly furnished to execute the office of a Mediator, and Surety. Which office He took not unto Himself, but was thereunto called by His Father, who put all power and judgment into His hand, and gave Him commandment to execute the same.

The Lord Jesus, in His human nature thus united to the divine, was sanctified, and anointed with the Holy Spirit—the anointing of the Holy Spirit came upon Him in His human nature, and came upon Him **above measure, having in Him all the treasures of wisdom and knowledge; in whom it pleased the Father that all fullness should dwell; to the end that, being holy, harmless, undefiled, and full of grace and truth, He might be thoroughly furnished to execute the office of a Mediator, and Surety.** The Holy Spirit came upon Christ; that is why He is called Christ or Messiah—He is anointed with the Spirit. Messiah (Hebrew), Anointed (English), *Christos* (Greek)—all have the same meaning. He is anointed to be empowered to undertake the office. This is in keeping with the teaching about the work of the Holy Spirit, who enables us to do the work to which God has called believers. There are many dimensions to the work of the Holy Spirit, and one is anointing, which is particularly concerned with enabling believers to fulfill the work that God has given us. The Holy Spirit comes upon believers to regenerate and to illumine the mind, but there is a redemptive work carried out through Christ that enables believers to fulfill their work. **Which office He took not unto Himself, but was thereunto called by His Father, who put all power and judgment into His hand, and gave Him commandment to execute the same.** Christ in the office of mediator as both God and man undertakes the office, and the Spirit enables Him to execute the office to complete the work of subduing all things unto Himself to the glory of God.[6]

SUMMARY ANSWER

The anointing of the Holy Spirit comes upon Christ in His human nature. The Holy Spirit enables Christ to complete the work of mediator.

QUESTION 42

How is redemption accomplished by the Mediator?

IV. This office the Lord Jesus did most willingly undertake; which that He might discharge, He was made under the law, and did perfectly fulfill it; endured most grievous torments immediately in His soul, and most painful sufferings in His body; was crucified, and died, was buried, and remained under the power of death, yet saw no corruption. On the third day He arose from the dead, with the same body in which He suffered, with which also He ascended into heaven, and there sits at the right hand of His Father, making intercession, and shall return, to judge men and angels, at the end of the world.

In Reformed theology, a distinction is made between redemption accomplished and redemption applied. We should underscore the word *accomplished*. A central part of the work of Christ as mediator is to accomplish redemption. Notice again the word "office"—**This office the Lord Jesus did most willingly undertake**—He did not put Himself forward, He was called to that office, and once called, He willingly undertook it. **That He might discharge [the office], He was made under the law.** He was made under the law to redeem human beings, including

---

6. *1 Corinthians 15:28.*

those under the Mosaic law. He **did perfectly fulfill [the law]**, which is one aspect of the requirement of the covenant of works—man was to obey every command given by God, so Jesus perfectly obeyed God's law. Moreover, He **endured most grievous torments immediately in His soul, and most painful sufferings in His body; was crucified, and died, was buried, and remained under the power of death, yet saw no corruption.** Christ fulfilled God's will both by His active obedience (doing all that God required), and His passive obedience (submitting to all that God put upon Him—"nevertheless, thy will be done"[7]). He accomplished redemption by standing in the place of believers, to *undo* what Adam did (suffer the penalty for sin) and *do* what Adam failed to do (perfectly obey all that God commanded). He accomplished redemption by obeying and submitting to the point of crucifixion, death, and burial. He had to do more to apply this work of redemption—**On the third day He arose from the dead, with the same body in which He suffered, with which also He ascended into heaven, and there sits at the right hand of His Father.** Part of His work as mediator is **making intercession,** and part of His work is that He **shall return, to judge men and angels,** at the end of the world.

SUMMARY ANSWER

Redemption accomplished: Christ perfectly fulfilled the covenant of works by active obedience (obeyed all that God required), and passive obedience (submitting to all God placed upon Him). The mediator stood in our place by undoing what Adam did (suffering the penalty on our behalf by death on the cross) and doing what Adam failed to do (perfect obedience). Redemption applied required His ascension and session, to make intercession for us, to rule at the right hand of God, and return to judge at the last judgment.

---

7. *Luke 22:42.*

QUESTION 43

How is justice satisfied in redemption?

V. The Lord Jesus, by His perfect obedience, and sacrifice of Himself, which He, through the eternal Spirit, once offered up unto God, has fully satisfied the justice of His Father; and purchased, not only reconciliation, but an everlasting inheritance in the kingdom of heaven, for all those whom the Father has given unto Him.

The idea of satisfying God's justice needs to be underscored in this section of the Confession. If sinners are to be forgiven, the penalty has to be paid, and God's justice must be satisfied. This is the core idea that separates Christianity from Islam and separates Christianity from post-biblical interpretations of Judaism. Is God just? How is the justice of God satisfied? Must the justice of God be satisfied? Is He infinitely, eternally, and unchangeably just? If so, can His justice be set aside, or must it be satisfied? These questions go back to the very nature of God: Is God infinite, eternal, and unchangeable in His justice? Answering this one question is sufficient to settle the disputes with other theistic religions.[8] Does Islam have anyone to pay the penalty? It does not believe Christ died on the cross; it does not see the need for atonement.[9] Do the Jews believe that there is one to come who will die for their sins? How do they believe atonement is made? In the Old Testament it was made through the animal sacrifice. So the question is, is the animal sacrifice the reality, or is it a sign? Neither Judaism nor Islam affirm the need for vicarious atonement. In Christianity, mercy satisfies justice through Christ—the Son of God—by means of His vicarious atonement on the cross.

---

8. Gangadean, *Philosophical Foundation*, 185-198.
9. Gangadean, "Paper No.91: Christianity and Islam," in *The Logos Papers*, 479-484.

SUMMARY ANSWER

Must the justice of God be satisfied, or can it be set aside? This question applies to the very nature of God. Addressing this question can settle the disputes between Judaism, Christianity, and Islam. This question separates Christianity from Islam and Judaism. Neither Judaism nor Islam affirm the need for vicarious atonement. In Judaism, the Messiah comes to overcome the enemies of Israel, not to satisfy divine justice. In Islam, there is no need for payment. Allah sets aside justice and forgives without payment. In Christianity, payment for divine justice is required to satisfy the demands of infinite justice. God, as infinitely just, cannot set aside the requirement of justice (payment) without at the same time denying His justice as infinite—it is an act contrary to the nature of God. Thus in Christianity, mercy satisfies justice through Christ—the Son of God.

QUESTION 44

How is the efficacy of redemption applied?

VI. Although the work of redemption was not actually wrought by Christ till after His incarnation, yet the virtue, efficacy, and benefits thereof were communicated unto the elect, in all ages successively from the beginning of the world, in and by those promises, types, and sacrifices, wherein He was revealed, and signified to be the seed of the woman which should bruise the serpent's head; and the Lamb slain from the beginning of the world; being yesterday and today the same, and forever.

Section 8.6 of the Confession introduces the application of redemption. **Although the work of redemption was not actually wrought by Christ till after His incarnation, yet the virtue, efficacy, and benefits thereof were communicated unto the elect, in all ages successively from the beginning of the world, in and by those promises, types, and sacrifices,**

wherein He was revealed. God giving Adam the coats of skin was a revelation that through the death of another sin is covered. That sin is covered through the death of another is affirmed when Abel, Noah, Abraham, and Moses offered sacrifices. The offering of sacrifices is the doctrine of representation. Through the death of the animal, which represents what we deserve, our sin is covered. The sacrifice is a sign forsignifying what would come. Redemption was accomplished when Christ was incarnated and died on the cross. How are those who lived before Christ forgiven? The promise of forgiveness through Christ was given to the people of God before Christ came, and God knowing the surety of redemption accomplished, applied the benefits of redemption to the people before Christ was actually sacrificed. By faith they were saved. Christ is spoken of as the Lamb of God slain from before the foundation of the world in the plan of God.[10] It was God's sure plan that Christ who was **signified to be the seed of the woman** would come. This was the promise from the Garden before they were expelled: "the seed of the woman shall crush the head of the serpent."[11] Throughout the Old Testament, the sacrifices foresignified Christ to come.

If Judaism were to understand the sacrifice properly, the Jews would see that redemption must be fulfilled through the seed of the woman. The Jews do not believe that Jesus is the Christ, yet, they believe in redemption, the Messiah, and atonement. They should be asked what is atonement for and what connection does atonement have with the Messiah? Does the animal in the sacrifice atone? Moreover, we should ask about representation. Does Adam represent all mankind? Should we expect the one, coming in place of Adam, who failed, to accomplish redemption by means of atonement? A more basic, and necessary, question to be asked of professing Jews is, who is the Messiah, and what is He to do? This question is asked from within their own framework, and if they believe with any understanding, they will need to respond to this question.

For Islam the more basic question is, is God both just and merciful? Is He infinite, eternal, and unchangeable in His justice and mercy? These are easy questions to ask. If we get back to the more basic, we can connect easily enough. In other words, to come into a discussion

---

10. *Revelation 13:8.*
11. *Genesis 3:15.*

with Jews or Muslims on a less basic issue is like breaking in through a window. But if we come in through what is most basic, it is like going in through an unlocked door. Why break through a window when we can enter through the front entrance that is well lighted and awaiting with a sign that says "Enter Here." This is Rational Presuppositionalism at work.

SUMMARY ANSWER

Although redemption was accomplished by Christ after the Incarnation, redemption was applied through all previous ages. Those who lived before the Incarnation had the promise through symbolic means foreshadowing the atoning work of Christ. God knowing the surety of redemption, applied the benefits to believers. Christ is the Lamb of God slain from before the foundation of the world.

QUESTION 45

Explain the relation of the work of redemption to the unity of the person.

VII. Christ, in the work of mediation, acts according to both natures, by each nature doing that which is proper to itself; yet, by reason of the unity of the person, that which is proper to one nature is sometimes in Scripture attributed to the person denominated by the other nature.

Section 8.7 affirms that there is a unity in the person of Christ. He is both God and man, yet one person—therein consists the unity. Some statements made in Scripture about Christ may seem puzzling, which the Confession addresses next. **Christ, in the work of mediation, acts according to both natures, by each nature doing that which is proper to itself; yet, by reason of the unity of the person, that which is proper to one nature is sometimes in Scripture attributed to the person denominated by the other nature.** The Scripture speaks about the Son of God shedding His blood. In the divine nature, He has no body and no blood, but what is true of the human nature is attributed to the divine according to the unity of the person. When Christ is tempted, He is not tempted as the Son of God; He is tempted as man. That is why He replied, "Man does not live by bread alone."[12] When it says that He is tempted in all points as we are,[13] it is properly referring to the human nature in the one person.

SUMMARY ANSWER

There is unity in the person of Christ. What is proper to one nature is sometimes in Scripture attributed to the person denominated by the other nature, e.g., the temptation and the shedding of blood.

QUESTION 46

How is redemption effectually applied and communicated to the elect?

VIII. To all those for whom Christ has purchased redemption, He does certainly and effectually apply and communicate the same; making intercession for them, and revealing unto them, in and by the Word, the mysteries of salvation; effectually persuading them by His Spirit to believe and obey, and governing their hearts by His Word and Spirit; overcoming all their enemies by His almighty power and wisdom, in such manner, and ways, as are most consonant to His wonderful and unsearchable dispensation.

Christ prays for believers before they are converted. The Confession says, **To all those for whom Christ has purchased redemption, He does certainly and effectually apply and communicate the same; making**

---

12. *Matthew 4:4.*

13. *Hebrews 4:15.*

intercession for them. He ever lives to make intercession for us, because He is our high priest. It is one of the offices He fulfills, and as such, the high priest prays for believers. Then, having been brought to the Father through Him, He further prays for our sanctification, which is also part of the work of the high priest. He applies redemption by **making intercession for them, and revealing unto them, in and by the Word, the mysteries of salvation; effectually persuading them by His Spirit to believe and obey, and governing their hearts by His Word and Spirit; overcoming all their enemies by His almighty power and wisdom, in such manner, and ways, as are most consonant to His wonderful and unsearchable dispensation.** Christ prays for, reveals, and effectually persuades believers—notice the connection between the Word and Spirit—to the end that they may believe and obey. In addition, He overcomes all their enemies by His almighty power. The enemies of the people of God are the world, the flesh, and the devil.[14] The world with all its lusts, temptations, and circumstances includes the false prophet, the harlot, and the beast.[15] The harlot is the world in its seductive power. The beast is the world in its systems of laws, regulations, and restrictions applied to believers. The false prophet is all the false teaching, communication, and propaganda that goes on in the world. The false prophet influences through the worldly system of education from grade schools, to colleges and universities, through the arts, media, entertainment, and in other ways. In addition to the world as our enemy, there remains the flesh, the old nature remaining in believers. They are always there; Satan rules over the world and dangles what is tempting in front of us, and sometimes believers do not protect themselves from temptation.

The world, the flesh, and the devil are the enemies, and there are different aspects of the world and the flesh—the lust of the eyes, the lust of the flesh, and the pride of life—which are part of the sinful nature. The devil is a liar and the father of lies; he is the accuser of the brethren; he is the killer.[16] We can see all three of these enemies in three different ways in which these enemies operate. In contrast, Christ works in believers to bring them to Himself, sanctify them, and overcome their

---

14. *1 John 2:16; James 3:15.*

15. For a fuller exposition, see: Gangadean, *The Book of Revelation.*

16. *John 8:44; Revelation 12:10; 1 Peter 5:8.*

enemies. To what extent have believers overcome their enemies? How does the battle go today? Are we aware that there is a battle? Have you been praying? Christ is going to work in believers to overcome. Christ is our mediator, and who He is, what He does, how He does it, and the necessity for His work is explained in this section. Christ is the true prophet—He reveals God to us. He is the true priest—He applies redemption in believers' lives and sanctifies them. And, He is the true king—He enables believers to obey the will of God. Does humanity need someone like Christ to make God known, to sanctify believers, to rule over and help them do the will of God, and to overcome their enemies? This is the work of the mediator. It is absolutely essential.

SUMMARY ANSWER

Those whom Christ redeemed, He applied His redemption and effectually called to believe in Him. As a priest, Christ ever lives to make intercession for our salvation and sanctification. Through the work of the Spirit, He rules in our lives to overcome the world (false prophet—the world in false belief systems; the harlot—luxury and indulgence; and the beast—the world in its system of laws and regulations opposed to the law of God), the flesh (the lust of the eyes, the lust of the flesh, and the pride of life), and the devil (liar and accuser of the brethren). Christ is the mediator in three offices: the prophet who reveals the truth of God, the true priest who sanctifies us through the truth, and as the true king who enables us to obey God's will.

Chapter 9

OF FREE WILL

QUESTION 47

What is meant by the natural liberty of the will?

I. God has endued the will of man with that natural liberty, that is neither forced, nor, by any absolute necessity of nature, determined to good, or evil.

The expression **endued the will of man with that natural liberty** concerns the reality of free will or liberty of the will. **God has endued the will of man with that natural liberty, that it is neither forced, nor, by any absolute necessity of nature, determined to good, or evil.** By contrast, human volition is not caused by anything external to us, nor are we determined to act in one way or another. As *imago dei*, humans have a rational nature, but humans are not determined by that rational nature to use reason to see what is clear. Some animals are determined by their nature (instinct), but human beings have a will that is not determined—neither externally forced nor internally determined. Humans are free. It is interesting to note that the Confession discusses free will directly after the section on Christ the mediator. One would hardly think that free will is something that needs to be discussed, but it needs to be discussed. People have had all kinds of misunderstandings about free will. The Confession corrects these misunderstandings by stating that there is natural liberty of the will, which by its very nature, is free so that it is not forced externally nor internally determined to be good or evil.

SUMMARY ANSWER

There is a natural liberty of the will that is neither externally determined by force, nor internally determined to good or evil. We have a rational nature, but we are not determined by our nature to use reason, unlike animals who act by necessity.

QUESTION 48

What is the relation of liberty and ability in man's fourfold state?

II. Man, in his state of innocency, had freedom, and power to will and to do that which was good and well pleasing to God; but yet, mutably, so that he might fall from it.

III. Man, by his fall into a state of sin, has wholly lost all ability of will to any spiritual good accompanying salvation: so as, a natural man, being altogether averse from that good, and dead in sin, is not able, by his own strength, to convert himself, or to prepare himself thereunto.

IV. When God converts a sinner, and translates him into the state of grace, He frees him from his natural bondage under sin; and, by His grace alone, enables him freely to will and to do that which is spiritually good; yet so, as that by reason of his remaining corruption, he does not perfectly, nor only, will that which is good, but does also will that which is evil.

V. The will of man is made perfectly and immutably free to good alone, in the state of glory only.

The remaining four sections of chapter 9 of the Confession speak about the four different states of man. It is vital to note that the different states of man are commonly missed by philosophers, and non-philosophers alike. Notice section 9.2, **Man, in his state of innocency, had**

freedom, and power to will and to do that which was good and well pleasing to God; but yet, mutably, so that he might fall from it. Two words stand out—*freedom* and *power*. Is freedom to be identified as liberty or ability? *Freedom* is to be identified with *liberty* in section 1, and *power* has to do with *ability*. The word *ability* is used explicitly in sections 3 and 4.

This passage of the Confession calls for an explanation of the freedom of the will and the four states of man. The first state is *innocency* before Adam fell, the second is his *fallen* state, the third is his *regenerate* state, and the fourth is his *glorified* state.[1] Liberty remains constant through all four states, but ability fluctuates widely. Freedom is to be identified with liberty, not with ability. If we understand freedom as liberty, we can make our way through many common objections against the doctrine of election. In addition, we will not fall into the traps that philosophers such as Immanuel Kant, William James, Alvin Plantinga and others fell into when they identify freedom with ability.[2]

Concerning seeking, do we want to seek or do we not want to seek? We have to speak about ability in connection with liberty. We are always free to seek, but we may not want to. We always do what we want, so that even in our fallen state we turn away from God, not because we are forced by something outside of ourselves or determined to turn away, but because we want to in our natural liberty. Liberty is to be connected with *want,* not *can.* Do not let *can* stand in front of *want* as in saying, "I can't want...." It is always, "If we want to use our reason we can use our reason." In the first state, man has 100% liberty and 100% ability to obey God. In the fallen state, he has 100% liberty and 0% ability. In the regenerate state, he has 100% liberty and 1-99% ability. In the glorified state, he has 100% liberty and 100% ability. What remains the same is 100% liberty in every state—we do what we want.

Section 9.3 describes the fallen state of man with 0% ability to obey God. **Man, by his fall into a state of sin, has wholly lost all ability of will to any spiritual good accompanying salvation. . . .** Remember that by the fall, man is utterly indisposed, disabled, and made opposite to all good. It is not just disabled, but disabled and *indisposed.* No one can ever say, "I'm disposed to obey God, but I'm not able." In the

---

1. Gangadean, *History of Philosophy*, 113-114.

2. Gangadean, *Philosophical Foundation*, 66, 167-168.

fallen state, he has **lost all ability of will to any spiritual good accompanying salvation: so as, a natural man, being altogether averse from that good, and dead in sin, is not able, by his own strength, to convert himself, or to prepare himself thereunto.** If we ask, "If man is not able to obey, how can you hold him responsible," our mind is slipping from freedom as *wanting* to freedom as *ability.* The mind continually slips. Perhaps some may say we are not able to want—we can try to leapfrog in this way. Do we want to be able to want? How far are we going to go down this road? Suppose we are quadriplegic and we are not able to get from where we are sitting into the kitchen. Are we not free? We are free to want to, and we can ask someone to help, and we will get there.

In the order of salvation, grace may be applied, we are given a new heart, and we now want to obey. We are re-created with a new heart (regeneration), and from the new heart, we want to please God. Some might ask, "Why have you made me so?" The answer given in Scripture is, "Can the thing formed say to the one who formed it, why have you made me so?"[3] Can we question our own nature? Can we say, "Why has He made me with reason? I do not like being a rational being." We cannot question our nature. Yet, this is where a lot of this discussion often goes.

Philosophically, we can take the issue of free will further by showing that making liberty based on ability (could have done otherwise) requires uncaused events,[4] and any uncaused event is an absurdity. If we say we could have done otherwise than we did, then in essence we are saying our act is not caused. This is libertarian or contra-causal freedom, where we end up with uncaused events. This is the direction Immanuel Kant went.[5] He avoided causes in the *noumenal* realm (the world as it is in itself) in order to guarantee freedom in the *phenomenal* realm because he assumes freedom is ability. This is also where William James went. He ended up saying if it makes the universe absurd, I guess it's absurd. I'd rather have a universe where there's freedom than necessity (what he calls the Block universe). Alvin Plantinga also goes the way of libertarian free will. The basic point being made here is that there

---

3. *Romans 9:20.*

4. Gangadean, *Philosophical Foundation,* 66, 167-168.

5. Gangadean, *History of Philosophy,* 113-114.

is a difference between freedom and ability, and we can have freedom even when we do not have ability.

Section 9.4 gives us the third state of man, **When God converts a sinner, and translates him into the state of grace, He frees him from his natural bondage under sin; and, by His grace alone, enables him freely to will and to do that which is spiritually good; yet so, as that by reason of his remaining corruption, he does not perfectly, nor only, will that which is good, but does also will that which is evil.** Humans have mixed motives in the third state; that is why it is said that ability changes from 1-99%. Sanctification is never 100% complete in the third state.

In the fourth state **the will of man is made perfectly and immutably free.** Please note, he is made perfectly and immutably free **to good alone, in the state of glory only.** Mutability is not the same as freedom, nor is it necessary for freedom. We could be *not* mutable, and yet be free. In the state of glory, believers will not be able to turn away from God. We will be perfectly and immutably free to will good alone in the state of glory only. This is the whole point of the covenant of works and grace—that in ourselves, we are changeable, but in Christ, in the covenant, we are unchanging. Is God immutably free to do good only? Is God infinite, eternal, and unchangeable in His truth? Can God lie? Scripture says He cannot lie, and yet He is utterly free. He does whatever He pleases, whatever He wants—that is where freedom is located. In the final state, believers will do what we please too, but we will only want what is good. Someone in spiritual death (in the bottomless pit) can begin to use their reason if they want to. They can begin to see what is clear if they want to. But left to ourselves, we will not want to. Fallen humanity is utterly indisposed, and we never get anything contrary to what we want, all things considered. There is no basis for complaint.

SUMMARY ANSWER

Freedom should be identified with liberty (want) and not ability. Liberty remains constant in the fourfold states while ability fluctuates.

Fourfold state of man:

1. Innocence: before the Fall (*posse peccare*—possible to sin) 100% liberty and 100% ability.

2. Fallen: after Fall (*non posse non peccare*—not possible not to sin) 100% liberty and 0% ability.

3. Regenerate: regenerated from Fall (*posse non peccare*—possible not to sin) 100% liberty and 1-99% ability.

4. Glorified: after death (*non posse peccare*—not possible to sin) 100% liberty and 100% ability.

Chapter 10

OF EFFECTUAL CALLING

QUESTION 49
What is effectual calling?

I. All those whom God has predestinated unto life, and those only, He is pleased, in His appointed and accepted time, effectually to call, by His Word and Spirit, out of that state of sin and death, in which they are by nature, to grace and salvation, by Jesus Christ; enlightening their minds spiritually and savingly to understand the things of God, taking away their heart of stone, and giving unto them a heart of flesh; renewing their wills, and, by His almighty power, determining them to that which is good, and effectually drawing them to Jesus Christ: yet so, as they come most freely, being made willing by His grace.

Fallen humanity is in a state of sin and death. Believers are brought out of that state to grace and salvation by the Word and Spirit of Christ renewing our minds, affections, and will, **by His almighty power, determining them to that which is good, and effectually drawing them to Jesus Christ: yet so, as they come most freely, being made willing by His grace.** When believers are re-created, they have a new self and a new desire. With regeneration comes understanding, desire, and will. We must be born again. Being born again comes before believing, conversion, repentance and faith, and conviction of sin and death. In the *Ordo Salutis*,[1] the order is as follows: regeneration, conviction of

---

1. Gangadean, *The Westminster Catechisms*, 39-49, 179-214.

sin, repentance and faith, justification, adoption, sanctification, and glorification. People are called in this life by those who proclaim the gospel, and if the gospel is proclaimed without the working of the Spirit, it is not effective. The Spirit regenerates, and the Word is ordinarily used in that process. There is an outward aspect to this call by the Word, and when it is accompanied by the Spirit to change the heart, both together constitute effectual calling. It accomplishes the effect of a response.

SUMMARY ANSWER

In regeneration, we are recreated in mind, emotions, and will. We are born again or recreated. Regeneration comes prior to believing, conversion, repentance, and conviction of sin and death.

QUESTION 50

How is effectual calling by grace alone?

II. This effectual call is of God's free and special grace alone, not from anything at all foreseen in man, who is altogether passive therein, until, being quickened and renewed by the Holy Spirit, he is thereby enabled to answer this call, and to embrace the grace offered and conveyed in it.

God, through the working of His Spirit, has enabled believers to receive His call. Regeneration consists of all three aspects of human nature (mind, soul, strength) but begins with being brought out of darkness, where the mind that was darkened is enlightened. Section 10.1 affirms this and says, "enlightening their minds spiritually and savingly to understand the things of God." Then the desires are changed, "their heart of stone" is changed. And, with the desires, the will is also renewed.

Being born again is not man's decision. In addition, it is not the decision of a parent or someone in the church. Being born again is something done by God, "That which is born of flesh is flesh; and that which is born of Spirit is spirit."[2] Many people use the words "born again," but they mean something different, as if one believes and then is born again. No, one is born again, and then believes. Nicodemus asked, "How can a man be born again when he is old?"[3] This doctrine has been misunderstood. Can we see where others in the Christian faith have different views about regeneration? Do we choose God? Yes, we choose God once we are born again, i.e., after He has chosen us through regeneration. But did we choose to be born again? No, God chooses sovereignly. Salvation is by grace alone.

SUMMARY ANSWER

Regeneration is not a decision of man; it is the sovereign act of God. It is not from what man possesses in himself, but by God alone. It entails a change in the triune personality of man (intellect, then emotion, then will).

QUESTION 51

How are those incapable of being outwardly called, effectually called?

III. Elect infants, dying in infancy, are regenerated, and saved by Christ, through the Spirit, who works when, and where, and how He pleases: so also are all other elect persons who are incapable of being outwardly called by the ministry of the Word.

Regeneration is a sovereign work of God, and God is able to regenerate a child apart from the outward call. Remember, the effectual call is outward plus inward. God is able to inwardly call someone and regenerate them apart from the outward call of the preaching of the gospel. An infant of six months old that cannot understand anything could

---

2. *John 3:6.*

3. *John 3:4.*

be regenerate. If, as some believe, regeneration depends on hearing the Word and believing, then babies dying in infancy would be left in spiritual death, unless we want to say they are neutral (and not spiritually dead), in which case they go to limbo or some other place.[4] Jesus said, "Unless you are born again, you cannot enter the kingdom of heaven."[5] A six-month-old infant or someone from conception could be born again. That is a comfort to us because there are times that babies die before they come to birth. We trust God's goodness and promises to believers and their children that God will work in that child's life. Many questions may arise here. "How do I know if my child is among the elect?" God gives a promise to us and our household. What if one becomes a believer later in life? We are to leave that in God's hands. Some have questions about the spiritual status of the 60+ million children that have been aborted since abortion became legal. The Confession says, **elect infants, dying in infancy, are regenerated, and saved by Christ.** Does that mean every infant is among the elect? I do not know that we could say that. We leave it in the hands of God, who is wise and good and knows everything. Is that sufficient? For believers, there is special reason to hope concerning children that die in infancy before they are outwardly called and come to believe.

SUMMARY ANSWER

God can regenerate inwardly those incapable of being outwardly called. Regeneration comes from God, apart from our choosing.

---

4. This is the accommodation developed by Roman Catholicism to allow for a lesser punishment for unbaptized children. It is the result of a double error: denial of God's sovereignty in election and the belief in regenerational baptism.

5. *John 3:3.*

QUESTION 52

What is the state of the non-elect with or without the outward call?

IV. Others, not elected, although they may be called by the ministry of the Word, and may have some common operations of the Spirit, yet they never truly come unto Christ, and therefore cannot be saved: much less can men, not professing the Christian religion, be saved in any other way whatsoever, be they never so diligent to frame their lives according to the light of nature, and the laws of that religion they do profess. And, to assert and maintain that they may, is very pernicious, and to be detested.

The non-elect may or may not have the outward call of the gospel. We might ask, "What about all those people in distant lands who have never heard the gospel?" "Are those who have never had the outward call not elect?" "Could not there be an elect person at the ends of the earth?" Yes, there could be an elect person at the ends of the earth, and if the message is not brought to them, an angel could go to them and tell them where to get the message (angels do not proclaim the gospel, the people of God do). God has worked it out in providence that ordinarily—by ordinary means—the elect are born in places fairly close to where they can hear the gospel.

The non-elect, without the outward call, will perish because they have the general call of general revelation. They have clear general revelation, and they are responsible for it. **Others, not elected, although they may be called by the ministry of the Word, and may have some common operations of the Spirit, yet they never truly come unto Christ, and therefore cannot be saved.** Some people come forward, pray to invite Christ into their lives, outwardly conform their lives to the gospel, go to church, and yet are not saved because they never truly come to Christ. They never had an effectual calling, a true conviction of sin and death, or a saving understanding of the gospel.

Furthermore, **much less can men, not professing the Christian religion, be saved in any other way whatsoever, be they ever so diligent to frame their lives according to the light of nature, and the laws of that religion they do profess.** If they were truly diligent to frame their lives according to the light of nature, they would know what is clear from general revelation. And, they would obey the law that is written on their hearts. Though we may appear to be diligent, like Saul of Tarsus, we may not be truly seeking and understanding. Do a lot of people profess that they are seeking? Before we were believers, did we think we were seeking? Did we think that we were interested in the truth? We may have thought we were, and appeared to others to be, but in actuality, we were not interested in truth. This is contrary to the doctrine held in some segments of the Church that says, a good Hindu living according to the duties of Hinduism may be saved. The Confession rejects this claim. A good Hindu has a clear revelation before them that all is not one, yet, he believes that all is one. He is not a good human being because he is not seeking the good. He is not seeking what is clear. What about people who are more virtuous than some Christians? What about grandma, who is nice? One can be nice without being good or knowing the good. This is what is being affirmed in this section of the Confession.

SUMMARY ANSWER

The non-elect may or may not have the outward call. The non-elect without the outward call perishes in their sin for their culpable ignorance. The non-elect, although called outwardly by the ministry of the Word, yet without inward regeneration, are not saved—regardless of how diligently they frame their lives according to the light of nature.

Chapter 11

OF JUSTIFICATION

QUESTION 53

What is justification?

I. Those whom God effectually calls, He also freely justifies: not by infusing righteousness into them, but by pardoning their sins, and by accounting and accepting their persons as righteous; not for anything wrought in them, or done by them, but for Christ's sake alone; nor by imputing faith itself, the act of believing, or any other evangelical obedience to them, as their righteousness; but by imputing the obedience and satisfaction of Christ unto them, they receiving and resting on Him and His righteousness, by faith; which faith they have not of themselves, it is the gift of God.

The doctrine of justification has been, and continues to be, disputed within the Church, with more controversies recently developing. Justification was a considerable dispute in the Book of Acts and Galatians, and in the Medieval Church. This seems to be an ever-recurring dispute in the history of the Church, but it need not be. **Those whom God effectually calls, He also freely justifies: not by infusing righteousness into them, but by pardoning their sins, and by accounting and accepting their persons as righteous; not for anything wrought in them, or done by them, but for Christ's sake alone; nor by imputing faith itself, the act of believing, or any other evangelical obedience to them, as their righteousness; but by imputing the obedience and satisfaction of Christ unto them, they receiving and resting on Him and**

His righteousness, by faith; which faith they have not of themselves, it is the gift of God. Justification is free to the believer, at no cost to ourselves. The Roman Catholic Church says that justification follows a change that makes us increasingly righteous by infused grace. The Confession denies this position by saying justification is not **by infusing righteousness into them,** or **by anything wrought in them,** or **by them.** Righteousness is not by infusion; it is by imputation.

The doctrine of justification is disputed in our day again. The New Perspective on Paul, and rethinking justification, is an example. Advocates of the New Perspective raise questions about the nature of imputation. If we understand that the sin of Adam is imputed to us, we can understand that the righteousness of Christ is likewise imputed to believers. Righteousness is not infused, or by anything wrought in them, or by them. The act of believing, or any other evangelical obedience is not counted as righteousness. Rather, righteousness is by the imputation of the obedience and satisfaction of Christ unto believers, and receiving and resting on Him and His righteousness by faith. And, even that faith is a gift of God. It is not quite accurate to say that justification is by faith alone. Instead, it should be understood that in justification one is accounted righteous on the basis of the righteousness of Christ, which is imputed to believers and received by faith. It is not faith plus works. We need to notice this.

Being accounted as righteous (through imputation) involves a change in the believer, but a prior change of regeneration has already occurred. In addition, there has been conviction of sin and death, the emptiness of life without God, and upon that, there is repentance of our sin and faith in Christ, and on that basis, there is justification. The righteousness of Christ is imputed to us and received by faith alone. Believers are not justified by faith, but receive justification by faith.

In Catholicism, there is a collapse in the distinction between justification and sanctification. In sanctification, a change in righteousness occurs. There is a process of being made actually righteous. But in justification, we are not being made actually righteous; we are being accounted/regarded/treated as righteous, even though we are not righteous. Some might object by saying, "this is like putting a covering of snow on a pile of manure"—and yes, we can put it that way. It is rotten inside. But this does not mean regeneration and faith have not taken place. There is a distinction between accounting someone righteous and righteousness being infused into the person. In Catholicism, this is where the sacramental system of salvation occurs (the sacraments bring grace, grace removes sin, then sin returns and negates grace). There is a revolving aspect in the sacramental system. This is why Luther was so distraught. What happens if, after having received communion, we look at a woman and lust after her in our heart (committing mortal sin) and then fall going down the stairway, break our neck, and die? Does this mortal sin remove our hope of salvation?

The doctrine of infusion is supposed to make us actually righteous. Imputation does not change anything in the person, but accounts them as righteous. It is sometimes spoken of as a legal or forensic term. It is like a judge saying, "not guilty" and we are declared not guilty. Being declared not guilty before God is not on the basis of our righteousness but on the basis of Christ's righteousness. He paid the penalty, and His righteousness is put down to our account. We are declared free. We are justified and this is by the grace of God, and it is received by faith alone, not on the basis of any works we do. And this is for Christ's sake alone. Justification by faith alone entails triple imputation: (1) Adam's sin is imputed to all. (2) Our sin is imputed to Christ. (3) Christ's righteousness is imputed to believers. Believers receive and rest on Christ and His righteousness by faith; righteousness is imputed as Adam's sin was imputed. Justification is not faith plus works. We are not made righteous but are counted as righteous. In Catholicism, the righteousness is infused by the sacraments and makes the person actually "not guilty." The Confession denies this position.

SUMMARY ANSWER

Justification is by Christ's imputed righteousness, not by infused righteousness (Catholicism and The New Perspective on Paul). Infusion is making the person righteous, while imputation is being counted as righteous through the righteousness of another. We are not justified by faith, but we receive justification by faith. We are counted righteous by the imputed righteousness of Christ. Justification by faith alone entails triple imputation: (1) Adam's sin imputed to all (2) Our sin imputed to Christ (3) Christ's righteousness imputed to believers.

QUESTION 54

What is the doctrine of faith alone *(Sola Fide)*?

II. Faith, thus receiving and resting on Christ and His righteousness, is the alone instrument of justification: yet it is not alone in the person justified, but is ever accompanied with all other saving graces, and is no dead faith, but works by love.

The Confession affirms that, **Faith, thus receiving and resting on Christ and His righteousness, is the alone instrument of justification.** There is no other way by which we receive justification than by faith alone—alone in the sense that it is the alone instrument of justification. A common misunderstanding arises by claiming, "since it is by faith alone, if I have faith, then it doesn't matter what I do now." But the next part of 11.2 addresses this claim by saying, **yet it is not alone in the person justified, but is ever accompanied with all other saving graces, and is no dead faith, but works by love.** The doctrine of *Sola Fide* refers to the instrument by which believers are justified, they are received by faith alone. It does not say that there are no works as a response of the faith of the believer. In addition, the Confession does not say that we are justified by faith itself. Rather, faith is an instrument by which believers receive justification. The Confession clarifies this point to avoid misunderstanding.

SUMMARY ANSWER

Faith is the instrument by which we are justified, and it is accompanied by works done in love.

QUESTION 55

What is God's purpose in justification?

III. Christ, by His obedience and death, did fully discharge the debt of all those that are thus justified, and did make a proper, real, and full satisfaction to His Father's justice in their behalf. Yet, inasmuch as He was given by the Father for them; and His obedience and satisfaction accepted in their stead; and both, freely, not for anything in them; their justification is only of free grace; that both the exact justice and rich grace of God might be glorified in the justification of sinners.

The purpose of justification is the glory of God—that the glory of God, in His justice and mercy, may be seen. **Christ, by His obedience and death, did fully discharge the debt of all those that are thus justified, and did make a proper, real, and full satisfaction.** We should notice how the word *satisfaction* is emphasized further by the qualifiers *proper, real,* and *full* satisfaction, **to His Father's justice in their behalf.** The Confession goes on, **yet, inasmuch as He was given by the Father for them; and His obedience and satisfaction accepted in their stead; and both, freely, not for anything in them; their justification is only of free grace; that both the exact justice**—underscore this phrase, *exact justice*—**and rich grace**—underscore this also—**of God might be glorified in the justification of sinners.** We should recall from earlier: God elects some for the praise of His glorious grace and leaves some for the praise of His glorious justice.[1] The way in which God brings man to salvation magnifies both His justice and His mercy—a revelation that would not have come apart from sin, death, and redemption by Christ.

---

1. *WCF 3.3.*

SUMMARY ANSWER

The magnification of God's glory: His justice and mercy—a revelation that would not have been seen apart from sin and redemption by Christ.

QUESTION 56

When are believers justified?
Was it different before Christ?

IV. God did, from all eternity, decree to justify all the elect, and Christ did, in the fullness of time, die for their sins, and rise again for their justification: nevertheless, they are not justified, until the Holy Spirit does, in due time, actually apply Christ unto them.

VI. The justification of believers under the Old Testament was, in all these respects, one and the same with the justification of believers under the New Testament.

Believers are justified when the Holy Spirit applies Christ to them. Justification is not from eternity past, and it is not only after Christ actually died, but justification is applied by the Holy Spirit even to believers before the time of Christ. Christ purchased salvation and the salvation is applied through the Holy Spirit. All believers since Adam have been saved by the same covenant of grace. The same atoning work of Christ is applied to all the elect throughout history. It is important to see that justification is a doctrine that presupposes other doctrines (e.g., covenant representation, covenant theology, election, and the economic trinity). Salvation is only by the imputation of Christ's vicarious atonement—before and after the coming of Christ.

SUMMARY ANSWER

Believers are justified when the Holy Spirit applies the righteousness of Christ to them. It was the same before Christ.

QUESTION 57

What need is there for repentance of sin under the state of justification?

V. God does continue to forgive the sins of those that are justified; and, although they can never fall from the state of justification, yet they may, by their sins, fall under God's fatherly displeasure, and not have the light of His countenance restored unto them, until they humble themselves, confess their sins, beg pardon, and renew their faith and repentance.

Section 11.5 of the Confession addresses the question: If a person is justified, and once justified remains justified, is further repentance of sin necessary? **God does continue to forgive the sins of those that are justified; and, although they can never fall from the state of justification, yet they may, by their sins, fall under God's fatherly displeasure, and not have the light of His countenance restored unto them, until they humble themselves, confess their sins, beg pardon, and renew their faith and repentance.** We will not lose our justification by sin, but we can fall under God's fatherly displeasure. From an earthly perspective, we can know what it is to be under our father's displeasure until we come back to repentance. How much more so in a heavenly way? We cannot say: Since we are justified and will never fall away, we do not need to be concerned with sin and repentance. Believers need to be very concerned. Otherwise, we will be under God's fatherly displeasure. We may die in the wilderness as a believer, but we are dying *in the wilderness.* We are not going into the Promised Land; in other words, we may die as a believer and not have contributed to the work of advancing the kingdom of God in our lifetime. We may die as a result of partaking of the Lord's Supper unworthily—we may be saved but get sick and die prematurely because we are under God's displeasure.

By sinning we will not lose our justification, but will be under the displeasure of God by not repenting of sin; and we will fail to attain the fullness of life found in the work of the kingdom in fulfilling the dominion mandate and the Great Commission.

SUMMARY ANSWER

By sinning, we do not lose justification but incur God's fatherly displeasure by not repenting of sin. We may die in the wilderness and yet be saved.

Chapter 12

OF ADOPTION

QUESTION 58

What are the several benefits of adoption?

I. All those that are justified, God vouchsafes, in and for His only Son Jesus Christ, to make partakers of the grace of adoption, by which they are taken into the number, and enjoy the liberties and privileges of the children of God, have His name put upon them, receive the Spirit of adoption, have access to the throne of grace with boldness, are enabled to cry, Abba, Father, are pitied, protected, provided for, and chastened by Him, as by a father: yet never cast off, but sealed to the day of redemption; and inherit the promises, as heirs of everlasting salvation.

All those that are justified, God vouchsafes, in and for His only Son Jesus Christ, to make partakers of the grace of adoption, by which they are taken into the number, and enjoy the liberties and privileges of the children of God. What are the graces and benefits of adoption? (1) We **have His name put upon** us. When we adopt someone into our family, they carry the family name. Believers are children of God, and we carry His name. The name of Christ is upon us, and we are Christians. This is not something that is only on paper, so to speak, but there is an added reality to that in the next point. (2) Believers **receive the Spirit of adoption.** Not only is the paperwork for adoption done, but there is the spirit of adoption. It is not the case that we are just barely received; we really are received by the Spirit. (3) In connection with the spirit of adoption, believers **have access to the throne of grace with boldness.** We do not stand back as if we were second-class persons in the family. We go directly to the throne of God as His children. (4) We **are enabled to cry, *Abba,* Father.** And the Father's response to our adoption is that (5) We are **pitied, protected, provided for . . . by Him, as by a Father.**

Believers are not orphans in this universe. We are children of the Creator of heaven and earth. What more could we ask for? But there is more. Psalm 103 speaks about the pity of a father.[1] Recall that fatherly displeasure is incurred if we continue in sin. In contrast, believers are pitied—He does not always treat us according to our sins. He protects us and provides for us, and (6) He **chastens** us. This is part of being in the family of God. And if we were not chastened, corrected, and dealt with as a child of God, then we would have to say that something is wrong. Do you have children, and do you chasten them? And you do this because you love them. Do you need chastening? "Whom the Lord loves, He chastens. And scourges every son He receives."[2] This can sound like serious chastening for serious sin. But He scourges every son whom He receives. Sometimes if He scourges us, we may think He is not treating us as a father, but He is. Scourging is like a whip that comes down on us. God is not angry with us; He is chastening us. (7) We are **not cast off** in this chastening, but the spirit of adoption seals us to the day of redemption. Believers never lose their standing as children of God once they have been adopted. We should find much comfort in God's dealing with us as a father. We need comfort on a cold, rainy, and difficult day—in the dark shadows of life. The fatherly displeasure is real, the chastening is real, but the pitying, the protecting, and providing for us is also real. And He hears our cries when we call out to Him. How did our Lord Jesus Christ's life end? He cried out, "Father, into your hands I commit my spirit."[3] Just as He, as the Son, had access to the Father, so we have access to our Father by His Spirit that is upon us.

We are really, truly children of God. Do you want to be in the family? Some may have brothers or sisters they do not care too much

---

1. *Psalm 103:8-17.*

2. *Hebrews 12:6.*

3. *Luke 23:46.*

about. They annoy you. It is not a family that is fully sanctified. It is dysfunctional, particularly among siblings. But God is going to chasten us and make us functional. We sometimes may want to walk out and have little to do with them. There are brothers and sisters throughout many churches across the land—the children of God. And in addition to this: (8) We **inherit the promises, as heirs of everlasting salvation.** Inheritance is also real. Believers will inherit the kingdom prepared for us from the foundation of the world. Christ is the heir of all things, and we have completeness in Him. We may not inherit much from our earthly parents, but we have the inheritance that counts. When we die, we go to our inheritance in part, and when the resurrection from the dead occurs, we have the fullness of the inheritance—we have a body with which to enjoy it all—a body that matches the inheritance. Is that not a great arrangement? Believers are adopted, and this is in addition to being justified. God does not only justify, but He brings us near to Him as children. He makes us members of the body of Christ and works to cleanse us, having justified us. There has been real change—it is like a seed that has been planted and is now growing.

SUMMARY ANSWER

We are adopted in the name of Christ. We receive the spirit of adoption, granting access to the throne of God in boldness as children of God, and we can cry out to God as our father. In response, God as our father pities, protects, provides, and chastens us.[4] We receive an inheritance as heirs of everlasting salvation. At death, we receive a partial inheritance, and at the resurrection we inherit the kingdom and a body to enjoy it.

---

4. *Psalm 103; Hebrews 12:6.*

Chapter 13

OF SANCTIFICATION

QUESTION 59

What are the basis, means, process, extent, and end of sanctification?

I. They, who are once effectually called, and regenerated, having a new heart, and a new spirit created in them, are further sanctified, really and personally, through the virtue of Christ's death and resurrection, by His Word and Spirit dwelling in them: the dominion of the whole body of sin is destroyed, and the several lusts thereof are more and more weakened and mortified; and they more and more quickened and strengthened in all saving graces, to the practice of true holiness, without which no man shall see the Lord.

They, who are once effectually called, and regenerated, having a new heart, and a new spirit created in them, are further sanctified. Being sanctified has to do with being set apart to God. This begins with effectual calling or regeneration (having a new heart). In connection with this beginning, as well as imputed righteousness (justification) and adoption, there is a further grace of sanctification. Believers are set apart once and for all by justification, and we are further sanctified—made holy and devoted to God. We **are further sanctified, really and personally.** While there is no righteousness infused into believers with justification, believers are made actually righteous now by sanctification. Actual righteousness is on the basis of **the virtue of Christ's death and resurrection.**

The means of sanctification are **by His Word and Spirit dwelling in them.** Notice how often it is stated that the work of the Spirit is by and with the Word. Sanctification is not just by the Word, not just by the Spirit, but by the Word and Spirit dwelling in them.

The dominion of the whole body of sin is destroyed, and the several lusts thereof are more and more weakened and mortified. The process of sanctification is that the dominion of the whole body of sin is destroyed. The root in the heart has been changed, and the old has been taken away. Believers are re-created in knowledge, holiness, and righteousness. Unbelief, unholiness, and unrighteousness at the core of our being are removed at the time of regeneration. Furthermore, the effects of the dominion of the whole body of sin, which remain in believers' lives, are increasingly weakened and mortified. Notice the process—**more and more**—this speaks about the gradual element of sanctification. This does not happen all at once—we are not totally sanctified. With sin remaining, we do not give our whole heart to the Lord. At best, we can say that we give all that we know of to the Lord, which may not be very much because we may not know ourselves very deeply.

Some people support the idea of total sanctification, such as the higher life movement and Methodism, which then influences the Holiness movement, Pentecostalism, and Perfectionism in Christianity. Each holds to a faulty doctrine of sanctification. Distortion in doctrine occurs because believers are still in the process of sanctification and have a mixture of belief and unbelief remaining within them. Negatively, **the whole body of sin is destroyed, and the several lusts thereof are more and more weakened and mortified,** which is where we take up our cross daily and follow Christ. Sin is mortified by crucifixion. We are to crucify the flesh with the affections and the lusts thereof. None of the flesh goes down gladly and willingly. It goes down kicking and screaming. It does not look pretty. This is how sanctification occurs. Crucifixion is not gentle. In this, we are unlike Christ, who submitted as a lamb led to the slaughter.

The lusts are more and more weakened and mortified, **and they more and more quickened and strengthened in all saving graces.** Sanctification is a gradual process, and the extent of it is in all saving graces. Holiness has to do with devotion, seeking, and desiring. It goes to other elements of our personality, but the element of feeling is particularly brought out in holiness. Holiness is by knowing the truth, "Sanctify them through thy truth."[1] And the Lord said: "If you continue in my Word, then you are my disciples indeed, and you shall know the truth and the truth shall set you free."[2] Truth sanctifies. Correct doctrine understood sanctifies. Those who try to get to holiness through zeal or piety for the Lord apart from knowledge are not undergoing true sanctification. There are many faulty views of spirituality and holiness in the Church that must be addressed. The ultimate end of sanctification is that we might see/understand God. We are chastened that we might be partakers of His holiness, without which no one shall see the Lord. In holiness we must have understanding. By seeking we come to knowledge, which leads to obedience by continuing in His Word, by which believers know the truth more fully, and become holier in an ongoing cycle.

SUMMARY ANSWER

Basis: We are set apart by justification. Means: We are further made righteous by sanctification of Christ's death and resurrection through His Word and the Holy Spirit (use of ordinary means). Process: Unrighteousness and unbelief are gradually removed yet being neither immediate nor total. Sanctification is in and by the Word working with the Spirit. None of unbelief goes gently; it is a mortification and crucifixion of the flesh. Extent: Holiness entails full devotion to God through the truth. End: Holiness leads us to seeing God (seeking God more fully).

---

1. *John 17:17.*
2. *John 8:31-32.*

QUESTION 60

Explain the subjective manifestation of the process of sanctification.

II. This sanctification is throughout, in the whole man; yet imperfect in this life, there abiding still some remnants of corruption in every part; whence arises a continual and irreconcilable war, the flesh lusting against the Spirit, and the Spirit against the flesh.

Section 13.2 of the Confession states, **This sanctification is throughout, in the whole man; yet imperfect in this life, there abiding still some remnants of corruption in every part.** A person may not be aware of remaining corruption, but remembering original sin and regeneration, there are some remnants of corruption in every part of our being—intellectually, emotionally, and volitionally. The subjective side of corruption is felt as **a continual and irreconcilable war, the flesh lusting against the Spirit, and the Spirit against the flesh.** We cannot have it both ways. We cannot sit on the fence forever. It has to go one way or the other. We have to choose between the two ways. This choice is experienced as a continual and irreconcilable war. "The things that I would I do not, and the things that I would not that I do, wretched man that I am."[3] The war within ourselves is the struggle of sanctification. Some people try to deny that Paul is referring to sanctification in this passage, rather this is Paul's thinking before he was a believer. They say, "If you are really sanctified, you will not have this internal struggle. There is a place where the eagles do not fly, far above all of this." The response is that believers do not get to that place in this life. Those who speak this way do not recognize sin remaining and the struggle of sanctification. Believers do not reach perfection in this life, but that does not mean that we simply resign. We are not perfect in holiness, but we are to perfect holiness in the fear of the Lord—this comes out in section 13.3. Section 13.2 speaks of the subjective manifestation of

---

3. *Romans 7:24-25.*

the process of sanctification—an irreconcilable war. The Spirit does not leave us alone in this, but He wars against the flesh, and the flesh against the Spirit. The flesh does not want to go—it is like pulling a donkey that does not want to move. It seems impossible, but believers are made able by the Spirit to change. The subjective side of sanctification is the spiritual war going on within each of us.

SUMMARY ANSWER

Corruption remains in our lives in every part of our being (intellect, emotion, and will). A continual and irreconcilable war of the flesh against the Spirit. Although perfection remains unattainable, we must strive to perfect holiness in sanctification.

QUESTION 61

What is the progress of sanctification?

III. In which war, although the remaining corruption, for a time, may much prevail; yet, through the continual supply of strength from the sanctifying Spirit of Christ, the regenerate part does overcome; and so, the saints grow in grace, perfecting holiness in the fear of God.

Some reject the need for progress, thinking they are already saved. Others doubt the possibility of progress, thinking the flesh will always remain the same. No, the flesh can be weakened more and more, and the Spirit's demands and graces strengthened more and more. It is a process of progress. Sanctification is a gradual process, increasing more and more. Sanctification is imperfect in this life. And lastly, the process is uneven. We might like to think of a simple, gradual, and steady progress, going straight up, as opposed to uneven progress. In these times, we are pressed to believe that God will continue the work. There are times in this war when the flesh has the upper hand, **In which war, although the remaining corruption, for a time, may much prevail; yet, through the continual supply of strength from the sanctifying Spirit** of Christ, **the regenerate part does overcome; and so, the saints**—all believers, not a special group of believers—**grow in grace, perfecting holiness**—improving it, continuing it, growing in it, becoming more and more mature—**in the fear of God.** In this process of sanctification, we learn to fear the Lord and to seek Him, to know Him, and be devoted to Him.

The process is that we are adopted, and are being sanctified. It is a gradual, imperfect process in this life, and it is uneven. But progress is made. Does this sound close to the reality of the Christian life? It does not mean that we should give up if the corrupt part prevails for a time. Remember, from section 5.5, persons are left for a time to the corruption of their hearts so they may be humbled. And from 6.4, we are utterly indisposed, disabled, and opposed to all good, and wholly inclined to all evil, in terms of the corruption that remains. That old nature does not change; it can be weakened, crucified, and mortified more and more. The Scripture says, "if you through the Spirit put to death the deeds of the body, you shall live."[4] Believers put to death the deeds of the flesh by the power of the Holy Spirit, not by our own power. And in this, believers have to use the means of grace, by the Word and Spirit, which includes the preaching of the Word, the teaching of the pastor-teachers (the past achievements), fellowship with other believers, prayer, and all other ordinary means.

SUMMARY ANSWER

Sanctification is gradual, imperfect, and uneven. The saints grow in grace, perfecting holiness in the fear of God.

---

4. *Romans 8:13.*

Chapter 14

OF SAVING FAITH

QUESTION 62

How does faith originate and increase?

I. The grace of faith, whereby the elect are enabled to believe to the saving of their souls, is the work of the Spirit of Christ in their hearts, and is ordinarily wrought by the ministry of the Word, by which also, and by the administration of the sacraments, and prayer, it is increased and strengthened.

Saving faith comes through the work of the Spirit and the Word. The Spirit regenerates, illuminates, and sanctifies by bringing us to know the truth. Believers grow by diligence in the use of the means of grace. We continue to grow by the Word and the Spirit, and **by the administration of the sacraments, and prayer.** The primary context of the Word is through hearing the preaching on the Lord's Day. We must come to the preaching duly prepared, on time, and able to stay focused for the entire church service. Additional means of grace include fellowship with other believers, personal devotions (reading of Scripture and prayer), and making use of the work of the pastor-teachers who have spoken and written on the Word. Furthermore, we ought to prepare to observe the sacraments, take the vows to walk according to them, and grow in grace. These are all means by which our faith increases.

SUMMARY ANSWER

Saving faith comes from the Holy Spirit and increases through the Word, sacraments, and prayer—the use of ordinary means of salvation.

QUESTION 63

What are the object, acts, and principal acts of saving faith?

II. By this faith, a Christian believes to be true whatsoever is revealed in the Word, for the authority of God Himself speaking therein; and acts differently upon that which each particular passage thereof contains; yielding obedience to the commands, trembling at the threatenings, and embracing the promises of God for this life, and that which is to come. But the principal acts of saving faith are accepting, receiving, and resting upon Christ alone for justification, sanctification, and eternal life, by virtue of the covenant of grace.

We should distinguish between the object of faith, the acts of faith, and the principal acts of faith. **By this faith, a Christian believes to be true whatsoever is revealed in the Word, for the authority of God Himself speaking therein.** The object of faith is the Word of God, and whatsoever is revealed in the Word. We can distinguish elements in saving faith. The traditional distinctions are: *notitia, assensus,* and *fiducia. Notitia* is the conception of what is being said. *Assensus* is our assenting to it. *Fiducia* is acting accordingly.

Next, we come to the act of faith, which faith **acts differently upon that which each particular passage thereof contains.** In some cases, it is **obedience to the commands,** in others it is **trembling at the threatenings,** and in others, it is **embracing the promises of God for this life** and receiving the comfort of the Scripture. The Scripture speaks in many ways, and we respond according to each particular. When it says,

"I can do all things through Christ who strengthens me,"[1] we embrace the promise of God here (it is not a command).

Finally, **the principal acts of saving faith are accepting, receiving, and resting upon Christ alone for justification, sanctification, and eternal life, by virtue of the covenant of grace.** The principal acts of faith include accepting, receiving, and resting upon Christ for salvation. The principal acts are not all of the acts of faith; it is the beginning of faith. *Fiducia*, which involves trust and obedience, may be looked at in terms of the principal act. Some churches may be concerned only with this principle act—whether or not we have received Christ as our savior and whether we are resting only on Him for salvation—without thinking about the need for sanctification and obedience in all of life. Saving faith includes obedience to the whole Word of God. Salvation is more than regeneration, repentance and faith, justification, adoption, and sanctification. It involves glorification as well.

SUMMARY ANSWER

The object of faith is the Word of God. The principal act of faith is accepting, receiving, and resting upon Christ for salvation. Traditional distinction on the elements of faith: *Notitia* refers to the content of faith, or conception of what is being said. *Assensus* is our conviction that the content of our faith is true. *Fiducia* refers to personal trust, reliance, and acting accordingly. Scripture speaks in many ways, and we are to respond in accordance to every particular passage: obedience, trembling, embracing the promises, and receiving the comfort of Scripture.

---

1. *Philippians 4:13.*

QUESTION 64

Explain the degrees of faith.

III. This faith is different in degrees, weak or strong; may be often and many ways assailed, and weakened, but gets the victory: growing up in many to the attainment of a full assurance, through Christ, who is both the author and finisher of our faith.

The Confession affirms that faith comes in degrees stating, **this faith is different in degrees, weak or strong,** and furthermore, it **may be often and many ways assailed, and weakened.** Faith can be strong at one time and later assailed and weakened. For example, we may be exposed to situations with which we are not prepared to deal. We may associate with people who influence us in negative ways. We may have all the proper resources available to us and, yet, find ourselves weakened and backsliding. We have to nurture and protect (not simply shelter) ourselves from being exposed to temptation. There comes a time when our faith is stronger, and we can take on difficult challenges, such as those presented by Wittgenstein, Quine, Carnap, Derrida, Foucault, and others.

There are degrees of faith, and it can be assailed and weakened. When we yield to temptation, we fall into a pit from which we may have a difficult time recovering. We ought not wallow in melancholy and self recrimination when we fall into sin, to do so is a form of pride. We have been saying, in principle, we are utterly indisposed toward anything good. Our faith may be often and in many ways assailed and weakened. But next, the Confession says our faith **gets the victory: growing up in many to the attainment of a full assurance, through Christ, who is both the author and finisher of our faith.** Christ is not only the author but also the finisher of our faith, bringing us to maturity. We need to remember that the Confession is a summary of the understanding of the pastor-teachers in Church history communicated to us.

SUMMARY ANSWER

There are degrees of faith: weak or strong, assailed or weakened.
We ought to protect ourselves through the use of ordinary means.

Chapter 15

OF REPENTANCE UNTO LIFE

QUESTION 65

What distinguishes the evangelical view of salvation?

I. Repentance unto life is an evangelical grace, the doctrine whereof is to be preached by every minister of the Gospel, as well as that of faith in Christ.

The doctrine of repentance unto life is what distinguishes evangelical teaching over and against other systems and ways in which salvation is supposedly wrought. The Confession affirms that **repentance unto life is an evangelical grace, the doctrine whereof is to be preached by every minister of the Gospel, as well as that of faith in Christ.** We are to preach "repent and believe." Historically, there have been many churches that have not preached repentance and belief. Rather, they teach that we come into the church, work through the system, and then we will be saved. Repentance unto life is not preached. The sacramental system in the Medieval Church did not declare the evangelical view of salvation. We may go to confession for sin, but confession of sin is not the same as repentance unto life. Christ came preaching, "Repent, the kingdom of heaven is at hand."[1] We are to repent of sin and believe the gospel. Preaching repentance may look different in practice. It may appear one way when preached to non-believers, and another when preached to covenant children, who grow up being taught and instructed in the faith, and who may not have had a crisis conversion.

---

1. *Matthew 4:17.*

But those who have not previously been in the covenant are particularly to be called to repent and believe. Repentance and belief unto life is the first stage of sanctification. Subsequent repentance is for the whole of our life to attain to maturity in the faith. The preaching of repentance unto life is what characterizes evangelicalism. Evangelicalism is simply the evangel or the gospel, the good news of salvation. And we proclaim that people receive salvation by repenting and believing. The next section of the Confession explains what it means to repent.

SUMMARY ANSWER

Preaching repentance unto life distinguishes the evangelical view of salvation. It ought to be preached by every pastor—repent and believe the gospel.

QUESTION 66

Explain repentance in the various aspects of the heart.

II. By it, a sinner, out of the sight and sense not only of the danger, but also of the filthiness and odiousness of his sins, as contrary to the holy nature, and righteous law of God; and upon the apprehension of His mercy in Christ to such as are penitent, so grieves for, and hates his sins, as to turn from them all unto God, purposing and endeavoring to walk with Him in all the ways of His commandments.

Section 15.2 of the Confession presents repentance in each of the threefold aspects of the human heart, including intellect, emotion, and will. First, the intellectual aspect of repentance is rooted in understanding, as seen in the statement, **By it, a sinner, out of the sight and sense not only of the danger, but also of the filthiness and odiousness of his sins, as contrary to the holy nature, and righteous law of God; and upon the apprehension of His mercy in Christ. . . .** The word for repentance is *metanoia*, which means to change one's mind or to have a change in thinking. We are to have an awareness of sin, not just in a bare technical sense, we are to have an understanding of sin and the effects of sin. We are to have the sight and sense that brings us to see the danger of sin, the death it produces, and its offensiveness to God. We are to see the filthiness and odiousness of sin, as contrary to the holy nature and righteous law of God. We tend to think of some things as filthy and odious, but the filthiness and odiousness of root sin is apart from fruit sins, which are also filthy and odious. An example of the odiousness of root sin is seen in Romans, "For although they knew God, they neither glorified Him as God nor gave thanks to Him, but their thinking became futile and their foolish hearts were darkened."[2] Another example of root sin occurred in the Garden when they stopped seeking and understanding, leading to the fruit sin of eating of the tree of the knowledge of good and evil. This was not a filthy, odious act in the way we ordinarily speak about fruit sin. In the Church at large, there has been a shift in primarily applying the characterizations of **filthiness and odiousness** to fruit sins, which is not the sense of sin described in this section of the Confession. Sin is odious in its root and fruit because all sin is contrary to the holy nature and righteous law of God. Our awareness is not just of sin, but the comprehension of what sin deserves and God's mercy in forgiving us as the Confession states, **upon the apprehension of His mercy in Christ to such as are penitent.** Repentance includes our thinking, awareness, and comprehension, which penetrates to our attitude. The intellectual comprehension of sin is one part of the heart, not the whole of it.

The second aspect of repentance of sin applies to the emotions. A sinner **so grieves for, and hates his sins.** Grief and hatred are the emotional aspects of repentance. Biblical repentance involves awareness of the filthiness and odiousness of sin as well as the mercy of God in Christ, which produces in us a grief and hatred of our sin.

The third aspect of repentance of sin applies to the will in that we **turn from [all sins] unto God, purposing and endeavoring to walk with Him in all the ways of His commandments.** We turn away from all our sins and turn unto God, in principle, as far as we know. We purpose, intend, and endeavor (even if we take baby steps) to walk with Him—notice the personal dimension of this—sin is against God and

---

2. *Romans 1:21.*

we want to walk with Him, and not just with Him apart from His Word, but with Him in all the ways of His commands.

The fullness of repentance is to be preached by every minister of the gospel, calling people to repent of their sins. We must recognize sin as sin, know its nature, understand the mercy of God, grieve and hate sin, and turn from all sin unto God. The Church tends to emphasize one aspect or another of sin without keeping the three aspects of intellectual, emotional, and volitional repentance together. Some people emphasize grief and hatred for sin by using graphic examples to produce an emotional repentance. Or they preach the consequence of sin to stir people's emotions. Others may attempt to get people to change their ways without much awareness of grief and hatred for sin. But appeal to emotions or attempt to change the will directly is not a true apprehension of sin. All three aspects of the heart must be involved in repentance and should not be separated.

SUMMARY ANSWER

Intellectual aspect of repentance is coming to awareness of sin and death in an existential sense; sin affects us and is contrary to the holy nature of God. Repentance is of both root sin (omission) and fruit sin (commission). The emotional aspect of repentance is grief and hatred of sin and death. The volitional aspect is turning from our sins and purposing, endeavoring and intending to walk with God in all the ways of His commands.

QUESTION 67

Explain the necessity of repentance for pardon.

III. Although repentance is not to be rested in, as any satisfaction for sin, or any cause of the pardon thereof, which is the act of God's free grace in Christ; yet is it of such necessity to all sinners, that none may expect pardon without it.

Section 15.3 corrects the assumption some people have that repentance is the cause of our pardon. Repentance is not the cause of our pardon because repentance itself is not the satisfaction for our sin. Christ is the satisfaction for sin. Some people think that if they ask for forgiveness, God forgives on the basis of their asking. Asking for forgiveness is not the basis of pardon, as if asking is all there is to being pardoned. Justice must be satisfied. **Although repentance is not to be rested in, as any satisfaction for sin, or any cause of the pardon thereof, which is the act of God's free grace in Christ.** . . . Repentance is neither the satisfaction for sin nor the cause of pardon, but forgiveness is of Christ's free grace alone, and, **is it of such necessity to all sinners, that none may expect pardon without it.** God may be ready to give pardon, and while Christ may pray, "Father forgive them for they know not what they do,"[3] we do not receive the pardon until we repent. Similarly, we are to forgive those who have sinned against us, but the pardon is not received until there is actual repentance. There is yet another step connected with repentance that needs to be addressed.

SUMMARY ANSWER

Repentance is not the cause of our pardon. Repentance itself is not the satisfaction for sin. Yet pardon is not to be expected until actual repentance takes place.

QUESTION 68

Are there limitations to the content and extent of repentance?

IV. As there is no sin so small, but it deserves damnation; so there is no sin so great, that it can bring damnation upon those who truly repent.

---

3. *Luke 23:34.*

V. Men ought not to content themselves with a general repentance, but it is every man's duty to endeavor to repent of his particular sins, particularly.

Some people may think that there are some sins so small that we do not need to repent of them. The Confession affirms that **there is no sin so small, but it deserves damnation.** Was eating the fruit in the Garden a small sin? A libertarian might say because it does not hurt anyone, eating the fruit is all right. And, yet, this act damned the whole human race. Given the covenant, eating the fruit is a big sin. There is no sin so small that it does not deserve damnation and therefore does not need repentance. Some people may say that their sin is too great, they are damned, and they do not repent. There is no limitation on repentance of the smallest or greatest of sins. Could Hitler repent and be saved? Sometimes people talk as though salvation for some is impossible because sin is seen as an act against us rather than against God.

Having covered the content of repentance, what is the extent of repentance? Notice how the Confession puts it: **Men ought not to content themselves with a general repentance, but it is every man's duty to endeavor to repent of his particular sins, particularly.** We should have a reasonable sense of the particular sin needing repentance.

SUMMARY ANSWER

No sin is so small that it does not need repentance, yet no sin is so great that it can damn those who repent. Our duty is to repent of particular sins particularly.

QUESTION 69

Explain the relation between repentance and confession of sin.

VI. As every man is bound to make private confession of his sins to God, praying for the pardon thereof; upon which, and the forsaking of them, he shall find mercy; so, he that scandalizes his brother, or the Church of Christ, ought to be willing, by a private or public confession, and sorrow for his sin, to declare his repentance to those that are offended, who are thereupon to be reconciled to him, and in love to receive him.

Repentance is the confession and forsaking of sin, and **every man is bound to make private confession of his sins to God.** All sin is first and fundamentally against God, but it is also against our fellow humans. And, **praying for the pardon thereof; upon which, and the forsaking of them, he shall find mercy; so, he that scandalizes his brother, or the Church of Christ, ought to be willing, by a private or public confession, and sorrow for his sin, to declare his repentance to those that are offended, who are thereupon to be reconciled to him, and in love to receive him.** If someone has offended their brother, they need to confess their sin to their brother. They must confess their sin to whomever it is they have offended. The offended party should be reconciled to the person repenting and receive them in love. In the Lord's Prayer we ask, "Forgive us our debts as we forgive our debtors."[4] If a sin is public and scandalizes the church, confession should be made to the church. If someone sins by breaking the marriage bond resulting in divorce, and they return and repent, they are to be forgiven. They are to be reconciled and received as a brother or sister, but not necessarily as a spouse again. Reconciliation with someone as a fellow believer can occur without necessarily having restoration to all that was in the relationship before. Decisions about the extent of restoration have to be

---

4. *Matthew 6:12.*

made based on the wisdom of God and Christ and by receiving input from others. With prayer and input we can make a decision, before God, with which all parties can live. As far as forgiving the person, we are called to forgive if they truly repent.

In general, when we forgive someone we do not hold their sin against them. The restoration process may take time, but we are not to hold the sin against them, and we are not to bring it up against them later. If they sin in the same way again, we are to forgive seventy times seven. Yet, rebuilding trust may take some time. Reconciliation takes little time, but rebuilding trust takes time. We can receive someone in love and in love desire them to go from where they are to the next step, and the next step, and so forth. Some sins can go outstanding, not being confessed for decades, but they will not go away. That is why particular sins should be repented of particularly. Given the length of time that sins can go unconfessed, we should see repentance is a real door of hope. Biblical repentance, which begins with an awareness that our sin is first and foremost against God, is the door that is always open, no matter how small or great the sin. We should never lose hope in any situation. If there is repentance, there can be reconciliation, which is a condition we should desire. If we can be reconciled to God through repentance, then we can certainly be reconciled to others through repentance. This is a comforting doctrine. There is real grace in the forgiveness of sins, but there is also real grace in sanctification and repentance. This is God's way regarding our redemption.

SUMMARY ANSWER

All repentance requires private confession to God and either private or public confession to those whom we wronged. Repentance is a real door of hope toward reconciliation. Through repentance we can be reconciled to God and others. Reconciliation takes little time, but rebuilding trust takes longer. Once reconciliation occurs, we are not to hold that sin against them.

Chapter 16

OF GOOD WORKS

QUESTION 70

What are the divine limits of good works?

I. Good works are only such as God has commanded in His holy Word, and not such as, without the warrant thereof, are devised by men, out of blind zeal, or upon any pretense of good intention.

Section 16.1 affirms, positively, that good works are *only* such as what **God has commanded in His holy Word.** And, negatively, which is the most common way to deviate from good works, **not such as, without the warrant thereof, are devised by men, out of blind zeal, or upon any pretense of good intention.** Warrant for works devised by men is lacking because they are not rooted in the Word. Zeal and good intentions do not guarantee or make for good works. Many people substitute works as a means of their justification because they intended good. Do they search the Word for God's command, or do they act out of blind zeal? We must keep in mind the good works derived from the Word. Blind zeal and good intentions are no substitutes for what the Word of God says. Focus on the Word addresses quite a bit of misunderstanding and gets proper works focused quickly—**only such as God has commanded.** Notice that if we had good intentions, we would be going to the Word to know what God would have us do.

SUMMARY ANSWER

Good works are only such as God has commanded in His Word.
Zeal and good intentions are not the basis for good works.

QUESTION 71

Explain the basis and fruits of good works.

*II. These good works, done in obedience to God's commandments,
are the fruits and evidences of a true and lively faith: and by them
believers manifest their thankfulness, strengthen their assurance, edify
their brethren, adorn the profession of the Gospel, stop the mouths of
the adversaries, and glorify God, whose workmanship they are, created
in Christ Jesus thereunto, that, having their fruit unto holiness, they
may have the end, eternal life.*

Faith is the basis of good works. **These good works, done in obedience
to God's commandments, are the fruits and evidences of a true and
lively faith.** Section 16.2 highlights the connection between faith and
works. Good works are the fruits and evidences of **a true and lively
faith.** Those who have faith will bear the fruits of good works. What
are the fruits of good works? The fruits of good works, in the life of
the faithful, **manifest their thankfulness, strengthen their assurance,
edify their brethren, adorn the profession of the Gospel, stop the
mouths of the adversaries, and glorify God.** The end of the fruits of
good works is eternal life—the knowledge and enjoyment of God.
Good works are the fruits of faith, and good works bear fruit in ones
life in a manifold sense.

SUMMARY ANSWER

The basis of good works is faith; good works are the fruits and
evidences of faith. By good works, believers manifest their thankfulness, strengthen their assurance, edify their brethren, adorn

the profession of the gospel, stop the mouths of the adversaries, and glorify God by acting for the good.

QUESTION 72

Explain the origin and operation of the ability to do good works.

III. Their ability to do good works is not at all of themselves, but wholly from the Spirit of Christ. And that they may be enabled thereunto, beside the graces they have already received, there is required an actual influence of the same Holy Spirit, to work in them to will, and to do, of His good pleasure: yet are they not hereupon to grow negligent, as if they were not bound to perform any duty unless upon a special motion of the Spirit; but they ought to be diligent in stirring up the grace of God that is in them.

The the Holy Spirit actively sustains and enables us to do good works, according to His good pleasure. The Confession affirms that the **ability to do good works is not at all of themselves, but wholly from the Spirit of Christ. And that they may be enabled thereunto, beside the graces they have already received, there is required an actual influence of the same Holy Spirit, to work in them to will, and to do, of His good pleasure.** Some may say that if the ability to do good works is up to us, we, in our sin, will become negligent. Yet, the Confession says, **yet are they not hereupon to grow negligent, as if they were not bound to perform any duty unless upon a special motion of the Spirit; but they ought to be diligent in stirring up the grace of God that is in them.** Some may say that they do not feel moved by the Spirit or feel the Spirit moving in them to do some good work. We are not to wait; we are to be diligent in stirring up the grace of God in us. In other words, God gives us means, and we are to stir up that grace by using the ordinary means. We are to put one foot in front of the other, without waiting for a special motion of the Spirit.

SUMMARY ANSWER

The ability to do good works is not at all of ourselves, but wholly of the Holy Spirit. We are not to become negligent in the use of the ordinary means. We need not wait for special movement by the Spirit to act. We are to seek God diligently.

QUESTION 73

What is the extent of the achievement of good works?

IV. They who, in their obedience, attain to the greatest height which is possible in this life, are so far from being able to supererogate, and to do more than God requires, as that they fall short of much which in duty they are bound to do.

Section 16.4 of the Confession addresses the mistaken doctrine of supererogation, which was a widespread belief in the Medieval Church and in Martin Luther's day. The doctrine affirms that some people, called "saints," so fully obey God that they achieve and build up merit for others, and that merit is dispensed to those in need of merit by the church through the sacramental system. The Confession affirms that in this life we do not fully obey, that supererogation is not possible. We need to understand that the extent of the achievement of good works is never full in this life. We come short of what we are called to do, and we do not go over and above our duty. In other words, we never exceed our duty, and we often come short of our duty. Furthermore, because it is our duty there is no special merit to be built up in obeying. Supererogation is denied in doctrine and in the extent of the achievement of good works.

SUMMARY ANSWER

The attainment of good works is never full (vs. supererogation). When we do our duty, we receive no additional merit. We never exceed our duty.

QUESTION 74

What merit or reward is there in good works?

V. We cannot by our best works merit pardon of sin, or eternal life at the hand of God, by reason of the great disproportion that is between them and the glory to come; and the infinite distance that is between us and God, whom, by them, we can neither profit, nor satisfy for the debt of our former sins, but when we have done all we can, we have done but our duty, and are unprofitable servants: and because, as they are good, they proceed from His Spirit; and as they are wrought by us, they are defiled, and mixed with so much weakness and imperfection, that they cannot endure the severity of God's judgment.

VI. Notwithstanding, the persons of believers being accepted through Christ, their good works also are accepted in Him; not as though they were in this life wholly unblamable and unreproveable in God's sight; but that He, looking upon them in His Son, is pleased to accept and reward that which is sincere, although accompanied with many weaknesses and imperfections.

We cannot merit pardon of sin or eternal life by our works. Forgiveness of sin is not a matter of our merit. The Confession explains we cannot merit pardon of sins because of **the great disproportion that is between them and the glory to come; and the infinite distance that is between us and God, whom, by them, we can neither profit, nor satisfy for the debt of our former sins, but when we have done all we can, we have done but our duty, and are unprofitable servants: and because, as they are good, they proceed from His Spirit; and as they** are wrought by us, they are defiled, and mixed with so much weakness and imperfection, that they cannot endure the severity of God's judgment. For all of these reasons, there is nothing that we merit by our good works. Is there a reward for good works? The Confession speaks about reward in a particular sense by stating, **notwithstanding, the persons of believers being accepted through Christ, their good works also are accepted in Him; not as though they were in this life wholly unblamable and unreproveable in God's sight; but that He, looking upon them in His Son, is pleased to accept and reward that which is sincere.** We do not earn our reward by merit, we receive it by God's gracious condescension, although our works are **accompanied with many weaknesses and imperfections.** Perhaps God rewarding our sincerity is like a child bringing a drawing to a parent, and the parent saying, "Oh, my dear, how wonderful!" Objectively speaking, it may be another matter. We cannot merit anything for many reasons, yet, we do good works, imperfect as they are, and they are accepted and rewarded by God in light of Christ's work.

SUMMARY ANSWER

We merit nothing for our good works. The rewards are given by God's gracious condescension in light of the atoning work of Christ.

QUESTION 75

Can the unregenerate do good works?

VII. Works done by unregenerate men, although for the matter of them they may be things which God commands; and of good use both to themselves and others: yet, because they proceed not from a heart purified by faith; nor are done in a right manner, according to the Word; nor to a right end, the glory of God, they are therefore sinful, and cannot please God, or make a man meet to receive grace from God: and yet, their neglect of them is more sinful and displeasing unto God.

The Confession affirms the position that the unregenerate cannot please God with their works, yet, their condition is worse if they neglect to do good works. What are some of the good works that unbelievers do? Parents bringing a child into the world and nurturing him, would be considered a good work. Cain and his descendants developed music, which is an accomplishment. Those who first raised cattle, and invented the wheel, also did good works.[1] There is a sense in which unbelievers do good works in that they contribute to the work of dominion, but the next point addresses why it is not accounted good works. **Works done by unregenerate men, although for the matter of them; they may be things which God commands, and of good use both to themselves and others: yet, because they proceed not from an heart purified by faith; nor are done in a right manner, according to the Word; nor to a right end, the glory of God, they are therefore sinful, and cannot please God, or make a man meet to receive grace from God.** For these reasons, the works of unbelievers cannot please God or prepare them for salvation. The Confession goes on to say, **and yet, their neglect of them is more sinful and displeasing unto God.** Even though an un-believer's works may serve God's purpose and are not pleasing to God because of how and why they are done, their neglect is more sinful and

---

1. *Genesis 4:20-22.*

displeasing to God. The works are good in that they are of good use to themselves and others but not good in the sense of pleasing God or in making them suitable to receive grace from God.

SUMMARY ANSWER

The unregenerate cannot do good works, but their neglect of good works is more displeasing to God. Works done by the unregenerate cannot be good, because they are not for the right reason—the glory of God. Although their works may serve the purpose of God, they are not pleasing to God.

Chapter 17

——

OF THE PERSEVERANCE OF THE SAINTS

QUESTION 76

What is the perseverance of the saints?

I. They, whom God has accepted in His Beloved, effectually called, and sanctified by His Spirit, can neither totally nor finally fall away from the state of grace, but shall certainly persevere therein to the end, and be eternally saved.

We need to understand why the doctrine of the perseverance of the saints had become an issue to be addressed in the Confession. After addressing the *Ordo Salutis* the question arises: Can a person fall from salvation? If we are predestined and brought to Christ on the basis of election, can we fall away? This is not quite the level at which we ought to ask the question. The question becomes clearer when in section 17.1 we examine the context of the state of grace. Can we fall from the state of grace? If we understand the meaning of the state of grace, we can avoid some of the problems arising from a great segment of Christianity (Arminian evangelicals and Catholic sacramentalists) who do not believe in the perseverance of the saints in the state of grace. They do not affirm perseverance of the saints because they do not believe that salvation begins by election and effectual calling, which is the sovereign work of God. Instead, Arminian theology affirms salvation depends on man's decision or man's will, fundamentally. In this view, since man's decision is subject to change, he may fall away and lose his salvation.

On the contrary, the Confession affirms that salvation depends solely on God by way of effectual calling (*ordo salutis*), God choosing without any foreseen condition in the person, and God sovereignly working to bring us from death to life, and so affirms that we will persevere in the state of grace by the work of the Holy Spirit. Once God's work of redemption in a person is done, it will not be undone. **They, whom God has accepted in His Beloved, effectually called, and sanctified by His Spirit, can neither totally nor finally fall away from the state of grace but shall certainly persevere therein to the end, and be eternally saved.** The doctrine of the perseverance of the saints is that we can never totally nor finally fall away, but we persevere in the state of grace. We will need to analyze more thoroughly and more clearly the state of grace.

In the Confession, the term "saint" is used synonymously with believers. It is not a special group of people (as in the Roman Catholic Church). The word is scripturally used for all believers at all times. Furthermore, the term is connected with sanctification; God sanctifies us, He makes us holy, and from the term sanctification, we have the word saint.

SUMMARY ANSWER

Can we fall away from the state of grace? Catholic sacramentalism and Arminian evangelicalism (decisional regeneration) deny the perseverance of the saints. On the contrary, the Confession affirms it. Election is a sovereign work of God depending on God alone—not for anything in man or done by man. Once the work of salvation is done, it cannot be undone. The elect can neither totally nor finally fall away from the state of grace but shall certainly persevere in the state of grace until the end to be eternally saved.

QUESTION 77

On what does perseverance depend?

II. This perseverance of the saints depends not upon their own free will, but upon the immutability of the decree of election, flowing from the free and unchangeable love of God the Father; upon the efficacy of the merit and intercession of Jesus Christ, the abiding of the Spirit, and of the seed of God within them, and the nature of the covenant of grace: from all which arises also the certainty and infallibility thereof.

Section 17.2 addresses the objection to the perseverance of the saints from the ordinary experience of believers who seem to fall away. The Confession affirms **the perseverance of the saints depends not upon their own free will, but upon the immutability of the decree of election.** When God decrees the elect, His decree does not change. His decree flows **from the free and unchangeable love of God the Father.** The immutability of the decree and election flow from the unchangeable love of God the Father, which is the first point of this section.

The second point is that perseverance of the saints is based **upon the efficacy of the merit and intercession of Jesus Christ.** Christ's death on the cross was efficacious, and it merited salvation. It is an objective fact that He purchased redemption. Those who struggle with the question of assurance, addressed in the next chapter, *Of the Assurance of Grace and Salvation,* must consider this reality. Notice also that perseverance of the saints depends on the intercession of Jesus Christ. He ever lives to make intercession for us.[1] He was reckoned with His priestly ministry as the High Priest who intercedes for believers. The third point is that perseverance of the saints depends upon the work of the Spirit—**the abiding of the Spirit, and of the seed of God within them.** God the Holy Spirit not only implants the seed of redemption, but He abides with us to uphold it. Just as we speak of the efficacy, merit,

---

1. *Hebrews 7:25.*

and intercession of Christ, which is the ongoing work of God the Father, Son, and Holy Spirit, so the Confession affirms the perseverance of the saints is a work of the Father, Son, and Holy Spirit. The work of God in establishing the saints in the state of grace is according to the covenant of grace. God has established the covenant of grace beginning with Adam and has continued the covenant. The immutable decree of God, the Father, the efficacy and merit of Christ's death on the cross and intercession, and the Holy Spirit planting the seed of redemption and abiding in the believer, all give rise to the certainty and infallibility of the perseverance of the saints.

SUMMARY ANSWER

Perseverance does not depend on man's will, but on the work of the Godhead. It depends upon the immutable decree of God the Father, upon the efficacy and merit of Christ's death on the cross and intercession, and upon the Holy Spirit planting the seed of redemption and abiding in the believer.

QUESTION 78

How does perseverance appear to be qualified?

III. Nevertheless, they may, through the temptations of Satan and of the world, the prevalency of corruption remaining in them, and the neglect of the means of their preservation, fall into grievous sins; and, for a time, continue therein: whereby they incur God's displeasure, and grieve His Holy Spirit, come to be deprived of some measure of their graces and comforts, have their hearts hardened, and their consciences wounded; hurt and scandalize others, and bring temporal judgments upon themselves.

We may speak of the state of grace in degrees in that we may grow in grace or backslide. Perseverance in the state of grace may be diminished greatly. Section 17.3 speaks about temptation, sin, and the consequences for believers. A person who falls into sin may seem to themselves no longer a Christian. Chapter 18 addresses the topic of assurance of salvation, which is the subjective aspect of the perseverance of the saints, while section 17.3 addresses the objective side of perseverance and Scriptural teaching.

The Confession says believers may fall into grievous sins **through the temptations of Satan and of the world, the prevalency of corruption remaining in them, and the neglect of the means of their preservation.** Notice the temptations come from the world, the flesh, the devil, and not using the ordinary means. Can we think of a relevant example of someone who fell into grievous sin? Consider the example of David.[2] Scripture says:

> And it came to pass . . . at the time when kings go forth *to battle*, that David sent Joab, and his servants with him, and all Israel . . . And it came to pass in an eveningtide, that David arose from off his bed, and walked upon the roof of the king's house: and from the roof he saw a woman washing herself; and the woman *was* very beautiful to look upon.

In the absence of seeking God and use of the ordinary means (kings going off to battle), David fell into temptation and sin. As a result, his assurance was greatly shaken.

We confess that we have sin and corruption remaining within us, yet the Confession speaks here of notable sins that **incur God's displeasure, and grieve His Holy Spirit.** In this situation, a sinner then comes **to be deprived of some measure of their graces and comforts.** Having one's graces and comforts diminished is a subjective state. Falling into sin, they may **have their hearts hardened, and their consciences wounded.** Towards God, they incur displeasure by grieving the Holy Spirit, depriving themselves of some measure of grace and comfort. Within themselves, their hearts are hardened, their consciences are wounded, and they **hurt and scandalize others, and bring temporal judgments upon themselves.** Temporal judgment may come to the point of physical death, as Scripture says of those who partake of the Lord's Supper unworthily, "For this cause, many are weak and sickly among you, and many sleep."[3] A person may have sin in their life, aggravate their

---

2. *2 Samuel 11-12; Psalm 51.*

3. *1 Corinthians 11:30.*

sin by unrepentantly coming to the Lord's table, and bring judgment upon themself as a result.

Did the people of Israel in the wilderness lose their salvation? Many think they did. Aaron died in the wilderness along with many others. They did fall into grievous sins. Some of them were struck down. Some of them were not believers, but some of them were. We may not be able to say in any particular case who was a believer and who was not. They brought temporal judgments upon themselves, but did they fall away from the state of grace? Phrasing the question that way makes us want to say yes, because there is an obvious sense in which they fell away from the state of grace. But the critical question is: *did they totally and finally fall away from the state of grace?* Do we see how the question of degree of grace comes in? The question of whether a believer can be utterly destitute of the seed of God and the life of faith will be revisited in section 18.4. All of the Israelites in the wilderness ended up in the spiritual wilderness, and some died in a state of unbelief. Even when there are appearances to the contrary, the truth of the perseverance of the saints still stands. Perseverance of the saints is a doctrine that is commonly neglected and denied in the greater part of the Christian community. Basing our beliefs upon experience leads to the abandonment of sound doctrine.

Perseverance of the saints includes those whom God has accepted, effectually called, and sanctified. Yet, how do we know who they are? Some people profess outwardly and then fall away from their profession. Did they have grace to begin with? We may not always know for sure. We can look at the end of a person's life and conclude that they seem devoid of faith. On the other hand, as in the case of David, we see instances of a person who made a profession, was truly called, seems to have fallen away, but has not totally fallen away. Biblical examples oppose experience-based theology.

SUMMARY ANSWER

In the state of grace, there are varying degrees of grace mitigated by sin and temptation. Through the temptations of the world, the flesh, and the devil, believers may fall into grievous sins— Aaron, Moses, David, Solomon, Peter—where they grieve the

Holy Spirit, hurt and scandalize others, and bring temporal judgments upon themselves.

Chapter 18

OF THE ASSURANCE OF GRACE AND SALVATION

IF WE DO NOT BELIEVE IN THE PERSEVERANCE of the saints, it will be difficult to believe in the assurance of grace. In the ancient Christian world, some people delayed baptism until the time of death because they thought grace comes through baptism that may be applied at death to ensure salvation. Some of the ancients did not have a proper understanding of these doctrines. Many people begin with the assumption that we cannot have assurance because we do not know what will happen in the future, and one could fall away. They therefore think that anyone that claims to have assurance is presumptuous. They think, there is no perseverance, therefore, all talk of assurance is presumptuous. Now, ask yourself: Do you have assurance of faith? Do you know that you are a Christian? And if so, on what basis? These are subjective questions. You may acknowledge perseverance of the saints, but you may wonder whether you ever came into the state of grace, or whether you will persevere in grace. Assurance of grace is subjective assurance that you are in, and will remain in, the state of grace.

On the other hand, there are many who are presumptuous about assurance of grace. There are some people who claim to be saved that are not actually saved, as Scripture affirms: "Many will say to me in that day, Lord, Lord, have we not prophesied in thy name? and in thy name have cast out devils? and in thy name done many wonderful works? And then will I profess unto them, I never knew you: depart from me, ye that work iniquity."[1] Today, it may come out, "My parents

---

1. *Matthew 7:22-23.*

are Christians, I was raised in the church, and I attended church all the days of my life. I even sang in the choir." This is the sort of profession and attitude that needs to be addressed in chapter 18 of the Confession.

QUESTION 79

Is the assurance of being in a state of grace presumptuous?

I. Although hypocrites and other unregenerate men may vainly deceive themselves with false hopes and carnal presumptions of being in the favor of God, and estate of salvation (which hope of theirs shall perish): yet such as truly believe in the Lord Jesus, and love Him in sincerity, endeavoring to walk in all good conscience before Him, may, in this life, be certainly assured that they are in the state of grace, and may rejoice in the hope of the glory of God, which hope shall never make them ashamed.

For some people, the assurance of being in a state of grace is not presumptuous. Those who **truly believe in the Lord Jesus, and love Him in sincerity, endeavoring to walk in all good conscience** have good reasons for their assurance, which is not a small thing. They may attain assurance in this life. There is much false hope and false assurance in the Church because people rest on a faulty foundation. Nevertheless, false hope does not nullify real assurance.

SUMMARY ANSWER

The assurance of being in a state of grace is not presumptuous for some. It is not presumptuous for them who truly believe, sincerely love God, and endeavor to walk in good conscience before Him.

QUESTION 80

On what factors is the infallibility of assurance based?

II. This certainty is not a bare conjectural and probable persuasion grounded upon a fallible hope; but an infallible assurance of faith founded upon the divine truth of the promises of salvation, the inward evidence of those graces unto which these promises are made, the testimony of the Spirit of adoption witnessing with our spirits that we are the children of God, which Spirit is the earnest of our inheritance, whereby we are sealed to the day of redemption.

The Confession affirms that there is a basis for the certainty of our salvation. Some people wrestle much to find this certainty. Martin Luther had no assurance, and in the sacramental system that he held to, he could not have assurance. His struggle with assurance led him to search for and eventually find it, but it required a reformation of the system. It is also true that some people, on the basis of Arminian theology, cannot have assurance. They claim assurance is possible, but subjectively, they cannot attain it, which leads to an inconsistent theology. Both Roman Catholic sacramentalism and Arminianism struggle with the doctrine of the assurance of salvation.

There are three factors on which the infallibility of assurance is based: (1) **the divine truth of the promises of salvation;** (2) **the inward evidence of those graces unto which these promises are made.** The inward graces include believing, having faith, repentance, obedience, walking in love, increasingly obeying the law of God, and seeing the inward evidences of these graces by which the promises are made. This is the objective Word, and we have the subjective awareness that these graces are operating in us by the testimony of the Holy Spirit of adoption. And (3) **the testimony of the Spirit of adoption witnessing with our spirits that we are the children of God.** The Holy Spirit working with the Word enables us to know the promises, see the evidence, and make the connections to come to the certainty of assurance. Certainty cannot be achieved apart from these promises and evidences.

It is commonplace at funerals for people to claim, "This person has gone to a better place." People who make this claim often do not consider the many assumptions and implications involved. Many people tend to deceive themselves about salvation, and therefore, do not give heed to true repentance and faith. How many people have, by means of deception, avoided hearing the gospel? Avoiding hearing the gospel on the basis of self-deception has serious consequences. We should ask ourselves: On what basis do I believe that I am saved? This is not a question about how we are saved, but whether we are saved? Can you identify the scriptural promises of salvation? Can you see the grace of God working in your life? Do you see, at a subjective level, the connection between the scriptural promises and God working in your life? Is the Spirit of God working in you to call God "Father"? Some people call God "Father" without the grace of God operating. Did the Jews call God "Father"? Some encourage everyone to call God "Father," as in, "The fatherhood of God and the brotherhood of men." We must distinguish between calling God "Father" in general, and calling God "our Father" in the Spirit, through Christ. To call God "our Father" requires us to recall the promises of God. We do not want to separate calling upon God as "Father" from understanding the truth about His fatherhood. If we go through the process of understanding the truth of the promises while having a saving understanding of them, with the grace of God in our life, and the Spirit of God enabling us to see and call upon God, we will have the certainty of the truth of the promises of God and have certainty of our salvation. Certainty is consequential, and we should have it because the promises are true.

SUMMARY ANSWER

Infallibility of assurance is based on the following factors: the truth of the promises of salvation, the inward evidence of those graces, and the testimony of the Spirit of adoption.

QUESTION 81

Explain the necessity, means, obligation, and effects of assurance.

III. This infallible assurance does not so belong to the essence of faith, but that a true believer may wait long, and conflict with many difficulties before he be partaker of it: yet, being enabled by the Spirit to know the things which are freely given him of God, he may, without extraordinary revelation, in the right use of ordinary means, attain thereunto. And therefore it is the duty of everyone to give all diligence to make his calling and election sure, that thereby his heart may be enlarged in peace and joy in the Holy Ghost, in love and thankfulness to God, and in strength and cheerfulness in the duties of obedience, the proper fruits of this assurance; so far is it from inclining men to looseness.

Assurance of salvation is not necessary for being saved, and while we are obligated to have it, assurance is not present in every believer. We can be a believer and not have infallible assurance, as the Confession affirms, **this infallible assurance does not so belong to the essence of faith, but that a true believer may wait long, and conflict with many difficulties before he be partaker of it.** We may be a believer and not have assurance, yet there is an obligation to have this assurance. The Confession continues, **yet, being enabled by the Spirit to know the things which are freely given him of God, he may, without extraordinary revelation, in the right use of ordinary means, attain thereunto.** The means of assurance are spoken of as ordinary and not extraordinary. Assurance of salvation is not reserved for a special category of people, but it is for those who, by the Holy Spirit, use the ordinary means. The Confession declares, **And therefore it is the duty of everyone to give all diligence to make his calling and election sure.** The Apostle Peter gives a specific command "to make your calling and election sure."[2]

---

2. *2 Peter 1:10.*

Not "sure" in the sense of securing it eternally, but sure to ourselves subjectively. It is often the case that someone who hardly reads Scripture and perhaps does not attend church regularly, says: "I have always believed in Jesus Christ. I am a Christian." They make this claim, but they have not been assured. They may be a believer, but they do not have a basis in their lives to claim to be a Christian. Is it appropriate for someone who attends church as an adherent to be asked: Are you a Christian? Why do you think that you are a Christian? Do you understand the promises? Do you see evidence of the grace of God in your life? Oversight must examine people seeking to join the church to see that they are making a credible profession of faith. The response of the adherent is not to become defensive and ask: "Well, who are you to judge me?" Those who claim to be a believer must make use of the ordinary means for a credible confession of faith.

Many errors arise by seeking assurance by the wrong standards. Some during the colonial period thought the blessing of God was identified with diligence in one's calling. Success in this world was taken as the blessing of God. The blessing of wealth was identified as a mark of election.[3] Some may look for a special feeling or experience as a mark of election. We devise false standards instead of the right use of ordinary means. Assurance of salvation is not essentially connected to faith. We may partake of many difficulties and wait long, but anyone who is a true believer and lacks assurance will be troubled by it and will diligently use the ordinary means. The Confession says one may **wait long.** Perseverance in uncertainty is not casual, it requires active seeking and searching the Scriptures.

I have heard some say that they do not think they are Christian even though they have the marks of being a Christian. A person may arrive at this belief by being hyper-critical of themselves. They lack a certain peace and assurance because they do not feel the love of God. A person may resolve in their mind: "If God damns me, then to God be the glory." This sort of lack of assurance may be mixed with a degree of low self-esteem. A person may believe, "Nobody loves me, nobody could love me, and God does not love me." A person may be caught up in a form of perfectionism and think that they can only be loved if they are

---

3. Max Weber, *Protestant Ethic and the Spirit of Capitalism* (Saint Louis: Forgotten Books, 2017).

sinless. These feelings may become exaggerated when a person encounters trials, "Whom the Lord loves He chastens, sure . . ., right . . ., He must really love me!" People have moments of doubt, and so the Confession says, **therefore it is the duty of everyone to give all diligence to make his calling and election sure, that thereby his heart may be enlarged in peace and joy in the Holy Ghost.** We are not merely to grit our teeth and bear it. As we have assurance, we have peace and joy in the Holy Ghost. With assurance comes love and thankfulness towards God, and **strength and cheerfulness in the duties of obedience,** which are **the proper fruits of this assurance.**

We should notice that peace and joy are in the Holy Ghost, and do not originate in our natural consciousness. Some may have "Charismatic" peace, joy, and assurance apart from the Holy Ghost. We need to discern between the Holy Spirit and the human spirit. Assurance of salvation results in **love and thankfulness to God.** Someone who does not have assurance and does not know the love of God is not likely to have love for God. Lacking love for God, a person may act out of duty in deontology, or they may act cheerfully in performing their duties but this cheerfulness does not emanate from their love for God. Love and thankfulness are some of the effects of assurance, and we will not manifest those effects without assurance. We may try to fake love and thankfulness, but without the reality it will not last. For example, Pelagius believed that unless people felt that they had to work to earn their salvation and that they could lose it, they would become relaxed and casual in the faith. To bring earnestness into a person's life, we must not allow the presumption of assurance without seeing the effects of peace and joy in the Holy Ghost, love and thankfulness of God, and cheerfulness in obedience and good works. Our response in faith is to affirm that we love God because He first loved us.

SUMMARY ANSWER

Necessity: We can be a believer and not have awareness of assurance of salvation. Means: The right use of ordinary means as opposed to extraordinary means given to a special people. Obligation: To give all diligence to the use of ordinary means. Effects: Peace and joy in the Holy Ghost, love and thankfulness of God, and cheerfulness in obedience and good works, which are the fruits of assurance.

QUESTION 82

How and to what extent may assurance be shaken?

IV. True believers may have the assurance of their salvation divers ways shaken, diminished, and intermitted; as, by negligence in preserving of it, by falling into some special sin which wounds the conscience and grieves the Spirit; by some sudden or vehement temptation, by God's withdrawing the light of His countenance, and suffering even such as fear Him to walk in darkness and to have no light: yet are they never so utterly destitute of that seed of God, and life of faith, that love of Christ and the brethren, that sincerity of heart, and conscience of duty, out of which, by the operation of the Spirit, this assurance may, in due time, be revived; and by the which, in the meantime, they are supported from utter despair.

We may work long and hard, or wait long and come through many difficulties, before we are partakers of the assurance of salvation. Yet, having partaken of assurance, we may lose the assurance of salvation, without losing salvation itself. A person's assurance may be **shaken, diminished, and intermitted**—notice the degrees—**by negligence in preserving of it, by falling into some special sin which wounds the conscience and grieves the Spirit; by some sudden or vehement temptation, by God's withdrawing the light of His countenance, and suffering even such as fear Him to walk in darkness and to have no light.** Consider the example of Job who was pressed to the point of cursing the day on which he was born while being the most righteous man in his day. In our Christian walk, we often hear stories about people that turn away from God because of difficulties of their life.

There is an account of a missionary couple who went to a village in Africa. The wife died in the mission field, and the husband turned away from God in bitterness and gave himself up to drinking. When the wife died, their daughter was given up for adoption. Eventually, the daughter discovered who her parents were, went back to Africa, and found her mother's grave. The mother's grave was held sacred by the people that lived in the village because through her parents' ministry, a boy that traded eggs was taught by her mother, became a believer, and later a teacher in the village. Through the boy's witness, the entire village, including the leadership, converted to Christ. The mother's legacy came to be revered by the locals. When the daughter found the effect that her parents' witness had, she searched for her father to relate her findings. The daughter brought the good news to the father, who had fallen into despair. She showed him the fruit of their labor by bringing him to the village. His assurance was shaken, diminished, and intermitted for a time, and in due time he was revived.

As we get older, we have to struggle harder to find hope. We are familiar with the characterization of the bitter old man. He is bitter because as time goes by, the things that he hoped for did not come to pass. Old men especially have to struggle to keep hope, **yet are they never so utterly destitute of that seed of God,** that is, the Word of God implanted in them by regeneration, **and life of faith.** They never outwardly renounce and denounce Christ. They never fully lose the **love of Christ and the brethren, that sincerity of heart, and conscience of duty,** however diminished they may be. This is where the objective side of perseverance in the faith and the subjective diminished assurance come together, **out of which, by the operation of the Spirit, this assurance may, in due time, be revived; and by the which, in the meantime, they are supported from utter despair.**

Assurance can be greatly diminished in our own lives as well as in the lives of our brothers and sisters. In times of doubts of assurance, we are called to discern: Was this person ever a believer? Or is this person a believer whose assurance has been shaken? We do not always know, but we can say that the Lord calls us to have certainty of our assurance of salvation. He shows us the way we should walk, and walking thus is how we have assurance. We do not have to figure out whether or not this person was really ever a believer or not; at any given time, someone is unsure. Objectively, we have the way of life through Christ before us. We are to embrace Him and walk in the gospel. The question becomes more focused: How and to what extent can assurance be shaken? Assurance may be shaken to the point of perplexity but not utter despair. Paul speaks of being perplexed but not in despair.[4] We may be struck down, but not cast out. We carry about in our bodies the marks of our Lord Jesus Christ.

SUMMARY ANSWER

The assurance of salvation can be shaken, diminished, and intermitted by negligence, grievous sin, or God withdrawing the light of His countenance—examples: Job, Elijah, Peter, etc. Although our assurance may be shaken to the point of perplexity, yet not utter despair such that we outwardly curse and renounce Christ.

The unpardonable sin is a sin against the Holy Spirit by persistently attributing to the devil the work of the Spirit. A sin unto death is a sin in which God terminates our life.

---

4. *2 Corinthians 4:8-10.*

Chapter 19

OF THE LAW OF GOD

THERE ARE DISPUTES IN THE BODY OF CHRIST regarding the law of God. The Jews, historically, have tried to be accepted before God through obedience to the law. Saul of Tarsus is a case in point. Luther raised objections to the sacramental system where justification comes from a combination of works and grace. Today there are disputes regarding the teaching of Paul on justification and whether justification is through infused or imputed grace.[1] This dispute is not to be settled by looking at the words of the New Testament. The idea of imputation is what is at stake. Is there such a thing as imputation? We first encounter the doctrine of imputation in Adam being our representative head, and his sin is imputed to all by natural generation. Christ is the second representative head, and His righteousness is imputed to believers. The idea of imputation is inferred this way. There is a powerful tendency to approach salvation through the law, yet such an approach, known as legalism, while claiming to be very strict in adherence to the law, it is anything but strict when it comes to the real meaning of the law. Jesus said: "Unless your righteousness exceeds that of the scribes and the Pharisees you will by no means enter into the kingdom of heaven."[2] Legalism does not get us to the strictness of the law.

The other side of legalism is called antinomianism—the opposite of law. *Anti-nomos* is anti-law. Legalism goes to the right and antinomianism to the left. Both are errors in understanding the law. These two basic errors about the law are widespread and rampant in the Church. One of the ways in which we can see they are rampant is that believers do

---

1. N. T. Wright, *Justification: God's Plan & Paul's Vision.* (Downers Grove: Ivp Academic, 2016).
2. *Matthew 5:20.*

not understand and apply the law in all areas of life. What if believers understood and obeyed the law? What would be the discernible outcome? The Church would be the head and not the tale of the culture, and the world would come to believe. We have to seriously consider the effects of legalism and antinomianism in understanding the law.

QUESTION 83

What is the original character, content, and consequence of God's law?

I. God gave to Adam a law, as a covenant of works, by which He bound him and all his posterity to personal, entire, exact, and perpetual obedience, promised life upon the fulfilling, and threatened death upon the breach of it, and endued him with power and ability to keep it.

The covenant of works is the context in which the law was originally given to Adam. The law of God is written on the hearts of all men and it is through the law that the covenant of works was to be obeyed. The Lord established the covenant of works to establish mankind in a permanent relationship. It was an act of condescension on the part of God to bless mankind.

Besides the original context, what else applies to the character of the law? Notice how the Confession states the character of the law is **personal, entire,** and **exact.** Let us look at each of these aspects of the character of the law. The law is **personal**, having to do with a personal relationship between us and God. How do we respond to God as a person? Not how do you personally respond to the law, but how do you personally respond to God? We are to see the difference. In obeying all the Commandments, we are responding to not just a principle but a person.

The law is **entire**, in terms of its breath. It is **exact**, being very particular, yet comprehensive. The law encompasses the entirety of our life in breadth and depth. We are to meditate on the law so as to strive for the deeper meaning of the commandments. There is a superficial meaning to "Thou shall not kill." And then Jesus brings out the depth of meaning in calling our brother *raca,* which is equivalent to murder.[3] There is a surface level of "do not commit adultery," which is sexual/outward; there is a deeper level of the meaning of the command including indulging in lustful thoughts, and there is a spiritual dimension of adultery where we love the creature more than the Creator. The law is **personal, entire,** and **exact.** It gets down to details. And we should be able to distinguish between the precepts and ordinances of God.

The law is *universal,* for all men, because it is in all men according to their nature. It is perpetual, there is no other standard. The law was the original standard that continues to be the standard. There is no standard that is higher; none that supersedes it.[4] Some juxtapose the law and love, seeing them in conflict. Is love higher than the law? Or are law and love one and the same? We are to love God with all our heart and love our neighbor as ourself. This is the law and the Commandments. We have the law of God given to Adam; it is given in his heart, and it is given to all men. Every human being has the law written on their heart.[5] Therefore, it is universal. It is perpetual for all time, and there is no higher standard. It is total for all areas of life and spiritual in terms of all depth.

The *unity* of the law is where the personal character of the law is seen. Obeying or not obeying is our response to God. The unity of the law is such that if we break it at one point we are breaking it in all points.[6] Finally, the law is *teleological*—goal oriented.

What should we say to Immanuel Kant or to John Stuart Mill who try to speak of ethical standards which aim at duty or happiness apart from God? Kant's theory allowed for conflict between moral laws. How do we choose between competing moral duties in Kantian ethics? For example, we promised to hold a gun for a friend and give it to him when he asks for it, but he wants to use the gun to shoot his wife. Do we keep the promise, or do we save her life? Kant does not see the law teleologically, as goal oriented and understood in relation to the good.

---

3. *Matthew 5:22.*

4. Gangadean, *The Westminster Catechisms,* 222-225.

5. *Romans 2:14-15.*

6. *James 2:10.*

The law is *teleological* and *doxological*. It is focused on the good as the knowledge of God and giving all glory to God.

The Confession sketches the character, content, and consequence of the law. The content of the moral law written on the heart is the same as the Ten Commandments, which is a summary of all that God requires of us. The consequence of obedience to the law brings spiritual life, and the consequence of disobedience brings spiritual death. These consequences were the original consequences in the Garden and were expressed in two ways symbolized by the two trees (the tree of life and the tree of the knowledge of good and evil), and the spiritual reality of the law continues since.

SUMMARY ANSWER

Character: the covenant of works is the context in which the law was given. It is personal: relating to God as a person. Entire: encompasses all areas of life. Exact: specific implications to every thought, word, and deed. Perpetual: forever, for no higher standard replaces it nor supersedes it for the law is the same as love. Universal: for all men, since it is in all men, it is given in our natures—written on our hearts. Total: every area of life. Spiritual: comprehends all depths of life. Teleological: goal oriented. Doxological: to give all glory to God. Content: the same as the Ten Commandments, which is a summary of what God requires of us. Consequence: Obedience brings spiritual life, and disobedience brings spiritual death.

QUESTION 84

What is the relation of this law to the law given at Sinai?

II. This law, after his fall, continued to be a perfect rule of righteousness; and, as such, was delivered by God upon Mount Sinai, in ten commandments, and written in two tables: the first four commandments containing our duty towards God; and the other six, our duty to man.

Dividing the law into duties towards God and towards man is one approach to understanding the law, but we do not want to simply insist on this approach. Clearly, there is a prominence of the focus on God in the first four commandments and the focus on man in the last six. But sin is always against God. If you steal, this sin is not only against man but against God. Sin against God and man are intimately connected.

The law given at Sinai is the same as that given in all men's hearts. Do we factor into our worldview that the moral law is clear, comprehensive, and critical? As part of our worldview, we are to understand and apply the law to all areas of life, including political theories, ideologies, and responsibility for knowing. That the law is written on the hearts of all men and that we are responsible for knowing the law is unequivocally true. To what extent do we uphold human dignity as made in the image of God with the capacity and responsibility for knowing? Is this part of our thinking? We must work into our thinking and worldview that the law is written on the hearts of all men, it is the same in content as the Ten Commandments, it is universal, and we must understand all its implications.

The Confession affirms these standards and implications. These are not things that we are teaching on our own; it is present in this great document passed down to us. The Confession affirms that the law given in the hearts of all men is the same as the one given to Moses as summed up in the Ten Commandments.[7]

SUMMARY ANSWER

The moral law is one and the same as the Ten Commandments.

QUESTION 85

What is the purpose and permanence of the ceremonial and the civil law?

III. Beside this law, commonly called moral, God was pleased to give to the people of Israel, as a church under age, ceremonial laws, containing several typical ordinances, partly of worship, prefiguring Christ, His graces, actions, sufferings, and benefits; and partly, holding forth divers instructions of moral duties. All which ceremonial laws are now abrogated, under the New Testament.

IV. To them also, as a body politic, He gave sundry judicial laws, which expired together with the State of that people; not obliging any other now, further than the general equity thereof may require.

Besides the Ten Commandments, God gave many other laws. The Ten Commandments were specially delivered, spoken directly by God, written on stone tablets, and given to Moses. But God gave other laws that are called civil laws (pertaining to the nation of Israel) and ceremonial laws (pertaining to the temple and worship). We thus make the distinction between the moral law, the civil law, and the ceremonial law. While the term "law" encompasses all of these, how do we relate the moral law to the civil and the ceremonial laws? What were their purposes?

First, the ceremonial law was given to the people of God **under age**, because Christ had not yet come, and it reveals some of the fullness

---

7. *Deuteronomy 30:11-14; Romans 2:14-15.*

of the law. The Confession says, **ceremonial laws, containing several typical ordinances, partly of worship, prefiguring Christ, His graces, actions, sufferings, and benefits; and partly, holding forth divers instructions of moral duties. All which ceremonial laws are now abrogated, under the New Testament.** Worship through sacrifices was a typological ordinance tied to the shadow. The types and shadows were done away with when Christ came. We do not bring animal sacrifices any more. The system of going into the Tabernacle, into the Holy of Holies, and sprinkling the blood of the lamb once a year is done away with. And the priesthood that administers in that system has likewise been done away with. This does not mean they are completely done away with. We should inquire into the permanence of the ceremonial and the civil law. What was in type and shadow is done away with, but when the reality comes, the reality abides. For example, Christ has now entered the most holy place, into heaven itself, with His own blood. That is an abiding truth. Imagine that someone has a picture of you, but the picture is not the reality. They treat the picture with special care and reverence, looking at it, and imagining all kinds of things. It would be strange for them to continue to treat the picture with care and reverence with you—the reality—in their presence. What you would expect is that the picture is put aside once the reality has come. In that sense, there is an abiding and permanent reality. The kosher food laws and ceremonial cleansing are done away with, but the point being taught in those laws remains. There is a permanence to what is being taught, but the outward way in which it is practiced is done away with. We affirm there is permanence in the ceremonial law. The substance remains, while the outward form vanishes.

Section 19.4 affirms the same permanence to the civil law. **To them also, as a body politic, He gave sundry judicial laws, which expired together with the State of that people; not obliging any other now, further than the general equity thereof may require.** Whereas the ceremonial law guided worship, the civil law includes applications of the moral law to civic life. For example, how should the law treat adulterers? In the Old Testament, adulterers were to be stoned. Remember the instance of the woman caught in adultery and Christ was approached: "Master, this woman was caught in the act of adultery. Moses in the law commanded us, that such should be stoned: but what do you say?"[8] And Jesus said: "He that is without sin among you, let him cast the first stone."[9] So the question is: Should we stone adulterers today? How about rebellious teenagers? How about witches? The Confession affirms there is a principle in the civil laws that must be kept.

It is important to understand the context that justified excommunication by death in the Old Testament. Excommunication was from the State and the Church. That is why it was by death. The boundaries of the State and the Church were one and the same in the Old Testament. The same number of members in the people of God (the Church) was the same number in the State. The exact number. Are we in the same context today? Are the Church and the State one and the same in terms of members? No, something changed with the New Testament. We are to keep the principle of excommunication, but it is not excommunication by death. Today we still excommunicate people from the State by death (murderers, rapists, etc.). Excommunication by death is to be done through the State only. Excommunication from the church is to be practiced but applied differently in light of the change in context. The State today bears the physical sword whereas the Church bears the spiritual sword.

How does the general equity thereof apply to adulterers in the State today? In the Old Testament, they were killed and therefore were dead. Today, we do not actually kill adulterers, but we may treat them as if they were dead. For example, dead people do not have visitation rights with their children. Dead people have no property rights. So the moral law upholds the general equity of the civil law by affirming that the adulterer leaves the marriage without any personal rights concerning the children or any property rights. The principle is upheld, while the application differs in light of the context. Wisdom and understanding are required to discern the general equity of the civil law.

Segments of the Church from time to time have tried to put the Old Testament civil law into practice. This is where the practice of witch burning arose. The Old Testament civil law practiced the execution of homosexuals, adulterers, and rebellious teenagers. We do not stone people anymore. Rather, there are natural sanctions inherent in

---

8. *John 8:4-5.*

9. *John 8:7.*

breaking the law, the first of which is spiritual death. Yet, there may also be civil sanctions, such as physical death carried out by the State. The law carries certain sanctions.

The moral law is what we need as the source of unity within and among human beings.[10] All human beings can unite on the basis of this and no other law. The law starts with the first commandment. Yet, not everyone will agree on the first commandment, which is why the Westminster Divines make a distinction between the first four and the last six commandments. Still, those last laws are written on the heart of all men and can be the basis of civil law today. All human beings can be called to obey the second tablet of the law. Particularly, we can apply those laws as they more immediately pertain to our relations with one another.

So where is the world heading? We are coming together, but we are struggling. What laws will prevail? The more believers understand the moral law and how it applies, the more we can speak it and teach it to all nations. That is the purpose and permanence of the civil and ceremonial laws. We are not to make the Old Testament civil law binding upon all in society, as the Confession affirms, **He gave sundry judicial laws, which expired together with the State of that people; not obliging any other now, further than the general equity thereof may require.** Theonomists seek to require the sanctions of the Old Testament civil law in contemporary society. The Confession does not affirm the teaching of the Theonomists. The Confession upholds the general equity of the law but not the particular laws themselves.

SUMMARY ANSWER

The law of God encompasses the moral law, ceremonial law, and civil law. The ceremonial law prefigures Christ's graces, actions, sufferings, benefits, and some moral ordinances. There is a permanence in the ceremonial law; what is a precursor (types and shadows) is done away with when the reality comes—it remains perpetually in Christ.

---

10. Gangadean, *Philosophical Foundation*, 171-183; Gangadean, *On Natural and Revealed Theology*, 33-39.

The civil law is the moral law applied contextually. Although the law is perpetual, its application is contextual. The union of Church and State contextualized the application of the moral law in Israel. When the context changed, so did the application of the law. In the NT, the Church is distinct from the State. Although the application of the law varies with context, the substance or equity of the law continues in perpetuity. The application of the moral law requires wisdom and the use of good and necessary consequence to faithfully apply the law of God to every context and circumstance. In wisdom, the law is applied in the concrete particular.

Examples of continuity of substance and general equity are adultery, rebellious teenagers, excommunication, etc.

QUESTION 86

What obligation is there to the moral law under the gospel?

V. The moral law does forever bind all, as well justified persons as others, to the obedience thereof; and that, not only in regard of the matter contained in it, but also in respect of the authority of God the Creator, who gave it. Neither does Christ, in the Gospel, any way dissolve, but much strengthen this obligation.

We are obligated to obey the law, both for its content and for the one who delivered it, both under the Old Testament as well as under the gospel in the New Testament. The obligation to obey the law is for believers and unbelievers. Christ does not in any way dissolve the law for those under Him in the gospel, **but much strengthen this obligation.** There is a greater obligation to obey under Christ, which is easy to affirm until we hear objections being raised. We may have heard the expression, "We are not under law; we are under grace. Christ has freed us from the law." This is antinomianism. In order to address this objection, we have to look at the law in terms of its context.

We previously addressed the context of the law in discussing the character, content, and consequence of God's law.[11] We now return to the question of context in the question raised about law and grace. There is a law, and there is a context in which the law is to be regarded. The context may change, but the law remains the same. The proper context is not law or grace, but rather the covenant of works or the covenant of grace. The law remains the same under the covenant of works and the covenant of grace, but there is a difference from one context to the other. Thus, the Confession affirms that the law **forever binds all,** which is another way of saying that the law is perpetual because it is written on the hearts of all men. Section 19.5 of the Confession is written in opposition to those who try to make a distinction between law and grace.

SUMMARY ANSWER

There is a full obligation to the moral law under the gospel. The law remains the same, although the context differs. The Confession opposes antinomianism which claims that we are under grace and not law—where the law no longer applies.

---

11. *See Question 83.*

QUESTION 87

Of what use is the moral law to the true believer?

VI. Although true believers be not under the law, as a covenant of works, to be thereby justified, or condemned; yet is it of great use to them, as well as to others; in that, as a rule of life informing them of the will of God, and their duty, it directs and binds them to walk accordingly; discovering also the sinful pollutions of their nature, hearts, and lives; so as, examining themselves thereby, they may come to further conviction of, humiliation for, and hatred against sin, together with a clearer sight of the need they have of Christ, and the perfection of his obedience. It is likewise of use to the regenerate, to restrain their corruptions, in that it forbids sin: and the threatenings of it serve to show what even their sins deserve; and what afflictions, in this life, they may expect for them, although freed from the curse thereof threatened in the law. The promises of it, in like manner, show them God's approbation of obedience, and what blessings they may expect upon the performance thereof: although not as due to them by the law as a covenant of works. So as, a man's doing good, and refraining from evil, because the law encourages to the one, and deters from the other, is no evidence of his being under the law; and, not under grace.

The law has always been, and will always be, the standard and rule for life, which does not change, though the context changes from the covenant of works wherein we are accepted by God through our own efforts, to the covenant of grace wherein we are accepted by the imputed righteousness of Christ. What is the use of the law under the covenant of grace and the gospel? The law informs believers **of the will of God, and their duty, it directs and binds them to walk accordingly; discovering also the sinful pollutions of their nature, hearts and lives; so as, examining themselves thereby, they may come to further conviction of, humiliation for, and hatred against sin, together with a clearer sight of the need they have of Christ, and the perfection of** his obedience. The law shows us our true condition. Part of our condition is that we harbor hostility in our hearts towards the law of God. We are confronted with the law, and because the law says "do not do it," there is something in us that wants to do it, as Paul affirms when he says, "The law entered, sin revived, and I died."[12] Again, "For what I want to do, I do not do, but what I hate, I do."[13] This attitude shows something about our true condition and brings conviction upon us, humiliation for and against sin, and makes us aware of the need for Christ. The law is not only the standard to direct us, but the law exposes our actual condition and our need for Christ. We recognize how perfect His obedience was when we see how far short we come.

Furthermore, the law **is likewise of use to the regenerate, to restrain their corruptions, in that it forbids sin: and the threatenings of it serve to show what even their sins deserve; and what afflictions, in this life, they may expect for them, although freed from the curse thereof threatened in the law.** This section of the Confession speaks of the curse that comes from the covenant of works. Because of the change in context, believers are freed from this curse. In Christ, we are no longer under the covenant of works. The content remains the same, but the context has changed.

The Confession goes on to say the law restrains believers in sin and shows them **what afflictions, in this life, they may expect for them, although freed from the curse thereof threatened in the law. The promises of it, in like manner, show them God's approbation of obedience, and what blessings they may expect upon the performance thereof: although not as due to them by the law as a covenant of works.** Please note the distinction between the *context* of the law and the *content* of the law. I hope that it can help you move beyond the difficulty there has been in those opposing law and grace. There is no conflict between law and grace in the Scriptures, but there is a conflict between the covenant of works and the covenant of grace and the law in each of them. They are different and distinct. So do not confuse the *content* with the *context*. And just using those two words has helped me to clarify what I want to think and communicate about this difficulty.

---

12. *Romans 7:9.*

13. *Romans 7:15.*

There are afflictions that result for not obeying the law. But these afflictions are not part of the law as the covenant of works. It is not the curse. We understand the curse somewhat differently, as we have previously spoken. Believers have a different motivation for obeying the law of God. We obey out of love for God. Our motive for obedience is not justification or to avoid condemnation. We must notice that the context of the law also affects our motive for obedience.

SUMMARY ANSWER

The law provides several uses for the believer: It is a rule of life to inform us of our duty and the will of God; it further directs and binds us to obedience; it shows us our true condition; it cultivates hatred against sin; and raises awareness of our need for Christ. It also restrains the corruption of the believer and manifests God's approbation and blessing upon obedience.

QUESTION 88

What is the relation between law and grace?

VII. Neither are the forementioned uses of the law contrary to the grace of the Gospel, but do sweetly comply with it; the Spirit of Christ subduing and enabling the will of man to do that freely, and cheerfully, which the will of God, revealed in the law, requires to be done.

The Confession sees no tension between law and grace. We may put it this way: The law shows us our need for grace, and grace enables us to keep the law. This is a quick, easy, fairly tight connection between the two. The law shows us our need for grace, but that is not the end of the law. Grace enables us to keep the law. There is no tension between grace and law. There is a tension between the law in the covenant of works and the law in the covenant of grace. There is a difference in the *context*, and there is an opposition between the two, but not in the *content*. The conflict lies between the covenant of works and the covenant of grace. The content, context, and motives connected with each ought to be distinguished. Under the covenant of works, we act righteously to fulfill the requirements of the covenant—to attain justification. Under the covenant of grace, obedience is done as an act of reverence and love for God—not to attain justification. The context affects the motive.

SUMMARY ANSWER

There is no tension between law and grace. The law shows us our need for grace; in turn, grace enables us to keep the law. Law leads us to grace, and grace leads us to law. The law and grace are in harmony. There is no conflict between the law and grace.

Chapter 20

OF CHRISTIAN LIBERTY, AND THE LIBERTY OF CONSCIENCE

QUESTION 89

In what does Christian liberty consist?

I. The liberty which Christ has purchased for believers under the Gospel consists in their freedom from the guilt of sin, and condemning wrath of God, the curse of the moral law; and, in their being delivered from this present evil world, bondage to Satan, and dominion of sin; from the evil of afflictions, the sting of death, the victory of the grave, and everlasting damnation; as also, in their free access to God, and their yielding obedience unto Him, not out of slavish fear, but a childlike love and willing mind. All which were common also to believers under the law. But, under the New Testament, the liberty of Christians is further enlarged, in their freedom from the yoke of the ceremonial law, to which the Jewish church was subjected; and in greater boldness of access to the throne of grace, and in fuller communications of the free Spirit of God, than believers under the law did ordinarily partake of.

Christian liberty is a blessing from Christ. Liberty in Christ was purchased for believers under the gospel, which is why it is titled "Christian liberty" not liberty of believers in general. We are to notice the particulars of section 20.1 and address them one by one. The first three go together and include, **freedom from the guilt of sin, the condemning wrath of God, and the curse of the moral law.** The Confession then speaks about being **delivered from this present evil world, bondage to Satan, and dominion of sin.** The world, Satan, and their own sinful nature are enemies of believers. Christian freedom includes freedom from those things having dominion over us. In addition, we have freedom from **the evil of afflictions.** Afflictions can work for good or evil. In our natural state, affliction is seen as evil. By the grace of God, we are freed from that form of affliction and can view affliction as God's chastening or correcting. We are freed from **the sting of death.** Though believers die physically, yet the sting of death as spiritual death is removed. In Christ, the sting of death is removed, in that we shall be raised from the dead in newness of life. We should have that glorious liberty of the children of God unhindered by sin—the victory over the grave and everlasting damnation. We may speak of the **evil of afflictions, the sting of death, the victory of the grave, and everlasting damnation** as going together. In addition, Christians, as against believers under the Old Testament, have **free access to God, and their yielding obedience unto Him, not out of slavish fear, but a childlike love and willing mind.**

The Confession continues, **under the New Testament, the liberty of Christians is further enlarged, in their freedom from the yoke of the ceremonial law.** We no longer have to bring an animal sacrifice to the Temple every time we need to confess our sin. Christians are freed of the yolk of **the ceremonial law, to which the Jewish church was subjected; and in greater boldness of access to the throne of grace, and in fuller communications of the free Spirit of God, than believers under the law did ordinarily partake of.** Notice the words **ordinarily partake of.** Some did partake of the Spirit of God in the Old Testament, but ordinarily, most did not. Since the Spirit was poured out at Pentecost, we do not have to go through the priest to come to God. Christ is our mediator. We do not have to go through the sacrifice; we freely come to the very throne of God by His grace.

SUMMARY ANSWER

Christian liberty consists of the following blessings: freedom from the guilt of sin and the condemning wrath of God; the curse of the law; deliverance from the enemies of the believer—the world, the flesh, and the devil; the evil of afflictions, since we can discern the benefit of affliction in chastising; and the removal of the sting of death by resurrection unto eternal life. Under the new covenant in Christ, we have free access to God and freedom from the ceremonial law.

QUESTION 90

What is the basis of true liberty of conscience?

II. God alone is Lord of the conscience, and has left it free from the doctrines and commandments of men, which are, in anything, contrary to His Word; or beside it, if matters of faith, or worship. So that, to believe such doctrines, or to obey such commands, out of conscience, is to betray true liberty of conscience: and the requiring of an implicit faith, and an absolute and blind obedience, is to destroy liberty of conscience, and reason also.

God created within us the inward guide of conscience. Conscience can, and often does, bring condemnation and shame. We need to reckon with the reality of justice and how it operates, and not overextend or underestimate it. Instead, we should heed what is stated in the Confession, **God alone is Lord of the conscience**, and in God, the Lord of conscience, we have true liberty of conscience. Special attention must be paid that God is the Lord of conscience and that conscience is not lord. This requires further explanation: We are never to go against our conscience, but if our conscience permits something, that does not mean we should do it. If conscience forbids us from doing something, we should not do it. Conscience is a negative guide, not a positive guide. Violating one's conscience results in sin. Conscience can be misinformed due to being conditioned by upbringing. Yet, as a negative guide, we should not violate conscience even when it is misinformed. This does not mean we should follow conscience if it does not forbid us. We can and should inform our conscience through the Word of God and the use of the ordinary means.

Another ethical dimension of conscience concerns how we relate with those of weaker conscience. Paul instructs us to use Christian liberty to build up a brother or sister with a weaker conscience. Many occasions give rise to making judgments, and we differ over eating, drinking, or even celebrating holidays. In all of our differences, we are to remember that God alone is Lord of conscience, and we are free from the imposition of human beings. The Confession says that we are **free from the doctrines and commandments of men, which are, in anything, contrary to His Word.** Thus the Church cannot bind us on whether we should eat meat or observe certain days. Because God is the Lord of conscience, we are **free from the doctrines and commandments of men** on matters **of faith, or worship. So that, to believe such doctrines, or to obey such commands, out of conscience, is to betray true liberty of conscience: and the requiring of an implicit faith, and an absolute and blind obedience, is to destroy liberty of conscience, and reason also.** For example, some United States justices would swear total obedience to the Pope in matters of doctrine and ethics. We are not supposed to bind our conscience that way. That **is to destroy the liberty of conscience, and reason also.**

The law is a guide for liberty, and it is not to be obeyed out of slavish fear. The basis for true liberty is that God is the Lord of conscience, and we are not bound by anything other than or besides His Word. Suppose someone says that women should wear head coverings. There is a place in the Word that says women should cover their head, yet, it has been interpreted differently by the Church. One believing this may become quite distressed due to the requirements of their conscience. Occasionally, someone will raise a concern regarding freedom of conscience, expecting others to acquiesce. What if someone believes that you should not use contraceptives? Is this what the Lord commands? If not, then one's conscience is bound by something other than the Word. People are prone to making rules and regulations that usurp the commands of God, but this must not be allowed. Much care must be taken before we seek to bind the consciences of others. What about courtship? Should we court or date? These kinds of questions must be addressed in light of the revealed will of God and the moral law. What is central is that God is the Lord of conscience; He left us free from the doctrines and commandments of men, which are anything contrary to His Word, and besides it in matters of faith and worship. If courtship is called for in the Word of God, we will learn to put it into practice. If it is not, we may have to go through a process of discussion to settle the question and determine whether or not it is consistent with the moral law and prudence.

God is the Lord of conscience, and therein lies liberty of conscience. Some people make rules and regulations regarding worship, others do not. Should we sing only the psalms in worship? Should we read from the *Book of Prayer*. The Puritans did not bind the conscience in these matters. There are many occasions for discerning the lawful pursuit of Christian liberty. Some people relax Christian liberty, and some make it stringent. If you read the Scriptures and are convicted that something is wrong, you should not do it. Whatsoever is not of faith is sin.[1] If you think something is wrong before God, and while believing it is wrong you still do it, then you are not showing respect for God, and, therefore, you have sinned. This is what it means to say the law is personal. If your conviction grows, then your conviction must undergo the process of discussion before seeking to extend what you have been convicted of to others. The process of much discussion, particularly with those who have been placed in authority over you in the church, is important so as not to act out of zeal without knowledge.

We must be mindful that the Christian Church did not come into existence overnight; that many attempts have been made to impose the doctrines and commandments of men on the church, yet responses have been given, and we are to build upon that cumulative insight. This church did not just wander into doctrine; we adopted what is revealed in the three foundations of general revelation, special revelation, and the Historic Christian Faith, to settle disputes. Exclusive psalmody is one of the practices deduced from the light of nature, from the regulative principle of worship, and from historic practice. It is an old practice, though it may be new to people today. Many currently disputed topics will have to be examined, discussed, and provided justification for from the philosophical, theological, and historical foundations.

SUMMARY ANSWER

God is the Lord of conscience. Conscience is not lord. Conscience is a negative guide, not a positive guide. We should never go against our conscience, but if our conscience approves, it does

---

1. *Romans 14:23.*

not mean it is right. Conscience can be wrong because it is subject to the measure of our understanding/faith. Conscience can and should be informed. Our conscience is bound to the Word of God alone and not to any man or church.

QUESTION 91

How is Christian liberty abused?

III. They who, upon pretense of Christian liberty, do practice any sin, or cherish any lust, do thereby destroy the end of Christian liberty, which is, that being delivered out of the hands of our enemies, we might serve the Lord without fear, in holiness and righteousness before Him, all the days of our life.

We are to remember that God frees us from the power and penalty (condemnation) of sin. Yet, we may abuse Christian liberty by using it to indulge our sin. We may, **upon pretense of Christian liberty** practice sin. People often indulge their lusts in the name of liberty. Again and again this has been done in the history of the Church. In the name of Christian liberty, some have used "love" as an excuse to allow for self-indulgence. They may justify themselves with the thought, "God is a God of love. He is very accepting and does not require the same standards as in the past." Christian liberty is abused when used to indulge in sin. The general principle to be followed to avoid man-made rules, and to avoid indulgence, in that whatever is done must be done unto edification.[2] What is done unto edification is what is done for the glory of God.[3] For example, the question of whether to drink alcohol has led to many discussions in the history of the Church. Some have used alcohol for self-indulgence while claiming to use it unto the Lord, while others have forbid the use of alcohol to indulge their self-righteous legalistic tendencies by binding the conscience of others. Both

---

2. *1 Corinthians 14:26.*

3. *1 Corinthians 10:31.*

abuses can and should be discerned by the general rule of God's glory and edification. Our concerns and lifestyle should have everything to do with bringing all glory to God.

SUMMARY ANSWER

Christian liberty is abused when liberty is used to indulge in sin and not used unto edification and the glory of God.

QUESTION 92

How is Christian liberty related to civil and ecclesiastical authority?

IV. And because the powers which God has ordained, and the liberty which Christ has purchased, are not intended by God to destroy, but mutually to uphold and preserve one another, they who, upon pretense of Christian liberty, shall oppose any lawful power, or the lawful exercise of it, whether it be civil or ecclesiastical, resist the ordinance of God. And, for their publishing of such opinions, or maintaining of such practices, as are contrary to the light of nature, or to the known principles of Christianity (whether concerning faith, worship, or conversation), or to the power of godliness; or, such erroneous opinions or practices, as either in their own nature, or in the manner of publishing or maintaining them, are destructive to the external peace and order which Christ has established in the church, they may lawfully be called to account, and proceeded against, by the censures of the church (and by the power of the civil magistrate).

Given that we have liberty, what is the proper place for the rule of authority in the Church and in the State? Christian liberty and the authority that is ordained by God are not opposed. They are not intended to destroy each other, but to mutually uphold one another. They complement one another in the good. Notice that Section 20.3 speaks about the pretense of those who indulge their sin in the name of liberty. Section 20.4, addresses the pretense of liberty in the outward manifestation ecclesiastically and in civil law. The Confession warns, **they who, upon pretense of Christian liberty, shall oppose any lawful power, or the lawful exercise of it, whether it be civil or ecclesiastical, resist the ordinance of God.**

Christian liberty is not against lawful authority in the Church or the State. There may be, and often is, unlawful authority in the Church. Unlawful authority may become authoritarian when it does not rule by the Word of God and asserts authority without insight. Lawful authority always leads by the standard of the law of God. Lawful authorities are not to be opposed under the **pretense of Christian liberty.** The peasant revolt during the Reformation is an illustration of opposing ecclesiastical and civil authority under the pretense of Christian liberty. In addition, **for their publishing of such opinions, or maintaining of such practices, as are contrary to the light of nature, or to the known principles of Christianity (whether concerning faith, worship, or conversation), or to the power of godliness; or, such erroneous opinions or practices, as either in their own nature, or in the manner of publishing or maintaining them, are destructive to the external peace and order which Christ has established in the church, they may lawfully be called to account, and proceeded against, by the censures of the church.** Lawful authority is not opposed to Christian liberty, whether in the Church or the State. But we need to reckon with the reality of unlawful authority. Even in doing so, we must be careful. For example, civil authority may not be lawful, yet, it is one thing if it does not require me to violate the law, while allowing others to violate the law (e.g., abortion). It is another thing if it requires me to break the law. If civil law should require us to commit abortion, then it must be resisted. Similarly, requiring us to bow down to Caesar must also be resisted. Christian liberty does not permit believers to do that which is contrary to the revealed will of God. But if something is lawful but does not require you to sin, then you must submit to legitimate authority. For example, submission is required in the husband-wife relationship. A husband may do things that are not according to the law of God, but he may not require his wife to sin. The moment that he requires her to sin, she goes against the law of God. In addition, the wife cannot yield to obeying what is sinful in the name of keeping the peace. The moral law, as the revealed will of God, provides the basis and parameters by which we are to judge what is lawful or unlawful.

SUMMARY ANSWER

Christian liberty is not opposed to lawful authority in the Church or State. Lawful is that which is in accordance with the law of God.

Chapter 21

OF RELIGIOUS WORSHIP, AND THE SABBATH DAY

QUESTION 93

How is worship regulated by general and special revelation?

I. The light of nature shows that there is a God, who has lordship and sovereignty over all, is good, and does good unto all, and is therefore to be feared, loved, praised, called upon, trusted in, and served, with all the heart, and with all the soul, and with all the might. But the acceptable way of worshiping the true God is instituted by Himself, and so limited by His own revealed will, that He may not be worshiped according to the imaginations and devices of men, or the suggestions of Satan, under any visible representation, or any other way not prescribed in the Holy Scripture.

The regulative principle of worship[1] limits worship to the revealed will of God. The justification for the regulative principle of worship is not derived only from Scripture, but it can and should be defended from general revelation.[2] The first part of Section 21.1 says, **the light of nature shows that there is a God,** which is known from reason and general revelation. General revelation also shows that we are to respond

---

1. Appendix 9.
2. Gangadean, "Paper No. 134: Worship, the Sabbath, and the Church," 679-682; Gangadean, "Paper No. 135: On Worship," in *The Logos Papers*, 683-684.

to God through worship. General revelation may be used to teach us other things regarding worship, yet it is limited to the general content of worship. We must rely on special revelation for the specific content of worship that is acceptable to God. The Confession says, **the acceptable way of worshiping the true God is instituted by Himself, and so limited by His own revealed will, that He may not be worshiped according to the imaginations and devices of men, or the suggestions of Satan, under any visible representation, or any other way not prescribed in the Holy Scripture.** In this section, the Confession explicitly defends the regulative principle of worship.

Though we are not going to present a full apologetics for the regulative principle of worship here, we affirm that it is taught in the Scriptures, in the second commandment, the Confession, and the Shorter Catechism.[3] The Old Testament provides examples from which we can infer the regulative principle of worship. The Lord commands Moses, "See to it that you make [the Tabernacle] after the pattern that I showed you in the mountain. Do not add or take away from it."[4] The acceptable way to worship God **is instituted by Himself, and so limited by His own revealed will,** which means the way we worship must be explicitly or implicitly commanded from Scripture. To determine an implicit command requires the use of good and necessary consequence. There are some things that are forbidden in worship, some things that are commanded, and some things that are neither forbidden nor commanded. The regulative principle of worship restricts worship only to what is commanded. It is limited to what is instituted by God, explicitly or by good and necessary consequence. The regulative principle particularly applies to corporate worship. By and large, the modern church has moved away from practices of the Church of the past such as the singing of psalms. Failure to worship God as He is results in distortions in our understanding of God, divisions in the Church, apostasy, cultural decay, and collapse.

---

3. Gangadean, *The Westminster Catechisms*, 59-60, 223-237.

4. *Exodus 25:40.*

SUMMARY ANSWER

General revelation shows there is a God, and we should respond to Him by adoring and worshiping Him in a general manner. The specifics of worship are contained in Scripture. Scripture institutes and limits worship. The regulative principle of worship limits worship to what is explicitly commanded or deduced by good and necessary consequence from Scripture.

QUESTION 94

To whom is religious worship to be given?

II. Religious worship is to be given to God, the Father, Son, and Holy Ghost; and to Him alone; not to angels, saints, or any other creature: and, since the fall, not without a Mediator; nor in the mediation of any other but of Christ alone.

Our tendency is to give some degree of worship to the creature. Roman Catholic theology distinguishes between *dulia, hyperdulia,* and *latria.*[5] The saints, seen as mediators in part, receive a measure of reverence. But the Confession says that reverence is **to be given to God, the Father, Son, and Holy Ghost; and to Him alone; not to angels, saints, or any other creature: and, since the fall, not without a Mediator; nor in the mediation of any other but of Christ alone.** Mary is not a mediator. Strictly, explicitly, the Confession says there is one God and only one mediator between God and man, Christ Jesus, to whom worship is to be given. Worship is to be given to God alone. In the *Book of Revelation,* worship is explicitly given to the Son.[6] Thus, the Son who is with God, is to receive our worship.

---

5. *Latria:* An act of adoration or worship due to God alone. *Hyperdulia:* An act of respect towards the Virgin Mary. *Dulia:* An act of respect towards the saints.

6. *Revelation 5-6.*

SUMMARY ANSWER

Worship is to be given to God alone (not any creature—angels, saints, etc.), and not in the mediation of anyone besides Christ (vs. Mary or saints).

QUESTION 95

What are the requirements in worship for prayer?

III. Prayer, with thanksgiving, being one special part of religious worship, is by God required of all men: and, that it may be accepted, it is to be made in the name of the Son, by the help of His Spirit, according to His will, with understanding, reverence, humility, fervency, faith, love, and perseverance; and, if vocal, in a known tongue.

IV. Prayer is to be made for things lawful; and for all sorts of men living, or that shall live hereafter: but not for the dead, nor for those of whom it may be known that they have sinned the sin unto death.

Prayer is required by God of all men. And to be accepted, it must be made **in the name of the Son, by the help of His Spirit, according to His will, with understanding, reverence, humility, fervency, faith, love, and perseverance; and, if vocal, in a known tongue.** These are required components of prayer and, if lacking, they are sins of omission. We are to approach God as He has prescribed. Our hearts are humbled by realizing that we come short. Notice that the Confession says, **if vocal, in a known tongue.** This requirement rules out praying in tongues. Tongues are not permitted because the practice is not consistent with the nature of prayer.[7]

How does one know if one is praying in tongues or making ecstatic utterances? Praying in tongues is highly intuitive and usually based on experience. Given the subjective experiential approach, correcting

---

7. Gangadean, *On Natural and Revealed Theology,* 223-228.

the practice will be difficult for individuals to work through. Once a person believes they have prayed in tongues they will continue to believe that they pray in tongues. Yet, how do we distinguish what is of the Spirit and what is of the human spirit, such as ecstatic utterances or emotions moving us in a certain way? Paul says: "I thank my God I speak with tongues more than ye all,"[8] and he goes on, "but in the assembly I pray with my understanding."[9] The gift of tongues that Paul references has ceased. He says in 1 Corinthians 13, in the famous love passage, "that which is complete is come and that which is in part is done away with."[10] In Paul's context, tongues plus interpretation was revelation. When the Scriptures are complete, the signs of revelation are done away with. This is similar to the Israelites having manna while they were going through the desert, but when they came to the promised land, manna ceased. The pattern in Scripture is that supernatural events take place at the establishment of the new order, yet after the order is established, those things fall away.[11]

Charismatics claim that *glossolalia* happens today. The charismatics are blazing like wildfire through certain parts of the world. Some think that this is a significant advancement of the Church. How may one explain speaking in tongues in human terms? Speaking in tongues are ecstatic utterances that may occur for some people experiencing certain emotions. People that are not Christians may speak in tongues as well. Some things are of the Spirit, and some things are from the human spirit. Just as there is true prophecy from God, there is also false prophecy from men who think that they are bringing new prophecy (e.g., Muhammad in Islam). The appeal to an experience is not sufficient for belief.[12]

The position the Confession affirms is cessationism.[13] If a person does not speak in the name of God, consistent with the nature of God

---

8. *1 Corinthians 14:18.*

9. *1 Corinthians 14:19.*

10. *1 Corinthians 13:10.*

11. For a more complete response to Charismatic theology, see: Gangadean, "Paper No. 122: Contra Charismatic Distinctive," in *The Logos Papers*, 651-653; Gangadean, *On Natural and Revealed Theology*, 223-228.

12. Gangadean, *Philosophical Foundation*, 26-27.

13. Gangadean, "Paper No. 122: Contra Charismatic Distinctive," in *The Logos Papers*, 651-653; Gangadean, *On Natural and Revealed Theology*, 223-228; O. Palmer Robertson, *The*

known from general revelation, and they do not present a miracle, sign, or wonder which comes to pass, then we are not to believe what they say. For example, in India, Sai Baba did all kinds of miracles, which are supposed to prove that he is an incarnation (Avatar) of Shiva. He claimed to be the first avatar of Shiva. Vishnu had many avatars, but never Shiva. How should we respond? Do we accept Sai Baba's claims? He does not speak consistently with the name of God.

The Confession rules out any prayer for the dead. We are encouraged to pray for the living, for our children, and grandchildren, **not for the dead, nor for those of whom it may be known that they have sinned the sin unto death.**[14] The sin unto death is the persistent denial of the work of the Spirit. It is attributing the work of the Holy Spirit to the Devil. The Pharisees attributed the work of the Spirit to Beelzebub.[15]

SUMMARY ANSWER

Prayer is required by God of all men; it should be made in the name of the Son, by the help of His Spirit, according to His will, with understanding, reverence, humility, fervency, faith, love, and perseverance; and, when in public in a tongue known to the hearer. Prayer is for things lawful, for the living and those who shall live, but not for the dead.

Final Word: A Biblical Response to the Case for Tongues and Prophecy Today (Carlisle: Banner of Truth, 1993).

14. *1 John 5:16-17.*

15. *Matthew 12:22-30.*

QUESTION 96

What are the ordinary and special forms and content of worship?

V. The reading of the Scriptures with godly fear, the sound preaching and conscionable hearing of the Word, in obedience unto God, with understanding, faith and reverence, singing of psalms with grace in the heart; as also, the due administration and worthy receiving of the sacraments instituted by Christ, are all parts of the ordinary religious worship of God: beside religious oaths, vows, solemn fastings, and thanksgivings upon special occasions, which are, in their several times and seasons, to be used in an holy and religious manner.

We are to distinguish between the form and content of worship. The form of worship is known from general revelation, and the content comes from special revelation. This distinction helps provide clarity. For example: singing is the form, the Psalms are the content. General revelation provides the form for expressing praise. From general revelation, we can and should know that we ought to sing unto the Lord and praise God. The content for singing is provided by Scripture in the Book of Psalms.

The reading, preaching, and hearing of Scripture, singing, and administering the sacraments are part of the **ordinary religious worship of God.** In addition to these, some other ordinances not done regularly include **oaths, vows, solemn fastings, and thanksgivings upon special occasions.** This section of the Confession gives us the form and the content of religious worship.

SUMMARY ANSWER

The form of worship comes from general revelation; the content comes from special revelation. Singing is a form of worship (in general revelation); The Psalms is the content of worship (in special revelation). Ordinary religious worship includes hearing and preaching the Word, singing the Psalms, and the sacraments.

QUESTION 97

How is God to be worshiped in spirit and truth under the gospel?

VI. Neither prayer, nor any other part of religious worship, is now, under the Gospel, either tied unto, or made more acceptable by any place in which it is performed, or towards which it is directed: but God is to be worshiped everywhere, in spirit and truth; as, in private families daily, and in secret, each one by himself; so, more solemnly in the public assemblies, which are not carelessly or willfully to be neglected, or forsaken, when God, by His Word or providence, calls thereunto.

Christ, speaking to the woman at the well in Samaria says, "Woman, believe me, the hour is coming when you will neither on this mountain, nor in Jerusalem, worship the Father . . ., God *is* Spirit, and those who worship Him must worship in spirit and in truth."[16] The Confession affirms **Neither prayer, nor any other part of religious worship, is now, under the Gospel, either tied unto, or made more acceptable by any place in which it is performed, or towards which it is directed.** We are not required, as in the Old Testament, to pray towards the Temple in Jerusalem, "But God is to be worshipped everywhere, in spirit and in truth."[17] The content of worshiping God in spirit and in truth is through family devotions **in private families daily,** and through personal devotions **in secret, each one by himself,** and in public assemblies. There may be additional times that God calls us to worship individually or corporately.

16. *John 4:21, 24.*
17. *John 4:24.*

SUMMARY ANSWER

God is to be worshipped everywhere in spirit and in truth—in daily family devotions, personal devotions, and corporately.

QUESTION 98

What is the requirement of time and day for worship under the gospel?

VII. As it is the law of nature, that, in general, a due proportion of time be set apart for the worship of God; so, in His Word, by a positive, moral, and perpetual commandment binding all men in all ages, He has particularly appointed one day in seven, for a Sabbath, to be kept holy unto Him: which, from the beginning of the world to the resurrection of Christ, was the last day of the week; and, from the resurrection of Christ, was changed into the first day of the week, which, in Scripture, is called the Lord's Day, and is to be continued to the end of the world, as the Christian Sabbath.

We are to set aside time to worship God. We are specifically called to set aside one whole day in seven to be kept holy unto Him. The week is instituted by God as part of the creation ordinance. The Sabbath was established as the seventh day of the week before Christ, and it is the first day of the week after Christ. The new cycle, where the Sabbath is the first day of the week, is connected with redemption and the renewal of things. Redemption was completed when Christ was raised from the dead. Thus, we observe the Sabbath rest on Sunday on the basis of His resurrection. God instituted the first Sabbath at the completion of the work of creation, and it is changed when Christ completed the work of redemption in His resurrection. The principle of work and rest remains the same, but the application changed from the last day of the week to the first day because the work of redemption was accomplished on the first day of the week.[18]

SUMMARY ANSWER

One whole day in seven is to be set aside for worship—Sunday. The Sabbath changed from Saturday to Sunday. The principle of work and completion remains. God created in six days and rested on the seventh. Christ accomplished redemption on Sunday.

QUESTION 99

How is the Sabbath day kept holy unto the Lord?

VIII. This Sabbath is then kept holy unto the Lord, when men, after a due preparing of their hearts, and ordering of their common affairs beforehand, do not only observe an holy rest, all the day, from their own works, words, and thoughts about their worldly employments and recreations, but also are taken up, the whole time, in the public and private exercises of His worship, and in the duties of necessity and mercy.

We are to keep the Sabbath with preparation. Part of preparation is coming to worship service on time. We should not let our circumstances and life conditions hinder us. By attending worship on time, we let others know this is part of our preparation. It is noticeable when congregants come in late. It is better to come in late than not, yet what is called for is due preparation. In addition to arriving on time, we are to come with our hearts prepared for worship.

Keeping the Sabbath entails resting from all employment and recreation for the whole day. We rest and let others rest on the Sabbath by not participating in commerce. I do not like bringing up these

---

18. Edwards, Jonathan. *The Perpetuity and Change of the Sabbath* (Classic Domain Publishing, 2014).

particulars, but some of us need to get the particulars in place. We may need to do some works of necessity and mercy on the Lord's Day. Nonetheless, if these things can be done on another day, they should be. The Confession mentions two exceptions for resting on the Sabbath: works of necessity and works of mercy. For example, firefighters, police officers, and people working on the power grid may need to work on the Sabbath. Yet, some people become legalistic about keeping the Sabbath and shut down the electricity in the house. We are not to go to the right or to the left. Remember, the purpose of the Sabbath is to rest from the work of dominion, to know God and make God known, and to rejoice in that work.

The Sabbath is a day to be prepared for the worship service, to be renewed in worship, to confess our sin, and to be renewed in covenant commitment to do the work. When we hear the truth preached, we are to say amen, confess the truth, be obedient, and commit ourselves to doing what is according to the truth.

The Sabbath is an opportunity to reflect on the previous week, how God has led and upheld us, and to anticipate the coming week. The entire day is to be for rest. What a blessing it is to have an entire day of rest. The day is not meant for relaxing and engaging in recreation, but a day set aside to be with the Lord. Keeping the Sabbath is how the Lord renews our focus and our goal. One entire day in seven is set aside to remind us of our origin, destiny, and hope in private and public worship. If we observe the Sabbath with this in mind, the Sabbath will be our greatest source of hope. It is a reminder that just as God completed His work,[19] so we will complete the work of dominion, and in the end the earth shall be filled with the knowledge of the glory of the Lord as the waters cover the sea.[20] Notice how the Sabbath goes back to the beginning in the Garden when the work was completed, and then God rested. It is very likely that if we understand the Sabbath in its fullness and give ourselves to the work, we will make great progress.

---

19. Genesis 2:2; Gangadean, "Paper No. 134: Worship, the Sabbath, and the Church," in *The Logos Papers*, 679-682.

20. *Isaiah 11:9; Habakkuk 2:14.*

SUMMARY ANSWER

We are to order our affairs and prepare our hearts for the Sabbath. We are to abstain from regular work and recreation, taking up the whole day in fellowship and worship. Acts of necessity and mercy are permitted. The purpose of the Sabbath is the completion of the work and rejoicing in the Lord.

Chapter 22

OF LAWFUL OATHS AND VOWS

WITHIN THE CONGREGATION, WE HAVE TAKEN VOWS. The vows that we are most familiar with are: church membership vows, baptismal vows, and marriage vows.[1] In the contemporary context, some may ask, why do we take vows? When are we called upon or required to take vows? What happens when we do not observe our vows? Some people break their membership vows. If they do not break them outwardly, many come short of keeping their vows. Coming short of keeping one's vow is breaking it. Given the pervasive breaking of vows, we may ask: Why take vows at all? In responding to these questions, we must keep the larger context in mind.

QUESTION 100

What is an oath and when is it warranted?

I. A lawful oath is a part of religious worship, wherein, upon just occasion, the person swearing solemnly calls God to witness what he asserts, or promises, and to judge him according to the truth or falsehood of what he swears.

---

1. Appendix 11.

II. The name of God only is that by which men ought to swear, and therein it is to be used with all holy fear and reverence. Therefore, to swear vainly, or rashly, by that glorious and dreadful Name; or, to swear at all by any other thing, is sinful, and to be abhorred. Yet, as in matters of weight and moment, an oath is warranted by the Word of God, under the New Testament as well as under the Old; so a lawful oath, being imposed by lawful authority, in such matters, ought to be taken.

Oaths or vows are a means of declaring the truth by swearing solemnly and calling upon God to witness that what we say is the truth. Vows are required when there is a significant long-term commitment between people. We do not take oaths or vows for a short term relationship. Vows are appropriate for church membership, which is a long-term relationship requiring significant commitment from the parties involved. Exercising oversight within the church body requires significant time and attention. The person coming into the church body is establishing a relationship with the oversight and the rest of the congregation. In taking a vow, we make a definite reciprocal commitment to and with others before God. A significant commitment is the justification for membership vows. Baptismal vows and marriage vows are justified under the same principle. There may be other vows besides these three, but these three vows are most commonly taken within the church.

When we swear, we should swear solemnly, i.e., thoughtfully, with due awareness of the implications. That is why we spell out some of the specifics and administer these vows after due consideration. We allow time for people to become aware of what is entailed in a vow to reflect deeply upon what their commitment means. We ask: Do you understand why vows are needed? Is requiring vows agreeable with Scripture? Is the taking of vows something that we can wholeheartedly commit to? In the relationships of church members, spouses, and parents, we are asserting and promising commitment to the truth, to one another, and to certain duties. In addition, we are asking God to judge us if we depart, which is why we take an oath before God.

The third commandment applies to the taking of vows by stating that we should not take the name of the Lord our God in vain.[2] We are

---

2. Gangadean, *The Westminster Catechisms*, 237-240.

not to lightly and thoughtlessly treat the name of God, for God will not hold him guiltless who takes His name in vain. Keep in mind that we have a lawyer against us, our adversary, the devil—he is a lawyer from hell. He accuses us before the Lord day and night by pointing out our faults and shortcomings. It is not as if God is bound to Satan, but God's justice is called into question if He does not follow through when we call God to witness and hold us accountable for our commitments. When we break our vow, our adversary will seek to expose us. God cannot neglect the breaking of a vow, and "He will not hold him guiltless who takes His name in vain."[3]

The context in which we begin discussing vows is the third commandment. But, more than that, the third commandment encompasses our entire life; it extends to anything by which God makes Himself known, all of His works of creation and providence. The third commandment binds our whole life, from taking a vow, which is the most thoughtful thing we can do, to the ordinary means of daily living. We should be sober-minded and not lightly and thoughtlessly go through life. We must recognize that taking a vow stands at the opposite end of the spectrum of not seeking. On the one hand, our inclination is not to seek, yet God calls us not to be thoughtless and disregard all that by which He reveals Himself. We have to be aware and understand how objective clarity applies to oaths and vows because we are so inclined to be thoughtless. We are so inclined to say and not do and let things slip. We must bind ourselves before God to each other to enter into a long-term relationship. If there were no sin and we did what we said we would do, as Jesus said, "Simply let your 'Yes' be 'Yes,' and your 'No,' 'No,'" we would have no problem, "Anything beyond this comes from the evil one."[4] Vows are necessary because of our sinful propensity to not live according to the Word of God, and our common failure to not live by knowing and acknowledging the truth. For these reasons, we call upon God to witness the truth or falsehood of what we swear. Sometimes we say, "may God deal with me be it ever so severely if I say this and do not do it." We have the explicit statement in the law that God does not hold us guiltless if we take His name in vain.

---

3. *Exodus 20:7.*
4. *Matthew 5:37.*

If we take an oath or vow, we are to swear by the name of God with holy fear and reverence. We are not **to swear vainly, or rashly, by that glorious and dreadful Name.** Nor are we to swear at all by any other thing, for to do so is sinful. The attitude that we ought to have when taking oaths and vows is holy fear and reverence because it is taken in the name of God. The taking of a vow by any other name than God's is not only sinful; it is to be abhorred. Some may attempt to avoid taking vows altogether. In the self-life, one may be inclined to think because a vow is so serious, I better not take it. Or, I better wait until I am near my deathbed before I take a vow to be sure I cannot break it.

Not only does God not hold us guiltless for breaking vows, but those in oversight in the church are to treat persons accordingly. Discipline can and should be brought by oversight if a person breaks their vow in certain respects. The vow for church membership is the basis for church discipline. Thus, vows are warranted under the Old and New Testaments. An oath may be imposed by a lawful authority, which is where we get the question of **warranted** or necessary. Civil magistrates may require an oath or a vow as in cases where we take an oath of allegiance or swear to tell the whole truth in a court of law. Perjury occurs when we break our oath, which we swore not to break. Perjury is more serious than ordinary lying and exists because we are not inclined to live by our oaths and vows.

An oath may be required when we cannot get to the truth, yet we want to settle a dispute. An oath settles a dispute between contending parties by saying, "God be my witness, and may God deal with me be it ever so severely if I am not speaking the truth." There are times when oversight has to require an oath from church members to attest that what they are saying is the truth in a given situation because we are not able to discern it. We ask a person to bind themselves by an oath under the appropriate circumstance. An oath is not required for a minor inquiry. Rather, an oath is required for what has long-term consequences for the welfare of the parties involved and their relationship to the church.

SUMMARY ANSWER

An oath is part of religious worship. In an oath, a person calls upon God to judge him according to what he/she swears. Oaths are taken when there is a long-term relationship and wholehearted commitment between two persons. It is warranted on just occasions: marriage, baptism, and church membership. Oaths are needed because of our sin. An oath is a means to protect ourselves and those with or for whom the vow is taken. God cannot neglect the breaking of a vow—God will not hold him guiltless who takes His name in vain.

QUESTION 101

What is the attitude toward and content of an oath?

III. Whosoever takes an oath ought duly to consider the weightiness of so solemn an act, and therein to avouch nothing but what he is fully persuaded is the truth: neither may any man bind himself by oath to anything but what is good and just, and what he believes so to be, and what he is able and resolved to perform. Yet is it a sin to refuse an oath touching any thing that is good and just, being imposed by lawful authority.

IV. An oath is to be taken in the plain and common sense of the words, without equivocation, or mental reservation. It cannot oblige to sin; but in anything not sinful, being taken, it binds to performance, although to a man's own hurt. Nor is it to be violated, although made to heretics, or infidels.

V. A vow is of the like nature with a promissory oath, and ought to be made with the like religious care, and to be performed with the like faithfulness.

A person's attitude in coming to take an oath or vow must be thoughtful, according to the truth, it must be sworn in accordance with **what is good and just, and what [one] believes so to be.** In addition, one must be **able and resolved to perform** the oath or vow taken. Are we able and resolved to keep our marriage vow? Premarital counseling is needed to see whether the persons approaching marriage are able and resolved to keep the vows they will take. Concerning the content of oaths and vows, the Confession says, **An oath is to be taken in the plain and common sense of the words, without equivocation, or mental reservation.** In our sin, we attempt to ambiguate the meaning of words, and we may dispute every word, making statements such as, "Depends on what the meaning of is, is."[5]

An oath or vow **cannot oblige to sin** or bind us to sin. It can only bind us to **what is good, just,** and what we believe to be so, even to our **own hurt.** Someone may have a different idea about the meaning of the marriage vow. If their idea of the marriage vow is something sinful, it cannot bind us. If we have taken an oath or vow for anything not sinful, we are bound to carry it out, even to our own hurt. We must keep oaths and vows, even if made to unbelievers if it is within the boundary of what is good.

There are times when a person may take an oath or vow and it is overridden by a person(s) in authority. Yet, if the person in authority knows about an oath that has been taken by one under his care, and he allows it to be made, the oath is binding. This principle applies to the headship of a husband over his wife. Before taking an oath, one is to be sure that those in authority are properly informed. A husband may override an oath made by the wife. His consent is required. Similarly, the father has parental authority over his daughter and her decision to take a marriage vow. The Confession continues, **a vow is of the like nature with a promissory oath, and ought to be made with the like religious care, and to be performed with the like faithfulness.** There is a close connection between vows and oaths.

SUMMARY ANSWER

An oath ought to be taken in reverent and holy fear, in the name of God only, thoughtfully, in accordance with the truth, and being able and resolved to keep it. Oaths are not to be for anything sinful, nor are they binding for anything evil. The content of an oath must be taken in the plain and common sense of the words, without equivocation or mental reservation.

---

5. A reference to President Bill Clinton's Grand Jury Testimony as an illustration.

QUESTION 102

What is acceptable and forbidden in an oath?

VI. It is not to be made to any creature, but to God alone: and, that it may be accepted, it is to be made voluntarily, out of faith, and conscience of duty, in way of thankfulness for mercy received, or for the obtaining of what we want, whereby we more strictly bind ourselves to necessary duties; or, to other things, so far and so long as they may fitly conduce thereunto.

VII. No man may vow to do anything forbidden in the Word of God, or what would hinder any duty therein commanded, or which is not in his own power, and for the performance whereof he has no promise of ability from God. In which respects, popish monastical vows of perpetual single life, professed poverty, and regular obedience, are so far from being degrees of higher perfection, that they are superstitious and sinful snares, in which no Christian may entangle himself.

This section of the Confession addresses what is acceptable and forbidden in an oath. A vow is not to be made under coercion. Vows are to be made to God alone, involving nothing prohibited by the Word of God. Outside of baptism, marriage, or membership, we have a certain amount of freedom in taking other oaths or vows. Yet, they should always be taken **in way of thankfulness for mercy received, or for the obtaining of what we want.** In the Scripture, we have the example of Hannah saying, "O Lord Almighty, if you will only look upon your servant's misery and remember me, and not forget your servant but give her a son, then I will give him to the Lord for all the days of his life, and no razor will ever be used on his head."[6] No one required this oath of Hannah, but she freely initiated it. The Confession continues, **no man may vow to do anything forbidden in the Word of God, or what would hinder any duty therein commanded.** Hannah giving her

---

6. *1 Samuel 1:11.*

son unto the Lord was not a necessary duty, yet it accords with other duties. In another example from Scripture, Jephthah violates the qualifications by vowing to the Lord, "And Jephthah made a vow to the Lord: 'If you give the Ammonites into my hands, whatever comes out of the door of my house to meet me when I return in triumph from the Ammonites will be the Lord's, and I will sacrifice it as a burnt offering.'"[7] His daughter came out of the door of his house. A vow is not to be made rashly, and it is only in matters of weight and moment which are necessary. Jephthah's vow was not made in any of these contexts.

Once we bind ourselves in marriage by our vow, irrespective of how unhappy we may be, we are morally obligated to continue in marriage. There are grounds for divorce, but apart from them, we are bound. In the wedding ceremony, the pastor is obligated to mention that the vow is for better or for worse. The content of the marriage vow is there for a good reason.[8] Marriage can be difficult and trying, but under God, we are called to persevere and learn. The Confession addresses the marriage vow, and the vow is to be upheld by the oversight of the church. This explanation should help prospective couples who seek to be married in the church to anticipate the standards set by the moral law, Scripture, and Historic Christianity. The propensity, in our sin, to break our vows necessitates that this issue be addressed in the Confession. The breaking of vows has troubled the church in the past, and it is very relevant to us in our day. It is very good that we have a section like this in the Confession, and we should be thankful for it.

SUMMARY ANSWER

Oaths are to be made to God alone, and oaths cannot be made for anything prohibited by the Word of God.

---

7. *Judges 11:30-31.*

8. I, _____, take you, _____, to be my lawfully wedded (husband/wife), to have and to hold, from this day forward, for better, for worse, for richer, for poorer, in sickness and in health, until death do us part.

Chapter 23

OF THE CIVIL MAGISTRATE

I T IS A GREAT BLESSING THAT THE CONFESSION addresses such topics as the civil magistrate. While we acknowledge that the Confession is not infallible, it is the ordinary means that we use to guide doctrine and life. We need to understand its content, know it well, and not differ with it lightly.

QUESTION 103

What is the origin and function of the civil magistrate?

I. God, the supreme Lord and King of all the world, has ordained civil magistrates, to be, under Him, over the people, for His own glory, and the public good: and, to this end, has armed them with the power of the sword, for the defense and encouragement of them that are good, and for the punishment of evildoers.

The origin of the civil magistrate is from God and for God's glory. Civil magistrates rule for the public good and have the power of the sword. As such, we ought to acknowledge their origin and purpose. We need to be on guard against pietism which tends towards the inward life and tends to play down relations and responsibilities to the State. We should be careful about a pietistic attitude. In contrast, we should note that the civil magistrate is ordained by God. God instituted that office, structured it in our being, and as sin became more manifest, He made the rule of magistrates more explicit after the flood. Yet, the office of the civil magistrate was there before the flood.

Some have questioned whether the civil magistrate is an institution that originated because of the Fall. Given the nature of the sword and its use (which is to restrain evil-doers), it assumes the reality of sin. In this respect, the discussion of the civil magistrate is connected with the sword and the Fall. The Fall is the origin of the institution of the State, unlike the Social Contract theories of John Locke, Thomas Hobbes, and Jean-Jacques Rousseau, where the State originates as a social contract from men coming out of the state of nature. These men speculate about and create constructions of the original state of mankind. There is a biblical and historical reality that accounts for government as ordained by God. Just as marriage is ordained by God, even among those who do not recognize the existence of God, because of the moral law in the hearts of men, so the civil magistrate is another institution that is ordained by God even though the non-believer does not recognize it as such.

SUMMARY ANSWER

Origin: Civil magistrates originated after the Fall to restrain sin (crime). It did not originate in the Social Contract (Locke, Rousseau, Hobbes). Function: Civil magistrates are ordained by God for His glory, and for the public good, and they have the power of bearing the sword (retributive justice).

QUESTION 104

What is the relation of the believer to the State and to war?

II. It is lawful for Christians to accept and execute the office of a magistrate, when called thereunto: in the managing whereof, as they ought especially to maintain piety, justice, and peace, according to the wholesome laws of each commonwealth; so, for that end, they may lawfully, now under the New Testament, wage war, upon just and necessary occasion.

The Christian can serve in the office of a magistrate. The civil magistrate is not to uphold an unwholesome law, i.e., a law that is destructive of human life. Whether a law is wholesome can be known from general revelation. Unwholesome laws that support racism, Nazism, apartheid, and slavery, among others, are not to be upheld by Christians serving as civil magistrates. This also applies to the fetus in the womb. We have to think about the connection between civil laws and the moral law, and determine whether or not a law is wholesome. We are to maintain piety and peace. What does maintaining piety mean? And how much can the magistrate get involved with maintaining piety? Some things are sacred that are not to be desecrated. Some symbols that partake of the reality, like the flag, among other holy things, are often desecrated.

The magistrate is to uphold **piety, justice, and peace, according to the wholesome laws of each commonwealth; so, for that end, they may lawfully, now under the New Testament, wage war, upon just and necessary occasion.** The Confession assumes the idea of a just war. The Confession does not teach pacifism, although some have attempted to say that the early church was pacifist. We need to distinguish the personal passivity of a Christian in the sense of not taking up arms against the State, and those times when citizens are called to serve in the armed forces **upon just and necessary occasions.** In the former, taking up arms is rebelling against the authority established by God; in the latter, one is defending the boundaries of nations as established by God. The State bears the sword, Christians are under the State, and are called to uphold and support it. Responsibility to serve should not obscure the fact that all wars are rooted in the failure to engage in the spiritual war. We should recognize that wars come about because believers have not been salt and light; they have not been waging the intellectual war. Although war results from the accumulated failure to use reason on both sides, there are occasions under which we may wage war justly. Cumulative intellectual failure does not deny the necessity to wage war when just occasion arises.

In the context of citizens being called upon by the State to go to war, a particular individual may be a conscientious objector. A person's conscience may be such that they choose not to bear the sword for particular reasons. For example, ministers of the gospel are called not to bear the sword because of their office. David was not permitted to build the Temple because he had engaged in war.[1] Certain offices are understandably exempt from battle if they wish to be exempt. Historically, this has been practiced.[2] Particular individuals may abstain from war for particular reasons. They may be called to serve in other ways (e.g., the medical corps.). We often hear people speak about war and the evils of war, yet there is a long history of understanding and applying the principles and basis upon which a just war can be waged.

SUMMARY ANSWER

It is lawful for Christians to serve as magistrates to maintain piety, justice, and peace. Christian magistrates can wage war upon just and necessary occasions (vs. pacifism).

---

1. *1 Chronicles 22:8-10.*

2. Currently, chaplains in the United States Military are excluded from bearing arms. They may be present with the troops in battle, but they are not to engage in physical war.

QUESTION 105

What is the relation of the Church and the State?

III. Civil magistrates may not assume to themselves the administration of the Word and sacraments; or the power of the keys of the kingdom of heaven; or, in the least, interfere in matters of faith. Yet, as nursing fathers, it is the duty of civil magistrates to protect the church of our common Lord, without giving the preference to any denomination of Christians above the rest, in such a manner that all ecclesiastical persons whatever shall enjoy the full, free, and unquestioned liberty of discharging every part of their sacred functions, without violence or danger. And, as Jesus Christ has appointed a regular government and discipline in His church, no law of any commonwealth should interfere with, let, or hinder, the due exercise thereof, among the voluntary members of any denomination of Christians, according to their own profession and belief. It is the duty of civil magistrates to protect the person and good name of all their people, in such an effectual manner as that no person be suffered, either upon pretense of religion or of infidelity, to offer any indignity, violence, abuse, or injury to any other person whatsoever: and to take order, that all religious and ecclesiastical assemblies be held without molestation or disturbance.

There is a positive and negative aspect to the role of the civil magistrates in relation to the Church. The negative side of the relationship is what the magistrates are not to do. The magistrates are not to assume religious offices nor hinder the exercise of religious offices and church function. The magistrates are not to hinder the Church in the least. This principle has been violated in many times and places.

Positively, **as nursing fathers, it is the duty of civil magistrates to protect the Church of our common Lord, without giving the preference to any [particular] denomination of Christians above the rest, in such a manner that all ecclesiastical persons whatever shall enjoy the full, free, and unquestioned liberty of discharging every part of**

their sacred functions, without violence or danger. The Confession addresses the relationship between the civil magistrates and the Church particularly in light of conflicts between factions of the Christian church during the Wars of Religion (1618-1648).

The civil magistrates are to protect the Church without giving preference. Some may say that during the St. Bartholomew's Day massacre (1572), the Huguenots were not considered part of the Church and so should not be protected. Yet, according to the Confession, even infidels are to be protected by the civil magistrates. The civil magistrates are not to hinder, but to uphold and help the Church. The point is that the magistrates are not to give preference to any one denomination of Christians above the rest. This is also the sense of the first clause of the First Amendment of the U.S. Constitution that "Congress shall make no law respecting an establishment of religion, or prohibiting the free exercise thereof . . ."[3] The civil magistrates are not to prohibit the free exercise of religion nor establish a religion thereby excluding others. In other words, the civil magistrates are not to do things that tend to the establishment of a religion at the expense of other religions or denominations. This prohibition entails not showing preference, for example, promoting Episcopalians over Lutherans. The State is not to favor any one religion or denomination. The intent of this law is to uphold the Church rather than hinder it. Given the historical context, treatment by the civil magistrates of non-Christians is not addressed in this portion of the Confession. The focus is on magistrates not hindering the Church and upholding the Church.

There are many questions regarding the role of the State in the preservation of piety, particularly in the history of the United States. For example, should the Decalogue be on display in courthouses? Should the phrase "under God" be in the pledge of allegiance? Should prayer be allowed in public schools? Should one be obligated to work on Sunday at risk of losing one's job? To answer these questions we should ask: What is it to maintain piety? And what is it to exercise the keys of the kingdom in the Church? The role of the Church is to disciple its members and bring discipline where there is sin. The role of the State is to bring discipline for crime. The State is not to punish for impiety or sin.

---

3. https://constitution.congress.gov/constitution/

Not establishing one religion over another is like not establishing Anglicanism in England or Lutheranism in parts of Germany and taxing the public to support the religion. Yet, the non-establishment of religion does not mean one cannot mention, or even discuss, God in the public schools. There are applications that may be discussed further, but we have identified the main idea being addressed in this section of the Confession. The State is not to interfere with the exercise of the offices in the church.

The Confession continues, **it is the duty of civil magistrates to protect the person and good name of all their people, in such an effectual manner as that no person be suffered, either upon pretense of religion or of infidelity, to offer any indignity, violence, abuse, or injury to any other person whatsoever.** The State is to protect the person and good name of all their citizens, irrespective of one's religious affiliation, unbelievers included. Furthermore, magistrates are to rule such that **no person be suffered, either upon pretense of religion or of infidelity, to offer any indignity, violence, abuse, or injury to any other person whatsoever.** The Confession is pretty clear, and Section 23.3 is good work that has been practiced historically, upon which we can build.

SUMMARY ANSWER

The State is not to take offices of the church or meddle in matters of faith. It ought to protect the Church without giving preference to any particular denomination or denominations. The State is not to punish impiety or sin; it is to punish crime.

QUESTION 106

What honor is due to the magistrate?

IV. It is the duty of people to pray for magistrates, to honor their persons, to pay them tribute or other dues, to obey their lawful commands, and to be subject to their authority, for conscience' sake. Infidelity, or difference in religion, does not make void the magistrates' just and legal authority, nor free the people from their due obedience to them: from which ecclesiastical persons are not exempted, much less has the pope any power and jurisdiction over them in their dominions, or over any of their people; and, least of all, to deprive them of their dominions, or lives, if he shall judge them to be heretics, or upon any other pretense whatsoever.

The Apostle Paul specifically commands us to pray for those who rule over us.[4] We should underscore that because, in many cases, prayer for our rulers has been treated as an option rather than a duty. It is our duty to pray for those in authority. **To honor their persons** means to speak respectfully to them, and even when we differ, to speak respectfully about them. Believers have a tendency to fall into the pattern of the world where contempt and abuse are cast upon those in authority. The Scriptures say specifically that Michael the Archangel did not speak contemptuously against the devil. He said: "The Lord rebuke you."[5] Therefore, care must be taken to respect authority as established by God. We are not to be casual, and we are not to fall into our own worldly desire to get rid of the authorities who rule over us. In addition, we are not to fall into the worldly thinking that encourages disregard for authority. Believers are not pagans and should not emulate them. We are not rude, backwoods people, which is what "pagan" means. Some in America, such as the frontiersmen, held to a particular view

---

4. *Romans 13.*

5. *Jude 1:9.*

of freedom that exalted autonomy rather than freedom under the law and under the authority instituted by God.

We have the duty **to pray for magistrates, to honor their persons, to pay them tribute or other dues.** We are to obey their lawful commands within the context of God's law. We are to be subject to their authority not merely outwardly, but inwardly before the Lord. If our leaders are infidels or of a different religion, that does not make void the magistrates' just and legal authority. So let us agree among ourselves[6] to hold one another accountable whenever we hear someone making disparaging comments about those in authority. We are not to do that. We are calling attention to the standard so that we can put it into practice, starting among us here and now. If we have not prayed for them lately, do not utter a word about them. Will that help us to become more consistent in submitting to God's sovereign rule through the existing authorities?

The Confession goes on to say, **from which ecclesiastical persons are not exempted, much less has the pope any power and jurisdiction over them in their dominions.** Historically, the rule of the church over the State has been a problem. The highest recognized authority in the Roman Catholic Church is still subject to the civil law. The Pope does not have jurisdiction over the magistrates in their dominion, or over their citizens as such, so as to put them under ban, to restrict communion, or other privileges of the Christian life. Nor can the Pope **deprive them of their dominions, or lives, if he shall judge them to be heretics, or upon any other pretense whatsoever.** Hundreds of thousands died during the wars of religion due this the error of ecclesiastical overreach.

One must exercise wisdom in engaging in and opposing political causes. One must deliberate: Is this the hill that I am willing to die on? Many are prone to identifying instances where the State is undermining other cultural institutions, claiming that this or that as an intrusion. We have to be thoughtful about these claims. There are important issues involved in this section of the Confession that have been covered elsewhere, and we want to keep what has been contended for in the past in mind.[7] Discerning further application of the relationship between

---

6. This statement was made to the congregants of Westminster Fellowship Church attending Pastor Gangadean's original study of the WCF. The intention of the statement is greater unity in the faith.

7. Gangadean, *Philosophical Foundation,* 171-284.

the civil magistrates and the church will require further discussion on a case-by-case basis. What is important is that we have a base in the Confession from which to work.

SUMMARY ANSWER

It is a duty to honor and pray for State leaders and to speak respectfully of them. We are to guard against speaking contemptuously of civil magistrates as the pagans do. We are to obey lawful commands, pray for civil magistrates, and pay taxes.

Chapter 24

———

OF MARRIAGE AND DIVORCE

QUESTION 107

What is marriage and why was it ordained?

I. Marriage is to be between one man and one woman: neither is it lawful for any man to have more than one wife, nor for any woman to have more than one husband, at the same time.

II. Marriage was ordained for the mutual help of husband and wife, for the increase of mankind with a legitimate issue, and of the Church with an holy seed; and for preventing of uncleanness.

The opening line of chapter 24 of the Confession provides answers to questions that we are dealing with today. It also deals with polygamy and polyandry, which are questions that may be on the horizon. **Marriage is to be between one man and one woman; it is monogamous.** That it is so is deduced from the light of nature—the law written on the heart. The definition of marriage as between one man and one woman is exemplified for us in the Scriptures, and the principle is written on our hearts.[1] The nature of marriage is derived from the nature of humans as persons with dignity, made in the image of God, and as a body/soul unity. The origin of our being is from the sexual union of our parents (one male and one female). This definition of marriage is opposed to same-sex marriage or same-sex unions. Marriage in this context is intimately connected with, and not to be separated from, the family. We

---

1. Gangadean, *Philosophical Foundation*, 245-248.

have to keep this context in mind: Marriage is the unit that embodies and produces the family.

To ask, "What about those who cannot have children?" is to raise an exception; let us first establish the rule. To address the exception without first establishing the rule is a red herring. The origin of our being is by virtue of the sexual union of one man and one woman. Is there any question in the mind about that? This does not mean that marriage is always productive of children, but no other relationship is productive. What is being protected in this application of the seventh moral law is the family.

Given recent challenges and the condition of the culture, the Church is called to give an apology in defense of marriage.[2] Proper boundaries acknowledging equality among institutions should be respected. The State cannot redefine the institution of the family, and marriage is part of that institution. Likewise, the family cannot redefine the institution of the State, and neither can the State nor the family redefine the institution of the Church. These institutions are distinct, equal, and have been established and ordained by God. The origin, nature, and function of each institution are structured in our being.[3]

Section 24.2 addresses the question, why was marriage ordained? In understanding the definition of marriage, we must factor in the broader contexts of the family and the work of dominion. Marriage is not only limited to those who can produce children but includes those who can assist in the whole process of nurturing and educating, and all that goes with raising children. Not all people who marry can have children, but they can be involved in nurturing and teaching children, and they may be invested in upholding and protecting the institution of marriage which is productive of children.

The work of dominion requires fruitfulness and increase in number so as to carry out the work of naming and ruling over the creation. God says, "Be fruitful, and multiply, and replenish the earth, and subdue it; and have dominion . . ."[4] The work of dominion necessitates a helper suitable for its accomplishment. Dominion is a work given to all of

---

2. Gangadean, "Paper No. 27: The Limits of the State," in *The Logos Papers*, 165-169.

3. Gangadean, *Philosophical Foundation*, 171-284; Gangadean, *History of Philosophy*, 61-69; Gangadean, *The Westminster Catechisms*, 227-267; Gangadean, *On Natural and Revealed Theology*, 127-139, 166-178.

4. *Genesis 1:28.*

mankind. The Confession includes the statement marriage is **for the increase of mankind with a legitimate issue, and of the Church with an holy seed.** . . . In our fallen nature, we tend to reverse the order of things. A helper suitable is broader than just mutual help—I help you, and you help me. A helper suitable is in the context of what God has called mankind to do, and cannot be separated from that context. Marriage is distorted when not understood in connection to the work of dominion. In the 1950s and 60s, marriage was centered on creating a haven for the husband, where the wife and family sought to make the husband's life comfortable and peaceful. This is self-serving and counterproductive of the good. Distortion of marriage, in that context, gave rise to resentment by women, the rise of feminism, and a discarding and rejecting of a distortion of marriage. Basically, women responded by telling the men, "Go to hell." Men acting in a self-serving way will result in women reacting in a self-serving way, and women acting in a self-serving way will cause men to respond in a self-serving way. As marriage is increasingly separated from the original goal, it goes down the toilet—where waste goes. We need to keep the goal of marriage in mind as well as the results of the failure to do so.

Some mistakenly think the purpose of marriage is having children, and in light of that false assumption, claim that "The more children, the better." This position may be justified by taking out of context the claim that "children are a blessing." Children in the Lord are a blessing.[5] If a couple has more children than for whom they can provide through dominion, they are contributing to overpopulation. The number of children a couple has should be commensurate to the level of dominion that they have achieved. There must be a balance between multiplying and being fruitful and having dominion. These two (fruitful and multiply) should not be separated. Bringing children into the world and educating them well for the work of the kingdom go together. Do you know how much work is involved in educating a child? Do you realize how much work is involved in getting a child to speak? Many students that come to college do not have much of a vocabulary; it is like talking with fourth graders sometimes. Invested, deliberate, sacrificial service is what is required to develop the potential latent in the child so as to engage in dominion. This is achieved by faithful education for many

---

5. Gangadean, "Paper No. 139: The Blessing of Children," in *The Logos Papers*, 701-702.

years. In addition to expanding their vocabulary, you must help them to use reason. "Use reason?" some will ask. "Where does it say that in the Bible?" We know this by good and necessary consequence.

Section 24.2 concludes that marriage is also for the **preventing of uncleanness.** There should be no uncleanness, no sexual immorality. Sex and love constitute marriage, and there is to be no sex apart from love. Love, in terms of commitment, should not be separated from the sexual act. It is unclean to separate the two. This is why Paul says: "It is better to marry than to burn."[6] And, this is why the Confession says marriage is to prevent uncleanness. Sex is never to be separated from love.

SUMMARY ANSWER

Marriage is monogamous—between one man and one woman. The institution of marriage is known from GR and illustrated in SR. No other relationship is productive of the family—children. Marriage is ordained for the mutual help of husband and wife, reproduction, and preventing uncleanness. Yet the most fundamental goal of marriage is dominion for the glory of God. Marriage is to be understood in light of the knowledge of God through the work of dominion. Determining the number of children is proportionate to the level of dominion attained. No institution is total. No institution can redefine another institution. All institutions are established by God with their limits and functions.

---

6. *1 Corinthians 7:9.*

QUESTION 108

Who can marry, and what is it to be married in the Lord?

III. It is lawful for all sorts of people to marry, who are able with judgment to give their consent. Yet is it the duty of Christians to marry only in the Lord. And therefore such as profess the true reformed religion should not marry with infidels, papists, or other idolaters: neither should such as are godly be unequally yoked, by marrying with such as are notoriously wicked in their life, or maintain damnable heresies.

IV. Marriage ought not to be within the degrees of consanguinity or affinity forbidden by the Word. Nor can such incestuous marriages ever be made lawful by any law of man or consent of parties, so as those persons may live together as man and wife.

Section 24.3 of the Confession addresses the question, "Who is permitted to marry?" It is lawful for all persons who are able with sound judgment to yield their consent to marry. We must be old enough to give thoughtful consent. Thoughtful consent includes understanding what the vows mean and entail. In addition, the person administering the vow should know whether those taking the vow understand and are able to keep the vow. Assenting to the marriage vow is not just a bare affirmation; rather, those assenting must be **able with judgment to give their consent.** Is that not a good, succinct requirement? Marriage has to be between a man and a woman, and they must give thoughtful consent. These are the necessary conditions for entering into the marriage relationship.

The Confession continues, **yet is it the duty of Christians to marry only in the Lord. And therefore such as profess the true reformed religion should not marry with infidels, papists, or other idolaters.** In this section, we get a sense of the fight that was going on when the Confession was written. Christians are only to marry other Christians.

Infidels are those who are not believers. And, Reformed Christians are not to marry those who are followers of the religion taught by the Pope or anyone else who is an idolater. Rather than getting into contentions regarding whether a Reformed person marrying an Arminian or a popular believer is a sin, we should consider, minimally, that it is unwise. Rather than emphasizing the minimum in approaching marriage, we should strive for the maximum, which is nothing but a shared vision of the good as the knowledge of God.

The spirit of this section is that we should marry those who share our fundamental commitment. The clearer our long-term commitment is, the more we desire the same in the other. Because, in marriage, after the initial emotions have settled, the fundamental commitment will be manifested. We want to have that in place prior to marriage and not put ourselves in a situation where we are hoping to bring about change in the other person. It is true that love changes things, but it is a love that is patient and long-suffering, which may have to endure for many years before the change comes. Given the reality of fallen human nature, some changes occur quite slowly. We should have that understanding upfront, and if we go through the normal process of getting counsel/wisdom from others (premarital counseling), we will have that understanding.

The last portion of the Confession 24.4 refers to those who should not marry. Incestuous marriages are forbidden.

SUMMARY ANSWER

Only those who share a common view of the good should marry. The more we are aware of our fundamental commitment, the more we desire it in the other. After the initial attraction, the basis for lasting unity lies in the commitment to basic things. Although change in the other is possible, it takes significant time to occur.

QUESTION 109

What are the grounds for divorce and remarriage?

V. Adultery or fornication committed after a contract, being detected before marriage, gives just occasion to the innocent party to dissolve that contract. In the case of adultery after marriage, it is lawful for the innocent party to sue out a divorce: and, after the divorce, to marry another, as if the offending party were dead.

It is noteworthy that the Westminster Divines address the issue of divorce and remarriage. It was an issue in the Church which has continued. They came to these conclusions after much discussion. There are many other views that had to be rejected. Yet, what the Confession says here is the Holy Spirit speaking through the pastor-teachers in the Church. It is not on the same level as Scripture, but the Confession is an ordinary means by which we become established in the faith.

From the time of engagement to taking the marriage vows, one can dissolve the arrangement. After the marriage vows are taken, in the case of adultery, it is lawful for the innocent party to sue out a divorce and after the divorce to marry another **as if the offending party were dead.** The offending party has no rights and no claims in the marriage or estate. By implication, the innocent party can remarry, yet the guilty party is not free to remarry. Today, in the Church, attention must be given to this question. The Church is not free to disregard the teaching that there is a guilty and an innocent party in a divorce. To be married and divorced—on grounds other than adultery or willful forsaking of the marriage bed such as the Church and the State cannot reconcile— is to be guilty and not free to remarry. The guilty party loses certain rights and is to be treated as if they were dead. Dead people do not take with them property, bank accounts, retirement funds, etc. And if there are children, dead people do not claim custody or visitation rights. In this principle, the general equity of the civil law is maintained. We no longer practice excommunication by death, but the general equivalent of excommunication under the moral law is continued by accounting the guilty party as dead. Being the guilty party to divorce invites re-strictions. The guilty party is not absolutely forbidden to remarry, but there are issues that need to be addressed before they can remarry. One cannot simply get remarried. A failed marriage is an outward manifestation that there are deeply rooted problems that must be addressed.

SUMMARY ANSWER

Grounds for divorce are adultery and willful forsaking of the marriage. In adultery and in willful forsaking, the innocent party may remarry, but the guilty party cannot remarry unless the sin is dealt with. Determination of justified divorce under willful desertion must proceed under the consultation of the Church and State.

QUESTION 110

What due process is to be observed in divorce?

VI. Although the corruption of man be such as is apt to study arguments unduly to put asunder those whom God has joined together in marriage: yet, nothing but adultery, or such willful desertion as can no way be remedied by the church, or civil magistrate, is cause sufficient of dissolving the bond of marriage: wherein, a public and orderly course of proceeding is to be observed; and the persons concerned in it not left to their own wills, and discretion, in their own case.

The institutions of the Church and the State are invested in the insti-tution of marriage (family), which is why the due process observed in a divorce includes both the Church and the State. We are married both in the Church and in the State. It is not right to be involved in a church community and leave the church during a divorce, as if the church and community were not involved. Leaving a church requires much more.

In the event that our life is threatened by the other, a light of nature implication is that we should seek safety until peace has been restored. Yet, think of what has taken place, or has been neglected, for it to get to the point where one's life is threatened by their spouse. There must have been a certain amount of violation of due process coming into the marriage, and, in desiring a divorce, we hope to escape from the marriage, again, working apart from due process. Instead, those who lead in the church should encourage church members to learn to use the ordinary means which God intended for entering into marriage. The blessings of marriage are connected with the use of ordinary means as God has intended. People may, under certain circumstances, when their safety is threatened, withdraw from a harmful environment. There should be no question about that. But, even then, they should have some counsel and oversight from those in church leadership. To leave a marriage under such circumstances is a separation, not a divorce. During a separation, the couple is to undergo the process of discussion with oversight to see if the offense can be remedied.

Willful desertion is the context in which the brokenness in the marriage can in **no way be remedied by the church, or civil magistrate.** In other words, we have to seek remedies for problems that come up in marriages. Remedies may not just come from the Church, but the civil magistrate as well. There are financial concerns, and lawsuits during a divorce that involve the State. Because the State has an interest in the marriage, the State and the Church should seek to remedy the situation by providing counsel. Generally, the pattern is that the longer we stay married, the longer it takes to get out of a marriage. There are layers of counseling through which we may seek remedies prior to divorce, which include friends, parents, the Church, and the State. They all agreed to the marriage. The State agreed by granting a marriage license; they should be there to aid in times of trouble.

In the case of willful desertion of the marriage, if the other person wants to depart, let them depart. In the case of one party converting while married to an unbeliever, if the unbeliever does not want to live with the believer, then let them go. If a person has a sexual relationship with another while unmarried, on the face of it, they are obligated to marry. But if the other person does not want to live with the other as a believer, the believer must let them go.

Generally, the man is the one that is responsible for the sexual relationship begun prior to marriage. Even though the woman may actively seduce, the man is the one who carries a particular responsibility. This is a point the Church has not emphasized. On the face of it, Exodus 22:16-17 is the rule by which we are operating, which says, "If a man seduces a virgin who is not betrothed and lies with her, he shall give the bride-price for her and make her his wife. If her father utterly refuses to give her to him, he shall pay money equal to the bride-price for virgins."[7] The man has a *prima facie* obligation to marry unless the father overrules in the matter. A man who sleeps with a woman outside of marriage may be restricted by the Church. This restriction is to prevent common licentiousness and sleeping around casually. If these obligations and restrictions were understood, and the community and the Church were operating by them, then people would have to stop and think twice before engaging in premarital sexual relationships. We should not separate sex and love any more than we should separate our body from our soul and dehumanize ourselves. Perhaps you have questions about the passage from Exodus because it is in the Old Testament. What you should do is to inform others by telling them that: "If you sleep with her you are obligated to marry her, and the church is going to hold you to that." Who are we kidding? What games are we playing? This is serious and should be upheld.

How are we to proceed in divorce? We spoke of abuse, procuring counseling, backing up, and learning. There is not only a due process to getting out of the marriage, there is a due process for getting into a marriage. Even to this day, people are still getting hurt from not going through the process of courtship. They may learn from what has happened and not be hurt as much, but we need to go through the process of courtship and marriage. Let us start with the reality of the Fall and "every inclination of the heart is only evil continually."[8] God has called us back through the curse for our sin, self-deception, and self-justification. If we start with that and apply it consistently, then we can relax and not be surprised by sin or be overwhelmed. We should be wise by implementing the ordinances and letting them do the work rather than trying to hold up a dike from flooding us. If we want to see the

---

7. *Exodus 22:16-17*, ESV.

8. *Genesis 6:5.*

Church built up, we have to see discipline brought into people's lives. That is why the Scriptures state again and again to be sure to obey all the Commandments of God. The Lord is teaching us to obey all things whatsoever He has commanded us.

SUMMARY ANSWER

There is a due process for getting married (seek the good for self, seek the good for others, seek the good with others, finding ones compliment, courtship, vows, laws). The Church and the State have a vested interest in preserving and promoting marriage. Divorce is permissible either because of adultery or through the willful desertion of the marriage bed as cannot be remedied by the Church or the State. Counsel must be sought to act in wisdom.

Chapter 25

OF THE CHURCH

THE CHURCH, AS AN INSTITUTION, HAS FALLEN on hard times. People do not recognize the Church as particularly binding, and few churches require membership vows, which used to be a regular practice. Churches are very divided and are in a worse condition today than the Westminster Divines were at the time of the writing of the Confession some 370+ years ago. We desperately need to cling to what they say in this section, reflect on what we need, and apply it to our present-day circumstances. The common habit of our day, of casually joining and leaving a church, is not consistent with discipleship. The Church must be involved in discipleship, and the Church should not be divided. Discipleship and division are the two major issues that we are going to draw out of Section 25 of the Confession.

QUESTION 111

What is the Church invisible and what is the church visible?

I. The catholic or universal Church, which is invisible, consists of the whole number of the elect, that have been, are, or shall be gathered into one, under Christ the Head thereof; and is the spouse, the body, the fullness of Him that fills all in all.

II. The visible church, which is also catholic or universal under the Gospel (not confined to one nation, as before under the law), consists of all those throughout the world that profess the true religion; and of their children: and is the kingdom of the Lord Jesus Christ, the house and family of God, out of which there is no ordinary possibility of salvation.

The Church invisible consists of all the elect in every age that have been, are, and shall be. The key term is the *whole* number of the elect. The Church is catholic. The word "catholic" means universal. The Church is invisible because we do not know who is and who is not elect. We can see who professes faith in the visible church, but the invisible, no one knows. Some people minimize the visible church by claiming that they are a member of the invisible Church, which is a presumptuous claim. The response to this claim is that believers are members of the body of Christ, and the invisible Church does not have membership. Some may claim: "I know that I am elect, there is no question about it." This is a very difficult claim to make because as soon as we say, "I am elect," but not obeying the Word of God by being a member of the visible church, we become suspect. This is the same as saying: "I am elect, but I am not submitted to the authority of the Word of God." We come short, and we deceive ourselves. We should take the doctrine of the Church seriously by understanding what constitutes the invisible Church—all the elect, who **have been, are, or shall be gathered into one, under Christ the Head thereof; and is the spouse, the body, the fullness of Him that fills all in all.** Notice there is an organic connection in **the fullness of Him that fills all in all.** This fullness is the Church invisible.

The visible church consists of all that profess the true religion, and we should add to that—with a credible profession. A credible profession is contrasted with simply claiming to be a believer without showing by word and life that we know and acknowledge the Lordship of Christ in our life. The visible church includes **all those throughout the world that profess the true religion; and of their children: and is the kingdom of the Lord Jesus Christ, the house and family of God, out of which there is no ordinary possibility of salvation.** If we are not members of the visible church, we have no ordinary possibility of salvation. It is problematic for someone to say, "I am a member of the invisible Church, but I do not attend the physical church." According to the Confession, if we are not a member of the visible church, a physical local body, then there is no ordinary possibility of salvation. We are to be a member of a church that professes the true religion. To claim to be a believer and not be under the authority of the truth is inconsistent. The invisible Church includes all of the elect, and the visible church includes all those who profess the true religion and their children. Notice that their children are included, they are part of the kingdom of God. As children mature, they may remain in the church or they may depart. Nonetheless, the ordained way of the growth of the kingdom of God is through covenant children being raised in and remaining in the church.

SUMMARY ANSWER

The invisible Church is the elect throughout history—called invisible because no one knows the totality of who is elected, except for God. The visible church is all those throughout the world that credibly profess the true religion. For those outside the visible church, there is no ordinary possibility of salvation.

QUESTION 112

What is the ministry of the Church?

III. Unto this catholic visible church Christ has given the ministry, oracles, and ordinances of God, for the gathering and perfecting of the saints, in this life, to the end of the world: and does, by His own presence and Spirit, according to His promise, make them effectual thereunto.

What is the purpose of the Church? As an organization, is it necessary? The spirit of the age is opposed to institutions, particularly the Church. The keys of the kingdom of God are the preaching of the Word (gathering for worship), the sacraments, and discipline. These ordinances are given to the visible church, not to the invisible Church. The ordinances of God are given to the Church for the purpose of discipleship, and Christ makes the teaching of the Church effectual by His presence and the presence of the Holy Spirit. This is why church membership is essential. One is not merely to visit the church. One is not to attend for a few years and still not be ready to take vows. The adherence process for church membership is not to be taken lightly. People should attend church, and by the second or third time they visit, they should be considering whether they are going to seek membership. The adherence stage in pursuing membership should be about three months. By the end of three months, if we have been actively seeking, we should be ready for membership. Some cases may take longer because people are not prepared. For example, some may not have an understanding of the Confession and will need to go through a study before taking membership vows. Yet, a person should have sufficient understanding to make a decision regarding church membership within six months of attending and actively seeking to understand through study.

SUMMARY ANSWER

Discipleship requires membership vows and due preparation to make a thoughtful commitment.

QUESTION 113

What determines the purity of a church?

IV. This catholic Church has been sometimes more, sometimes less visible. And particular churches, which are members thereof, are more or less pure, according as the doctrine of the Gospel is taught and embraced, ordinances administered, and public worship performed more or less purely in them.

V. The purest churches under heaven are subject both to mixture and error; and some have so degenerated, as to become no churches of Christ, but synagogues of Satan. Nevertheless, there shall be always a church on earth, to worship God according to His will.

VI. There is no other head of the Church but the Lord Jesus Christ. Nor can the pope of Rome, in any sense, be head thereof.

Doctrine, sacraments, and discipline are often spoken of as the three marks of the true church. This involves public worship and the teaching of sound doctrine. The doctrine taught in a church must be embraced and not merely professed. As believers, our obligation is to find that branch of the visible church—understanding the reality of time and place—which is most pure, to the best of our knowledge, at the present time, and join ourselves to that branch. We judge the purity of a church in terms of doctrine, sacraments, and discipline, which ties them all together. Every Christian is morally obligated to be a member of such a church. We are not free to float from church to church. Notice that there are churches that **are more or less pure.** What is the basis of the doctrine taught in a church? It is not acceptable to say piously: "We just believe the Bible here." Many churches make this claim. The teaching of sound doctrine is based on the work of the pastor-teachers, those who have gone through the process of much discussion, out of which the Confession comes. We are to begin with the Scriptures, and in the history of the Church, if there is a difference between confessions, we are to ask which confession is closest to the Scriptures? We determine which confession to follow by diligently searching the Scriptures. We determine the purity of doctrine by heeding the work of Christ through the Holy Spirit in church history as it was modeled in Acts 15.[1] Christ said that through the Holy Spirit He will lead the Church into all truth, and the work of the pastor-teachers through church history is the process by which He does this.

The work of the pastor-teachers includes the Jerusalem Council in 50 AD, the Apostles' Creed, Nicaea, Chalcedon, and several others. The teachings contained in the creeds, councils, and Confession have been professed by the Historic Christian Church through the centuries, and

---

1. Gangadean, "Paper No. 60: The Spiritual War (Part II)," in *The Logos Papers*, 329-330.

is the foundation upon which we are to build.[2] Building on the foundation of Historic Christianity is the ordinary means by which Christ has established His Church and advanced its doctrine. He provided the Church with apostles, prophets, evangelists, pastors, and teachers.[3] Today, pastor-teachers continue the work of leading the Church.

Building on the Confession is the ordinary means for the Church to grow and the kingdom to advance. We are not to be boastful, yet we believe that the Confession is the last and most comprehensive confession of the Reformation era.[4] Therefore, the Confession is the high-water mark of Christian doctrine to date. Throughout history, we see the principle of pastor-teachers working in church history to respond to challenges. The Confession is the latest, clearest, and fullest work of the pastor-teachers. And so, in wisdom, we should build upon the Confession. The adoption of the Confession in a congregation has nothing to do with the person choosing it, whether we appear humble or proud, but it is about building on the cumulative insight embodied in the creeds, councils, and confessions. Adopting the Westminster Standards is the ordinary means to becoming established in the faith both as a church and for the individual believer. We need to think this principle over for ourselves, understand it, and believe it. Secondly, we need to bring this principle into focus for others. This is gradual idealism. It takes time to get the truth well established in our minds and then repeat it to others until they understand. We can come to understand. And, once we have gotten it well settled in our minds, once we are really convinced, the steps are as definitive as when presenting the argument that there must be something eternal.[5]

Christ said the Holy Spirit will lead us into all truth.[6] We see in the example of Acts 15, along with other examples in the history of the Church, the way in which He leads. It was after much discussion that "it seemed good to us and to the Holy Spirit," the truth was established,

---

2. Appendix 3.

3. *Ephesians 4:11-13.*

4. The WCF is the fullest confession in that while there have been other confessions after 1648, those confessions built upon the WCF, as did the Second London Baptist Confession (1689). The SLBC built upon the Westminster Confession and dropped a few key points.

5. Gangadean, *Philosophical Foundation*, 61-68.

6. *John 16:13.*

and the word was sent out to the churches.[7] The process of much discussion is how the Holy Spirit leads the Church into all truth. Furthermore, the Spirit leads in response to heresies and challenges. The Scriptures say, "For there must be also heresies among you, that they which are approved may be made manifest among you."[8]

The Confession is a historical document responding to historical challenges. History continues, and new challenges arise. New challenges need to be responded to, thus we should expect that future confessions will build upon the Confession and answer new challenges in light of what came prior. We believe in conciliar Christianity, which consists of church councils of elders, and that is why Westminster Fellowship Church is Presbyterian in doctrine. Presbyterianism is expressed both in doctrine and in the form of church government. Before we can speak of being Presbyterian in judicial form, we must be Presbyterian in doctrine. Before we speak of Presbyterian in discipline, we must be Presbyterian in doctrine. The more basic is expressed in doctrine.

There are challenges that have developed since 1648, and the Church needs to respond to those challenges. It will require a certain amount of work to bring these challenges to the attention of the broader Church. We will have to publish works that will raise many questions, and when the discussion gets heated enough, the need for resolution will be seen, and serious discussion will begin. Discussion is begun by making the issues known in a relevant way, not by the spirit of creating conflict. The whole period of Modernity (1650-1945) and of Postmodernity (1945-) needs to be addressed.[9] We can identify the challenges: the doctrine of clear general revelation vs. every form of non-theistic thought; faith vs. reason and the very nature of religion; the Church's otherworldliness vs. the this-worldliness of secular thought; and the good as grounded in human nature vs. all forms of autonomy.

Are there topics in the Confession that need further development? What we need to address is the conflict between good and evil, which is a foundational doctrine that needs further elucidation in the Confession. Root sin is evil understood in its radical form as not seeking, not

---

7. *Acts 15:28.*

8. *1 Corinthians 11:19.*

9. Gangadean, *History of Philosophy*, 131-191; Gangadean, *On Natural and Revealed Theology*, 127-139, 149-165.

understanding, and not doing what is right.[10] The definition of root sin is scriptural, yet it has not received proper attention in the Church, which is understandable, given the noetic effect of sin in man,[11] but it is not excusable. If the definition of root sin as not seeking, not understanding, and not doing what is right takes hold in the Church, in addition to the doctrine of the good as the knowledge of God and the earth being filled with the knowledge of God, then we will overcome many challenges that remain today. The foundational components of understanding good and evil and the goal of the Christian life will enable the settling of many disputes and divisions that have arisen since the Confession. The essential piece is getting it to the table to be discussed. Bringing the topics up for discussion among pastor-teachers within the Church is about 90% of the work; 5% is having discussion and finding agreement among the pastor-teachers by being led by the Holy Spirit; and the last 5% is getting the response to challenges written down to share with all the Churches.

Section 24.5 of the Confession, as well as the Scripture, speaks of churches becoming a synagogue of Satan.[12] These are groups that have denied basic doctrines to such a point that they become synagogues of Satan. This title is not restricted to some denominations within the visible Church. Human beings, being what they are, will go into decline and decay. When this occurs, we need to leave those churches. There are some churches that have openly advocated doctrines concerning sexual immorality. To remain in a "church" that openly endorses sin would be to identify as an apostate, as one that has departed from the true faith. Though many churches wax cold, **nevertheless, there shall be always a Church on earth, to worship God according to His will.** Though the church may degenerate, the Church will never cease to be. The Church becomes sometimes hidden, and less visible, as in Abraham's day, or Elijah's day when he believed that "I alone am left."[13] But there will always be a true church on the earth and we are to join ourselves with it.

---

10. *Romans 3:10-11.*

11. Appendix 7.

12. *Revelation 2:9.*

13. *1 Kings 18:22.*

What is stated in Section 25.6 is very plain and not meant to be disrespectful. To say **nor can the pope of Rome, in any sense, be head** of the Church is over and against the claim that "This is the only church and apart from this church there is no possibility of salvation," which has been a claim of the Roman Catholic Church for centuries. The Confession denies the claim that there is no possibility of salvation outside the Roman Catholic Church. Since some Catholics believe theirs to be the true church, they call for Protestants, "to come home to Mother Church." What we have to inquire about is whether or not Catholics are open to discussing our differences. We can approach this discussion by backing up and asking prior questions: Why should I be a Christian as against a Muslim or a Hindu? Is it clear that God exists? If so, what proof is there? We are to proceed presuppositionally. If we can address more basic questions that have been overlooked by the church at large, then we can address the sources of division between Christian denominations.

SUMMARY ANSWER

The purity of a church is determined by its connection with the Historic Christian Faith, whether it holds to the doctrine passed down by the pastor-teachers being led by the Holy Spirit. Along with doctrine, the sacraments and worship must likewise align. The three marks of the church are the preaching of the Word, the administration of the sacraments, and discipline. It is our moral responsibility to look for and join the church which most closely resembles our understanding of the Holy Catholic and Apostolic Faith.

Chapter 26

OF THE COMMUNION OF SAINTS

QUESTION 114

What is the communion of the saints and what are its obligations?

I. All saints, that are united to Jesus Christ their Head, by His Spirit, and by faith, have fellowship with Him in His graces, sufferings, death, resurrection, and glory: and, being united to one another in love, they have communion in each other's gifts and graces, and are obliged to the performance of such duties, public and private, as do conduce to their mutual good, both in the inward and outward man.

II. Saints by profession are bound to maintain an holy fellowship and communion in the worship of God, and in performing such other spiritual services as tend to their mutual edification; as also in relieving each other in outward things, according to their several abilities and necessities. Which communion, as God offers opportunity, is to be extended unto all those who, in every place, call upon the name of the Lord Jesus.

Sections 1 & 2 of Chapter 26 address the communion that we have with God through Christ. Believers are united to Christ by the Spirit, and by faith, believers have fellowship with Him. There is a union and communion with the Lord. Additionally, believers **have communion in each other's gifts and graces,** and are obliged—notice that word "obliged"—**to the performance of such duties, public and private, as do conduce to their mutual good, both in the inward and outward** man. Believers are given gifts and graces that are brought to fruition by communion with God, and are to be shared in communion with fellow believers. God has given gifts to each one particularly, and those gifts are to be developed and nurtured for the sake of service in the body of Christ. We grow in grace from God by the ongoing communion with other believers. In addition, there are obligations that believers have to commune with and to serve others, both in an inward and outward manner.

Section 26.2 speaks about the communion of the saints. There have been prominent distortions of this doctrine. Communion of the saints is not advocating communalism, where all things are owned in common. In misapplying Acts 2:44, many groups throughout church history have sought to form communities where private property was abolished. Some went so far as to share wives in common. We are not to go to the left (absolute communalism) or to the right (autonomous individualism without regard for others). Believers have a special obligation to assist and support other believers throughout the world—all the more those who are suffering. We have an obligation to the Sudanese Christians, Chinese Christians, Indian Christians, European Christians, and Christians that were under the old Soviet state and who are still living under oppression emanating from the old anti-theist Soviet system. Believers have communion with Christians in all places.

We have an obligation to love our neighbor as ourselves. We are first humans, then we are Christians, and then we can go on from there (male/female, educated/uneducated, etc.). Our first identity is as human beings, and our second is as Christians. Having the identity as human beings and Christians, we have a double responsibility to show mercy to our fellow humans under affliction. The question of how much should be done through the Church in terms of charity and social services is a consideration of wisdom. In general, much more should be done privately than through the government. There are other agencies besides the Church, such as families and non-profit organizations, that can show mercy. The Church, along with other agencies related to the Church, can and should help. For example, Food for the Hungry is not a church, but it is an agency inspired by faith to go out and serve.

There are many ways in which we can and should serve. The government is the last resort. The government has an obligation to encourage and assist private agencies to do their work and not to get involved in and usurp their work. Some may object: "Doesn't the Bible teach that charity should be done through the Church?" Prior and more explicit biblical teaching is that the Church should not be divided. If there was unity in the Church, we would be salt and light, and the culture would not be in the decaying state that we presently see. A unified Church provides the only viable long-term solution against the social ills and afflictions of a culture in apostasy and moral decay. Unfortunately, the Church finds itself in a context where theological divisions hinder the ability to work together. Neither the preemptive work of redeeming the culture nor the practical assistance of those in need can be accomplished by the Church because it is divided. While acknowledging the need to assist others, one should always encourage the unity of the Church so that believers can work together to remedy short and long-term problems. It is the Church that is the pillar and ground of the Truth;[1] it is the Church that provides the basis for a lasting culture built upon the Truth.

SUMMARY ANSWER

There is a union and communion in Christ and with fellow believers. There is an obligation to maintain holy fellowship, partake in spiritual service tending to mutual edification, and relieving them in outward things, according to ability and necessity.

---

1. *1 Timothy 3:15.*

QUESTION 115

What are the errors in understanding the communion of the saints?

III. This communion which the saints have with Christ, does not make them in any wise partakers of the substance of His Godhead; or to be equal with Christ in any respect: either of which to affirm is impious and blasphemous. Nor does their communion one with another, as saints, take away, or infringe the title or propriety which each man has in his goods and possessions.

There are two parts to the communion of the saints: one related to God, and the other to fellow believers. The errors are twofold. The first error is in relation to communion with God. Some people take communion with God to mean we share in God's grace and power. Some segments of the Orthodox Church speak of salvation as "divinization"—becoming divine (*theosis*). The line between God (infinite, eternal, and unchangeable) and man (finite, temporal, and changeable) is blurred.[2] Mysticism also provides an occasion for blurring the distinction between God and man by making an appeal to mystical experiences where God indwells man as mystical ecstasy. This mystical experience is characterized as man becoming divine, a form of the beatific vision in the body. Communion with God does not mean that our being becomes one with God in this sense. We can be one with God in several senses, e.g., ethically, but not ontologically.[3]

The second error is in relation to communion with fellow believers. Some have claimed that Christians should share all things in common, including property, using the practice of Acts 2:42-47 as an example. Yet, that passage, speaking in the context of the early church in Jerusalem, when the Scripture says, "they had all things in common," those who sold their lands could have kept the profits from the sale.

---

2. Gangadean, *On Natural and Revealed Theology*, 9-39.

3. Gangadean, *History of Philosophy*, 40.

Peter says this explicitly to Ananias.[4] What Peter rebuked Ananias for in that passage was his lying about keeping the profit from the sale of the land. He wanted the privilege of public recognition but deceived others through false appearances. Therefore, Acts 2 does not diminish nor deny the legitimacy of private property in the Christian life. Private property should be understood as private stewardship.

SUMMARY ANSWER

People do not attain equality with Christ or the Godhead. This does not detract from private stewardship. Communion is not communalism (sharing all things in common). Communion is with the living and not with the dead, which is prohibited by Scripture. We partake in communion with the dead by partaking in their contribution to the work while they were alive.

---

4. *Acts 5:4*, "Didn't it belong to you before it was sold? And after it was sold, wasn't the money at your disposal? What made you think of doing such a thing? You have not lied to men but to God."

Chapter 27

OF THE SACRAMENTS

QUESTION 116

What is a sacrament?

I. Sacraments are holy signs and seals of the covenant of grace, immediately instituted by God, to represent Christ, and His benefits; and to confirm our interest in Him: as also, to put a visible difference between those that belong unto the church, and the rest of the world; and solemnly to engage them to the service of God in Christ, according to His Word.

As we work for the unity of the faith, we should be mindful that the Church has been divided by different understandings of the sacraments. This is something of importance to be underscored. If the more basic assumptions are kept in mind, we will be able to engage with all the distinctions and divisions that exist in connection with the sacraments. The distinction between sign and reality and the covenant of grace are basic teachings. A sacrament is a sign; it is not the reality. But it is also a seal that confers a definite benefit in terms of assurance of the gift being given. A seal is a visible recognition of a spiritual reality. A sacrament is a sign and seal of the covenant of grace. We covered the covenant of grace in Chapter 7.[1] As we go through the process of understanding the sacraments, we will identify several distinctions and divisions within the church, and we will be able to understand the origin of these divisions.

---

1. Chapter 7: Of God's Covenant with Man.

The sacraments confer benefits, confirm our union with Christ, and our being set apart from the world. Sacraments **put a visible difference between those that belong unto the Church, and the rest of the world.** The sacraments are signs that set a person apart, and state that the person belongs to a branch of the visible church. As we enter into the visible church, we partake of the sacraments. It is in the act of joining the visible church that we understand why the sign must be administered in a particular way, and why only certain people can partake of these signs. The sacraments put a visible difference between those who belong to the Church and those who belong to the world. In addition, we are to think of partaking of the sacraments as an affirmation of the covenant of grace. The sacraments affirm that we are readying ourselves for service in the kingdom so that we are solemnly engaged in **the service of God in Christ, according to His Word.**

Partaking of the sacraments is an act of covenant renewal. It is a commitment to live by the Word of God, and not live inconsistently with the truth of God. Reaffirmation of the covenant is a guard against hypocrisy. To partake of the sacraments without conformity to the law of God is to partake improperly.

A sacrament is a sign and seal of the covenant of grace that settles many major divisions that exist in the church. For example, Catholicism holds to baptismal regeneration, where the baptism itself washes away original sin, i.e., the sign *is* the reality. This is a failure to recognize that the sign is *not* the reality. Baptists, on the other hand, profess decisional regeneration; the decision to be baptized makes one a believer. Baptists fail to recognize that baptism is a sign and seal of the covenant of grace and that there is one covenant of grace continuing from the Old Testament to the New Testament.[2] The words of the Confession go a long way towards settling disputes regarding the sacraments. What are the sacraments? The sacraments are a sign and seal of the covenant of grace. Other particulars follow in this section of the Confession. The sacraments are instituted by God, **to represent Christ, and His benefits; and to confirm our interest in Him.** The sacraments mark a visible difference between those who belong to the Church and those who do not, and they are meant to engage us in the service of God and Christ.

---

2. Gangadean, "Paper No. 140: Argument for Paedobaptism," in *The Logos Papers*, 703-704.

The fundamental teaching of this section is that a sacrament is a sign and seal of the covenant of grace.

Prior to partaking in the Lord's Supper, it is a believer's duty to engage in self-examination. Whether our self-examination makes manifest something great or small, we are to recognize that we are forgiven by God, that we ought to confess our sin, and that we are to accept His forgiveness and partake of the sacrament. Our partaking is contingent upon knowing that we are endeavoring to walk in the newness of life before God. But if there is a notable outstanding sin in our life, it must be addressed in accordance with biblical guidelines prior to partaking of the sacrament. Once this sin is resolved, we are free to partake of the sacrament. We are to guard against operating under the guidance of a conscience that is not well informed by the law of God. A misinformed conscience can lead to focusing on microscopic matters that overlook more basic infractions of the moral law. We are not to strain at gnats and swallow camels; we are to inform our conscience so as to understand the weightier matters of the law and not be hindered by legalism and/or pietism. It is possible to become legalistic. I say this with much care, for it is good to have a sensitive conscience, but it must be well-informed. The emphasis on informing our conscience is to make righteous judgments.

SUMMARY ANSWER

Sacraments are holy signs (not the reality) and seals (confers definite benefit) of the covenant of grace. They put a visible difference between those who belong to the Church and those who do not, and they are an act of covenant renewal. Sacraments affirm that we are endeavoring to live in conformity with the law of God.

QUESTION 117

Explain the relation of sign and seal in a sacrament.

II. There is, in every sacrament, a spiritual relation, or sacramental union, between the sign and the thing signified: whence it comes to pass, that the names and effects of the one are attributed to the other.

III. The grace which is exhibited in or by the sacraments rightly used, is not conferred by any power in them; neither does the efficacy of a sacrament depend upon the piety or intention of him that does administer it: but upon the work of the Spirit, and the word of institution, which contains, together with a precept authorizing the use thereof, a promise of benefit to worthy receivers.

Sections 27.2-3 may be the occasion for many questions. It is important to keep in mind that the sacraments are the sign and seal of the covenant of grace. Having said that, the question that naturally follows is: What is the relation between the sign and the seal? For example, Christ says in instituting the Lord's Supper, "This is my body, which is broken for you . . ., this is the blood of the new covenant."[3] When Christ gave them wine and said this is my blood, was Christ saying that the wine is literally His blood? Or is this according to the statement **that the names and effects of the one are attributed to the other** because of the spiritual relation in the sacramental union? We affirm the latter. This is what is meant by saying the sign is not the reality. Equating the sign with the reality has led to the Catholic error known as transubstantiation. In transubstantiation, the physical bread and wine of the Lord's Supper are actually the body and blood of Christ. Therefore, in order to be taken truthfully, it is said that the elements of bread and wine literally undergo a transformation. It goes through a change of substance or transubstantiation. The substance is changed from bread and wine to the body and the blood of Christ. There are many other

---

3. *Matthew 26:26-28.*

assumptions and beliefs that are used to justify this claim. One would have to deny the idea of essences and the law of identity to affirm the doctrine of transubstantiation. The distinction between sign and reality in the Confession should bring us to a greater appreciation of the insight provided by the Westminster Divines.

A second erroneous interpretation of the sacrament of the Lord's Supper is known as consubstantiation. This view was held by Luther and is continued by the Lutherans. In consubstantiation, it is said that the physical bread and wine are not literally the body of Christ, but the body of Christ is literally "in and with" the bread and wine. "Consubstantiation" means the substance is with.

The sacrament of the Lord's Supper is a sign, and there is a sacramental union between the sign and the thing signified, and they are conceptually distinguishable. That is why we can speak about the reality of one and the other. There are some things that can be considered natural signs and seals. For example, beauty is a sign of goodness, but it is not necessarily accompanied by the reality. A smile is a sign of friendliness, but we can smile and be a villain (e.g., Iago). Sex is a sign and seal of love, yet the sign may be separated from the reality; we can have the sign without the reality. We often use these signs and attribute to them their natural reality. This is a failure on our part to operate without noting that the sign is not the reality.

Section 27.3 affirms that there is grace in the sacraments, that it is conferred, but not by any power in the sacraments themselves and goes on to say, **neither does the efficacy of a sacrament depend upon the piety or intention of him that does administer it.** The grace conferred by the sacrament is not in the things themselves, nor by the piety or the intention of him that administers it. We may add a qualifier to this statement by saying that the one administering the sacrament must be a professing believer and appropriately called to that position. Not everyone and anyone can administer the sacraments.

The grace conferred by the sacrament depends **upon the work of the Spirit, and the word of institution, which contains, together with a precept authorizing the use thereof, a promise of benefit to worthy receivers.** Jesus said: "Do this in remembrance of me,"[4] which is a precept with a promise of benefit to worthy receivers. The sacrament

---

4. *1 Corinthians 11:34.*

is made effectual by the Spirit, for those who partake rightly. Efficacy does not depend on the sacramental elements themselves, or on the intention or piety of the one administering it. Instead, it depends on the Holy Spirit, who makes it effectual for those who rightly partake of it. There must be faith/understanding on the part of those who partake, and it is made effectual by the Holy Spirit—both must be present.

SUMMARY ANSWER

Grace is not in the elements themselves nor in the piety of the administrator. The sacraments are made effectual by the Holy Spirit to those who partake in a worthy manner, with understanding.

QUESTION 118

What are the sacraments of the Old and the New Testaments?

IV. There are only two sacraments ordained by Christ our Lord in the Gospel; that is to say, Baptism, and the Supper of the Lord: neither of which may be dispensed by any, but by a minister of the Word lawfully ordained.

V. The sacraments of the Old Testament, in regard to the spiritual things thereby signified and exhibited, were, for substance, the same with those of the new.

Under the Old Testament, the sacraments were immediately instituted by God. Under the New Testament, they are immediately instituted by Christ, and are **Baptism, and the Supper of the Lord: neither of which may be dispensed by any, but by a minister of the Word lawfully ordained.** Only those called to the ministry of the Word are to baptize. A fuller explanation of this principle will be given in the chapter on church offices and councils. The Confession affirms that there are two sacraments; there are not seven as in the Roman Catholic Church.

Section 27.4 affirms the reality that there were two sacraments in the Old Testament, which were circumcision and Passover. The Scriptures speak about circumcision as being applied to the heart signifying regeneration when it states, "Circumcise your heart and not your flesh."[5] A person can be circumcised outwardly in the flesh, but not in the inner reality of the heart. The Holy Spirit circumcises the heart where and when He wills.

Since there are only two sacraments, it follows that marriage is not a sacrament, and therefore non-believers may be properly married, though not through the Church. Marriage in the State does not have to be administered by someone in the church. Neither marriage nor several other claims to sacraments by the Roman Catholic Church, are sacraments. Furthermore if the sacraments are one and the same between the Old and the New Testaments, infants were included in the sacrament of circumcision in the Old Testament. Thus, baptism, representing the same reality as circumcision is to be applied to infants under the New Testament. In addition, baptism is extended to female infants as it is understood that females are included in the household of faith even though the sign (circumcision) was not applied to them in the Old Testament.

SUMMARY ANSWER

The two sacraments instituted by God in the Old Testament are circumcision and Passover. In the New Testament, Christ instituted Baptism and the Lord's Supper.

---

5. *Deuteronomy 30:6.*

Chapter 28

___

OF BAPTISM

QUESTION 119

What is signified by baptism?

I. Baptism is a sacrament of the New Testament, ordained by Jesus Christ, not only for the solemn admission of the party baptized into the visible church; but also, to be unto him a sign and seal of the covenant of grace, of his ingrafting into Christ, of regeneration, of remission of sins, and of his giving up unto God, through Jesus Christ, to walk in newness of life. Which sacrament is, by Christ's own appointment, to be continued in His Church until the end of the world.

Baptism is a sacrament of the New Testament; it is different from the Old Testament in sign but not in substance. The Old Testament sign is circumcision; the New Testament sign is baptism. Both signify the need for a new heart. Baptism is ordained by Jesus Christ. We are united with Christ with the circumcision of our heart in regeneration, which is the beginning of our spiritual and covenantal life. If we were to underscore anything, it is that baptism signifies regeneration—being brought from death to life—and our union with Christ. Baptism teaches the truth about being born of the Spirit, the reality of sin and death, and the need to be brought out of spiritual death into spiritual life.

SUMMARY ANSWER

Baptism signifies the beginning of covenantal life and signifies regeneration—the sovereign work of the Spirit.

QUESTION 120

What are the manner, mode, and subject of baptism?

II. The outward element to be used in this sacrament is water, wherewith the party is to be baptized, in the name of the Father, and of the Son, and of the Holy Ghost, by a minister of the Gospel, lawfully called thereunto.

III. Dipping of the person into the water is not necessary; but Baptism is rightly administered by pouring, or sprinkling water upon the person.

IV. Not only those that do actually profess faith in and obedience unto Christ, but also the infants of one, or both, believing parents, are to be baptized.

Historically, there has been no dispute about water being used as the element in the sacrament of baptism. Some have raised the question as to whether baptism is only to be done in the name of Christ. The historical understanding has been that baptism is to be in the name of the Father, the Son, and the Holy Spirit, which is explicitly stated in Matthew 28:18-20. The element is water, and we are to be baptized in light of the Trinity. There are other forms of baptism: the baptism by the Holy Spirit Himself and the baptism by fire. The latter is the suffering that comes as we live as Christians both in terms of crucifying the flesh and persecutions that come through trials of faith. Baptism by fire is connected with our cleansing/sanctification. But in this section, we are focused on baptism as a sacrament which is a sign of regeneration by the Spirit.

Section 28.3 addresses the mode of baptism. Some, interpreting the Scriptures in a certain way, have concluded that baptism requires literal submersion underwater of the person being baptized. The Confession does not require submersion, but endorses **pouring, or sprinkling water upon the person.**

Section 28.4 addresses who is to be baptized. Disputes have been raised about whether infants are to be baptized. Historically, the practice is that infants are included in baptism. Baptism points to our union with Christ under the covenant of grace. Since there is only one covenant of grace, and since the substance of the sacrament is the same from the Old to the New Testament, this should settle the dispute. The Old Testament sign is circumcision. Infants were circumcised. The New Testament sign is baptism. Infants should be baptized. In some Christian circles, a split is made between the Old and the New Covenant. The Old Testament/Covenant is a covenant of works, and the New Testament/Covenant is a covenant of grace.[1] To be consistent with other assumptions, this view cannot allow that both the Old and New Testaments are the same covenant of grace. We need to understand from where the split between Old Covenant and New Covenant has come and what the thinking process is that leads to this split.

Some object that the New Testament does not require one to be baptized because there is no command. Yet, if we understand the Old Testament in light of the covenant of grace, which is a previous point, and the covenant of grace continues to the New Testament, and people are saved in one and the same way—through faith in the death of Christ—the sign of circumcision in the Old Testament is now replaced with the sign of baptism in the New Testament, that settles the question. Sometimes there are doubts in a person's mind, and we have to go through various arguments to bring it into focus.

Another division involves the Pentecostal and Charismatic churches who speak of the baptism of the Holy Spirit as a distinct experience separate from one's conversion where one may have to wait for the experience. Waiting for the baptism of the Holy Spirit is a misunderstanding of Scripture, which takes that which is transitional between the Old and the New Testaments to be permanent. Some who were believers in the transition between the Old and New Testaments had

---

1. Chapter 7: Of God's Covenant with Man.

a separate, miraculous experience as a sign to confirm that Christ has come. But for new believers, after Christ's ascension, there are no instances in the New Testament of waiting for the Holy Spirit and of a separate experience.

At Pentecost, all the believers present were under the Old Testament. The Holy Spirit was not given until Christ ascended. Believers then had to have a separate experience through the pouring out of the Holy Spirit. Given that it was separate, it was accompanied by speaking in tongues. It was something supernatural and manifested because of what the disciples and followers of Christ were called to do. They needed the power of the Holy Spirit to go and make disciples of all the nations, baptizing them, and teaching them to obey all that Christ has commanded.[2]

As the peoples of the world were scattered from Babel by the confusion of tongues in Genesis 11, now, in Acts 2, tongues are being manifest at the beginning of the ingathering of the people from all the nations. Pentecost marks the reversal of Babel. It was right after Babel that Abraham was called by God,[3] and the focus became on Abraham and his descendants—one person and one nation. Now the Word is going out beyond one person and one nation to the whole earth, so it is appropriate and fitting for those who traveled from all the nations to Jerusalem for the festival of ingathering, to hear the gospel preached in their own tongues.[4] From Jerusalem, the gospel was to go out to the whole world to fulfill the Great Commission. In the Old Testament, the gospel was contained within the people of God in the nation of Israel. Others were able to join and become part of that nation by living according to the laws and regulations of God. But, under the New Testament, believers are to engage in the Great Commission, taking the gospel to the ends of the earth. The coming of Christ brought about this change, and God had prepared the ground for this commission and sent the Holy Spirit to enable them. The expansion of the gospel

---

2. Matthew 28:19-20 Jesus says: "Therefore go and make disciples of all nations, baptizing them in the name of the Father and of the Son and of the Holy Spirit, and teaching them to obey everything I have commanded you. And surely I am with you always, to the very end of the age."

3. *Genesis 12.*

4. *Acts 2:1-12.*

to all the nations was one among a number of things that was changed by the coming of Christ.

SUMMARY ANSWER

Manner: with water, by a lawfully ordained minister, and in the name of the Father, Son, and Holy Spirit. Mode: by pouring and sprinkling water. Subject: infants of believing parents and new believers.

QUESTION 121

Explain the necessity and efficacy of baptism.

V. Although it is a great sin to contemn or neglect this ordinance, yet grace and salvation are not so inseparably annexed unto it, as that no person can be regenerated, or saved, without it; or, that all that are baptized are undoubtedly regenerated.

VI. The efficacy of Baptism is not tied to that moment of time wherein it is administered; yet, notwithstanding, by the right use of this ordinance, the grace promised is not only offered, but really exhibited, and conferred, by the Holy Ghost, to such (whether of age or infants) as that grace belongs unto, according to the counsel of God's own will, in His appointed time.

This section of the Confession affirms that a person can be regenerated and saved without having been baptized. Some within the church believe in baptismal regeneration, that we are regenerated through the administration of the sacrament. To believe this is to confuse the sign with the reality. The point being made in Section 28.5 is that it is a sin to neglect the ordinance of baptism, but one can be regenerated and saved without being baptized. Baptism is not necessary for salvation; one can have the reality of regeneration without the sign. Nonetheless, it is important to observe the ordinance.

Section 28.6 affirms that **the efficacy of Baptism is not tied to that moment of time wherein it is administered**. A person may be baptized and may have been born regenerated, or may be regenerated within minutes after or before the baptism. Or, regeneration could have happened before baptism in terms of months and years, or regeneration can happen after baptism in terms of months and years. A baptized child may not be regenerated until they are 5 or 10 or 25, or 30. Hopefully, by the time they are 30, they are regenerated. But for that matter, it could be even later. If regeneration happens later in life, and a person's baptism was properly administered as a child, their baptism is valid even when they have been explicit in their unbelief for decades. There is hope that the Lord will bring the reality of baptism (regeneration) into the life of a covenant child.

Proper administration of the ordinance of baptism is contingent upon the parents being professing believers when the child was baptized, and the church in which the baptism took place was a branch of the visible church. If those two factors were not present, then the baptism was not administered properly. For example, the Mormon faith is not considered evangelical in terms of truly believing in Christ as Lord and Savior. Even more basic, they do not believe in God the Creator. Therefore, Mormon baptism is not accepted as having been properly administered. Nor is Roman Catholic baptism accepted as properly administered. Those converting from a Mormon or Catholic background will need to be baptized.

SUMMARY ANSWER

Necessity: A person can be regenerated and saved without baptism. Yet, it is important to observe. Efficacy: by the Holy Spirit.

QUESTION 122

Can baptism be administered more than once?

VII. The sacrament of Baptism is but once to be administered unto any person.

The Confession denies that baptism can be administered more than once. The question is whether something that is called baptism is actually baptism. Anabaptists, and those waiting to be baptized as an adult upon profession of faith, are not acting according to the teaching of the Confession nor of the Scriptures.

SUMMARY ANSWER

Baptism can only be administered once.

Chapter 29

OF THE LORD'S SUPPER

QUESTION 123

What is signified by the Lord's Supper?

I. Our Lord Jesus, in the night wherein He was betrayed, instituted the sacrament of His body and blood, called the Lord's Supper, to be observed in His Church, unto the end of the world, for the perpetual remembrance of the sacrifice of Himself in His death; the sealing all benefits thereof unto true believers, their spiritual nourishment and growth in Him, their further engagement in and to all duties which they owe unto Him; and, to be a bond and pledge of their communion with Him, and with each other, as members of His mystical body.

We grow in grace through the sacrament of the Lord's Supper. As we feed on Christ, by partaking in the sign, we affirm our union with Christ. Of particular emphasis in this section is our nourishment and growth in Christ, remembering His sacrifice and death, and our union and communion with Him. Notice that regeneration is not what is emphasized in the meaning of the Lord's Supper. Instead, it is the remembrance of His life and His atoning sacrifice on our behalf. The benefits of partaking this sacrament are our nourishment and growth in Christ, as well as the engagement in all the duties that we owe to Him. Both Baptism and the Lord's Supper speak about our union with different aspects of the life of Christ. Each sacrament is administered differently. Baptism is administered once because we are regenerated once, but we regularly observe the Lord's Supper to feed on Christ and to be regularly nourished by Him.

SUMMARY ANSWER

The Lord's Supper represents our union with and growth in Christ.

QUESTION 124

How is commemoration opposed to the real sacrifice?

II. In this sacrament, Christ is not offered up to His Father; nor any real sacrifice made at all, for remission of sins of the quick or dead; but only a commemoration of that one offering up of Himself, by Himself, upon the cross, once for all: and a spiritual oblation of all possible praise unto God, for the same: so that the popish sacrifice of the mass (as they call it) is most abominably injurious to Christ's one, only sacrifice, the alone propitiation for all the sins of His elect.

Section 29.2 addresses a challenge that arises from Catholicism in the teaching that the sacrament of the Lord's Supper is literally the body and blood of Christ. If this is the case, the sacrifice of Christ occurs again every time the sacrament is observed. The nature and meaning of the Lord's Supper is a core distinction between the Protestant and Catholic Church. The mass is a deep-seated Roman Catholic tradition, with the eucharist as its central focus. Catholics regard the Lord's Supper as a real sacrifice, the Confession affirms the Lord's Supper is a commemoration.

The Confession is very pointed when it says, **so that the popish sacrifice of the mass (as they call it) is most abominably injurious to Christ's one, only sacrifice, the alone propitiation for all the sins of His elect.** We cannot minimize or set aside the error the Confession names in this section. The repeated sacrifice of Christ through transubstantiation and the Catholic eucharist implies that Christ's sacrifice on the cross was not sufficient for salvation. It means that the work of redemption was not completed when Christ was sacrificed on the cross and said, "It is finished."[1] Also implied in the Catholic eucharist is that human beings, by their own work, can make satisfaction through sacrifice, which is a distortion deeply rooted in our fallen nature. It is the universal human tendency to seek to justify ourselves by our own deeds. Once transubstantiation is adopted, a whole system of theology follows. We see how emphatically the Confession rejects the Lord's Supper as a sacrifice. We can conclude that commemoration is opposed to the real sacrifice.

SUMMARY ANSWER

Commemoration of Christ's death (done once), is not an offering up of Himself to His Father (real sacrifice). The Roman Catholic understanding maintains that one sacrifice was not enough.

QUESTION 125

How is the Lord's Supper to be observed?

III. The Lord Jesus has, in this ordinance, appointed His ministers to declare His word of institution to the people; to pray, and bless the elements of bread and wine, and thereby to set them apart from a common to an holy use; and to take and break the bread, to take the cup, and (they communicating also themselves) to give both to the communicants; but to none who are not then present in the congregation.

IV. Private masses, or receiving this sacrament by a priest, or any other, alone; as likewise, the denial of the cup to the people, worshiping the elements, the lifting them up, or carrying them about, for adoration, and the reserving them for any pretended religious use; are all contrary to the nature of this sacrament, and to the institution of Christ.

---

1. *John 19:30.*

Section 29.3 describes how the Lord Lord's Supper is to be observed. The Lord's Supper is to be observed very simply and straightforwardly. Remember the way in which it was observed by Christ and the believers present with Him.[2] We are also to remember the idea of our union with Christ through the sign of bread and wine. In the history of the Roman Catholic Church, the cup was denied to the people in order to avoid spilling the wine (because it is considered the literal blood of Christ). But the sacrament includes both the bread and the wine, which are signs. In the institution of the Lord's Supper, so much of the elements are set aside from an ordinary to a sacramental use, and then afterward, one may dispose of what is left over. If the bread and wine have become the literal body and blood of Christ, disposing of the remaining elements becomes problematic due to the unnecessary hindrance of the doctrine of transubstantiation.

Section 29.4 describes how the Lord's Supper is not to be observed. The Roman Catholic practice of receiving communion alone or in private masses is not permitted. Communion is an aspect of the public worship of the corporate body of Christ. The move to adore the sacraments arose from the belief in the real presence of the elements. Worship of the elements is not permitted. We are not to partake of the Lord's Supper alone or take the bread only; and we are not to lift up the elements for adoration or reserve the elements for any pretended religious use.

SUMMARY ANSWER

The Lord's Supper is to be observed very simply. It is not to be observed in private masses (alone), nor is the cup to be denied, nor the elements adored.

---

2. *Matthew 26:17-30.*

QUESTION 126

How are sign and seal opposed to change of substance?

V. The outward elements in this sacrament, duly set apart to the uses ordained by Christ, have such relation to Him crucified, as that, truly, yet sacramentally only, they are sometimes called by the name of the things they represent, to wit, the body and blood of Christ; albeit, in substance and nature, they still remain truly and only bread and wine, as they were before.

VI. That doctrine which maintains a change of the substance of bread and wine, into the substance of Christ's body and blood (commonly called transubstantiation) by consecration of a priest, or by any other way, is repugnant, not to Scripture alone, but even to common sense, and reason; overthrows the nature of the sacrament, and has been, and is, the cause of manifold superstitions; yes, of gross idolatries.

Sections 29.5-6 discuss the nature of the sign and seal of the Lord's Supper. Because of the sacramental union and spiritual relation between them, the bread and wine are called the body and blood. A miracle is a violation of a law of nature; a miracle is not and cannot be a violation of a law of reason. In the miracle at Galilee, when Jesus changed water into wine, that change was not a violation of reason (the laws of thought); rather, it is a violation of a law of nature, which laws are created and under the rule of God. The laws of reason cannot be violated, as they are part of the very being of God. When Jesus changed the water into wine, it is a sensible change—it looked, smelled, and tasted like wine. Jesus' miracle is different than the Roman Catholic doctrine of transubstantiation that postulates a change in substance, while the essential properties remain unchanged. In the Roman Catholic mass, the wine still looks, smells, and tastes like wine. In this sense, the doctrine is repugnant to reason, common sense, and Scripture. We are asked to believe that wine is not wine. We are asked to believe that the substance of the wine has been changed while the essential properties of wine are still present, but the essential properties of human blood are not present.

As we go through the discussion of disagreement among believers, unless we get back to the more fundamental reality of sin and death, we will make little progress in settling doctrinal disputes. As believers, we are to avoid getting stuck in less basic disputes, and we should instead engage at a more fundamental level to work towards the unity of the faith. We are not to start a discussion with the doctrine of the Lord's Supper, but we are to start with sin and death, repentance, and faith in Christ. If we proceed presuppositionally by going back to the most basic in a discussion and agreeing on it, it should not be that difficult to secure the unity of the faith. This is Rational Presuppositionalism[3] applied: If we agree on what is more basic, we will agree on what is less basic. This should be affirmed strongly—categorically. When there is a difference, it is because there is a difference in something more basic. Let us keep that in mind and not get discouraged. And, when we find that we cannot move forward in a discussion, we should move back to what is more basic. There is true hope in this approach to discussion and settling disputes.

SUMMARY ANSWER

The sign and seal point to the spiritual reality (union with Christ). The spiritual reality is effectual upon those partaking in faith. A change in substance overthrows the nature of the sacrament (sign and seal). Transubstantiation is repugnant to Scripture, common sense, and reason (a change in substance requires a change in essential properties).

---

3. Appendix 6; Gangadean, *History of Philosophy*, 22-23.

QUESTION 127

How is Christ present and received in the Lord's Supper?

VII. Worthy receivers, outwardly partaking of the visible elements, in this sacrament, do then also, inwardly by faith, really and indeed, yet not carnally and corporally but spiritually, receive, and feed upon, Christ crucified, and all benefits of His death: the body and blood of Christ being then, not corporally or carnally, in, with, or under the bread and wine; yet, as really, but spiritually, present to the faith of believers in that ordinance, as the elements themselves are to their outward senses.

What is stated in Section 29.7 presupposes Section 27.2 regarding the nature of the sacraments. There is in every sacrament a spiritual relation or sacramental union between the sign and the thing signified. The spiritual reality is present in faith just as the elements are present in outward senses. This is an illustration of how the Confession addresses a specific issue at length because it was a source of conflict and subject to much discussion. This depth of discussion is what is to be expected as there is an increased awareness of issues that need to be resolved.

SUMMARY ANSWER

The Lord's supper is spiritually received and fed upon representing Christ crucified, and all benefits of His death.

QUESTION 128

Who may partake or be admitted to the Lord's Supper?

VIII. Although ignorant and wicked men receive the outward elements in this sacrament; yet, they receive not the thing signified thereby; but, by their unworthy coming thereunto, are guilty of the body and blood of the Lord, to their own damnation. Wherefore, all ignorant and ungodly persons, as they are unfit to enjoy communion with Him, so are they unworthy of the Lord's table; and cannot, without great sin against Christ, while they remain such, partake of these holy mysteries, or be admitted thereunto.

Section 29.8 denies the practice of some churches that all who would like to partake of the Lord's Supper may partake. This practice fails to provide a visible difference between those who are in Christ and those who are not. In addition, allowing all to the Lord's table denies the worthy receiving of the sacrament. Rather, the Lord's Supper is to be given only to members of the visible church who are in good standing. If someone is undergoing church discipline, they cannot, and should not come to the Lord's table. At times when sin is manifest in the life of a member of the church, they are not put out of the church, but are to be placed under discipline and restricted from partaking of the Lord's Supper. Furthermore, if someone is not under discipline, but is aware of sin in their life that needs to be dealt with, which has not yet been confessed and properly dealt with involving oversight, they should not partake. But those who are troubled by certain things remaining in their lives, if they have confessed it, asked for forgiveness, and have received it, should come to the Lord's table and partake.

If someone has not yet been baptized, and has not entered into the visible church, they should not partake of the Lord's Supper. People who are known to be believers in good standing in a branch of the visible church when visiting another church may partake. But for someone visiting the congregation who is not known to the oversight, for example, a friend of a member, they should not partake. If someone invites someone to church when communion is being observed and they want to partake, they should become known to the oversight. Becoming known to the oversight helps to avoid awkwardness for the visitor and for the pastor. Once their status is known to the oversight, the visitor can freely partake with the congregation; they are not unnecessarily excluded. Restricting the table may be a sensitive matter, and we do not want to cause offense, nor do we want people partaking in an unworthy manner. The pastor's preference is to see people come, but the pastor has a responsibility to watch over the Lord's Table and properly administer it. This practice is called "fencing" the Lord's Table. We put a fence around it so that it will be properly administered. The Table is fenced by words, not physically. If someone decides to partake and disregard what was spoken, they may be eating and drinking judgment unto themselves. Judgment may be to the extent of physical illness and death. This is why the Scriptures say: "For this cause many are weak and sickly among you, and many sleep."[4] If we judge ourselves, we will not be judged, but when we are judged we are chastened by the Lord that we should not be condemned with the world.

SUMMARY ANSWER

Those who are members of the visible church and in good standing, may partake of the Lord's Supper.

---

4. *1 Corinthians 11:30.*

Chapter 30

OF CHURCH CENSURES

QUESTION 129

What is the origin of church government and of the keys of the kingdom?

I. The Lord Jesus, as King and Head of His Church, has therein appointed a government, in the hand of church officers, distinct from the civil magistrate.

II. To these officers the keys of the kingdom of heaven are committed; by virtue whereof, they have power, respectively, to retain, and remit sins; to shut that kingdom against the impenitent, both by the Word, and censures; and to open it unto penitent sinners, by the ministry of the Gospel; and by absolution from censures, as occasion shall require.

The Apostle Paul, in Ephesians Chapter 4 affirms that Christ appointed church officers when he says, "And He Himself gave some *to be* apostles, some prophets, some evangelists, and some pastors and teachers."[1] Paul desires the appointment of elders in every church.[2] And, in the Pastoral Letters, he speaks about the appointment of elders—*episcopoi*—and presbyters, which are interchangeable terms. Furthermore, the Scriptures say, "Obey them that have the rule over you, and submit yourselves: for they watch for your souls, as they that must give account, that they may do it with joy, and not with grief: for that is

---

1. *Ephesians 4:11*, NKJV.
2. *Acts 14:23.*

unprofitable for you."[3] There is a prescribed way to order the visible church. The elders have oversight of the preaching of the Word, the administration of the sacraments, and discipline for church members. There is an ordered government in the Church, which is distinct from the civil magistrate.

Regarding church government, the Confession affirms, **to these officers the keys of the kingdom of heaven are committed.** The keys are not given to only one person, but **to these officers.** Wherever the visible church is, there are officers; and, to these officers, the keys of the kingdom of heaven are committed. The Westminster Divines understood the keys of the kingdom differently than is understood in the Roman Catholic Church, where the keys are given to one person—the Pope. Instead, the Confession affirms there is a government within the Church, and the keys are given to those who govern the Church. Wherever there is a legitimate branch of the visible church, those keys are being exercised.

The purpose of the keys is to regulate church membership. People are to be received into the visible church insofar as they have a credible profession of faith. If a profession of faith is not credible, that person is to be excluded from partaking in the blessings that accompany church membership. The exclusion is represented in the power of the keys. There is no mystery either for admission or exclusion from the visible church. It must be done in light of a credible profession of faith. Whenever a person is admitted to the visible church, that power is being exercised. The visible church is to carry out the three marks of a true Church. Insofar as church leadership faithfully preaches the gospel, administers the sacraments, and exercises godly discipline, that church is considered part of the visible church.

A person may be included or excluded from the Church in light of a credible profession of faith. If church members are living their lives in such a way that it can no longer be said that they have a credible profession, they will be excluded from church membership. If they are excluded, that person may continue to profess that they are a believer, but have no grounds to make that claim. Likewise, other members have no grounds for saying that the person excluded is a believer, if that person was excluded on the basis of discipline and they remain

---

3. *Hebrews 13:17.*

unrepentant. The Confession says church leaders are **to shut that kingdom against the impenitent, both by the Word, and censures; and to open it unto penitent sinners.** Let's say that a member of the church commits adultery and it is known to oversight and other members. Their act has been found out, yet they are not repentant, and they are not doing things in keeping with repentance. That person may be excommunicated from the Church. Another cause for excommunication is if a person displays conduct that divides the body of Christ in very obvious ways. In these examples, a person may be proceeded against. Let's say that a member comes to believe that God did not create the heavens and the earth and that the earth is coeternal with God. This belief shows a failure to understand who the true God is, which is cause for exclusion. Perhaps a person comes to believe that Christ is not the only begotten Son of God and thinks that we are all sons of God in the same way. This person may be excluded from the Church. People may run after strange doctrines that divide the body, which is cause for exclusion from the Church. Thus we see the purpose and the need for church censures.

What may happen is that one is going along living life, a problem develops, and a very notable sin manifests itself. This sin is not equivalent to a pimple; it is a boil. A boil is an indication of something more serious—speaking metaphorically. When adultery occurs in a marriage, that is a boil. Adultery is serious and has deep-seated causes which need to be attended to. In this case, the adulterer may be put under certain restrictions until the root cause is dealt with. Church oversight is to act as the Old Testament priests when a boil manifests: They declared the person unclean. Being unclean means that the problem that has become manifest goes deeper than skin-deep, it is deeply rooted in the self-life, and discipline needs to be brought against the person to help them address the root of sin. Often, church members bring restrictions upon themselves when sin is manifest. For example, if we are having quarrels in the home, we should not have people over to the house until we have dealt with the matter. We are to observe that something unclean is taking place and is the manifestation of a deeper spiritual problem. Self-life has an aroma to it, and people can sense it. Preventing exposing others to our self-life is a matter of self-discipline. It is proper to have self-discipline so that church discipline is not required.

Ordination is the means by which one is recognized as an officer in the church. There are two or three views of ordination. One view is apostolic succession, going back to the Apostle Peter. In this view, if a church is not in communion with the holy and apostolic church, they are not properly ordained. The Roman Catholic Church may say, "Outside of this church, there is no legitimate office." Others, such as the Episcopalians, may say that they have apostolic succession; whether Catholics recognize the claim is another matter. The standard Presbyterian practice of ordination is that the current elders of a church recognize a person for their preparation and service to the church. They lay hands on that person before the congregation, symbolizing their being set aside for the work of ministry. Conversely, a body of believers may recognize someone who is able and willing to lead. Ordinarily, ordination is by presbytery. But there are times in the church, as during the Reformation, when things were not yet up and running, when a person comes to lead by the recognition of the congregation. The congregation receives a person to serve in the office of pastor or elder because of their ability. This is what happened at the beginning of the Reformation with reformers such as John Knox and John Calvin. This is called congregational recognition for ordination, and usually, there is some relation between those who believe in the true faith and those administering ordination. Paul said to the people that were conferred under his ministry, "You are my letter of recognition."[4] Ordination of elders shows that the work is being done, and God is blessing it.

Not every group that claims to be a church is part of the visible church. The doctrine of that group must be according to what has been held historically. Making converts is not sufficient to be a visible branch of the Church. Muslims and Mormons make converts but are not part of the Church because the doctrine that they profess is not consistent with the Historic Christian Faith. There are safeguards even when a church is "congregational." Congregational churches have been recognized as part of the visible church when they hold to the Historic Christian Faith. In the United States, some of the Puritans were congregational, and some were Presbyterian. We recognize independent churches and accept their baptisms when that church is a branch of the visible church and someone who is recognized by that church has

---

4. *2 Corinthians 3:2.*

administered the sacrament. Otherwise, we may say that independent churches that have departed from the Historic Christian Faith are not considered a branch of the visible church.

SUMMARY ANSWER

The origin of the Church is from Christ (Eph. 4), who has established church government. To these officers, the keys of the kingdom are committed.

QUESTION 130

Why are church censures necessary, and how are they to be administered?

III. Church censures are necessary, for the reclaiming and gaining of offending brethren, for deterring of others from the like offenses, for purging out of that leaven which might infect the whole lump, for vindicating the honor of Christ, and the holy profession of the Gospel, and for preventing the wrath of God, which might justly fall upon the church, if they should suffer His covenant, and the seals thereof, to be profaned by notorious and obstinate offenders.

IV. For the better attaining of these ends, the officers of the church are to proceed by admonition; suspension from the sacrament of the Lord's Supper for a season; and by excommunication from the church; according to the nature of the crime, and demerit of the person.

If an offense arises within the congregation between church members, there is a process of reconciliation to be found in Matthew 18. There are three steps to Matthew 18. In the first step, the offended party is to pray until they have a focused question in mind, then they are to go to the person, inquiring, rather than accusing. They should ask: "You did this, or you said this; is this what you meant?" Then they are to allow the person to respond. In other words, you are inquiring for meaning, which is more basic than truth. You do not take step one of Matthew 18 ten times and then blow up after the tenth time. You do not go from step one to step three and tell it to the whole church. The purpose of discipline is to reclaim the person and to help them understand the seriousness of what they have done. If the offense is legitimate, and it is not cleared up after using step one, the offended party is to use Matthew 18, step two, which includes bringing one other person as a witness to the offending person. If the person is still unrepentant, and it progresses to Matthew 18, step three, the oversight of the church is told. The oversight then will communicate what is relevant to the congregation to inform and warn them. Sin is like a spiritual disease that can spread, and oversight wants to protect the flock. The three steps of Matthew 18 are necessary and are to be administered in stages. The stages are (1) go inquiring to the person, (2) bring a witness to the person, (3) involve the oversight in the matter so that oversight can protect the church. Depending on the seriousness of the offense and how much light they have had, they may be excommunicated from the church after step three.

When a person is excommunicated, there is to be no communication between church members and the excommunicated person. Just the awareness of the reality of excommunication and its implications is a deterrent. After excommunication is carried out, all members are responsible to be united in the process by abstaining from further contact with the excommunicated person. The congregation is to affirm the belief and practice of church discipline, they ought to stand together, because it is for the benefit of the excommunicated person. The door of repentance is always open. Repentance ought to come first through the oversight of the church, then to the affected parties.

SUMMARY ANSWER

Censures are necessary to exercise church discipline; for reclaiming and regaining offended brethren; deterring others from like offenses proceeding by admonition, suspension from Lord's Supper, and excommunication from church.

Chapter 31

OF SYNODS AND COUNCILS

QUESTION 131

What is the form and the function of church government?

I. For the better government, and further edification of the church, there ought to be such assemblies as are commonly called synods or councils: and it belongs to the overseers and other rulers of the particular churches, by virtue of their office, and the power which Christ has given them for edification and not for destruction, to appoint such assemblies; and to convene together in them, as often as they shall judge it expedient for the good of the church.

II. It belongs to synods and councils, ministerially to determine controversies of faith, and cases of conscience; to set down rules and directions for the better ordering of the public worship of God, and government of His church; to receive complaints in cases of maladministration, and authoritatively to determine the same: which decrees and determinations, if consonant to the Word of God, are to be received with reverence and submission; not only for their agreement with the Word, but also for the power whereby they are made, as being an ordinance of God appointed thereunto in His Word.

The general heading for Chapter 31 is "Of Synods and Councils," and these terms are used interchangeably within the chapter. There are three different forms of church government: hierarchical, presbyterian, and independent/congregational. The form of church government affirmed by the Westminster Divines is presbyterian. In Presbyterianism, the church is governed by the rule of the presbyters, elders, or overseers. The elders of each particular church appoint representatives to attend the assemblies of presbytery. Notice, this means that each church is not independent of the other, but each church is working together with the others. Church government is not hierarchical from the top, but is by the elders and church officers in the particular churches coming together. Those to whom Christ has given power, rule by virtue of their office. The oversight of particular churches agree with each other to appoint such assemblies and to convene together. The frequency of these councils and meetings can be agreed upon together. In some places, the standard practice is to meet yearly. In other places, meetings of presbytery may be less frequent.

Elders (also called presbyters or overseers) and deacons are the two offices recognized by the Scriptures and each has biblical qualifications. These two offices are distinctively identified in Timothy and Titus.[1] The elder/overseer has particular qualifications. They are to examine doctrine and life (morals). Deacons are to manage the general material well-being of the congregation. For example, in Acts 6, deacons are chosen to help serve at the tables and to make sure that there is a proper administration of the natural/physical needs of the people. The apostles said that it was not right for them to leave their responsibility of the ministry of the Word to wait on tables.

Within a congregation, among the elders/overseers, there is a distinction between those who labor in doctrine and word and those who rule. So there are teaching elders and ruling elders. The one that exposits the Word is particularly the teaching elder. The teaching elder gives himself to the preaching of the Word. Generally speaking, there has been one teaching elder in a congregation, although all elders are supposed to be able to teach. Within a congregation, one elder may be singled out for the office of teaching the Word, which has been the practice historically in churches throughout the centuries.

We see an example of a counsel being called in Acts 15.[2] There was a dispute in the early church regarding whether a person must be circumcised in order to be saved. Notice that a dispute arose among local

---

1. *1 Timothy 3:1–12; Titus 1:5–9.*
2. *Acts 15:1-4.*

churches, and they went up to Jerusalem to deal with the matter, and various churches participated along with the apostles. The council was not uniquely an apostolic act. In this counsel, after much discussion, they came to an agreement, and after the agreement was secured, letters were sent out to all the churches with the decision of the matter. When Paul went on his second missionary journey, he took the ruling of the elders to the various churches he visited. The use of councils is the ordinary means by which the unity of the faith is maintained, particularly in the face of challenges.

Early in the Reformation, the Synod of Dort assembled to address the question of what is necessary to be saved. The Synod of Dort presupposed the work that had been attained by previous creeds and councils, including the doctrine of salvation (Council of Orange), the incarnation of Christ (Council of Chalcedon), and the Trinity (Council of Nicea). Dort built upon doctrines that were previously settled by church councils in church history. We are to continue that pattern and hold to what has been ruled upon by synods and councils in centuries past, which embodies the substance of the Historic Christian Faith.

When the Westminster Divines met from 1643-1648, they were aware of what had gone before in the creeds and councils and affirmed their doctrines. They were also aware of departures from church councils, and of what had not yet been addressed in church councils. They saw what was contrary to Scripture that were hindrances to the life of the Church. The Divines came together to discuss what the Scriptures taught. They were able to discuss because they accepted certain basic things about the authority of Scripture and they were able to come to agreement on disputed matters by means of the Holy Spirit working through the pastor-teachers in the Church.

Section 31.2 says, **it belongs to synods and councils, ministerially to determine controversies of faith, and cases of conscience; to set down rules and directions for the better ordering of the public worship of God, and government of His church.** The purpose of meeting in synods and councils is to determine doctrine, address cases of conscience in moral matters, and to address questions regarding the law of God and its applications. In addition, synods address the worship of God as well as the government of the church.

Synods are also **to receive complaints in cases of maladministration.** There is a process of appeals for church members in the case of maladministration. When synods make a ruling, it becomes the law and order of the church. These decrees and determinations, if consonant with the Word of God, are to be received with reverence and submission. Yet, there may be times in which the ruling of synods are not consonant with the Word of God. These rulings, then, would not be received. We have to be very careful about rejecting a rule of synod, but at times, synods have erred. Ordinarily, if a ruling is consonant with the Word of God, it is to be submitted to with reverence, not only because of its agreement with the Word, but also for the authority whereby the decision was made. God has ordained this authority, and if it is within the boundaries of the Word, it is to be submitted to. This is the same way in which we speak of submitting to civil government. We are not to lightly disregard the government that God has established, whether in the Church or in the State.

There is an order by which decisions of synod are to be made. In judicial proceedings, given the context, there are times when that order may or may not be followed. Decisions are to be made according to the Word, and those making the decisions are to be in accord with one another, as exemplified by the ordinance of God appointed in His Word.[3] Matters of controversies are not made by one person, as in the Roman Catholic Church. They believe that if the Pope speaks in matters of faith and morals, which are matters of conscience, he binds the conscience of all Catholics. Furthermore, they believe that when the Pope speaks from the position of authority *ex-cathedra*, he speaks definitively and infallibly. The Confession does not grant infallibility to one person, nor to any group of persons, as in the case of synods and councils. The Confession explicitly says that synods and councils are fallible. Nevertheless, though men may err, synods are useful. The Scriptures are always the final authority.

SUMMARY ANSWER

Form: There are three forms of church government—hierarchical, presbyterian, and congregational. Function: Presbyters and elders (ruling and teaching) watch over doctrine and moral

---

3. *Acts 15:28.*

matters in the church, while deacons watch over material matters in the church.

QUESTION 132

What are the limits of synods and councils?

III. All synods or councils, since the Apostles' times, whether general or particular, may err; and many have erred. Therefore they are not to be made the rule of faith, or practice; but to be used as a help in both.

IV. Synods and councils are to handle, or conclude nothing, but that which is ecclesiastical: and are not to intermeddle with civil affairs which concern the commonwealth, unless by way of humble petition in cases extraordinary; or, by way of advice, for satisfaction of conscience, if they be thereunto required by the civil magistrate.

Councils are the ordinary means by which God intends to bring about the well-being and the good of the Church. Teachers are fallible, particularly those teachers that have not built upon those who have come before. There is a reality of historically cumulative insight. Just because a person is a teacher does not mean they are connected with the insight of the past. When someone is a teacher in the church, we should ask where are they in relation to the historically cumulative insight. Where are they in relation to the creeds? Where are they in relation to the Westminster Standards? In God's providence, the Westminster Standards are the summary of the striving of the Church to come to unity. Those in positions of authority within the church cannot neglect this reality. There has not been a document as extensive since the Confession. In fact, the Church has moved away from the fullness of the Westminster Standards. The fullness of the doxological focus of the Westminster Confession of Faith is the reason we hold to this Confession and not to some other confession. There are differences between the Reformed community and Lutherans including the question of the sovereignty of God over all of life, the relationship between Church and State, as well as differences in understanding the sacrament of the Lord's Supper. Yet, there is a lot of common ground between the Reformed and Lutheran community as well. The primary basis for judging a confession is its doctrine. And though other confessions are useful, and we should reckon with them, the Westminster Standards uniquely have a doxological focus.

Scripture says there needs to be controversies among you so that those that are proven be made manifest.[4] In this passage, we see controversies arise, questions are forced to the fore, and God has provided the means by which to address controversies by synods and councils. Synods and councils are the means by which the Holy Spirit leads the Church into all truth.

Section 31.4 reaffirms the separation between ecclesiastical rule and the civil magistrate. In the past, the Roman Catholic Church has made rulings about civil affairs. There is a separation between Church and State, yet both are equally under the moral law of God as it applies to each institution. So while synods and councils are only to deal with matters ecclesiastical and not intermeddle with civil affairs, they may, through humble petition in cases extraordinary, address the civil magistrate. The Church may see something urgent that merits the attention of the State, in which case synods and councils may make a humble petition to the government. Notice, the Church is not acting in an imperial way by saying: "We declare . . .," "We anathemize you . . .," or "We will excommunicate you if you do not act." But the Church, if it approaches the State, is to do so humbly. We may examine the way some of the reformers addressed and petitioned the civil rulers of their day to find examples. The reformers may have acted as individuals, but synods may petition humbly, in a similar way. On the other hand, the civil magistrate may request advice from the Church on a certain matter. The Confession affirms this when it says, **or, by way of advice, for satisfaction of conscience, if they be thereunto required by the civil magistrate.** We should be aware that the Westminster Assembly itself was convened by request of the English Parliament, which is the civil magistrate. Parliament wanted a unified teaching that could be disseminated to all the churches throughout England and Scotland.

---

4. *1 Corinthians 11:19.*

SUMMARY ANSWER

Synods and councils may err and have erred. Synods and councils are to deal with the Church only, but may humbly petition the civil magistrate.

Chapter 32

OF THE STATE OF MEN AFTER DEATH, AND THE RESURRECTION OF THE DEAD

C HAPTER 32 BRINGS US TO THE DOCTRINE of eschatology in general. "Eschatology" comes from the word "eschaton," the end, or last things. This chapter addresses what happens at death, after death, and at the end of death, or the resurrection.

QUESTION 133

What is the state of men after death?

I. The bodies of men, after death, return to dust, and see corruption: but their souls, which neither die nor sleep, having an immortal subsistence, immediately return to God who gave them: the souls of the righteous, being then made perfect in holiness, are received into the highest heavens, where they behold the face of God, in light and glory, waiting for the full redemption of their bodies. And the souls of the wicked are cast into hell, where they remain in torments and utter darkness, reserved to the judgment of the great day. Beside these two places, for souls separated from their bodies, the Scripture acknowledges none.

There are controversies about the state of the soul after the death of the body. The Church has a very definite position on the subject, but from time-to-time people forget the historic teaching. When the body dies physically, the soul does not die. People may sleep while in the body, but the soul does not sleep after death. The Confession is speaking against a view that says that we are unconscious after death (soul sleep). The soul neither dies nor sleeps. Notice that the soul returns to God immediately. What are the implications of this teaching for haunted houses or for those who believe that the dead wander the earth as in Greek literature or in Shakespeare's Hamlet? Or what about those who believe that you have to propitiate the dead? A little bit of doctrine goes far.

The Confession goes on to address what happens to the souls of the righteous, **the souls of the righteous, being then made perfect in holiness, are received into the highest heavens.** This statement needs to be unpacked. The souls are made perfect in holiness, which means that there is not a long purgatorial period to go through after death for further cleansing. Sanctification is imperfect in this life, but it is complete at death, immediately and instantly. The righteous are made perfect in holiness by means of a sovereign act of God. God could have made us perfect in holiness right after we were converted. But God does not do so because evil is removed gradually. Engaging in the struggle to overcome against evil is part of the work of dominion. God is able to fully sanctify, but does so in a particular way in keeping with His purpose.

Redemption is not completed at death; the righteous are waiting. The Confession affirms this by saying the righteous in heaven **behold the face of God, in light and glory, waiting for the full redemption of their bodies.** A question may arise: If the souls are waiting for the resurrection of the body, where are they waiting? In other words, where are these non-spatial beings in space? Does this question arise by way of curiosity or is it something vital? The Confession says they behold the face of God in light and glory. Let's address this section part by part. How are we to understand the expression, **they behold the face of God?** The statement cannot be understood literally, as God is a spirit and has no body, parts, or passions. Yet the expression is used. It was used in Scripture when the "Lord spoke to Moses face to face."[1]

---

1. *Exodus 33:11.*

Beholding the face of God has to do with seeing the essence of God, the very nature of God.

After death, the righteous are conscious and what they are particularly aware of is the face of God in the revelation of God. God is revealed in the things that are made and in what is taking place in history. God is known though creation and providence. The righteous behold the face of God through what is taking place in His providence.

The question may occur, how can the dead hear us or see us since they have no eyes or ears? We affirm that angels see the physical world. Is the only way to know the physical world through the senses? Can we have awareness of the physical world without physical eyes? The Confession says that the righteous see the face of God in light and glory. They are not asleep. They have communion with the Lord, and in that state, they are waiting for the full redemption of their bodies.

There is more that the Scriptures say about the state of the soul after death, but we are not pushed to address those matters now. In this section of the Confession, we do not have the sense that those who behold the face of God are in a grievous state. There is something lacking when you do not have your body, that is why they are waiting for it. With the body, we can once again participate in activities in a way that we could not in a disembodied state.

The Confession goes on to address the state of the souls of the wicked after death, who **are cast into hell, where they remain in torments and utter darkness, reserved to the judgment of the great day.** After death, there is a separation between believer and unbeliever. Unbelievers are cast into hell. Some may ask, how can there be a separation in a non-physical space? There is a separation in this life between believer and unbeliever. One is in the state of darkness of mind, and the other is enlightened by Christ. That state continues in the next life. The essence of the separation is spiritual death. "The wages of sin is death"[2] is present now and continues in the next life. The idea of being cast into hell suggests the idea of a spatial place, but the Scriptures speak of the lake of fire as the second death. Spiritual death is present now and continues into the next life. The wicked are in that state permanently now and irrevocably. While on this earth, we can be redeemed through regeneration, but in the next life, the wicked are left in the condition

---

2. *Romans 6:23.*

of unbelief. God does not call us back nor does God choose to bring anyone out of that state.

By saying, **beside these two places, for souls separated from their bodies, the Scripture acknowledges none,** the Westminster Divines deny that there is a third place for the souls of the dead, as in purgatory. There are two and only two conditions after death. The soul is not annihilated, it is not in soul sleep, and the soul has awareness. The righteous are made perfect in holiness. The dead are either in the state of growth in the knowledge of God (seeing the face of God) or they are in a state of darkness without the light of the knowledge of God.

SUMMARY ANSWER

The soul is aware—it does not sleep, nor is it annihilated. The believer continues in perpetuity knowing God vs. the unbeliever who is in perpetual "darkness".

QUESTION 134

When shall the resurrection take place, and in what manner?

II. At the last day, such as are found alive shall not die, but be changed: and all the dead shall be raised up, with the selfsame bodies, and none other (although with different qualities), which shall be united again to their souls forever.

III. The bodies of the unjust shall, by the power of Christ, be raised to dishonor: the bodies of the just, by His Spirit, unto honor; and be made conformable to His own glorious body.

The Confession simply says the resurrection will take place **at the last day, such as are found alive shall not die, but be changed. . . .** The change spoken of in this section is a reference to the rapture.[3] The Confession affirms the rapture in the sense that those who are alive at Christ's second coming are caught up with Him and are changed. But the Confession does not promote anything beyond this change at the rapture.[4] Notice that the change applies to all that are found alive. It does not say believers, but such as are found alive shall not die, but shall be changed. This is a little different than the rapture, which speaks of believers only, who are changed to be with the Lord.

The Confession continues, **and all the dead shall be raised up, with the selfsame bodies, and none other (although with different qualities), which shall be united again to their souls forever.** The Confession affirms that the resurrected body is the same body that we had before death, which is the body that God gave you: Rejoice and be glad.

The resurrection takes place after all things are subdued as Scripture affirms, "Then the end will come, when He hands over the kingdom to God the Father after He has destroyed all dominion, authority and power."[5] And, "the last enemy to be destroyed is death."[6] Death is subdued after all other things are subdued. The Confession goes on to tell us in what manner the bodies of the dead are raised. **The bodies of the unjust shall, by the power of Christ, be raised to dishonor,** in terms of their lives and function without God. And **the bodies of the just, by His Spirit, unto honor.** Those who are raised unto honor are made conformable to His own glorious body. Both bodies of believers and unbelievers are no longer subject to physical death.

Some wonder about the degree of consciousness that the unbeliever has. We would say that they are not with the Lord and other inferences can be made from that reality. When Paul was caught up to the third heaven, and saw things not lawful to be uttered, he said twice that whether in the body or out of the body he does not know. I do think that he was there, he experienced it, and he did not know whether he was in the body or out of the body. He says it twice with strong emphasis. Therefore, it is something for us to heed when we start talking about

---

3. *1 Corinthians 15:50-58.*

4. As in various premillennial views.

5. *1 Corinthians 15:24.*

6. *1 Corinthians 15:26.*

when, and where, and what will it be like. You could be there, as in his case, and whether in the body or out of the body, he does not know.

1 Corinthians 15 tells us when the resurrection will take place— when everything is subdued to Christ. Thus, the righteous in the Lord are now waiting until everything is subdued and the work of dominion is completed, and then the end will come. After death, we will still be concerned about what the Lord is concerned about, the earth being filled with the knowledge of His glory. As Christ unfolds His glory, the earth is being filled with the knowledge of His glory. Believers are beholding the face of God, which is being revealed in His works of creation and providence, and His glory is uncovered on the earth.

SUMMARY ANSWER

On the last day, when everything has been subdued to Christ.

Chapter 33

OF THE LAST JUDGMENT

QUESTION 135

What is the last judgment?

I. God has appointed a day, wherein He will judge the world, in righteousness, by Jesus Christ, to whom all power and judgment is given of the Father. In which day, not only the apostate angels shall be judged, but likewise all persons that have lived upon earth shall appear before the tribunal of Christ, to give an account of their thoughts, words, and deeds; and to receive according to what they have done in the body, whether good or evil.

There are several reasons Christ is in the position of judge of the world. Christ has the honor to preside over the last judgment because He is the Son of God incarnate who represents man and has been given the position of judge by God, and thus has authority to judge. In addition, in Him all fullness dwells. Furthermore, He is the one that has ruled in history and brought things to fruition by subduing all things. He has been given all authority in heaven and earth and that includes judging. All those who disregard Christ will stand before the Lord Jesus Christ in judgment. The final judgment includes not only the work of God the Father, but Christ Himself sits in judgment, giving honor and glory to Him. Mankind will respond with rejoicing as well as with awesome wonder and trepidation while all stand before the tribunal of Christ. In the judgment, all will **give an account of their thoughts,**

words, and deeds, which is why the Scriptures say that we will have to give an account of every idle word.[1]

In what sense can we call it a "day of judgment?" The last judgment certainly begins at a given point in time and continues until each one has given an account. This period of giving an account is the day of judgment or time of judgment. Some might ask, "Would the judgment not take longer than all of human history?" We do not know how long the judgment will take, especially if people start making excuses and they become interminable. Some may say: "You cannot remember every one of your thoughts?" You will have a perfect body, a perfect mind, and a perfect memory at that time.

In addition, each will **receive according to what they have done in the body, whether good or evil.** The day of last judgment comes only after the general resurrection. When the believer dies, they are waiting for the general resurrection, in the presence of God, in complete holiness. We are accepted in Christ; we have passed from death to life. We can never be cast out from the presence of the Lord or our enjoyment of Him diminished. Then comes the last judgment where all angels and men come before Christ to give an account of all their deeds.

SUMMARY ANSWER

All persons and apostate angels will stand before Christ to give an account.

---

1. *Matthew 12:36.*

QUESTION 136

What is the end of God's appointing this day?

II. The end of God's appointing this day is for the manifestation of the glory of His mercy, in the eternal salvation of the elect; and of His justice, in the damnation of the reprobate, who are wicked and disobedient. For then shall the righteous go into everlasting life, and receive that fullness of joy and refreshing, which shall come from the presence of the Lord; but the wicked who know not God, and obey not the Gospel of Jesus Christ, shall be cast into eternal torments, and be punished with everlasting destruction from the presence of the Lord, and from the glory of His power.

The last judgment is a manifestation to the whole universe of all that has been done in the providence of God, which becomes a public and universal record. It is not a scattered account with one person living a millennium ago and another living a millennium later. We grow more in the knowledge of God as we see all the details of history unfold. This is what was affirmed in Chapter 5 of the Confession—God decreed all things from the greatest to the least for the manifestation of His glory, and not apart from that. If we are focused on the knowledge of God, how intense would this universal account be? For example, James Joyce's book *Ulysses* allows the reader to see all that goes on in a person's life in a 24-hour period, which is a very rich revelation. If the last judgment is like this, how would we react? We would certainly see the justice of God and praise the justice of God. It certainly brings praise to the glory of God. Perhaps because of sin, we do not currently understand what the judgment will be like. An analogy is in movies, novels, and all the unfolding of stories. We can never have enough of stories; they are interminable. All of this is revelation.

Going back to Chapter 5 of the Confession, we understand that God created all things for the praise of His glory and He rules all things from the least to the greatest—all of it to the praise of His glory—every thought, word, and deed. In a movie, one look can reveal so much, and we get the satisfaction of capturing it. All of that subtlety will come out in the last judgment. The purpose of the last judgment is **for the manifestation of the glory of His mercy, in the eternal salvation of the elect; and of His justice.** At every point, we will see how in ourselves we are not good, but God, by His grace, brought redemption to completion. All things are for **the manifestation of the glory of His mercy** and of His **Justice,** which is what we mean by the doxological focus of the Confession. More than providing a worldview, the Confession reveals the glory of God. We need to build upon the foundation of the Historic Christian Faith of the Confession.

Believers will live in the presence of the Lord, in the understanding of His justice and His mercy, in every dealing that comes to pass. By contrast, **the wicked who know not God . . . shall be cast into eternal torment.** Eternal torment is to be understood spiritually, as life without meaning. We have spoken about spiritual death as meaninglessness, boredom, and guilt. The condition of meaninglessness, boredom, and guilt unendingly is "eternal torment." The wicked are left in that state forever and receive the justice of God.

They do not see and enjoy the knowledge of the glory of God. If they see in any sense, it is to acknowledge that God is just, and God is merciful, and that they rejected that mercy.

The Scriptures speak about the condition of the wicked as anguish and gnashing of teeth. Some people think of this as a physical condition rather than a spiritual condition, but they do not grasp the reality of the spiritual condition. And yet, we see the justice of God insofar as there is an exact connection between our torment and the things that we have done. Meaninglessness, boredom, and guilt are because we have been heedless and neglectful of truth, and we bypassed it, avoided it, and resisted it. All of these things will come back to us, and through them, the glory of God will be manifested, which is awesome. It is awful—full of awe and awesome. There is a kind of fear and trembling in the reality of God, His Word, and ruling in each life in its history, which is displayed forever and ever unendingly. Thus, judgment day is appointed, and the end of it is for the manifestation of the glory of His mercy and justice. Notice that both those attributes are magnified. We need to keep reminding ourselves that both justice and mercy are true in God.

SUMMARY ANSWER

The end of the last judgment is to reveal His glory (justice and mercy).

QUESTION 137

What is the intended effect of making the day of judgment known?

III. As Christ would have us to be certainly persuaded that there shall be a day of judgment, both to deter all men from sin; and for the greater consolation of the godly in their adversity: so will He have that day unknown to men, that they may shake off all carnal security, and be always watchful, because they know not at what hour the Lord will come; and may be ever prepared to say, Come Lord Jesus, come quickly, Amen.

The intended effect of making known the day of judgment is deterrence. If we just stop and consider the plausibility of coming in judgment before the Lord, it should cause a certain fear in us that will turn us away from sin. We should not lightly and thoughtlessly commit sin. Sin will have its inherent effect in us, and we will have to give an account to the Lord for committing sin. We need to understand more clearly and fully the connection between sin and death. We think of suffering and unhappiness, but we do not think of it as death, the spiritual misery connected with sin. We must see the connection between fruit sin and root sin. Root sin is not seeking, not understanding, and not doing what is right, and the consequences that come from that. Understanding our root sin is difficult for us to learn. When someone comes to Christ, there is conviction of the misery of existence and the emptiness of life without God, which is what turns a person to God. As spiritual life begins with the conviction of sin and death, so it will continue and grow with greater conviction and awareness of sin and death. This growth is how we put aside all sin.

Knowing that there will be a last judgment is not only to deter us from sin, but it is also **for the greater consolation of the godly in their adversity.** There is consolation in knowing there will be a last judgment in connection with the certainty of that day. Though it is certain, that day is unknown to all men. We all know that judgment will come to each one of us at the time of our death. There is a sense in which, at death, there is a kind of judgment in that we will be separated from God, or we will be in God's presence forever thereafter. We should live every day as if it could be our last day. In this way we avoid carnal security. We are called to **be always watchful, because they know not at what hour the Lord will come.** The Lord comes not only in the final judgment, but the Lord will come for us in this life. Death can come to us suddenly. We know not at what hour the Lord will come. The Lord may come in judgment upon nations and churches, and again, we do not know the day and the hour, yet we may know the time and the season. We know that the work of dominion must be completed in terms of the corporate work of the kingdom, which will happen before Christ returns. We are to be watchful and ever **prepared to say, Come Lord Jesus, come quickly, Amen.**

SUMMARY ANSWER

Knowing there will be a last judgment is to deter us from sin and is consolation for the godly. The day is unknown to men.

By the grace of God, with thanksgiving, we end this study. Amen.

—

APPENDICES

—

Appendix 1

———

THE DISTINCTIVES OF
WESTMINSTER FELLOWSHIP

WESTMINSTER FELLOWSHIP AFFIRMS Historic Christianity as it is summed up in the Westminster Confession of Faith of 1648. The Westminster Confession affirms the authority of Scripture, the Tri-unity of God, Father, Son, and Holy Spirit, the sovereignty of God in creation, history, and redemption, the continuity of the Old and New Testaments, the regulative principle of worship, and the law of God for all of life. The Confession of Faith sums up the work of the Holy Spirit, leading the Church into all truth. The Holy Spirit calls and enables the pastor-teachers to respond to challenges to the faith in every age. The modern age has challenged the Church's understanding of general revelation and of the goal of life. Faith has been opposed by reason; Scripture has been opposed by science; focus on heaven has been opposed by focus on this world.

The distinctives of Westminster Fellowship arise from a response to these challenges to the faith.

We affirm that creation and history are revelation of God's glory and that man's purpose is to know God's glory through the work of dominion, given to him in the beginning (*The Goal of the Knowledge of God*).

We affirm that eternal life is knowing God and Jesus Christ, whom He has sent.

We affirm that the eternal power and divine nature of God are clearly revealed, being understood from the things that are made, so that man's unbelief is without excuse (*The Clarity of General Revelation and the Inexcusability of Unbelief*).

We affirm that every thought raised up against the knowledge of God must be taken captive and made obedient to Christ (*Rational Presuppositionalism*).

We affirm the regulative principle and the singing of Psalms in the worship of God.

We affirm that the earth shall be full of the knowledge of the Lord as the waters cover the sea, as Christ subdues all things to Himself through the Church (*Postmillennial Eschatology*).

Appendix 2

THE DOXOLOGICAL FOCUS

of the

WESTMINSTER STANDARDS

expresses the

DISTINCTIVES OF WESTMINSTER FELLOWSHIP

THE CONFESSION TEACHES:

Although the light of nature, and the works of creation and providence do so far manifest the goodness, wisdom, and power of God, as to leave men inexcusable. (1.1)

God hath all life, glory, goodness, blessedness, in and of Himself; and is alone in and unto Himself all-sufficient, not standing in need of any creatures which He hath made, nor deriving any glory from them, but only manifesting His own glory in, by, unto, and upon them. (2.2)

By the decree of God, for the manifestation of His glory, some men and angels are predestinated unto everlasting life (to the praise of His glorious mercy); and others foreordained to everlasting death (to the praise of His glorious justice). (3.3)

It pleased God the Father, Son, and Holy Ghost, for the manifestation of the glory of His eternal power, wisdom, and goodness, in the beginning, to create, or make of nothing, the world, and all things therein whether visible or invisible, in the space of six days; and all very good. (4.1)

God the great Creator of all things doth uphold, direct, dispose, and govern all creatures, actions, and things, from the greatest even to the least, by His most wise and holy providence, according to His infallible foreknowledge, and the free and immutable counsel of His own will, to the praise of the glory of His wisdom, power, justice, goodness, and mercy. (5.1)

Our first parents, being seduced by the subtlety and temptations of Satan, sinned, in eating the forbidden fruit. This their sin, God was pleased, according to His wise and holy counsel, to permit, having purposed to order it to His own glory. (6.1)

THE SHORTER CATECHISM TEACHES:

Man's chief end is to glorify God, and to enjoy Him forever. (Q. 1)

The first commandment requireth us to know and acknowledge God to be the only true God, and our God; and to worship and glorify Him accordingly. (Q. 46)

In the first petition, which is, *Hallowed be thy name*, we pray that God would enable us, and others, to glorify Him in all that whereby He maketh Himself known; and that He would dispose all things to His own glory. (Q. 101)

WE BELIEVE THAT:

We are to glorify God in all that by which He makes Himself known, in all His works of creation and providence.

Appendix 3

———

HISTORICAL FOUNDATION
The Work of the Holy Spirit
Leading the Church Into All Truth

WESTMINSTER FELLOWSHIP HOLDS to Historic Christianity. Historic Christianity is the work of the Holy Spirit leading the Church into all truth,[1] through the centuries, through the work of pastor-teachers. Pastor-teachers are given to the Church by Christ to bring believers to the unity of the faith, to the full measure of the stature of Christ.[2]

Challenges occur in every age, to which the Church must respond in order to attain to the fullness of Christ, and to accomplish its task to disciple all nations. Without the teachings of Historic Christianity firmly established in the lives of believers, there is no ordinary basis for hope for attaining maturity in the fullness of Christ.

In every age, as the Church expands, new believers bring into the Church ideas and practices from their culture which challenge the truth of the Gospel. After much discussion, the pastor-teachers come to agreement on the teaching of Scripture in response to these challenges.

The First Church Council was held in Jerusalem in response to the challenge of Judaic legalism.[3] The early gentile converts were influenced by Greek dualism, and raised the challenge of Gnosticism, which was answered by the Apostles' Creed (*ca.* A.D. 180), recited in churches through the centuries. The Council of Nicea (A.D. 325) addressed

———

1. *John 16:13.*
2. *Ephesians 4.*
3. *Acts 15.*

challenges to the doctrine of the Trinity. The Council of Carthage (A.D. 397) identified all the books and only the books that constitute the Scripture of the New Testament. The Council of Chalcedon (A.D. 451) clarified the doctrine of the Incarnation (that Christ is fully God and fully man), and the Council of Orange (A.D. 529) affirmed the doctrine of sin (man is fallen in Adam) and salvation (man is saved by grace) in response to Pelagian and semi-Pelagian error.

The Westminster Confession of Faith (A.D. 1648) is the high-water mark of Historic Christianity at the beginning of the modern era. Building on the work of the pastor-teachers in the early Church councils, it responded to the challenges of systemic distortions in the Church at the time of the Reformation.[4]

It affirmed the authority of Scripture over against all other sources of special revelation. It affirmed the sovereignty of God over all, and its application in salvation through one covenant of grace over against all admixtures of grace with human effort.

It affirmed the work of the pastor-teachers meeting in synods/councils over against hierarchical and independent ecclesiastical authority. And it affirmed the regulative principle of worship, that the worship of God, which God has commanded in Scripture, must be kept pure and entire.

In the modern age, the Church has been challenged in terms of its claim to knowledge (reason and science vs. faith and scripture), and in its view of human purpose (life on earth vs. eternal life in heaven, the secular vs. the sacred).

The Church has not yet come to the unity of faith in meeting these challenges and has steadily been losing ground where it once led the culture in Western Civilization. Current globalization has intensified contact with non-western cultures and worldviews in Asia, Africa, and South America.

The more supernatural forms of Christianity growing in these areas are yet to face the acid tests of skepticism and secularism. By building on Historic Christianity, as summed up in the Westminster Confession of Faith, these challenges can be met.

---

4. Gangadean, "Paper No. 16: The Historic Christian Faith: The Holy Spirit Guides the Church into All Truth," in *The Logos Papers*, 103-114.

The challenge of reason and science vs. faith and scripture can be met by the Biblical teaching on the clarity of general revelation and the inexcusability of unbelief.[5]

The Westminster Confession opens with the affirmation of this teaching: "The light of nature [reason], and the works of creation and providence do so far manifest the goodness, wisdom, and power of God, as to leave men unexcusable . . ." Believers today are being challenged by skepticism to show the clarity of general revelation and to take thoughts captive which are raised up against the knowledge of God.[6]

Believers today are being challenged by secularism—life in this world vs. eternal life in heaven. This can be met by the Biblical teaching that eternal life is the knowledge of God,[7] and that man's purpose on earth is to fill the earth with the knowledge of God as the waters cover the sea.[8]

The Westminster Confession of Faith affirms that God's purpose in creation and providence is the revelation of His glory;[9] that the first commandment requires us to know and acknowledge God;[10] that the first petition in the Lord's Prayer is that God would enable us and others to glorify Him in all that by which He makes Himself known;[11] that man's chief end is to glorify God and enjoy Him forever.[12]

---

5. *Romans 1:18-20; 2:14.*

6. *2 Corinthians 10:4-5.*

7. *John 17:3.*

8. *Isaiah 11:9.*

9. *WCF. 4.1, 5.1.*

10. *SCQ. 46.*

11. *SCQ. 101.*

12. *SCQ. 1.*

Appendix 4

THE GOAL OF THE
KNOWLEDGE OF GOD

PART I:
Creation Is Revelation

1. *God created to make His glory known.* "It pleased God the Father, Son, and Holy Ghost, for the manifestation of the glory of His eternal power, wisdom, and goodness, in the beginning, to create, or make of nothing, the world, and all things therein whether visible or invisible in the space of six days; and all very good."[1] *God rules in history to make His glory known.* "God the great Creator of all things doth uphold, direct, dispose, and govern all creatures, actions, and things, from the greatest even to the least, by His most wise and holy providence, according to His infallible foreknowledge, and the free and immutable counsel of His own will, to the praise of the glory of His wisdom, power, justice, goodness, and mercy."[2]

2. *This revelation is not bare, but full.* The whole earth is full of His glory.[3] Revelation is not restricted to Scripture. Scripture is not an alternative to general revelation.

3. *Creation is revelation, necessarily.* A being is revealed in its acts; the acts of God in creation and providence reveal the nature of God. Every act of God reveals His nature. No act of God is above, apart from, or against His nature.

---

1. *WCF 4.1.*
2. *WCF 5.1.*
3. *Isaiah 6:3; Psalm 8, 29.*

4. *Creation is revelation, intentionally.* Creation is by the will of God, by His infinite, deliberate wisdom. What creation reveals, God intends to reveal. What God reveals, He intends to be known. God created and rules to reveal Himself.

5. *Creation is revelation, exclusively.* There is no knowledge of God apart from creation and history. There is no direct vision of God, no beatific vision of God in heaven apart from God's self-revelation in creation and history.[4] To see God face to face is to see His revelation clearly, without the distortion of sin. God is a Spirit, immortal, invisible, whom no man has seen nor can see.[5] There is no greater revelation of the glory of God than by His works of creation and providence, which includes Christ's work of redemption.

PART II:
General Revelation Is Clear

1. "Since the creation of the world, God's invisible qualities—His eternal power and divine nature—have been clearly seen, being understood from what has been made, so that men are without excuse."[6] Without clarity of general revelation, there is no inexcusability for unbelief and, therefore, no sin and no need for redemption.

2. The clarity of general revelation includes the existence and nature of God, as well as the law of God which is written on the hearts of all men.[7]

3. Although general revelation is objectively clear, no one, left to himself, sees it. All have sinned and come short of the glory of God.[8] There is no one righteous, not even one; there is no one who understands, no one who seeks God.[9]

---

4. Gangadean, "Paper No. 106: The Good and Heaven: The Good Is Not the Beatific Vision," in *The Logos Papers*, 547-556.

5. *1 Timothy 1:17; 6:16.*

6. *Romans 1:20; WCF. 1.1.*

7. *Romans 2:14-15.*

8. *Romans 3:23.*

9. *Romans 3:10-11.*

4. Without seeking, there is no understanding of what is clear about God. Without understanding what is clear about God, there is no understanding of sin and death, no understanding of the need for Scripture, and no understanding of Christ's redemption.

5. The wages of sin is death.[10] This death is spiritual, not physical. Spiritual death is the destruction of the soul, which is present and inherent in sin.[11] It begins in this life and lasts forever. It is called the second death or the lake of fire.[12] Individually, spiritual death consists in meaninglessness, boredom, and guilt. Corporately, it consists in the death of relationships, institutions, and cultures.

PART III:
Eternal Life Is Knowing God

1. From general revelation, the good for man as a rational being is understanding creation and providence, which reveal God; the good is the knowledge of God. Jesus said: "Now this is eternal life: that they might know you, the only true God, and Jesus Christ, whom you have sent."[13]

2. *Eternal life is the good for man.*[14] It was the good for man before the Fall, as well as after the Fall. Redemption is restoration to life. Eternal life is not heaven. It begins in this life and grows forever. Eternal life is more than salvation; understood as forgiveness of sins and justification.

3. *Man's chief end is to know God.* Man's chief end is to glorify God and to enjoy Him forever.[15] To glorify God is to understand His glory (the greatness of His wisdom, power, justice, and goodness) and to make His glory known.

---

10. *Genesis 2:17; Romans 6:23.*

11. *Ephesians 2:1, 4-5.*

12. *Revelation 20:6, 10, 14.*

13. *John 17:3.*

14. Gangadean, "Paper No. 4: The Cornerstone: Good & Evil – Life & Death: The Beginning of the Foundation," 21-25; Gangadean, "Paper No. 42: The Moral Law: The First Commandment," in *The Logos Papers*, 231-235.

15. *SCQ. 1.*

4. *The first commandment is to know God.* The first commandment requires us to know and acknowledge God to be the only true God, and our God, and to worship and glorify Him accordingly.[16]

5. *The first petition of prayer is to know God.* In the first petition of the Lord's Prayer which is *Hallowed be Thy Name*, we pray that God would enable us and others to glorify Him in all that by which He makes Himself known; and that He would dispose all things to His own glory.[17]

PART IV:
The Knowledge of God Is Through the Work of Dominion

1. "And God said, Let us make man in our image, after our likeness: and let them have dominion over all the earth."[18] The knowledge of God is through the work of dominion. In dominion, man is to be fruitful and multiply and fill the earth and rule over it.[19] The work of dominion is corporate, cumulative, and communal. It requires all of mankind, working together through all of history, to be achieved.[20]

2. *In dominion, man is to rule over the creation.* He is to develop all the powers latent in himself and in the creation.

3. *In dominion, man is to name the creation.* Naming requires grasping the nature of all beings in all their parts and relations so as to make known the glory of God. Man is to know the nature of all things created.

4. In knowing the creation, which reveals the glory of God, man comes to know God.

5. Sin does not cancel God's revelation or the work of dominion, but deepens the revelation and enlarges the work of dominion. The fullness of life is not attained in heaven apart from the completion of the work of dominion.

---

16. *SCQ. 46.*

17. *SCQ. 101.*

18. *Genesis 1:2.*

19. *Genesis 1.*

20. Gangadean, *Philosophical Foundation*, 207-219.

PART V:
The Earth Shall Be Full of the Knowledge of God

1. The Sabbath, from the beginning, signified hope that the work of dominion will be completed. As God completed the work of creation, man will complete the work of dominion. As creation is revelation, so dominion brings knowledge of this revelation.[21]

2. Since the Fall, God calls man back to himself through the curse and the promise.[22] Individually, the curse consists in toil and strife, and old age, sickness, and death. Corporately, the curse consists in famine, war, and plague. The curse is natural evil; it is imposed by God to restrain, recall from, and remove moral evil (sin). Moral evil includes not only not seeking and not understanding, but also self-deception and self-justification for sin.

3. The promise, given in Scripture, is that Christ will *undo* what Adam did, in paying the penalty for sin, and will *do* what Adam failed to do, to fill the earth with the knowledge of God.

4. In Christ, believers must take captive every thought raised up against the knowledge of God.[23] In Christ, believers must make disciples of all nations, teaching them to obey all that He has commanded.[24]

5. As a result of Christ's rule, "The earth shall be full of the knowledge of the Lord, as the waters cover the sea."[25]

---

21. *Genesis 2:1-3.*
22. *Genesis 3:14-24.*
23. *2 Corinthians 10:4.*
24. *Matthew 28:20.*
25. *Isaiah 11:9.*

Appendix 5

RATIONAL

PRESUPPOSITIONALISM

Critically Examining Assumptions for Meaning

RATIONAL PRESUPPOSITIONALISM IS AN epistemological method used to settle philosophical disputes by critically analyzing assumptions for meaning. It applies reason as a test for meaning to what is presupposed in a dispute.

Rational Presuppositionalism (RP) affirms that some things are clear. The basic things are clear. The basic things about God and man and good and evil are clear to reason.[1] RP is an answer to skepticism and fideism. It is an alternative to rationalism and to empiricism, both of which make uncritically held assumptions.[2]

Thinking is presuppositional. We think of the less basic in light of the more basic. We think of truth in light of meaning, experience in light of basic belief, conclusions in light of premises, and the finite and temporal in light of the infinite and eternal. If we understand what is more basic, we can understand what is less basic; if we agree on what is more basic, we can agree on what is less basic.

RP seeks to avoid needless disputes by examining if there is agreement on what is more basic. It seeks to avoid straining at gnats while swallowing camels. It looks at both the objective and the subjective aspects of knowledge and dialogue. Dialogue presupposes a commitment to reason along with an understanding of the nature of reason.

---

1. Gangadean, *Philosophical Foundation*, 287-292.

2. Gangadean, *History of Philosophy*, 131-149.

Having knowledge presupposes a concern to know, which presupposes integrity as a concern for consistency, both theoretically and personally. If there is commitment to reason, with integrity, disputes can be settled.[3]

Skepticism claims that knowledge is not possible. It is rooted in uncritically held assumptions, that if rationalism (for example, Descartes) and empiricism (for example, Hume) cannot give knowledge, then no knowledge is possible.[4] Consistently held, skepticism leads to nihilism, in which no distinction is clear, including the distinction of *a* and *non-a*, being and non-being, true and false, and good and evil.

Skepticism denies reason, makes dialogue impossible, and leads to silence as well as a cessation of all thought. It dissolves the meaning of its terms—*knowledge* and *possible*. Pragmatism cannot overcome the meaninglessness of skepticism.[5] And fideism (appeal to faith apart from proof based on understanding) becomes an arbitrary affirmation of one view from among many.

RP affirms that sense experience gives knowledge of appearance but not of reality, and that the data of experience (common sense, scientific or mystical) must be interpreted in order to be meaningful. RP does not allow the post-modern skeptical view that "it is all a matter of interpretation." Philosophy does not end with interpretation, but begins here.

Every interpretation can be, and must be, tested for coherence and meaning. RP affirms that the self-evident truths of rationalism (Descartes' *cogito* or Jefferson's self-evident truths) are not logically basic, even though they are taken as properly basic. The alternatives of absolute idealism and naturalism require a response.

Rational Presuppositionalism is to be distinguished from fideistic presuppositionalism, in which one moves from Scripture (the Triune God of the Bible) to reason. RP is to be distinguished from axiomatic presuppositionalism, in which one begins with the Scripture as one's set of axioms.

RP is to be distinguished from reformed epistemology, in which one begins with what is taken as properly basic beliefs.[6] RP is to be distin-

---

3. Gangadean, *Philosophical Foundation*, 287-292.

4. Gangadean, *History of Philosophy*, 9-12.

5. Gangadean, *Philosophical Foundation*, 117-118.

6. Gangadean, *History of Philosophy*, 175-179.

guished from evidentialism, in which one seeks to argue from miracles to God. RP is to be distinguished from common sense realism, in which the objective existence of the external world is assumed.[7]

RP affirms that the clarity of general revelation is necessary for the inexcusability of unbelief and undertakes to show what is clear from general revelation by showing the alternatives of unbelief are contrary to reason.[8] It is to be distinguished from all attempts to answer historical criticism of the Scriptures without first establishing the clarity of general revelation.

RP begins with an affirmation of the nature of reason based on the reality of thought. Reason is to be defined in itself, in its use, and in us.[9]

Reason in itself is the laws of thought. Most basically, these are the law of identity: *a* is *a*; the law of non-contradiction: not both *a* and *non-a*, at the same time and in the same respect; and the law of excluded middle: either *a* or *non-a*. Other laws of thought are based on these laws. To doubt these laws is to lose all distinctions and to cease to think.

Reason in its use is formative, critical, interpretive, and constructive. Reason is used to form concepts, judgments, and arguments, which are the forms of all thought. Whenever there are thoughts, reason is being used formatively. Reason is used critically as a test for meaning. It is applied especially to basic beliefs as a test for meaning. If a belief, upon analysis, violates a law of thought, it lacks meaning and cannot be true. Reason is used to interpret experience in light of one's basic beliefs. No experience is meaningful without interpretation, and every interpretation can and must be tested for meaning. And lastly, reason is used to construct a coherent world and life view upon one's basic belief. Worldviews are manifest in cultures. They are held more or less consciously and more or less consistently and, therefore, continually face the internal and external challenges of reason.[10]

Reason is always being used formatively. It is often used constructively, without first being used critically. It is sometimes used interpretively

---

7. Gangadean, "Paper No. 3: The Principle of Clarity, Rational Presuppositionalism, and Proof," in *The Logos Papers*, 15-20.

8. Gangadean, "Paper No. 3: The Principle of Clarity, Rational Presuppositionalism, and Proof," in *The Logos Papers*, 15-20; Gangadean, *Philosophical Foundation*, 71-161.

9. Gangadean, *Philosophical Foundation*, 10-15.

10. Gangadean, "Paper No. 19: Foundation for Philosophy of History," in *The Logos Papers*, 123-125.

without realizing it. Reason in itself is not fallible, but a person may fail to use reason critically and fully.

Reason does not succeed only if it persuades subjectively, but if it answers objections with an objectively sound argument. Many objections against reason and rationalism are really against what amounts to a failure to use reason.[11] Reason in itself must therefore be distinguished from reason in its use.

Reason in us is natural, ontological, transcendental, and fundamental. Reason is natural, not conventional. It is universal, the same in all persons. Reason as the laws of thought is the common ground among all thinkers. What distinguishes us is not reason, but the willingness to use reason. What distinguishes us is not our assumption, but the willingness to critically examine our assumption for meaning.

Reason is ontological. It applies to being as well as to thought. There are no square-circles, no uncaused events, no being from non-being. It applies to all being, including the highest being. God is not both eternal and not eternal, at the same time and in the same respect. Matter is not both extended and not extended, at the same time and in the same respect.[12] There is no noumenal realm or dimension in which reason does not apply, but to which faith gives access.[13] While the mysteries of faith do not originate in reason, they do not go against reason. Miracles are not against the laws of reason, but against a law of nature. Reason, as an aspect of God's being, is eternal. The laws of nature are created. Paradoxes are puzzling to reason insofar as assumptions present and at work are not yet critically examined and corrected. Finite beings cannot have exhaustive or comprehensive knowledge of anything, but the unknown is not against the laws of reason.

Reason is transcendental. It is authoritative and self-attesting. It is transcendental in that it stands above thought and makes thought possible. It cannot be questioned, but makes questioning possible. Statements about general and special revelation (Scripture) can and must be questioned, by reason, but reason itself as the laws of thought cannot be questioned. As transcendental, it cannot be argued for, even in a circular manner. In thought, what is of highest authority

---

11. Gangadean, *History of Philosophy*, 131-137.

12. Gangadean, *History of Philosophy*, 38.

13. Gangadean, *History of Philosophy*, 151-153; Gangadean, *Philosophical Foundation*, 109-110.

is self-attesting, and only reason is self-attesting.[14] Scripture assumes reason as that by which Scripture is to be understood. Scripture, if it is to be received, must be spoken in the name of God; that is, it must be consistent with the nature of God known from general revelation. There is not and cannot be any conflict between reason, general revelation, and Scripture. Scripture is set against all other forms of special revelation, not against reason and general revelation.

Reason is fundamental. It is fundamental to other aspects of human personality. Feelings are directed by belief about the good, and thought and feeling move the will to act. Feeling and will are not independent of or contrary to belief. Conflicts within the understanding are manifest in conflicts in feeling and will. Unnoticed, these misunderstandings, as conflicts within our thoughts, lead to apparent conflict between thought and feeling, etc. Our deepest need is for meaning. Our deepest misery is in the awareness of the lack of meaning. Meaninglessness is a fundamental aspect of spiritual death, and, sometimes, physical death is sought as an escape from spiritual death. Boredom comes from meaninglessness, in which the creation, apart from or in place of the Creator, cannot satisfy. Failure to be rational is experienced as guilt, from which escape is sought in the unending rationalizations of self-justification. Our greatest happiness is from the use of reason in understanding the creation, when this understanding leads to the knowledge of God.

The first application of RP is to the question *what is real?* It clarifies the subjective factors of integrity and commitment to reason as preconditions to knowledge. It prevents further discussion, which would be fruitless if these preconditions are not in place.

We begin with the question *what is real?* because existence is our most basic concept, and eternal existence (without beginning) is more basic than temporal existence (with beginning).

To show that *some is eternal* is true, we show that the contradiction *none is eternal* cannot be true. *None is eternal* implies that *all is temporal, all had a beginning, all came into being.* If all came into being, it would have come into being from non-being, which is impossible.

---

14. Gangadean, *Philosophical Foundation*, 298-299.

Hence, *none is eternal* cannot be true, and its contradiction *some is eternal* must be true. *All came into being from non-being* is not the same as creation *ex nihilo*, in which God is eternal and acted to create.[15]

By *non-being* is meant the absence of all being whatsoever, not just the absence of all visible being. An unending series of finite and temporal beings having the power to create *ex nihilo*, is not an objection that has been (or, upon analysis, can be) made.

If it is agreed that it is clear to reason that there must be something eternal, we can go on to the next step in showing what is clear.[16]

---

15. Gangadean, *Philosophical Foundation*, 61-68.

16. Gangadean, *Philosophical Foundation*, 71-284.

Appendix 6

———

THE CLARITY OF
GENERAL REVELATION

*God's Eternal Power and Divine Nature,
and the Moral Law*

G ENERAL REVELATION IS WHAT MAY BE KNOWN of God by all men,
everywhere, at all times. What is clear from general revelation is
His eternal power and divine nature and the moral law.[1]

The clarity of general revelation is the basis of the inexcusability of
unbelief and of the necessity of redemptive revelation in Scripture.[2]
Because general revelation is clear, those in unbelief regarding the
existence and nature of God and of the moral law have no reason for
their unbelief.

To deny what is clear requires the denial of reason. The clarity of
general revelation, under the condition of moral and natural evil, leads to
recognition of the necessity, content, origin, and existence of Scripture.
This further leads to the recognition of the transmission, completion,
translation, clarity, sufficiency, and interpretation of Scripture.[3] The
clarity of general revelation is necessary in order to avoid misinterpre-
tation of Scripture.

If non-believers are responsible for seeing through the inexcusability of their unbelief, believers are all the more so. If we have come to

---

1. *Romans 1:18-20; 2:14-15.*

2. Gangadean, "Paper No. 12: The Necessity for Scripture: General Revelation Requires Special
   Revelation," in *The Logos Papers*, 75-77.

3. Gangadean, "Paper No. 11: From General Revelation to Special Revelation: Prologue to
   Scripture," in *The Logos Papers*, 69-73.

understand what is clear, we should be able to show what is clear.[4] We should be able to take thoughts captive that are raised up against the knowledge of God.[5]

But believers still have sin and have to contend with the noetic effect of sin in themselves. Believers have to struggle to avoid being taken captive by prevailing unbelief in the culture in which they live. But by recognizing the need for the renewal of one's mind, by benefiting from the understanding already achieved in Historic Christianity, and by engaging with the remaining internal and external challenges to the Faith, believers can come to a mature understanding of the clarity of general revelation.

Rational Presuppositionalism is an epistemological method which seeks to settle disputes by thinking of the less basic in light of the more basic and critically analyzing assumptions for meaning. By Rational Presuppositionalism, we can understand the major steps in showing the clarity of general revelation.

1. Show the necessity for clarity in general against skepticism, and the necessity for clarity in particular for Christian theism, against fideism.

2. Show, by ontological argument, that there must be something eternal. This is a paradigm of what is clear to reason. Rational Presuppositionalism requires agreement here before going any further in metaphysics. If this cannot be known, nothing can be known and dialogue is not possible.

3. Show, by cosmological arguments, that only some (God) is eternal; that is, show theism vs. all forms of non-theism. This requires showing that matter exists and that matter is not eternal; that the soul/spirit exists and the soul is not eternal.

To show the material world is not eternal, it must be shown that the material world is not self-maintaining (vs. material monism—all forms of scientific materialism and cosmological naturalism).

---

4. Gangadean, "Paper No. 110: On Clarity: Concern for Consistency in Thought and Action," 577-578; Gangadean, "Paper No. 39: Clarity: And Its Application," in *The Logos Papers*, 217-220.

5. *2 Corinthians 10:4-5.*

To show that the soul exists, it must be shown that the mind is not the brain. To show the individual soul exists, it must be shown that there is not one mind only and its ideas (vs. spiritual monism—absolute or Vedantic idealism).

To show that the material world exists (vs. ordinary idealism), it must be shown that the cause of what is seen is not my mind or another mind, but outside all minds.

To show that the soul is not eternal (vs. all forms of dualism—Greek, Indian, Persian, and Mormon, and reincarnation), it must be shown that the soul experiences unique events.

4. Show, by teleological argument, that the natural order is by design (that is, show special creation) vs. all forms of evolution—natural and theistic.

5. Show, by teleological argument, that, in divine providence, moral and natural evil serve the divine purpose (that is, show the Ironic Solution to the problem of evil) vs. naturalistic and free will solutions.

6. Show the moral law, structured into human nature by creation, is clear, comprehensive, and critical, the same in content as the law given by special revelation.

7. Show the necessity, content, origin, and existence of special revelation (vs. deism). Further, show the transmission, completion, translation, clarity, sufficiency, and interpretation of special revelation.

8. Show Christian theism (vs. all forms of non-Christian theism—that is, Judaic and Islamic theism), based on general and on special revelation.

9. Show the response to past challenges to Christian theism, based on general and on special revelation, and summed up in the ecumenical and historical creeds (Gnosticism, Trinity, Incarnation, predestination).

10. Show the response to continuing external and internal challenges to Christian theism (faith vs. reason, otherworldliness and secularism vs. knowledge of God, continuing divisions within theism vs. unity of the faith).

Appendix 7

THE NOETIC EFFECT OF SIN

The Effect of Moral Evil on the Mind of Man

I T IS THE NATURE OF SIN (MORAL EVIL) TO NOT SEEK the good, to misunderstand the good, in ignorance to call good evil and evil good, to oppose the good in light of one's misconception, and to avoid and resist correction by self-deception and self-justification. The effect of moral evil on the mind of man is called the noetic effect. It began with the Fall of man and is removed gradually in the redemption of man.

Scripture (the biblical worldview of creation–fall–redemption) assumes the clarity of general revelation.[1] Sin begins in the failure to seek and understand what is clear about God. This sin is universal.[2] This sin is deep.[3] This sin is destructive.[4] The neglect of not seeking is set against the necessity for seeking: he that comes to God must believe that He is and that He is the rewarder of those that diligently seek Him.[5] The reward of diligently seeking God is knowing Him. Eternal life is knowing God.[6]

The noetic effect of sin is first seen in the Garden of Eden. Man is called to know God through the work of dominion. Left to himself, man turns from the knowledge of God as the good. When tested (regarding

------

1. *Romans 1:20.*
2. *Romans 3:10-11.*
3. *Jeremiah 17:9.*
4. *Romans 6:23.*
5. *Hebrews 11:6.*
6. *John 17:3.*

his understanding of good and evil, and life and death) he failed. He believed the falsehood: "You shall not surely die . . . you shall be like God knowing good and evil."[7] The outward act of eating of the tree of the knowledge of good and evil revealed the inward state of not seeking and not knowing God. He lost sight of the radical difference between God as Creator and man as creature in knowing good and evil. He had put himself in the place of God to determine good and evil.

Good for a being is based on the nature of that being. God knows good and evil, not by discovery, but by determining the nature of beings by the act of creation. Adam was to know good and evil by discovering the nature of beings. Man cannot be like God in knowing good and evil because man is a creature, not the Creator. He cannot determine the nature of things. Adam, by not seeking the knowledge of God as the good, failed to understand what is clear about God—that God is the infinite and eternal Creator, and that man is a finite, temporal creature. This, the original sin, is the origin of all sin in all men. Sin is the failure to understand what is clear about God.

As the inward act of sin of not seeking and not understanding is exposed by the outward act of unrighteousness (eating), man experiences shame in his nakedness. Shame is the first natural and inward call back from sin. It is the call of conscience. Man avoids this call back through self-deception, by covering his nakedness. God calls man back a second time, outwardly, by a call to self-examination in asking: where are you? Man resists the second call by self-justification, blaming the woman and God Himself for his own disobedience. God calls man back a third and final time by imposing on man the curse (toil and strife, and old age, sickness, and death) and by the giving of the promise (the seed of the woman will crush the head of the serpent).[8] Man responds to the third call by repentance and faith. He is justified by God in being covered with the coats of skin (forgiveness through the death of another), and is to be sanctified through suffering, by expulsion from the Garden to live under the curse.

Sin is permitted by God and is made to serve His purpose. It deepens the revelation of His justice and mercy. If it is removed abruptly, the revelation will not be deepened. If it is not removed, the revelation will

---

7. *Genesis 3:5.*

8. *Genesis 3:15.*

not be seen. Sin, as unbelief, is permitted to work itself out in human history in every form and degree of combination with belief. In this age-long and agonizing conflict, good overcomes evil. The seed of the woman crushes the head of the serpent, according to the promise.[9]

Although forgiven in Christ, sin remains in believers, along with its noetic effect. Believers continue to fail to understand what is clear about God from general revelation. This failure to seek and to understand the clarity of general revelation is overlooked in self-deception and resisted in self-justification. Natural evil (the curse) continues to call men back from moral evil (sin). Suffering calls men to stop and think about basic things, about meaning and purpose, about God and man, about good and evil, about life and death. Suffering the curse and agonies of the spiritual war of belief vs. unbelief continues as long as the noetic effect of sin remains.

The clarity of general revelation cannot be denied without denying the inexcusability of unbelief. But clarity cannot be affirmed without being required to show the clarity of general revelation. As a result, the doctrine of clarity has been left in the dark. Believers continue to show a disregard for the clarity of general revelation and a disinclination to show the inexcusability of unbelief.[10] This, and other closely connected doctrines, has been held more or less consciously, and more or less consistently.

Self-deception about diligently seeking to know God continues; self-justification for not knowing what is clear about God continues; the suffering of toil and strife, and old age, sickness, and death continues as God's call back to stop and think. Insofar as we do not stop and think, our understanding remains in darkness. What we profess to believe becomes emptied of meaning or filled with misunderstanding. One's entire worldview is affected by one's understanding of good and evil.

The failure to understand what is clear from general revelation continues in the failure to understand what is clear from special revelation. The divisions in the Church in understanding Scripture reflect the divisions in understanding general revelation. Sin has affected the entire Christian worldview by distorting understanding of foundational

---

9. Gangadean, *Philosophical Foundation*, 156-161.

10. Gangadean, "Paper No. 61: The Present and Future State of the Church: To and For the Church," 331-333; Gangadean, "Paper No. 62: The Next Reformation: Prepare the Way of the Lord," in *The Logos Papers*, 335-337.

teachings. The following briefly mention some of this misunderstanding, with further explanation below.

Moral evil is not seen as the failure to understand what is clear about God. It is seen as a willful act of disobedience of a command of God. Faith is not seen as based on understanding and evidence. It is seen as a choice to believe above, apart from, or against evidence. The wages of sin is not seen as spiritual death, present and inherent in sin. The wages of sin is seen as hell, which is future and imposed. Eternal life is not seen as the knowledge of God. It is seen as the absence of the curse in heaven.

1. The noetic effect affects our understanding of sin (moral evil).

Sin is the failure to seek and to understand what is clear about God (divine nature) and man, and good and evil (moral law). Sin is not fundamentally the willful outward act of disobedience of a command of God.[11] Adam believed what was false about God and about sin and death before he ate; and he ate because of his unbelief. Sin is coming short of seeing the glory of God. This is the sin which is universal, and of which all must repent. Yet, personally and corporately, the Church repents of fruit sin, but not root sin. We think of ourselves as concerned to know the truth even when we fail to know what is clear. We resist responsibility for knowing what is clear by denying clarity (no one knows), or making it impossible to know (reason is finite/fallen), or irrelevant to faith (deep down everyone knows). The noetic effect of sin is covered by hypocrisy through self-deception and self-justification. Integrity, by self-examination and by discipline, is necessary and sufficient to overcome hypocrisy, and to know what is clear about God.

What can be known of God is revealed by the Word of God. Man, in his fallen state, resists and rejects the Word of God in every form: in himself as reason;[12] in creation as general revelation;[13] in history as special/ redemptive revelation;[14] in person as Jesus Christ, the Word incarnate.[15]

---

11. Gangadean, "Paper No. 120: Contra Voluntarism: The Will Is Not Independent of the Intellect," in *The Logos Papers,* 611-647.

12. *John 1:4-5.*

13. *John 1:10.*

14. *John 1:11.*

15. *John 1:14.*

2. The noetic effect affects our understanding of spiritual death.

The wages of sin is death,[16] not hell as is commonly conceived. Death here is spiritual, not physical. Spiritual death is present and inherent in sin, whereas hell, as a literal lake of fire, is future and imposed. Hell, in biblical language, is a symbolic representation of spiritual death. It is called the second death.[17] Taken literally, hell, as a lake of fire, is without meaning. Spirits are not affected by physical fire. To appeal to a continual miracle in order to make the literal hell possible is to deny God's justice and to invite blasphemy.[18] The fear of hell (avoiding natural evil) is not the fear of God (avoiding moral evil). There is a necessary connection between sin (not seeking, and not understanding) and death (meaninglessness, boredom, and guilt). Understanding the connection between sin and death creates the fear of the Lord, which moves us to diligently seek Him. Thus, the fear of the Lord is the beginning of wisdom.

3. The noetic effect affects our understanding of the curse (natural evil).

The curse of toil and strife, and old age, sickness, and death, is God's call back from sin, not punishment for sin. There are two kinds of death as well as two kinds of resurrections: physical and spiritual.[19] The wages of sin is spiritual death, not physical death. It is part of the noetic effect of sin to avoid and resist the curse as God's call to repentance of failing to see what is clear.

Physical death is not original in the creation. Physical death is not inherent in sin. Physical death is imposed because of sin. It is the third and last call back from sin. (The first call back of shame is avoided by self-deception, and the second call back to self-examination is avoided by self-justification.) The noetic effect of self-deception and self-justification objectively require the curse and at the same time subjectively resist the curse. Although the curse is sometimes referred to as punishment and sometimes as chastening, it is not punishment in the strict or absolute

---

16. *Romans 6:23; Genesis 2:17; Ephesians 2:1.*

17. *Revelation 20:14.*

18. *Romans 2:24.*

19. *John 5:24-29; 11:25; Revelation 20:6.*

sense of the term. Physical death cannot (in the strict sense) be considered punishment for sin, in this life or the next. If physical death were punishment for the believer, then Christ did not bear the full penalty of sin. If physical death were punishment for the non-believer, there would be no resurrection for the bodies of non-believers. If the curse were punishment for both believers and non-believers, there would be some proportionality in its manifestation. But the most righteous, for example Job, often suffer more than others, and the wicked often prosper more than the righteous.[20]

The curse serves several purposes in relation to sin. Its serves to restrain all from sin, to recall non-believers from sin, and to remove the sin remaining in believers. In all the suffering of the curse, there is a call to stop and think deeply about good and evil, about the meaning and purpose of life. It is a call to know God. The curse is intensified in history to become famine, war, and plague. At death, there is no further call back. A person continues in the condition in which they died. The curse is fully removed, not at death, but at the end of this age in the resurrection, when all things have been subdued to Christ.[21] The last enemy to be destroyed is death.

4. The noetic effect affects our understanding of eternal life.

Eternal life is to know God.[22] Eternal life is not heaven. Eternal life begins in this life, at regeneration. Heaven begins after this life. God makes Himself known through His works of creation and providence (providence includes redemption in history). God is a Spirit, immortal and invisible, whom no man has seen nor can see.[23] God cannot be seen directly in heaven apart from His works. Creation is revelation, necessarily, intentionally, and exclusively. In heaven, after death, and before the resurrection, in the intermediate state, the fullness of blessing is not received, but is awaited. Departed believers await the completion of the work given to man in history.[24] Through the work of dominion,

---

20. *Psalm 75.*
21. *1 Corinthians 15:25-28.*
22. *John 17:3.*
23. *1 Timothy 6:16.*
24. *Hebrews 11:13, 39-40.*

the earth is to be filled with the knowledge of God as the waters cover the sea.[25]

Dominion (developing the powers latent in the creation—in one's self and in nature) is necessary for knowledge of the creation. And knowledge of the creation is necessary for the knowledge of God. The fullness of life is not absence of the curse, but the fullness of the knowledge of God. To expect life without knowledge of God is contrary to human nature. To expect fullness of life apart from the completion of dominion is false hope. To expect the work of dominion to be done by Christ at the Second Coming, supernaturally, apart from the Church, is to misunderstand the nature of knowledge through dominion.[26] To expect the knowledge of God through the work of dominion is true hope.

Due to sin and its noetic effect, the work of dominion is not set aside, it is deepened. The noetic effect is opposed by a spiritual war. With the curse in natural evil is given the promise in redemptive revelation: between good and evil (light and darkness, truth and falsehood, belief and unbelief), there is a spiritual war, which is age-long and agonizing, in which good eventually overcomes evil.[27] Every thought raised up against the knowledge of God will be made subject to Christ. Dominion now extends over sin.[28] The spiritual war is fought asymmetrically. Truth uses reason to persuade; falsehood uses threat and slander and the entire range of pseudo-arguments commonly called informal fallacies.[29] There is enmity, hostility, and hatred toward what exposes falsehood. Removal of this hostility requires a redemptive change of heart by regeneration. Truth prevails: "the light shines in the darkness and the darkness cannot overcome it or withstand it."[30] The rational requirements of human nature cannot be eradicated. The need for meaning, found only in the knowledge of God (eternal life), remains.

---

25. *Isaiah 11:9.*

26. Gangadean, *Philosophical Foundation*, 207-219.

27. *Genesis 3:15.*

28. *2 Corinthians 10:4.*

29. Gangadean, *Philosophical Foundation*, 45-48.

30. *John 1:5.*

5. The noetic effect affects all our basic beliefs.

The noetic effect affects our understanding of faith and reason and the inseparability of the two. It affects our interpretation of Scripture and of literature. It affects our understanding of good and evil, and why there is evil, and how evil serves the good. It affects our understanding of the moral law written on the hearts of all men and how the law serves the good. It affects our view of world history and Church history and human propensity toward apostasy. It affects our understanding of human conflicts and is the source of all conflicts and of every kind and degree of evil (in and between persons, in each household, in and between churches, in and between nations, and most comprehensively summed up between two ways, two kingdoms, two cities: the City of God and the City of Man). It affects our eschatology and our interpretation of all of life.

We can progress in overcoming the noetic effect:

1. by acknowledging the nature of sin at its root and its continued existence in us.

2. by acknowledging the curse (toil and strife, and old age, sickness, and death) as imposed by God as a continuing call to stop and think.

3. by acknowledging the good as the knowledge of God and the goal of filling the earth with the knowledge of God.

4. by acknowledge the work of the Holy Spirit leading us into all truth through the work of the pastor-teachers and summed up in the creeds of the Church.

5. by acknowledging the continuing internal and external challenges to the faith as God's call to take all thoughts captive which are raised up against the knowledge of God.

Appendix 8

———

POSTMILLENNIAL ESCHATOLOGY
The Earth Shall Be Full of the Knowledge of God

E SCHATOLOGY HAS TO DO WITH THE END. It has to do with our hope. It has to do with what we can expect in the future. Eschatology has a broader and a narrower aspect. The broader aspect has to do with the goal, or end, of human existence.

The first question of the Shorter Catechism is: "What is the chief end of man?" It is the more basic aspect of eschatology. The narrower aspect has to do with how and when this chief end of man is realized. If we understand what is more basic, we will understand what is less basic.

If we agree on the chief end of man, we can overcome the divisions regarding premillennial, amillennial, and postmillennial eschatologies. If we keep in mind the method of Rational Presuppositionalism and the problems of the noetic effect of sin, we can come to the unity of the faith in relation to eschatology.

From general revelation, from Scripture, and from Historic Christianity (summed up in the Westminster Confession of Faith) we can know that eternal life—the good for man—is the knowledge of God,[1] and that the earth shall be full of the knowledge of God as the waters cover the sea.[2]

We know that creation reveals the glory of God[3] and that knowledge of God's glory comes through the work of dominion given to man in the

———

1. *John 17:3.*
2. *Isaiah 11:9.*
3. *Isaiah 6:3.*

beginning. The hope of life in knowing God is assumed and affirmed throughout Scripture from the beginning to the end.

1. Sabbath

The Sabbath is the single, greatest, continuing affirmation of hope for mankind. Man is made in the image of God. As God worked and completed His work of creation, so man will work and complete his work of dominion. As creation is revelation, dominion brings knowledge of this revelation. As a result of the corporate work of mankind through the ages in ruling over the creation, the earth will be filled with the knowledge of God as the waters cover the sea.

2. The seed of the woman

In sin, man turned away from knowing God as the good. He put himself in the place of God to determine good and evil. God permits evil to serve the good—to deepen the revelation of His glory, especially His justice and mercy. His mercy is seen in the promise of redemption, and in the curse which restrains, recalls from, and removes moral evil. God established a spiritual war between believer and non-believer which is age-long and agonizing, with the promise that good (the seed of the woman) will overcome evil (crush the head of the serpent).

3. Noah

In the first age of human history, God permits evil to come to maximum expression. Yet His purpose is not frustrated. Noah, in faith and hope, builds the ark in which he preserves the promise of redemption and the work of dominion attained thus far. In doing so, he comforts us (mankind) in the labor and painful toil of our hands caused by the ground the Lord has cursed. Hope is preserved through the greatest darkness, and continues, with further restraints on evil by increased toil and diminished lifespan.

4. Abraham and the patriarchs

Apostasy has become worldwide again at Babel and further restrained by the division of mankind. While mankind is left to go on in apostasy,

God chooses to fulfill the promise of redemption for all of mankind through Abraham. In Abraham's seed all the families of the earth will be blessed. The promise continues through Isaac and Jacob and his sons, who are seeking the City of God, a city with foundations, which is the kingdom of God on earth, in the Promised Land.

5. Moses

Moses sought this City too. He left the power and glory of Egypt for the promise in Christ. He led the people out of Egypt by God's power and gave them the Law of God for the Kingdom of God. The way of life through atonement, sanctification, and service is taught, culminating in the feast of ingathering (of all peoples) and the full removal of all debt (jubilee).

6. Joshua

After the first generation leaving Egypt did not enter the Promised Land because of their unbelief, Joshua leads the next generation in the conquest of Canaan. Joshua's conquest is a pattern for the Church to overcome all worldviews of the nations raised up against the knowledge of God, rather than fear the giants of opposing systems of thought, and wander in the wilderness in unbelief.

7. David and the Psalms

David and others in the Psalms sing of the person and work of Christ, both in His suffering and His glory. Christ is raised from the dead and appointed to reign now.[4] All the ends of the earth will remember and turn to the Lord and all the families of the nations will bow down before Him. All of creation is brought to praise the Lord whose splendor is above the earth and the heavens.

8. The Prophets

All the prophets speak of God's judgment of famine, war, and plague on sin, and of God's restoration of His people. This restoration extends beyond the near future into the Gospel age, in which the nations are

---

4. *Psalms 2, 22, 67, 72, 110, 148, 150.*

brought into the house of God. All nations stream to it[5] until the earth is filled with the knowledge of God.[6] The comfort of restoration extends to the new heavens and the new earth.[7] Ezekiel sees the restoration in the vision of the dry bones[8] extending as a river from the Temple to all mankind.[9] Daniel sees the kingdom of God grow from the Rock that struck the image of the worldly kingdoms and became a huge mountain that filled the whole earth.[10] Jonah's life prefigures the resurrection of Christ and the call of the nations to repentance. Joel anticipates the outpouring of the Spirit on multitudes in the Valley of Decision.

9. Jesus

Jesus is the seed of the woman who came to destroy the works of the devil. He is the seed of Abraham in whom all the families are to be blessed. He is the Lamb of God who takes away the sin of the world. He is the anointed prophet, priest, and king, whose kingdom is to rule over all the earth. He is the Word of God, the Son of God, incarnate. He taught the character of the kingdom and the law of the kingdom in His Sermon on the Mount. He taught that the goal of the will of God and the coming of the kingdom is that the name of God would be hallowed (that God would be glorified in all that by which He makes Himself known). He taught that the kingdom will grow gradually to its fullness (as a mustard seed, and as leaven). Though few at first are saved, and though Jerusalem will be destroyed,[11] He commanded His followers to make disciples of all nations, and He sent the Holy Spirit to enable them to do this work.

---

5. *Isaiah 2.*

6. *Isaiah 11.*

7. *Isaiah 40, 66.*

8. *Ezekiel 37.*

9. *Ezekiel 47.*

10. *Daniel 2:34-35.*

11. *Matthew 23-24.*

10. Paul

The apostle Paul taught that where sin increased, grace increased all the more.[12] He taught that God placed all things under Christ who, through His body the Church, is to fill everything in every way,[13] that through the work of the Spirit in the ministry of pastor/teachers, the Church is to attain to the unity of the faith, to the whole measure of the fullness of Christ.[14] He taught that all Israel will be saved when the fullness of the gentiles has come in;[15] that Christ will reign until He has put all His enemies under His feet, the last enemy to be destroyed, at His second coming, is death.[16]

11. Peter

Peter exhorts his readers to be patient in suffering for the cause of Christ; that although false teachers are bold and arrogant, God rules, as in the days of Noah, when He brought that world to a sudden end. So too now the world of wickedness will be destroyed. Believers are to speed the coming of that day by their witness. The rule of spiritual forces of evil in the heavenly realms (the heavens) will be destroyed and the fundamental principles (the elements/*stoicheia*) of the world will be destroyed suddenly. In the place of the old, believers look for a new heaven and a new earth, in which the will of God is done.

12. John

John's Revelation brings the blessing of hope to all who read it and take it to heart. The time is near to readers in every age. After a seven-fold description of the state of the Church in John's age, the rule of God through the curse and the promise in an age-long spiritual war is unveiled in a seven-fold vision: the seven seals, the seven trumpets, the woman and the dragon, the seven bowls, the woman on the beast, the age-long spiritual war (Armageddon—fought with the sword coming

---

12. *Romans 5.*
13. *Ephesians 1.*
14. *Ephesians 4.*
15. *Romans 11.*
16. *1 Corinthians 15.*

out of the mouth), the thousand-year rule of believers (the millennium, in which all rule, who are raised from the dead spiritually—the first resurrection). Each vision covers the entire period of Christ's rule, from the first to the second coming. Each vision depicts the spiritual war between believers and non-believers under different aspects. Each vision shows the conquest of the kingdom of God over the kingdom of darkness. John's Revelation ends with the consummation of the kingdom of God. The work given to mankind in the Garden of Eden is completed by Christ through the Church. The City of God, perfected in beauty, comes down from heaven to earth. The river of life flows through the middle of the city, bringing blessing to all nations, life in its fullness. The hope of the Sabbath, of work and rest, is fully realized. The earth is filled with the knowledge of God as the waters cover the sea.

———

THE REGULATIVE PRINCIPLE
OF WORSHIP

According to the Revealed Will of God

G ENERAL REVELATION, SCRIPTURE, AND Historic Christianity (the
Westminster Confession of Faith) call us to worship God as He
is in truth, and not according to our own imagination. They call us
to worship God with all the heart and not merely outwardly, in vain.

"The light of nature shows that there is a God, who has lordship and
sovereignty over all, is good, and does good unto all, and is therefore to
be feared, loved, praised, called up, trusted in, and served, with all the
heart, and with all the soul, and with all the might. But the acceptable
way of worshiping the true God is instituted by Himself, and so limited
by His own revealed will, that He may not be worshiped according
to the imaginations and devices of men, or the suggestions of Satan,
under any visible representation, or any other way not prescribed in
the Holy Scripture."[1]

The principle which regulates worship limits worship to the revealed
will of God. The second commandment requires the receiving, observing,
and keeping pure and entire, all such religious worship and ordinances
as God has appointed in His Word.[2] It forbids the worshiping of God
by images, or any other way not appointed in His Word.[3] The second commandment affirms the regulative principle of worship which
limits worship to what God has revealed in His Word. The regulative

---

1. *WCF. 21.1.*

2. *SCQ. 50.*

3. *SCQ. 51.*

principle includes what is commanded; it does not include what is not commanded as well as what is explicitly forbidden. Jesus taught that God is Spirit, and His worshipers must worship in spirit and in truth.[4]

The book of Psalms in the Scriptures is given for singing, which is an ordinary part of public worship. "The reading of the Scriptures with godly fear, the sound preaching and consciable hearing of the Word, in obedience unto God, with understanding, faith, and reverence, singing of psalms with grace in the heart . . . are all parts of the ordinary religious worship of God."[5]

The Psalms alone, and not any songs of human composition, are to be used in singing in the corporate worship of God. Our own heart, which in this life remains affected by sin and comes short of the glory of God, is not sufficient to represent the truth of God, to be confessed immediately in singing by all. A broken and a contrite heart will not put its fallible thoughts of God in place of God's revelation of Himself.[6]

Biblical piety is in contrast to zeal without knowledge. We are sanctified by knowing the truth of God.[7] Singing the Psalms with understanding develops true spirituality. The Psalms affirm the nature of God as both just and merciful. They affirm the Biblical worldview of creation, fall, and redemption in all aspects. They affirm the will and purpose of God in history in His law and kingdom. They affirm, with hope, the full force of spiritual warfare faced by believers in every age. They are intimately acquainted with the whole range of human emotions. They are always God-centered and not self-centered. They are Christ-centered in His person and His work, on earth and at God's right hand.

Through singing the Psalms, the Word of Christ comes to dwell in us richly,[8] and we are filled with the Spirit.[9] The Psalms are to be sung, not as a matter of prudence or preference merely, but as the expression of love for God as He is in truth, not as we might imagine Him to be.

---

4. *John 4:24.*

5. *WCF. 21.5.*

6. *Job 42:5-6.*

7. *John 17:17.*

8. *Colossians 3:16.*

9. *Ephesians 5:18-19.*

Appendix 10

DISCIPLESHIP AT
WESTMINSTER FELLOWSHIP

"Go and make disciples of all nations . . ."
Matthew 28:20

The Church is the people of God, the body of Christ, the Kingdom of God expressing itself in all of culture. The Church consists of all those who make a credible profession of the Historic Christian Faith, and their children.

The Pillar and Ground of the Truth: Christ is the eternal Word of God (the Logos) incarnate who makes God fully known. The Logos is Truth in its fullness. The Church as the body of Christ is, therefore, the pillar and ground of the Truth to all mankind.

Man's Chief End: God created and rules over all things for His own glory. Man is created in the image of God. Man's chief end is to glorify God and to enjoy Him forever. Through the work of dominion given to mankind at creation, man is to fill the earth with the knowledge of God as the waters cover the sea.

Fall and Redemption: Mankind is fallen in Adam. Although they knew God, they glorified Him not as God.[1] Christ comes in the place of Adam to undo what Adam did (He is the Lamb of God who takes away the sin of the world) and to do what Adam failed to do (He is the Lord who rules to make God known).

---

1. *Romans 1:21.*

Worship and Discipleship: To worship God is to know and acknowledge Him as He has revealed Himself, and not in the imagination of one's own heart. The Church is gathered out of the world to worship God in spirit and in truth and to make disciples of all nations.

Salt and Light: The Church is the salt of the earth and the light of the world. As Christ makes known the Truth of God to the Church, the Church makes that Truth known to the world. Without the Truth, there is division and apostasy in the Church and decay and collapse in the culture.

Marks of a True Church: The marks of a true church are doctrine (Truth), sacraments (signs and seals of the Truth), and discipline through its oversight (upholding the practice of Truth in the Church). Churches are more or less pure according to the presence of each of the marks of a true church.

Truth in the Church: Christ, the Word of God (the Logos) incarnate, sends the Holy Spirit to lead the Church into all Truth: by reason, by the clarity of revelation in creation, and by Scripture; by its councils and creeds, by regeneration of unbelievers, and by the sanctification of believers.

From the Garden to the City of God: The Church is to grow from the Garden of Eden to the City of God, the Kingdom of God in its fullness. The Church must be taught to obey all that Christ has commanded. The Church is to take captive every thought raised up against the knowledge of God to the obedience of Christ.

The Discipline of Instruction: The Church is to be instructed in all knowledge, understanding, and wisdom, at every stage in the lives of its members in order to do its work. The Church is to be established on its philosophical, theological, and historical foundation by the discipline of instruction as called for by all vows made by its members. The Church must express the worldview built upon its foundation in all of culture, until man's work of dominion is completed.

Appendix 11

———

Vows

MEMBERSHIP VOW

1. Do you believe the Scriptures of the Old and New Testaments to be the Word of God, the only infallible rule for faith and life?

2. Do you believe in the one living and true God—Father, Son, and Holy Spirit, as revealed in the Scriptures?

3. Do you repent of your sin; confess your guilt and helplessness as a sinner against God; profess Jesus Christ, Son of God, as your Savior and Lord; and dedicate yourself to His service? Do you promise that you will endeavor to forsake all sin, and to conform your life to His teaching and example?

4. Do you promise to submit in the Lord to the teaching and government of this Church as being based upon the Scriptures and described in substance in the Bylaws of Westminster Fellowship? Do you recognize your responsibility to work with others in the Church and do you promise to support and encourage them in their service to the Lord? In case you should need correction in doctrine or life, do you promise to respect the authority and discipline of the Church?

5. To the end that you may grow in the Christian life, do you promise that you will diligently read the Bible, engage in private prayer, keep the Lord's Day, regularly attend the worship services, observe the appointed sacraments, and give to the Lord's work as He shall prosper you?

6. Do you purpose to seek first the kingdom of God and His righteousness in all the relationships of your life, faithfully to perform

your whole duty as a true servant of Jesus Christ, and seek to win others to Him?

7. Do you make this profession of faith and purpose in the presence of God, in humble reliance upon His grace, as you desire to give your account with joy at the Last Great Day?

BAPTISMAL VOW

1. Do you believe this child is a possession of God entrusted to your care?

2. In this light, do you promise to provide for his/her temporal well-being, to teach him/her to love God and His Word, the Bible, and to provide him/her with a God-centered education?

3. Do you promise to teach him/her of his/her sinful nature, of the plan of salvation which centers in Jesus Christ, and his/her own personal need of a relationship with Christ?

4. To the end that he/she may grow in the Christian life, do you promise to pray for him/her, and to train him/her to read the Bible, to pray, to keep the Lord's Day, and to understand the nature of the Church, the value of its worship and fellowship, and his/her need to seek communicant Scriptural Membership in the Church?

5. Do you promise to lead him/her by your example and parental discipline exercised in love, to seek first the Kingdom of God and His righteousness in all the relationships of life?

6. Do you make these promises in the presence of God, in humble reliance upon His grace, as you desire to give your account with joy at the Last Great Day?

Appendix 12

WESTMINSTER FELLOWSHIP
NOVITIATE
for
SELF-EXAMINATION

CHRIST THE LORD COMMANDED HIS FOLLOWERS to make disciples of all nations, by teaching them to obey all that He command-ed.[1] He gave to the church pastor/teachers to prepare God's people for works of service, so that the body of Christ may be built up, until we all reach unity the faith and in the knowledge of the Son of God and become mature, attaining to the full measure of the fullness of Christ.[2] We can go on to maturity only if the foundation is laid in our lives.[3] The purpose of the novitiate is to establish the foundation in our lives. The purpose of the self-evaluation is to help those in oversight know of your progress in having the foundation laid.

-----

1. *Matthew 28:20.*
2. *Ephesians 4:11.*
3. *Hebrews 6:1.*

On a scale of 1-5 (weak to strong) please evaluate how you are doing in each of the following. Use the other side of this paper to make comments and explanations.

Scripture

Diligently reading the Bible   _____
Memorizing the Psalms   _____
Memorizing Scripture   _____

Godliness

Personal/family devotions/and attending the worship services_____
Trusting and obeying God for my personal needs   _____
Walking in the Spirit and having the fruit of the Spirit   _____

Doctrine

Understanding the Westminster Standards   _____
Understanding our distinctives: clarity, the goal,
psalmody, the biblical worldview   _____
Other studies: Scripture, applications, general revelation   _____

Service

Duties and responsibilities in home   _____
Duties and responsibilities in work   _____
Duties and responsibilities in church   _____

Witness

Continuing witness already begun   _____
Witness to non-believers   _____
Witness to other believers   _____

Appendix 13

———

WESTMINSTER FELLOWSHIP BYLAWS: ADDENDUM A

Unity in the Church Through Discipline

BELIEVERS ARE TO DWELL TOGETHER in unity.[1] We are to be one that the world may believe.[2] We are to maintain the unity of the Spirit;[3] attain to the unity of the faith;[4] and operate in functional unity in the body of Christ.[5] Sin hinders unity, with God, and with man (fellowship/friendship).[6] If we confess our sins, He is faithful and just to forgive us our sins, and to cleanse us from all unrighteousness.[7] All sin is rooted in original sin.[8]

The church is for worship and discipleship. Discipline for discipleship[9] is due to sin remaining in the believer, covered up by self-deception[10] and self-justification.[11] In God's providence disputes arise to deepen the church's understanding.[12] Cleansing from unbelief requires

---

1. *Psalm 133.*
2. *John 17:21.*
3. *Ephesians 4:1-6.*
4. *Ephesians 4:7-13.*
5. Ephesians 4:14-16.
6. *1 John 1:7.*
7. *1 John 1:9.*
8. *Genesis 3:4-5; Exodus 20:3; Romans 1:20.*
9. *Luke 9:23.*
10. *Genesis 3:7.*
11. *Genesis 3:12.*
12. *1 Corinthians 11:19.*

truth in one's inward parts.[13] Through suffering—trials of faith—one is called to stop and think. Discipline in the church is based on our vows (membership vows, marriage vows, and baptismal vows). It is assumed that, as rational beings, made in the image of God, we can and should make vows— covenants of commitment—and that we can and should be held responsible for keeping our vows.

God's process to settle disputes is found in Scripture generally, and in Matthew 18:15-18 particularly. There are three steps in the process and there are prerequisites to begin to use this process. Matthew 18 is a general principle. Variations in applying the principle require wisdom (considering all things). Whenever there is doubt, one should come inquiring about how to apply the process, and not disregard the process. By this process oversight maintains the peace and purity of the church.

Authority in general, and in the church in particular, is based on insight, not might. It is rational, not personal (lording it over another). Insight is historically cumulative (summed up in the creeds of the Historic Christian Faith), not individual. Authority in the church (oversight) is legitimate if it is based on insight. Oversight without insight produces death rather than life and should be changed where possible. A request by oversight to meet, in the context of a dispute where correction in doctrine or life may be needed, is not arbitrary and is not to be disregarded. Disregard of such a request disturbs the peace and purity of the church, which is impermissible, and, as a breaking of one's vow, is sufficient grounds to terminate one's membership.

When an offence arises due to sin, (or to a perceived sin), the offended party should consider:

1. First, can I forbear in love, not just in outward behavior while being upset in heart? Love is patient and is kind, and also seeks the good for all.

2. If I ought to act, in love, have I examined myself first to see if there is a significant misunderstanding in me that contributes to my taking offence? Is it clear? Do I have ears to hear—am I listening/thinking literally and not thinking contextually, using good and necessary consequences? Do I have a relevant uncritically held assumption? Do I have a beam in my own eye (is there a deep level hypocrisy

---

13. *Psalm 51:6; John 17:17.*

in me)? Do I have the foundation sufficiently in place to apply the biblical understanding of good and evil?[14] If I do not have the first principles in place, am I straining at gnats while swallowing camels? Am I able and willing to use common ground to find meaning and settle disputes? Is it my aim to understand and apply Scripture, in this case, for the good of all?

3. If I do go any further, am I going (humbly) inquiring, or (presumptuously) judging?

4. If a person's discontent makes him uninclined to use Matthew 18 to settle his dispute, that person is legally free to withdraw his membership. That person is not morally free to stay and complain. It is unprofitable for him and for the peace and purity of the church.[15]

Matthew 18, Step One

A concern, issue or offence must be dealt with privately, between the parties immediately concerned. A party may be more than one person. Gossip and slander must be avoided. Distinction must be made between public and private, between doctrine and life. Clergy confidentiality is observed regarding private sins not affecting another person. In case there is doubt, the person concerned about privacy should inquire first.

Any concern of offence must be brought up in a timely manner: within one day if possible; within one week (before corporate worship); definitely before (monthly) communion. It becomes a matter of sin if it is not dealt with in a timely manner. The longer the delay the less obligation there is to hear a matter. Delay disturbs the peace and purity of the church, which is sin.

One should go, repeatedly if necessary, in order to define the concern clearly in terms of Scripture and its application. This is the time to clarify one's position by much discussion. It is reasonable to go up to three times, and wise to state the difference in writing.

There must be one issue only at a time. No change is to be made in the issue stated after going to the second step. It should be understood that the issue can go to step two after a few attempts to clarify

---

14. *Hebrews 5:11-6:3.*

15. *Hebrews 13:17.*

the issue. Declining a reasonable request to meet and discuss the issue automatically takes it to the next step.

Matthew 18, Step Two

In step two, one or two more persons are included in the process of resolution. This adds weight of more witnesses to the truth of Scripture and to the truth of the response of the parties involved. It makes it clear that the concern is in step two, and is a grave matter being taken seriously.

Focus of discussion should be on what does Scripture teach and how does it apply.

Discussion of the issue as defined from step one can go on until resolution or, if there is no resolution, until it is appropriate to go to step three.

Three attempts at resolution are reasonable. If there is no resolution at step two, witness to this should be sent up to step three, in writing. If there is resolution, there should be a stated agreement of both parties to avoid having to revisit the issue in the future.

Matthew 18, Step Three

Step three brings the dispute before the church. An action that affects the entire congregation must be done decently and in order, under the wisdom of oversight, and is not left to the discretion of individuals.

Oversight's judgment, representing the church, must consider and respond to objections to oversight's judgment raised by a group of peers (equivalent to a jury).

If after sufficient discussion there remains no reasonable objection to oversight's judgment in the matter, oversight's judgment, representing the congregation as a whole, will conclude the process of Matthew 18 step three. There is no further appeal beyond step three.

If the party is found guilty, and fails to repent, that failure terminates fellowship and membership in the congregation (Matthew 18:17-18). If the party is found not guilty, that must be declared so in order to terminate the matter. If the party is found guilty, and repents, he may continue his membership in the church in keeping with the fruit of repentance.

In case of termination of membership, a letter of standing summarizing the findings of the Matthew 18 process is to be drawn up and made available to others on a need-to-know basis.

After termination of membership, the door of repentance still remains open. Membership may be restored upon a credible expression of repentance.

GLOSSARY OF TERMS

act of faith — Trusting in God according to his nature and according to the promises of Scripture, which are grounded in his nature.

actual sin — The root and fruit sin that results from the imputed original sin of Adam (see also original sin, root sin, and fruit sin).

adoption — An act of God's free grace by which a believer comes under God's fatherly care, is received as a member of the family of God, and is a joint heir with Christ in his inheritance.

Allegoricalism — A hermeneutical method that uses foreign or arbitrary assumptions in interpretation to provide a deeper meaning as a response to the arbitrary constraints of literalism. Literalism and allegoricalism are antinomies that derive their strength from their mutual failure. Allegoricalism rejects that interpretation is bound by the clarity of general revelation, and maintains that there is no clear general revelation and that we cannot know what is clear from general revelation.

antinomianism — The error that, being set free from having to obey the law to be justified, God's law no longer binds and guides the conduct of believers. It is the rejection of God's law in favor of man's law (autonomy), whether private or by tradition, as the measure of holiness or piety. It denies the universal and perpetual nature of the law as the way of life.

antinomy   Contrary positions, both of which can be false at the same time because they share a common assumption. Examples include: capitalism and communism; this-worldly and other-worldly; all is eternal and none is eternal; skepticism and fideism; literalism and allegoricalism; virtue is the good and happiness is the good. Antinomies are a source of recurrent conflict within and between cultures.

Apocrypha, the   The books written before the coming of Christ between the Book of Malachi and the gospels. The word Apocrypha has come to mean non-scriptural or non-canonical and they are considered books of human authorship.

Arminianism   A theological response to Reformed Theology. Jacobus Arminius formulated its main views in his Remonstrance (1610). The core beliefs are contrasted with TULIP, which was formulated in the Synod of Dort (1618-1619). Arminianism affirms the belief in Conditional Election (foreknowledge of faith and acceptance of Christ), General Atonement (Christ's atonement was intended for all who choose to believe), Partial Depravity (man is sick or weakened in sin and holds some degree of ability to do good), Resistible Grace (fallen man can by his free will accept or reject the grace of God), and Possibility of Falling Away from Grace (salvation is contingent upon the will of the person to remain in the faith).

aseity   God's attribute of self-sufficiency and completeness. God as self-sufficient means that all of God's actions proceed from within Himself and not from any outside cause. The aseity of God enables us to understand how and why God acts. He acts for the manifestation of His own glory.

assensus   Personal commitment to the content of one's faith.

atonement   The required payment for sin.

ceremonial law The priesthood, offerings, laws of cleansing, dietary laws, and festivals of the nation of Israel. The ceremonial law prefigures Christ's graces, actions, sufferings, benefits, and some moral ordinances. All ceremonial laws are now abrogated under the New Testament. There is a permanence in the ceremonial law; what is a precursor (types and shadows) is done away with when the reality comes—it remains perpetually in Christ.

civil laws The laws given to and for the nation of Israel concerning justice and discipline with unique applications of the moral law for the Church before the coming of the Messiah. The 613 laws applied in the Israelite context, where the church and the state were the same. Only the general equity of the civil laws remains.

clarity Applied to basic beliefs; a belief is clear to reason if the contradiction is not logically or existentially possible; e.g., There must be something eternal; clarity is necessary for meaning, morality, and inexcusability; one knows what is clear if one can show what is clear; what is clear can be known by anyone who seeks to know.

clarity of general revelation The belief that God's eternal power and divine nature are clearly seen so that unbelief is without excuse. It is the basis of the inexcusability of unbelief and the necessity of redemptive revelation in Scripture.

conscience An inward moral sense in man, created by God, that judges man's moral action according to the moral law written on the heart. Conscience includes the notion of being blameworthy and deserving of punishment. The feeling of shame is an inward recognition by one's conscience that one has sinned and is blameworthy and deserves to be cut off (punished) for one's sin.

consequentialism The ethical theory that holds that the consequences of one's conduct are the ultimate basis for judgment about the rightness or wrongness of that conduct.

contextualism   A hermeneutical principle that is opposed to both literalism and allegoricalism. Contextualism uses good and necessary consequences derived from several ordered layers of context: first, clear general revelation; second, the biblical worldview of creation–fall–redemption in Genesis 1–3; third, the historical context of redemptive revelation; fourth, the book in historical context; then chapter; then verse; then word.

conversion   The outward effect of regeneration in which a person is convicted of sin, has repentance towards God, and has faith in Jesus as Lord.

cosmological argument   A philosophical argument that accounts for contingency, change, and motion in the universe by appealing to a first cause, a necessary being, or an eternal being as the ultimate source for the universe. The cosmological argument is used to settle the basic questions regarding the nature of reality.

covenant of grace   The doctrine that those who are fallen according to the covenant of works made with Adam must be redeemed by the terms of that covenant. The redeemer must perfectly obey in place of Adam and pay the penalty for sin required by that covenant. The grace of God does not negate but satisfies the justice of God. Yet the covenant is gracious in that God Himself fulfills the terms of the covenant in place of man. There are not two covenants by which man is redeemed, but one covenant of grace, differently administered under the Old and New Testaments.

covenant of works

A special arrangement made by God whereby Adam represents mankind. The covenant is deduced from Scripture by good and necessary consequences. The covenant has three parts: representation, probation, and manifestation. In representation, Adam is the covenant head of mankind—his actions will affect all. In probation, Adam is to continue in perfect obedience—seeking the knowledge of God as the good by carrying out the work of dominion. In manifestation, it was revealed that Adam did not continue in perfect obedience—Adam failed to know the distinction between God and man and good and evil. If Adam had obeyed God, righteousness would have been passed down to all his posterity. All not under the covenant of grace are under the covenant of works.

covenant representation

A special arrangement made by God, the purpose of which is to permanently establish mankind in righteousness. The means of covenant representation is one man representing all. The first representative was Adam, who fell, and in him, all are fallen. The second representative is Christ, who came to do what Adam failed to do (perfectly obey) and undo what Adam did (brought moral and natural evil upon the world). Christ represents the elect.

creed

A statement of belief, from the Latin word credo, which means "I believe."

culpable ignorance

The failure to know what is objectively clear to reason about God (and man, and good and evil) for which there is no excuse or rational justification. Objective clarity is sufficient for responsibility. Inexcusability is a matter of clear and present truth unacknowledged. It is set in contrast to voluntarism.

curse   Is natural evil, which encompasses the miseries of this life imposed upon man after the Fall by God in light of man's self-deception and self-justification. The curse is God's continuing and final call of repentance to man, a continuing and final call to stop and think. The curse serves to restrain, recall from, and remove sin. It consists of toil and strife, and old age, sickness, and physical death in all their manifestations—increased in war, famine, and plague (see also natural evil).

decalogue   The moral law. The word "decalogue" is derived from the Greek words "deka," meaning ten, and "logos," meaning word or principle. It is synonymous with the Ten Commandments delivered at Mount Sinai in Exodus 20.

deism   The belief that God created the world, but God does not actively rule it; God did not act after creation to bring about natural evil in the world or to give any redemptive revelation to mankind.

demiurge   In Plato's dualist cosmology, the being that makes the world. He is a maker, not the Creator.

discipleship   The process whereby a believer is sanctified (made holy) and taught to obey all that Christ has commanded (the law of God in all of life). It brings us to know and practice the truth (doctrine and life); it requires us to deny ourselves, take up our cross daily, and follow Christ. Discipleship is through the church, based on membership vows, the sound preaching of the Word, and the use of ordinary means accompanied by the inward work of the Holy Spirit. Discipleship is for the goal of attaining maturity (understanding of the foundation), fruitfulness (increase of understanding in others), unity (in all relationships in all spheres of life), and fullness (in all the riches of knowledge and understanding).

Dispensation-alism

The eschatological position that interprets biblical history progressively through different stages or dispensations. A dispensation is a period during which man is tested in respect of obedience to some specific revelation of the will of God. In each dispensation, God uses different means of grace to redeem his people in each successive age. There are three major forms: classical (1830-1950), revised (1950-1980), and progressive (1980 to present). Dispensationalism uses literalist hermeneutics, holds to two redemptive plans for Israel and the church, allows for 3-7 dispensations, and affirms pretribulation rapture and the fulfillment of a literal millennial kingdom.

dominion

The exercise of authority over oneself and the created order by naming and ruling. Man is to name the creation, which reveals God's glory, and he is to rule over it, which is to develop the powers latent in man and the creation. Naming the natural world is the realm of science; ruling over it is the task of technology. Naming the human world is the task of the humanities; ruling over it is the task of all forms of the arts of human culture. Dominion is directed toward the good as the knowledge of God, set in contrast to dominion as rule for self-interest.

dominion mandate

The original command of God in Genesis 1:28 to "Be fruitful, and multiply, and replenish the earth, and subdue it: and have dominion [over it]." The task of dominion is for the entire race throughout history. It requires the unity of all mankind in all aspects of man's diversity. The work of dominion will be completed when the earth is filled with the knowledge of God as the waters cover the sea.

doxological focus

The foundational doctrine that all of creation and providence manifest the glory of God and that man is to give all glory to God. It is contained in the Westminster Standards (WCF 1.1, 2.2, 3.3, 4.1, 5.1, 6.1, and SCQ. 1, 46, 101).

doxological postmillennialism	The eschatological position that good will triumph over evil, the curse will be gradually removed as moral evil is removed through the dominion and gospel mandates, and the end will come when the earth is filled with the knowledge of the glory of the Lord as the waters cover the sea (Isaiah 11:9; Habakkuk 2:14).
Doxological Reformed	The most conscious and consistent level of Reformed theology to date, based upon a reading of the Westminster Confession of Faith which emphasizes that all of creation and providence reveal the glory of God, and the end of the Christian life is the knowledge of the glory of God.
doxological understanding	The interpretive framework that God creates and rules to make His glory known and that man's work of dominion in all areas of life is for the goal of knowing and glorifying Him.
doxology	To give all glory to God.
dualism	The ontological position that reality consists of two distinct kinds of being—mater and spirit—both of which are eternal; affirmed in different forms of Greek thought by Plato and Aristotle; distinct from theism, although dualistic attitudes persist in popular forms of theism.
effectual calling	Also known as regeneration. It is the beginning of salvation in which a person is raised from spiritual death to life, which is to be regenerated by spiritual rebirth or recreated as a new creature in Christ. Effectual calling is wholly of God and not from man, either positively (by man's will cooperating with God's will) or negatively (by man's will not resisting God's will). By regeneration, a person is made both willing and able to seek and understand and to do the will of God so that regeneration precedes and naturally results in repentance and faith.
empiricism	The epistemological position that all knowledge arises from sense experience, affirmed by John Locke, David Hume, and in some claims made in the name of science; radical empiricism includes inner as well as sense experience.

equivocal   A term is equivocal if it has more than one meaning, which can be a source of ambiguity. In theology, to think of the nature of God equivocally is to think of God as totally other and thus unknowable (see David Hume's character Philo in Dialogues Concerning Natural Religion).

eschatology   The theological discipline that aims to explain the end of history (the end times), the second coming of Christ, the resurrection of the dead, and the last judgment. Eschatology has a broader and a narrower aspect. The broader aspect concerns the goal or end of human existence. The narrower aspect concerns how and when this chief end of man is realized. Understanding the narrower aspect presupposes the broader aspect.

eternal   What has no end and no beginning, which is also infinite.

Evangelical   The theological position concerned with "the evangel," the good news, and the gospel's advance in all the earth.

exclusive psalmody   The theological position that the Psalms alone, and not any songs of human composition, are to be used in singing in the corporate worship of God. The Psalms are to be sung, not merely as a matter of prudence or preference, but as the expression of love for God as He is in truth and not as we might imagine Him to be.

extraordinary providence   The rule of God beyond the use of ordinary means (e.g., miracles).

faith   The substance (underlying support/reality/hypostasis) of things hoped for, the evidence (proof/elenchus) of things not seen. Faith is a term that is applied to belief in general, which cannot be verified through sense experience; faith is not opposed to reason; as truth cannot be separated from meaning, faith cannot be separated from reason; faith grows as understanding grows; it is tested as understanding is tested.

fideism
Holds a belief without proof; proof is seen as either not relevant or not possible or may not actually be present; belief may either be theistic or non-theistic; fideism assumes basic things are not clear; belief without proof based on understanding loses all meaning.

fiducia
The aspect of one's faith that involves trust and obedience based upon understanding the character of God.

first cause
A cause that started everything. In theism, God is the first cause.

foundation
The most basic beliefs within a coherent system of beliefs. Christianity has philosophical, theological, and historical foundations that support the entire Christian worldview.

fruit sin
The unrighteousness arising from not seeking and not understanding (root sin). It is sins of commission such as autonomy, idolatry, hypocrisy, sloth, murder, anger, lust, lying, pride, greed, gluttony, and envy.

fullness
The theological doctrine that affirms God created the world with a fullness of kinds (substances and beings), that God created man in His image (rational) to carry out the work of dominion (the dominion/cultural mandate), that God permitted the gradual removal of evil which allows all forms of degrees and combinations of evil to come to expression in world history and be overcome (Ironic Solution), that man is to rule over sin by making disciples of all the nations (the gospel/mission mandate), and that in redemption, Christ is to fill everything in every way.

general revelation
What can be known of God by all persons, everywhere, at all times, through the ordinary means of knowing, in contrast to special revelation, the subject matter of natural vs. revealed religion. General revelation is known inferentially by reason: it is deduced from the nature of things created. It is objectively clear and accessible to all who care to know by seeking diligently.

glorification   The final stage of redemption which occurs immediately after death, wherein all remaining sin is removed and the believer is in the presence of the Lord.

glossolalia   The act of speaking in a language foreign to the speaker through the Holy Spirit, as in the day of Pentecost in Acts 2, which was a sign of the reversal of the confusion of tongues at Babel. The term also describes ecstatic utterances arising from the human spirit (rather than the Holy Spirit).

gnosticism   The position in epistemology that affirms esoteric knowledge vs. the clarity of general revelation. In metaphysics, the position is associated with dualism. In ethics, it is associated with the beatific vision, in which the good is achieved in the next life by a direct seeing of God or by divinization.

heresy   A theological view that departs from what has been agreed upon in the historic Christian faith (orthodoxy or right thinking) in its councils and creeds. It entails the denial of an essential doctrine to the coherence of Christian theism (e.g., creation ex nihilo, the Trinity, the incarnation, the dual nature of Christ, etc.).

historically cumulative insight   The body of knowledge that has been achieved through much discussion in response to challenges and preserved and passed down as wisdom in every area of life.

Historic Christian Faith   The truths of the faith that have been achieved by the pastor-teachers, through the process of much discussion, being led by the Holy Spirit until the church comes into the unity of the faith. Summed up in the great creeds and confessions of the faith. The Westminster Confession of Faith is the high watermark of Historic Christianity to date.

imago dei   Man as the image of God. Man is created a body/soul unity, a male/female unity, with a formal/larger aspect of the image of God, with a triune personality, and with dominion.

imputation   To ascribe, or to account, from one person to another. In the Fall, Adam's sin is ascribed to all those he represents. In redemption, the sin of the redeemed is ascribed to Christ, and Christ's righteousness is ascribed to the person redeemed.

inexcusability of unbelief   The doctrine that failure to know what is clear from general revelation, God's eternal power and divine nature, is without excuse.

justification   In philosophy, the giving of a reason, account, or argument in support of a conclusion. In theology, the need for justification shows that God has so made us that we are required to give an account for all our behavior.

knowledge   Justified true belief.

knowledge of God   Inferential knowledge of the existence and nature of God from the things that are made—all His works of creation and providence. In general revelation, it is the good. In Scripture, it is eternal life. In the Westminster Standards, it is man's chief end.

light of nature   The light of the Logos, the Word of God in all men—that by which we see and understand. Reason is the self-attesting light of nature in all men made in the image of God.

literalism The belief that understanding a text is free of interpretive assumptions, that preceding layers of context are not necessarily relevant, that meaning is explicit only and not also by inference, and that understanding language figuratively is to be avoided whenever possible. Based on non-rational empiricism, literalism fails to distinguish interpretation based on the biblical worldview of creation-fall-redemption (Rational Presuppositionalism applied in contextualism) from interpretation based on non-biblical or foreign/unwarranted (gnostic) assumptions used by allegoricalism. Literalism neglects, avoids, resists, and denies the logical distinction between less basic and more basic. It cannot understand the distinction because it undermines it. Literalism renders the distinction meaningless by making all things equally basic. In seeking to preserve literal meaning without contextual interpretation, literalism loses all meaning.

Logos The Word of God in its fullness. The Word of God, which is eternal, is in all men as reason, is in creation as general revelation, is in history as Scripture, is incarnate in Jesus Christ, by the Holy Spirit is in the Church as the Historic Christian Faith, and is in the believer by regeneration and sanctification. The Logos is Truth.

love Seeks the good for the other; love is a moral virtue, not the good sought for its own sake; set in contrast to romantic love in which the other is considered the good; in theism, to seek the good as the knowledge of God is to love God and to love oneself.

magisterial Authoritative. In theology, there is a debate about whether reason is authoritative (magisterial) or the handmaiden to theology (ministerial). Reason in itself, as the laws of thought, is transcendental and authoritative. It applies to all being (including the being of God) and thought.

magisterium Teaching. In theology, the teaching authority of the church.

material monism   The position that all is one substance—monism—and that this substance is matter. Matter, or the material universe, is eternal. It denies the existence of all non-physical being, in contrast to spiritual monism, dualism, and theism. There is no God, no soul, and no afterlife. Everything in the universe can, in principle, be explained in purely natural terms. Material monism is also called naturalism or materialism.

matter   That which has size and is not conscious; can be measured.

ministerial   Delegated authority. In theology, the position that reason is a servant (vs. judge). Reason has a role in the interpretation of Scripture and in judging other claims to Scripture, but is not to be the judge of Scripture.

modernity   Also known as the modern period or the modern world. The historical period between 1648 and 1950 was one in which new challenges in philosophy and theology arose, which the Historic Christian Faith has not yet addressed. These challenges include faith vs. reason, science vs. religion, and this-worldliness vs. otherworldliness.

moral evil   Is an act contrary to the nature of one's being; for man as a rational being, it is to neglect, avoid, resist, and deny reason in the face of what is clear; it is the failure to seek, and to understand, and to do what is right. It is also self-deception and self-justification for sin.

moral law   Revealed to man from the very beginning, from the time of his creation. The moral law is written on the heart of man so that its requirements are clearly revealed to all men. The moral law, being a requirement of God's nature and the nature of man as made in the image of God, cannot be added to or changed in any way; it is perpetual.

natural evil   In the context of an all-powerful and all-good Creator, natural evil is not original in the creation, nor inherent in moral evil; it is imposed by God to restrain, recall from, and remove moral evil; it consists in toil and strife, and old age, sickness, and death, and all amplifications of these in famine, war, and plague.

natural theology The branch of theology that shows what can be known of God and man and good and evil from general revelation. Natural theology precedes revealed theology, providing the basis for its necessity.

nihilism The loss of all meaningful distinctions in epistemology, metaphysics, and ethics; the inherent consequence of skepticism—the denial of all clarity; a position which cannot be maintained with integrity.

noetic effect The effect of moral evil on the mind of man. It began with the Fall of man and is removed gradually through man's redemption and sanctification. The noetic effect affects our understanding of sin, spiritual death, the curse, eternal life, and basic beliefs.

notitia The Conscious understanding or recognition of the object of faith.

noumenal Being as it exists in itself; inaccessible to the senses. Unknowable in Kantian philosophy.

ontological argument A philosophical argument from the idea of the greatest possible being (God) to the existence of that being. The revised ontological argument argues for the necessity of an eternal being.

ordinary means That which is regularly used to bring about a desired result. The ordinary means for sanctification are prayer, regular reading of the Word, family devotions, attending to the preaching of the Word, the sacraments, and fellowship with other believers.

ordniary providence The rule of God through the use of ordinary means.

ordo salutis The order of the application of redemption: effectual calling (regeneration), conversion (repentance and faith), justification (based on Christ's righteousness received by faith alone), adoption (having all the privileges of children of God), sanctification (being made holy through knowing the truth), and glorification (the removal of all sin at death and the removal of death by the resurrection of the body).

original sin   The first sin, the same in all, and the paradigm of sin. Original sin is root sin, and out of it proceeds fruit sin. Original sin is the failure to seek, understand, and do what is right in the face of what is clear. The objective effect is the imputation of original sin (root sin) through Adam—our covenant representative. The subjective effect of original sin is twofold: negatively, we are utterly indisposed to all good, and positively, we are wholly inclined to all evil. It does not mean we do all evil, but that we are wholly inclined towards all evil. All actual sin proceeds from original sin.

paedobaptism   The practice of applying the sacrament of baptism to infants of believers.

pastor-teachers   The leaders of the Christian Faith who have engaged with the most pressing theological issues in the history of the Church. They have served as the instrument of the Holy Spirit to respond to challenges of the Faith. The progress of the Faith in Church history is not merely the contributions of great men but the work of the Holy Spirit working through men through the process of much discussion. All those involved are counted among the pastor-teachers.

pelagianism   The position that affirms the innate goodness of human nature and the free will of man and denies original sin and predestination.

perspicuity   The affirmation of clarity. Applied to Scripture, the clarity of Scripture. Those passages of Scripture that seem less clear are made more clear when interpreted contextually.

pietism   The theological position that emphasizes personal devotion and holiness.

plenary   Full. The view that all of Scripture is fully inspired by God.

postmillennialism   The eschatological view that the millennium spoken of in the Book of Revelation is the time between the first and second coming of Christ, during which good overcomes evil, and the Kingdom of God overcomes the Kingdom of darkness.

postmodern world
Also known as postmodernity, is a cluster of skeptical responses to claims of objective truth in modern thought; it is anti-foundationalism, anti-realism, and anti-essentialism; it assumes reason is not ontological or transcendental, nor is thinking presuppositional; it privileges the subjective aspects of interpretation.

problem of evil
The objection to Theism that asks: if God is all good and all powerful, why is there evil?; if God is all powerful, he could create a world without evil; if he is all good, he would create a world without evil; the problem is intellectual, to make sense of an apparent contradiction, and not empty basic terms of meaning.

rationalism
A reliance on reason as a source of knowing the truth; to be contrasted with reliance on sense experience or intuition or testimony; also, to be contrasted with reliance on reason as a test for meaning (rational presuppositionalism).

Rational Presuppositionalism
Thinking is presuppositional; we think of the less basic in light of the more basic: less basic/more basic, truth/meaning, experience/basic belief, conclusion/premises, finite/infinite, etc.; reason is the test for meaning; if we agree on what is more basic, we can agree on what is less basic.

reason in its use
Reason in its use is formative—used to form concepts, judgments, and arguments, which are the forms of all thought; critical—used as a test of meaning; interpretive—used to interpret experience in light of basic belief; and constructive—used to construct a coherent worldview.

reason in itself
Reason in itself is the laws of thought: the law of identity—a is a; the law of non-contradiction—not both a and non-a; the law of excluded middle—either a or non-a; these laws make thinking possible; the common ground for all who think.

reason in us
Reason in us is natural—the same in all thinkers; ontological—applies to being as well as to thought; transcendental—authoritative, self-attesting, cannot be questioned but makes questioning possible; and fundamental—basic to all other aspects of human personality.

redemptive revelation   Scripture as redemptive revelation reveals how man is brought out of sin and death; scripture assumes all have sinned—no one seeks, no one understands, no one is righteous; all are in the state of spiritual death—meaninglessness, boredom, and guilt; redemption by vicarious atonement shows both divine justice and mercy.

Reformation, the   The return to the historic Christian faith in response to the challenge of sacramentalism and synergism. The Reformation consisted of three phases: (1) Luther, (2) Calvin, and (3) The Westminster Assembly. The first phase concerned the ultimate authority of Scripture vs. the teaching authority of the church; justification is by faith alone apart from works and sacrament; the priesthood of every believer vs. the need for priests as intermediaries with God. The second phase focused on the divine sovereignty over all aspects of life, the purity of worship apart from human traditions, and church order is synodical (the joint rule of all pastor-teachers) vs. hierarchical or local independence. The third phase focused on the clarity of general revelation and the inexcusability of unbelief, the use of reason (the light of nature and good and necessary consequences) to understand general and special revelation, the doxological focus on the knowledge of the glory of God, and the law of God for all of life.

regeneration   The first part of effectual calling. Regeneration is an act of the Holy Spirit in which a person is changed from a state of spiritual death to life. Conversion is the outward effect of regeneration in which a person is convicted of sin, has repentance towards God, and has faith in Jesus as Lord.

religion   The belief or set of beliefs used to give meaning to experience.

repentance   True repentance requires first, understanding of sin as truly evil, and of God's mercy in Christ, and is manifested in grief and hatred toward our sin and in the fruit of new obedience.

revealed theology The branch of theology that studies what can be known of God and man and good and evil from special revelation; presupposes natural theology.

root sin Is not seeking and not understanding what is clear about God. Root sin leads to fruit sin (not doing what is right). It is the original sin, is universal in all as unbelief, and is inexcusable in light of the objective clarity of general revelation. Root sin blinds man to all sin. Root sin is the first sin historically (in Eden), ontologically (in the First Commandment), and existentially (in human self-awareness).

sacramentalism The belief that the sacraments are necessary for salvation. Historic Christianity does not affirm but denies sacramentalism and affirms the sufficiency of vicarious atonement, apart from human effort.

sanctification The work of God's free grace, whereby we are renewed in the whole man after the image of God and are enabled more and more to die unto sin and live unto righteousness. The Holy Spirit illumines our minds to know God, through which truth we are sanctified. As we contemplate the glory of God, we are transformed into His likeness; we are set free from sin and made holy. Righteousness in conduct proceeds from this knowledge and holiness.

saving faith Is an understanding of the truth of the Word of God by which the Christian, through the work of the Holy Spirit, is convicted of sin and is brought to repentance and faith. The principal act of saving faith is accepting, receiving, and resting upon Christ for salvation. Differing in degrees, it is strengthened by using the ordinary means of salvation: the Word, sacraments, and prayer, but weakened by their neglect.

second causes An act of finite beings that occurs necessarily (according to the nature of a thing), freely (according to human desire), or contingently (without human forethought or intention). God uses all second causes to bring about his sovereign purposes.

seeking

Diligently using reason to understand the meaning of what is clear. This requires the full application of reason in its formative, critical, interpretive, and constructive uses; if one seeks, one will find—seeking leads to understanding, and understanding to doing what is right/good; set in contrast to neglecting, avoiding, resisting, and denying reason in the face of what is clear; the lack of seeking and understanding spirals downward into ever-increasing meaninglessness. The fear of meaningless existence leads one to seek diligently to understand.

self-attesting

What testifies to itself and cannot be testified to by another; reason in itself, as the laws of thought, is self-attesting and is, therefore, the highest authority in the realm and order of human thought/knowledge; it does not need justification and cannot be questioned because as the laws of thought, it makes questioning possible; it is immediately clear by test for meaning, not by proof for truth (it cannot be argued for, even in a circular manner); it is irrepressible and irresistible—it arises spontaneously so that we cannot cease from thinking, and any attempt to neglect, avoid, resist, or deny reason is futile: the light shines in the darkness, and the darkness cannot withstand it; only reason in itself, and nothing else (neither testimony—divine or human, nor common sense, nor intuition, nor empiricism, nor tradition), is self-attesting—their meaning is understood and analyzed by reason.

semi-pela-gianism

A modified Arminian doctrine that holds to the universality of original sin and affirms the necessity of grace for Christian life and action. Yet, the innate corruption of humankind is not so great that the initiative toward Christian commitment is beyond the powers of a person's native will. The focus is on the justice of God. If salvation depends initially and unilaterally only on God's free election of the saved, those not chosen could complain that the mere fact of being born dooms them. The Council of Orange (A.D. 529) affirmed the doctrine of sin (man is fallen in Adam) and salvation (man is saved by grace) in response to Pelagian and semi-Pelagian error.

sensus divinitatis   The immediate awareness of divinity present in human consciousness; variously understood, ranging from a sense of dependence on a higher power to awareness of God as Creator and ruler or as one having an innate sense of the qualities of infinite, eternal, and unchanging, which can only, upon analysis, be applied to God.

skepticism   The epistemological view that knowledge is not possible, that nothing is clear; consistently held, skepticism leads to nihilism, the loss of all meaning.

soteriology   The branch of theology dealing with the doctrine of salvation. It seeks to identify how mankind is brought from death to life, individually and corporately.

sovereignty   Is God's authority to rule freely, according to his nature, over all creation. As the only righteous ruler, divine sovereignty does not limit liberty but grants it.

special revelation   What is known of God through testimony and its transmission; usually contained in the form of scripture, the subject matter of revealed theology in contrast to natural theology or religion.

spirit   That which has no size and is conscious (also known as mind, soul, or consciousness).

spiritual death   Set in contrast to and analogous to physical death; the inward condition of meaninglessness, boredom, and guilt; inherent in moral evil as the failure to seek and to understand basic things that are clear to reason.

supereroga-tion

The doctrine that affirms that some may so fully obey their duty to God that they may act beyond their duty to achieve and build up merit for others, which is dispensed to those in need by the church through the sacramental system (i.e., indulgences, chastity, perfect charity, etc.). The Confession affirms that in our fallen state, we do not and cannot fully obey God, that in our disobedience, the extent of our duty to and achievement of good works in this life cannot be fulfilled, that there is no act in which we can fulfill which goes beyond our duty to God and Man, thus rendering the doctrine both inherently and existentially impossible.

teleological argument

A philosophical argument that argues from order in the world to the source of order. Historically, arguments have been made from the natural and moral order to the existence of a designer or God. Both versions of the teleological argument have faced significant objections. The revised teleological argument builds on the revised ontological and cosmological arguments, shows the ne-cessity for special creation (vs. naturalistic and theistic evolution), and addresses the problem of evil.

the good

The end in itself, chosen for its own sake and not for the sake of anything else; it is the highest good (the sum-mum bonum); it is the source of unity (in a person, be-tween two persons, and between groups of persons); set in contrast to virtue as means to the good and happiness as the effect of possessing the good.

The Great Commission

The highest eschatological command and promise given to mankind as a call to fulfill God's will and purpose. Summarized biblically in Matthew 28:18-20. Christ an-nounced his sovereignty over the creation, commanded his people to know God and make him fully known, to observe and obey his word to disciple the nations through his atoning sacrifice and rule by the work of the spirit, to fulfill the dominion mandate to fill the earth with the knowledge of God to advance his kingdom to its full-ness, with the promise that he will rule until that great work is accomplished.

theism Belief in God the Creator who brought the universe and all things in it into being; God is a Spirit, infinite, eternal, and unchangeable, in his being, wisdom, power, holiness, justice, goodness, and truth; in contrast to deism, God in theism is both Creator and ruler of mankind in history.

the principle of clarity Some things are clear, the basic things are clear, the basic things about God and man and good and evil are clear to reason; necessary for meaning and morality.

tradition A way of life handed down by and received on the basis of testimony, in contrast to reason, intuition, or sense experience; without critical analysis, traditions are affirmed to be equal, requiring radical pluralism, diversity, multiculturalism, cultural relativism, and tolerance.

univocal A term that has one and only one meaning. In theology, applied to God, He is totally like man, only with greater power (see David Hume's character Cleanthes in Dialogues Concerning Natural Religion).

vicarious atonement Payment of sin through the death of another. In Christianity, this payment is through a representative man.

virtue Is not the good, but the means to the good; there are different kinds of virtues: instrumental (money, house, car), natural (health, beauty, talent), and moral (wisdom, courage, love).

voluntarism A prevailing epistemological assumption in the Church that affirms that the will acts independently of and can be in opposition to the intellect (what one knows/understands); that we may know the truth and not do it—due to weakness of the will (akrasia); that we may know the truth and rebel against what we know (knowing the truth and willfully suppressing it); that we may knowingly do evil; and that knowledge is not sufficient for morality.

wisdom Is knowing the good and the appropriate means to achieve the good.

work of dominion   Man's work of dominion reflects God's dominion in creation; man is to form the creation by developing all the powers latent in the creation; man is to name the creation so as to know God who revealed his glory in creating; man is to fill everything in every way as the rule of God's kingdom over all. The task of dominion is for the entire race throughout history. The work will be completed when the earth is filled with the knowledge of God as the waters cover the sea. The Sabbath given to man signifies the goal and completion of this work.

worldview   Is how a person understands the world based on answers to the basic questions; each culture is shaped by a worldview held more or less consciously and consistently; a culture grows or declines as its worldview increases or decreases in its capacity to provide meaning.

BIBLIOGRAPHY

Bratt, James D. *Abraham Kuyper: A Centennial Reader.* Grand Rapids: William B. Eerdmans Publishing Company, 1998.

Edwards, Jonathan. *The Perpetuity and Change of the Sabbath.* Classic Domain Publishing, 2014.

Gangadean, Ashok. *Between Worlds—The Emergence of Global Reason.* New York: Peter Lang, 1998.

———. *Meditative Reason—Toward Universal Grammar.* New York: Peter Lang, 1993.

Gangadean, Surrendra. *History of Philosophy: A Critical Analysis of Unresolved Disputes.* Phoenix: Public Philosophy Press, 2022.

———. *Man, The Image of God: The Seven Aspects of Human Nature.* Phoenix: Logos Papers Press, forthcoming 2025.

———. *On Natural and Revealed Theology: Collected Essays of Surrendra Gangadean.* Phoenix: Logos Papers Press, 2023.

———. *Philosophical Foundation: A Critical Analysis of Basic Beliefs, Second Edition.* Phoenix: Public Philosophy Press, 2022.

———. *The Biblical Worldview: Creation, Fall, Redemption: Genesis 1–3: Scripture in Organic Seed Form.* Phoenix: Logos Papers Press, 2024.

———. *The Book of Revelation: What Must Soon Take Place: Doxological Postmillennialism.* Phoenix: Logos Papers Press, 2024.

———. *The Logos Papers: To Make the Logos Known.* Phoenix: Logos Papers Press, 2022.

———. *The Westminster Shorter and Larger Catechisms: A Doxological Understanding.* Phoenix: Logos Papers Press, 2023.

———. *Theological Foundation: A Critical Analysis of Christian Belief.* Phoenix: Logos Papers Press, 2024.

Khayyám, Omar. *The Rubáiyát of Omar Khayyám.* Boston: Little Brown and Company, 1900.

Kline, Meredith G. *Essential Writings of Meredith G. Kline.* Peabody: Hendrickson Publishers, 2022.

Robertson, O. Palmer. *The Final Word: A Biblical Response to the Case for Tongues and Prophecy Today*. Carlisle: Banner of Truth, 1993.

Ross, Hugh. *Creation and Time: A Biblical and Scientific Perspective on the Creation-Date Controversy*. Colorado Springs: Navepress, 1994.

Warfield, Benjamin B. *The Westminster Assembly and its Work*. Michigan: Baker Books, 2003.

Weber, Max. *Protestant Ethic and the Spirit of Capitalism*. Saint Louis: Forgotten Books, 2017.

Wright, N. T. *Justification: God's Plan & Paul's Vision*. Downers Grove: Ivp Academic, 2016.

INDEX

ABOUT THE AUTHOR

DR. SURRENDRA GANGADEAN (1943–2022) was a Professor of Philosophy at Phoenix College and at Paradise Valley Community College for 45 years. Additionally, he taught from the pulpit at Westminster Fellowship for almost 30 years and taught courses at Logos Theological Seminary for over 25 years. Courses he taught include: Introduction to Philosophy, Logic, Ethics, Philosophy of Religion, Eastern Religions, World Religions, Introduction to Christianity, Introduction to Humanities, Philosophy of Art, The Great Books, Philosophical Theology, Biblical Worldview, Biblical History, Church History, Systematic Theology, Biblical Hermeneutics, and Existential Hermeneutics. He received an M.A. degree in Literature from the University of Arizona, an M.A. degree in Philosophy from the University of Arizona, and a Ph.D. in Natural Theology from Reformed International Theological Seminary. He presented academic papers and public lectures on Natural Theology and the Moral Law. Dr. Gangadean was the organizing President of The Logos Foundation, which serves academic education in Liberal Arts and Theology.

www.ingramcontent.com/pod-product-compliance
Lightning Source LLC
Chambersburg PA
CBHW020428130626
46549CB00001B/26